ETHICS

Julie C. Van Camp

Publisher: Clark Baxter

Senior Sponsoring Editor: Joann Kozyrev

Development Editor: Florence Kilgo

Assistant Editor: Joshua Duncan

Editorial Assistant: Marri Straton

Market Development Manager: Joshua I. Adams

4LTR Press Project Manager: Kelli Strieby

4LTR Press Product Development Manager: Steve Joos

Content Project Manager: Jill Quinn

Art Director: Linda May

Manufacturing Planner: Sandee Milewski

Senior Rights Acquisition Specialist: Mandy Groszko

Production Service: Integra

Text Designer: Lachina Publishing Services

Cover Designer: Riezebos Holzbaur/Andrei Pasternak

Cover Image: ©David Muir/Photographer's Choice/Getty Images

Compositor: Integra

For product information and technology assistance, contact us at **Cengage Learning Customer & Sales Support, 1-800-354-9706**.

For permission to use material from this text or product, submit all requests online at **www.cengage.com/permissions**. Further permissions questions can be emailed to **permissionrequest@cengage.com**.

Library of Congress Control Number: 2012945751

ISBN-13: 978-1-133-30891-1

ISBN-10: 1-133-30891-0

Wadsworth
20 Channel Center Street
Boston, MA 02210
USA

Cengage Learning is a leading provider of customized learning solutions with office locations around the globe, including Singapore, the United Kingdom, Australia, Mexico, Brazil, and Japan. Locate your local office at **international.cengage.com/region**

Cengage Learning products are represented in Canada by Nelson Education, Ltd.

For your course and learning solutions, visit **www.cengage.com**.

Purchase any of our products at your local college store or at our preferred online store **www.cengagebrain.com**.

Instructors: Please visit **login.cengage.com** and log in to access instructor-specific resources.

Printed in the United States of America
2 3 4 5 6 7   16

Brief Contents

Gyuszkofoto/Shutterstock

Contents

Portrait Essentials/Alamy

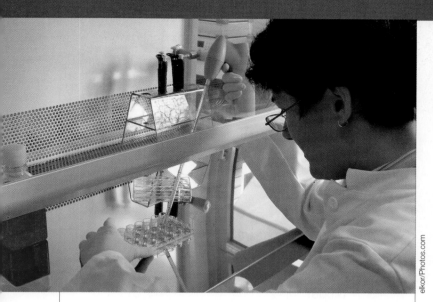

elkor/Photos.com

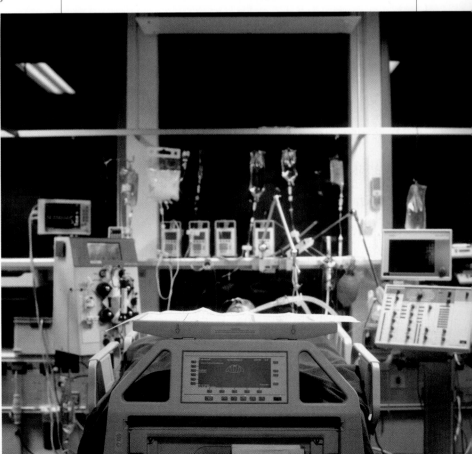

apply pictures / Alamy Limited

PART III: ETHICS IN THE PROFESSIONS

Lisa F. Young/Shutterstock.com

What Is Ethics?
How Do We Develop an Understanding of Ethics?

> At the descriptive level, certainly, you would expect different cultures to develop different sorts of ethics and obviously they have; that doesn't mean that you can't think of overarching ethical principles you would want people to follow in all kinds of places.

Peter Singer, Ira W. DeCamp
Professor of Bioethics, University Center for Human Values, Princeton University

> The problem is that no ethical system has ever achieved consensus. Ethical systems are completely unlike mathematics or science. This is a source of concern.

Daniel C. Dennett, Austin B. Fletcher
Professor of Philosophy, Tufts University

LEARNING OUTCOMES

After you complete this unit, you should be able to:

1-1 Explain what philosophy and ethics are, and how ethics fits into philosophical thinking.

1-2 State a working definition of what ethics is in everyday life.

1-3 Summarize different meanings of what people consider ethics to be.

1-4 Identify ethical issues that are currently most important to you.

1-5 State goals you would like to accomplish this term to develop an understanding of ethics based on personal exploration.

hould we stop to help a stranger who seems to be in trouble? Should we tell the clerk at the grocery store that she has given us more change than we deserve? Should we submit a paper in a college course that a friend wrote for us? Should we donate some of our hard-earned money to charity to help those worse off than we are? We all face ethical choices every day of our lives. Ethics examines the various ways in which we can work to answer those questions in our own lives. Our goal here will not be to provide a simple checklist of rules that will answer all of our questions but to develop ways of reasoning through the myriad ethical challenges each of us faces.

decide which actions are right or wrong? In this chapter, we will start by considering what philosophy itself is, especially because it is rarely studied in high school and is thus a new subject for almost all college students. We will then explore various ways of understanding *ethics* that we will refer to in the balance of this book. We will look at various approaches to ethics that have

Overview

Ethics is the branch of philosophy that studies value in human behavior. What does it mean to be a good or bad person? How should we

What do **you** think?

Ethics is an attainable, objective set of reasoning tools for deciding how to act in life.

Strongly Disagree						Strongly Agree
1	2	3	4	5	6	7

been promoted in the history of western philosophy. There is no one "right" way to pursue ethical inquiry and considering different approaches will help us better understand the ways in which we can address contemporary issues most effectively.

We will ask you to examine what you already know or might believe about ethics as you begin the course, and whether you might follow specific ethical rules and how you arrived at them. We will also ask you to identify those ethical issues that are most important to you at this stage of your life. We will then ask you to select a particular issue that you might be willing to discuss with your class as we work through the course and how it might be addressed with the reasoning tools we will learn about in this book. Finally, we will ask you to consider what goals you would most like to reach in developing a solid understanding of ethics and how it can help you deal with issues you face personally. The chapter will end with excerpts from *The Meno,* a famous dialogue by Plato, on the subject of whether virtue can be taught.

> **Philosophers study classic texts ... because these works ... give us valuable ideas and insights for how to develop our own views.**

1-1 WHAT IS PHILOSOPHY? WHAT IS ETHICS?

1-1a Major Branches of Philosophy

Traditionally, philosophy pursues timeless questions studied for thousands of years that fall into three major categories. First is **metaphysics**, or the study of reality, which asks what is real? What exists? Is physical existence the only reality? Are there also nonphysical realities? Ideas or concepts that exist independently of concrete things? Souls? Minds? In contemporary life, for example, metaphysical issues arise when we ask how "virtual reality" is different from "reality."

Second is **epistemology**, or the theory of knowledge, which asks what we know and how we know it. These questions are broader and more wide-ranging than you might encounter in a course in psychology or education. Do we acquire knowledge only from our sense perceptions? Are we born with innate ideas? How do we explain knowledge about human-created disciplines, such as logic and mathematics?

Third, **value theory** (sometimes called axiology) studies value and the distinction between value and fact. One branch of this discipline includes the study of values in human behavior, or ethics (defined more extensively further in the chapter). Another includes the exploration of values in the realm of art. What makes a work of art good or bad? Are aesthetic judgments objective or are they hopelessly subjective?

1-1b Philosophy as a Method of Inquiry

Philosophy is traditionally taught as intellectual history, which studies the writings of many great philosophers who have addressed these classic questions, and this remains a legitimate approach to studying philosophy. Philosophers study classic texts, not because they necessarily have the "right answers," but because these works have proposed ways of analyzing issues that give us valuable ideas and insights for how to develop our own views.

Metaphysics

Epistemology

Value Theory

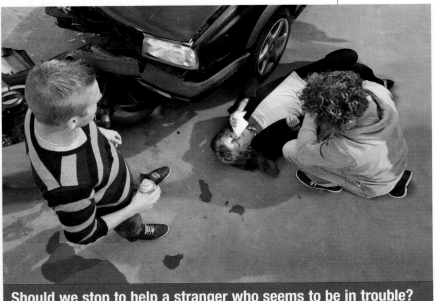

corepics/Shutterstock

Should we stop to help a stranger who seems to be in trouble?

Should we tell the clerk at the grocery store that he has given us more change than we deserve?

Hemera Technologies

Increasingly in recent decades, philosophers have refocused their understanding and teaching of philosophy to emphasize methods over content. Philosophers step back and ask the "big picture" questions. They look for broad perspectives and connections. What does science have in common with art? With religion? And philosophers remain especially focused on good reasoning, or critical thinking. They closely examine key terms and concepts; far beyond just looking something up in a dictionary, philosophers like to peel back the layers of such complex terms as *beauty*, *goodness*, *truth*, or *justice* and explore in great detail the many nuances of these important concepts. With this emphasis on good reasoning, philosophers explore just about any possible subject matter. Thus, we have witnessed the emergence of such areas of investigation as philosophy of sport, philosophy of religion, philosophy of science, philosophy of art, and so on. In all of these areas, philosophy emphasizes good reasoning.

1-1c What Philosophy Accomplishes

Although any philosophy course hopes to impart some factual knowledge, terminology, and context of the discipline, its more important purpose is to help acquire the skills of philosophical inquiry and analysis, good reasoning, and critical thinking. These skills are helpful in pursuing any other subject in college and beyond. Philosophy courses also show how to consider all sides of an issue, emphasize independent reasoning over dogmatic solutions, and thus open minds to unknown horizons.

In ethics courses, students should expect to become skilled at identifying ethical problems and framing them in ways that facilitate helpful analysis and discussion. Students should be able to see alternative solutions and understand the reasoning in support of different approaches to those ethical problems. Students should learn to apply competing ethical theo-

ries in testing out different solutions to ethical dilemmas.

Ethics instruction avoids preaching, propaganda, or dogmatic assertion of just one viewpoint. It steers clear of simplistic rules for conduct in life. It shuns the idea that there are easy "right answers," especially to challenging ethical dilemmas. Although professors of ethics courses understandably have personal views on the issues considered, they typically try to play devil's advocate to encourage students to look at all sides of an issue and not assume they must agree with the professor to get a good grade in the course.

Philosophers sometimes like to joke, when asked in the career-oriented educational world, what can you *do* with philosophy? What, they answer, can you do without it? If philosophy today is centrally concerned with good reasoning and independent thinking, they surely have a point!

In CourseMate, watch a video and take the quiz.

1-2 WHAT IS ETHICS IN EVERYDAY LIFE?

Every time we confront a choice that impacts the life of a person, we are facing an ethical choice. This might be a decision family members have to make when a loved one has been in a serious accident and is on life support equipment. Is it ethical to "pull the plug" and cause that life to end? If our family member has never given us any instruction, is it okay to agree to have their organs donated?

We sometimes have to make decisions that impact persons we have never met and probably never will. If we pollute the environment, we might impact the health of persons living in our town now or in the future. Do we have an ethical obligation to them?

Some would argue that our ethical obligations extend to nonhumans, including animals. Is it ethical to eat meat if that requires the termination of the life of a nonhuman animal?

And our ethical decisions can also arise in making choices that seem to impact only our own lives. If we smoke or drink or use illegal drugs or attempt suicide, are we harming only ourselves in violation of some ethical duty to ourselves? Are these actions truly "victimless crimes" that hurt only one self?

The most difficult ethical challenges often involve a clash of principles we hold dear. We might believe strongly

Should we donate some of our hard-earned money to charity to help those worse off than we are?

Michael Newman/PhotoEdit

1-3 VARIOUS MEANINGS OF ETHICS

Most philosophers consider **moral philosophy** to be synonymous with **ethics**. But you will likely encounter some who use the word *morality* to mean very specifically an ethical question involving sexual behavior. As with much of our language, different words can be used in different ways and there is no single "right" way to use these terms. The important thing is to look carefully at the context to see how someone is using a term and get clear on that usage to avoid unnecessary detours away from the substance of, and irrelevant disagreements in, a discussion.

You have likely met some people who consider ethics to be the concern only of fools. "Every man for himself," they say, and who cares about anybody else. But this misunderstands what ethics is as a field of study. Ethical theories encompass a wide range of often inconsistent views on what is ethical. **Egoism** is the theory that says that the only factor to take into account in deciding what is ethical is the consequences for oneself and nobody else. **Altruism** is the opposite, claiming that the only thing to consider is the consequences for others, never oneself. **Utilitarianism** holds that we should consider the consequences for everyone, including ourselves, in deciding what is ethical. All three of these theories are examples of **consequentialism**, as they all determine right and wrong action based on the consequences of those actions. The field of ethics does not say which of these positions is "correct." Rather ethics studies

that it is wrong to lie but also believe it is wrong to hurt the feelings of a close friend. If your roommate puts on an atrocious outfit for a job interview, should you tell the truth and hurt your roommate's feelings? Or should you lie and say it is a great outfit for an interview and save your hurtful comments for another day?

We make decisions all day long that impact many people. Yet we do not realistically have time to stop and reason through every decision the way we might do in a philosophy class. Instead, we pursue guiding principles that we establish as we mature and that help us make good decisions on a regular basis. As we think through a new dilemma, we learn to feel more comfortable pursuing the same action in the future, without starting from scratch in our consideration of the problem.

You find out that the girlfriend of a long-time friend who is your roommate has cheated on him with another roommate. What do you do? Do you speak up? Do you keep quiet about it?

Gary Conner/PhotoEdit

the pros and cons of these different approaches to ethics through reasoning.

Some think that ethical concerns are relevant only if others know what we are doing and we might get caught doing the wrong thing, that is, where consequences are of importance only if they risk exposing unethical actions to public scrutiny. Being known as an unethical business person would have severe consequences on one's reputation that would discourage future clients. But we might consider whether unethical conduct in private might catch up with us some day. The convicted con man Bernard Madoff was believed to be an ethical person because he donated much of his wealth to worthy charities, bringing in still more business. But his secret unethical behavior eventually was revealed, undoing whatever reputation he once had as an ethical person. In addition, one's hidden unethical behavior might also become a burden that one's conscience must struggle with, causing one stress and forcing one to engage in further unethical behavior to keep other unethical actions secret.

Philosophers sometimes like to look at ordinary language to further unpack what we mean by certain key concepts, that is, help give light to any complexities in these concepts and clarify these intricacies. Consider how you and your friends use the words *ethics* and *ethical person* and what you mean by it.

In CourseMate, practice what you learned by taking the chapter quiz.

1-4 MOST IMPORTANT ETHICAL ISSUES FOR YOU TODAY

Ethical issues uppermost in our minds vary considerably depending on our age, our life situation, and individual circumstances. In high school you might have been tempted to cheat on an exam, but worried about the consequences if you were caught. If your parents are struggling financially, you might wonder if you should forgo college and work to help

> [E]thics studies the pros and cons of these different approaches . . . through reasoning.

KEY TERMS

moral philosophy: a synonym for *ethics*

ethics: the study of human conduct impacting other humans

egoism: the ethical theory that right and wrong action depends on consequences for oneself only

altruism: the ethical theory that right and wrong action depends on consequences for other persons, but not for oneself

utilitarianism: the ethical theory that right and wrong action depends on consequences for everyone, including oneself

consequentialism: any ethical theory that determines right and wrong action based on consequences (including altruism, egoism, and utilitarianism)

Why is cheating on a test wrong?

lisegagne/iStockphoto.com

support the family for the time being. You might be facing difficult choices if your parents are elderly and you need to help them decide whether to sign a do not resuscitate (DNR) order at a nursing home. If you were raped by an uncle, you might be struggling to decide whether or not to seek an abortion if you become pregnant. You might also have struggled simply about whether to tell anyone about what happened.

Some of the ethical issues facing you personally are private and no one should force you to announce them to others, whether classmates or other acquaintances.

But, for the purposes of this course, you should think of some ethical issues in your life now that you are comfortable discussing with the class and instructor. You will be asked to identify one particular issue to be the springboard for personal reflection as the course progresses. You will have an opportunity to try out different reasoning tools and compare your approaches with those of classmates facing similar dilemmas.

In CourseMate, listen to the audio summary of the chapter.

1-5 YOUR PERSONAL GOALS

Virtually every college requires students to take a range of courses to broaden their education and give them the skills that will help them succeed in whatever career they pursue. Philosophy is rarely a course students rush to take on their own, especially with understandable concerns about landing a good job after college and worries that courses in philosophy and the other traditional

You realize that a threatening post on a famous social media outlet was authored by a close friend of yours. What do you do?

Michael Doolittle/Alamy

humanities are a mere sideshow that will not improve their employability.

Philosophy professors firmly believe that the reasoning skills you will develop this term will be helpful to you in all of your courses and in your current and future life. But you will also find this course more than an annoying hurdle to get beyond if you think about specific goals that will help you develop your personal ethics.

This means giving more thought to the most urgent ethical challenges in your life at the present time. But it also means coming to a better understanding of how to talk with friends and family about ethical issues that concern you. Perhaps you and your friends and family disagree strongly on the morality of abortion, euthanasia, or eating meat. Developing your personal ethical reasoning tools also means giving thought to how to accommodate yourself to an increasingly diverse population, with widely differing views on ethics, religion, politics, and a range of contemporary issues. Perhaps you feel strongly about a certain issue, such as environmental protection, animal rights, or the legalization of marijuana or marriage equality and want to be a more effective advocate in convincing others of the rightness of your views. Perhaps you are at a point in life where you are questioning traditional religious views of your friends and family and want to either clarify and strengthen those views or gradually move away from them and develop your own spirituality.

As with your most pressing ethical issues, some of your goals are personal and confidential, but many ethical issues you might be able to share with classmates and friends and will feel comfortable discussing in class. For example, discussing whether or not you have had an abortion might be a topic you want to keep private and you have that right. But what to do when you see another student cheating on an exam might be an issue easier to tackle with the class. In chapter 2, you will be asked to set specific goals to help you address the ethical issue you have identified. You will also be introduced to a tool, the critical thinking table, which will demonstrate, for each of the Part II chapters, how to apply methodical reasoning to work through an ethical claim. Step by step, an example pertaining to one of the chapter's topics will be examined: a sample claim will be subjected to the scrutiny outlined in the left-hand side of the table. From examining and clarifying key terms and concepts through confirming that the conclusions you draw are logical, the right-hand side explanations related to the chapter example will bring to light the mechanisms to enforce, the techniques to develop, the types of questions to ask, and the pitfalls to avoid.

Plato

One of the most influential philosophers of ancient Greece was Plato (429–347 B.C.E). He framed issues that shaped our philosophical dialogue in the West for the next two millennia, and even today. He asked questions about the nature of reality ("metaphysics"), knowledge ("epistemology"), and most importantly for us here, ethics. Plato urged us to think through problems with pure reason, shunning emotion. He believed that we all possess knowledge of universal truths, even though we are not aware of that knowledge. For Plato, philosophical dialogue is a process of bringing those universal truths to the surface of our understanding and awareness, drawing out the knowledge that he believed we all possess.

He never gave simple answers to questions of any sort, but challenged us to think things through for ourselves. This does not mean he was a relativist who thought any answer was as good as the next. To the contrary, he thought that absolute truth existed and could be achieved through reasoning. We might disagree with that strongly held position, but we can agree with his emphasis on reasoning to work through ethical and other dilemmas.

Plato wrote in a literary form called "dialogues" in which Socrates, his own teacher, engages in long discussions with other persons to draw out their ideas. This form of writing may be unusual for contemporary audiences, but it serves Plato's purpose in stressing the long careful process of raising questions and meticulously trying to move toward knowledge by answering them. The dialogues are not like the script for a play in the theater, but rather are an intellectual exercise intended to get at the truth on difficult questions. Knowledge, he posits, does not consist of rules and conclusions we passively memorize from others but is instead reasoning we draw from our own efforts.

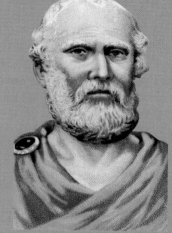

Photos.com

Why are Plato's writings still pertinent today?

CHAPTER 1 Case Study

Cheating

Almost all colleges and universities have honor codes that spell out rules against cheating and plagiarism. Some include requirements that students who witness another student cheating have an obligation to report that student to school authorities. Imagine that two of your best friends in one of your courses have paid an advanced graduate student to complete the written work for the course, including term papers and written assignments outside of the classroom. You are worried that the high quality of the work they are submitting will hurt your grade, as the professor said that no more than 15 percent of the students in the class will get A's for the course. You need to get a good grade in the course yourself so you can be admitted to the very competitive program in nursing at your university. Your friends suggest that you hire the same graduate student to complete your written work. Your university's policy says that students caught cheating can be expelled from school.

1. What is your immediate gut reaction to what you should do? Should you hire the same graduate student to do your written work? Should you report your friends to the professor?

2. Now think about the reasoning you would use to explain your initial gut reaction. Are you appealing to your self-interest? Are you worried about getting caught? Does your goal of a good grade outweigh your loyalty to your friends? Does your university's threat of punishment deter or discourage you from taking a chance on cheating? Are there principles that you are relying on to justify your "gut" reaction? In other words, what general principles can you state that would support your initial reaction?

3. Now that you have put into words your reasoning, do you want to change your mind about your decision on what you should do in this situation? What most influenced you to come to the same conclusion or to change your mind?

For additional case studies, please see the CourseMate for this text.

Reading Excerpt: Plato, *The Meno*

INTRODUCTION

In these brief excerpts from *The Meno*, one of his many dialogues, Plato asks whether virtue is a form of knowledge that can be taught. Before we can answer that question, he says, we must examine what virtue is. Meno is a young man in this dialogue with whom Socrates engages in discussion. Meno had previously studied with Gorgias, a Sophist who promoted false teaching, at least according to Socrates. Plato believed that everything has an essence, a something that makes it what it is. Socrates pursues the essence of "virtue" in early portions of these excerpts. Socrates also pursues his view of knowledge as recollection of knowledge that our souls have through eternity. These eternal concepts are known as Plato's "forms" or "ideas" that exist independently of us, whether or not we take notice of them. This excerpt from *The Meno* is adapted from a translation by Benjamin Jowett.

QUESTIONS FOR REFLECTION

1. Plato claims that there is an essence to virtue. How does he go about making his case? What do you think the essence of virtue is? Could we understand the meaning of a term if it did not have an essence?

2. What does Plato mean by *recollection*? If we possess all knowledge already, and only need to recollect it, what means should we use to accomplish this recollection? Has Plato made a persuasive case for his view of knowledge?

3. Reading Plato can be frustrating because he seems to raise more questions than answers. Is his method of drawing out knowledge helpful to you? Does his technique suggest different ways of learning than you have previously experienced?

4. What do you think *virtue* means? Do you believe that virtue can be taught or must we all develop our own sense of what virtue is?

READING

The Essence of Virtue

SOCRATES:...By the gods, Meno, be kind and tell me what you think virtue is. For I will be absolutely delighted to find that I have been mistaken, and that you and Gorgias [i.e., Meno's teacher]
5 have this knowledge, since, as I have been just saying, I never found anybody who had.

MENO: It will not be difficult, Socrates, to answer your question. Let us take first the virtue of a man—he should know how to administer the state in a way that benefits his friends and harms his enemies;
10 and he must also be careful not to suffer harm himself. A woman's virtue, if you wish to know about that, may also be easily described: her duty is to keep her house in order, and obey her husband. Every age, every condition of life, young or old, male or female, bond or free, has a different virtue: there are numerous virtues, and no lack of defi-
15 nitions of them; for virtue is relative to the actions and ages of each of us in all that we do. And the same may be said of vice, Socrates.

SOCRATES: How fortunate I am, Meno! When I ask you for one virtue, you present me with a swarm of them. Suppose that I carry on the metaphor of the swarm, and ask of you, What is the nature
20 of the bee? and you answer that there are many kinds of bees, and I reply: But do bees differ as bees, because there are many and different kinds of them; or are they distinguished by some other quality, such as beauty, size, or shape? How would you answer me?

MENO: I should answer that bees do not differ from one another,
25 as bees.

SOCRATES: And if I went on to say: That is what I want to know, Meno; what is the quality in which they do not differ, but are all alike; can you answer that?

MENO: I can.

30 SOCRATES: And the same for the virtues, however many and different they may be, they all have a common nature which makes them virtues; and he who would answer the question, 'What is virtue?' would do well to have his eye fixed on that.... And will virtue, as virtue, be the same, whether in a child or in a grown-up
35 person, in a woman or in a man?...Then all men are good in the same way, and by participation in the same virtues?

MENO: This is the inference.

SOCRATES: And they surely would not have been good in the same way, unless their virtue had been the same?

40 MENO: They would not.

nikolpetr/Shutterstock

What does the metaphor of the bee used by Socrates mean? What is important in the comparison of virtues with bees: their individuality or their common nature or both? Why?

Justice as a Virtue

SOCRATES: Now that the sameness of all virtue has been proven, try and remember what you and Gorgias say that virtue is....

45 MENO: If you want to have one definition of them all, I do not know what to say, except that virtue is the power of governing mankind.

SOCRATES: And does this definition of virtue include all virtue? Is virtue the same in a child and in a slave, Meno? Can the child govern his father, or the slave his master; and would he who governed 50 be any longer a slave?

MENO: I think not, Socrates.

SOCRATES: No, indeed; there would be small reason in that. Yet once more, fair friend; according to you, virtue is 'the power of governing;' but shouldn't you add 'justly and not unjustly'?

55 MENO: Yes, Socrates; I agree; for justice is virtue.

SOCRATES: Would you say 'virtue,' Meno, or 'a virtue'?

MENO: What do you mean?

SOCRATES: I mean as I might say about anything; that a circle, for example, is 'a figure' and not simply 'figure,' and I speak this way 60 because there are other figures.

MENO: I agree; and that is just what I am saying about virtue— that there are other virtues along with justice.

Other Virtues

SOCRATES: What are they? tell me the names of them, as I would 65 tell you the names of the other figures if you asked me.

MENO: Courage and temperance and wisdom and magnanimity are virtues; and there are many others.

SOCRATES: Yes, Meno; and again we are in the same place: in searching for one virtue we have found many, though not in the 70 same way as before; but we have been unable to find the common virtue which runs through them all.

MENO: Why, Socrates, even now I am not able to follow you in the attempt to get at one common notion of virtue as of other things.

> **"[W]e have been unable to find the common virtue which runs through them all."**

75 SOCRATES:…Why, did not I ask you the nature of virtue as a whole? And you are very far from telling me this; but you declare every action to be virtue which is done with a part of virtue; as though you had told me and I must already know the whole of virtue, and this too when frittered away into little pieces. And, 80 therefore, my dear Meno, I fear that I must begin again and repeat the same question: What is virtue? for otherwise, I can only say, that every action done with a part of virtue is virtue; what else is the meaning of saying that every action done with justice is virtue? Should I ask the question over again; for can any one who does not 85 know virtue know a part of virtue?

MENO: No, he cannot.

Acquiring Knowledge

MENO: And how will you enquire, Socrates, into that which you do not know? What will you suggest as the subject of enquiry? And 90 if you find what you want, how will you ever know that this is the thing which you did not know?

SOCRATES: I know, Meno, what you mean; but just see what a tiresome dispute you are introducing. You argue that a man cannot enquire either about that which he knows, or about that which he 95 does not know; for if he knows, he has no need to enquire; and if not, he cannot; for he does not know the very subject about which he is to enquire.

MENO: Well, Socrates, is not my argument sound?

SOCRATES: I think not.

100 MENO: Why not?

SOCRATES: I will tell you why: I have heard from certain wise men and women who spoke of things divine that—

MENO: What did they say?

SOCRATES: They spoke of a glorious truth, as I conceive.

105 MENO: What was it? and who were they?

Knowledge as Recollection

SOCRATES: Some of them were priests and priestesses, who had studied how they might be able to give a reason of their profession: there have been poets also, who spoke of these
110 things by inspiration…and many others who were inspired. And they say…that the soul of man is immortal, and at one time has an end, which is termed dying, and at another time is born again, but is never destroyed. And the moral is, that a man ought to live always in perfect holiness…. The soul,
115 then, as immortal, and having been born again many times, and having seen all things that exist, whether in this world or in the world below, has knowledge of them all; and it is no wonder that she should be able to remember all that she ever knew about virtue, and about everything; for as all nature is
120 akin, and the soul has learned all things; there is no difficulty in her eliciting or as men say learning, out of a single recollection all the rest, if a man is strenuous and does not faint; for all enquiry and all learning is but recollection. And therefore we ought not to listen to this sophistical argument about the
125 impossibility of enquiry: for it will make us idle; and is sweet only to the sluggard; but the other saying will make us active and inquisitive. In that confiding, I will gladly enquire with you into the nature of virtue.

MENO: Yes, Socrates; but what do you mean by saying that we
130 do not learn, and that what we call learning is only a process of recollection? Can you teach me how this is?…

Lipsky/Shutterstock

If "what we call learning is only a process of recollection," does that mean that the human race could keep a record of what is "recollected" in a big dictionary, for instance, that could help teach virtue?

SOCRATES: If the truth of all things always existed in the soul, then the soul is immortal. Therefore be of good cheer, and try to recollect what you do not know, or rather what you do not
135 remember.

MENO: I feel, somehow, that I like what you are saying.…

SOCRATES: Then, as we agree that a man should enquire about that which he does not know, shall you and I make an effort to enquire together into the nature of virtue?

140 Is Virtue Knowledge?

MENO: By all means, Socrates. And yet I would much rather return to my original question, Whether in seeking to acquire virtue we should regard it as a thing to be taught, or as a gift of nature, or as coming to men in some other way?

145 SOCRATES: Had I the command of you as well as of myself, Meno, I would not have enquired whether virtue is given by instruction or not, until we had first ascertained 'what it is.'…Let the first hypothesis be that virtue is or is not knowledge,—in that case will it be taught or not? or, as we were just now saying,
150 'remembered'? For there is no use in arguing about the name. But is virtue taught or not? or rather, does not every one see that knowledge alone is taught?

MENO: I agree.

SOCRATES: Then if virtue is knowledge, virtue will be taught?

155 MENO: Certainly.

SOCRATES: Then we have made a quick end to this question: if virtue is of such a nature, it will be taught; and if not, not?

MENO: Certainly.

SOCRATES: The next question is, whether virtue is knowledge or
160 something else?

MENO: Yes, that appears to be the question which comes next in order.

SOCRATES: Do we not say that virtue is a good?—This is a hypothesis which is not set aside.

165 MENO: Certainly.

SOCRATES: Now, if there be any sort of good which is distinct from knowledge, virtue may be that good; but if knowledge embraces all good, then we shall be right in thinking that virtue is knowledge?

> ## " [I]f there be any sort of good which is distinct from knowledge, virtue may be that good… "

170 MENO: True.

SOCRATES: And virtue makes us good?

MENO: Yes.

Is Virtue Beneficial?

SOCRATES: And if we are good, then we are beneficial; for all good
175 things are beneficial?

MENO: Yes.

SOCRATES: Then virtue is beneficial?

MENO: That is the only inference.

SOCRATES: Then now let us see what are the things which sev-
180 erally benefit us. Health and strength, and beauty and wealth—
these, and the like of these, we call beneficial?

MENO: True.

SOCRATES: And yet these things may also sometimes do us harm:
would you not think so?

185 MENO: Yes.

SOCRATES: And what is the guiding principle which makes them
beneficial or the reverse? Are they beneficial when they are rightly
used, and hurtful when they are not rightly used?

MENO: Certainly.

190 SOCRATES: Next, let us consider the goods of the soul: they
are temperance, justice, courage, quickness of apprehension,
memory, magnanimity, and the like?

MENO: Surely.

SOCRATES: And those things which are not knowledge, but of
195 another sort, are sometimes beneficial and sometimes hurtful;
as, for example, courage lacking prudence, which is only a sort of
confidence? When a man has no sense he is harmed by courage,
but when he has sense he profits?

MENO: True.

200 SOCRATES: And the same may be said of temperance and
quickness of apprehension; whatever things are learned or done
with sense are beneficial, but when done without sense they are
hurtful?

MENO: Very true.

205 SOCRATES: And in general, all that the soul attempts or endures,
when under the guidance of wisdom, ends in happiness; but when
she is under the guidance of folly, in the opposite?

MENO: That appears to be true.

SOCRATES: If then virtue is a quality of the soul, and is admitted
210 to be beneficial, it must be wisdom or prudence, since none of the
things of the soul are either beneficial or hurtful in themselves, but
they are all made beneficial or hurtful by the addition of wisdom or
of folly; and therefore if virtue is beneficial, virtue must be a sort
of wisdom or prudence?

215 MENO: I quite agree.

SOCRATES: And the other goods, such as wealth and the like, of
which we were just now saying that they are sometimes good
and sometimes evil, do they not also become beneficial or hurtful,
accordingly as the soul guides and uses them rightly or wrongly;
220 just as the things of the soul herself are benefited when under the
guidance of wisdom and harmed by folly?

MENO: True.

SOCRATES: And the wise soul guides them rightly, and the foolish
soul wrongly.

225 MENO: Yes.

SOCRATES: And is not this universally true of human nature? All
other things hang upon the soul, and the things of the soul herself
hang upon wisdom, if they are to be good; and so wisdom is inferred
to be that which profits—and virtue, as we say, is beneficial?

230 MENO: Certainly.

Is Virtue Wisdom?

SOCRATES: And thus we arrive at the conclusion that virtue is
either wholly or partly wisdom?

MENO: I think that what you are saying, Socrates, is very true.

235 SOCRATES: But if this is true, then the good are not by nature
good?… And if the good are not by nature good, are they made
good by instruction?

MENO: There appears to be no other alternative, Socrates. On the
supposition that virtue is knowledge, there can be no doubt that
240 virtue is taught.

Were you ever taught virtue formally when you were in school? If no class you ever attended was called *Virtue*, was there any class that taught a subject matter that discussed the concept of virtue?

SOCRATES: Yes, indeed; but what if the supposition is erroneous?

MENO: I certainly thought just now that we were right.

SOCRATES: Yes, Meno; but a principle which has any soundness should stand firm not only just now, but always.

245 MENO: Well; and why are you so slow in believing that knowledge is virtue?

SOCRATES: I will try and tell you why, Meno. I do not retract the assertion that if virtue is knowledge it may be taught; but I fear that I have some reason in doubting whether virtue is knowledge: 250 for consider now and say whether virtue, and not only virtue but anything that is taught, must not have teachers and disciples?

MENO: Surely.

Can Virtue Be Taught?

SOCRATES: And conversely, may not the art of which neither teach-255 ers nor disciples exist be assumed to be incapable of being taught?

MENO: True; but do you think that there are no teachers of virtue?

SOCRATES: I have certainly often enquired whether there were any, and taken great pains to find them, and have never succeeded; …

260 SOCRATES: Then virtue cannot be taught?

MENO: Not if we are right in our view. But I cannot believe, Socrates, that there are no good men: And if there are, how did they come into existence? …

SOCRATES: Good men are necessarily useful or beneficial. Were 265 we not right in admitting this? It must be so.

MENO: Yes.

SOCRATES: And in supposing that they will be useful only if they are true guides to us of action—there we were also right?

MENO: Yes.

270 SOCRATES: But when we said that a man cannot be a good guide unless he have knowledge, this we were wrong.

Is True Opinion the Same as True Knowledge?

MENO: What do you mean by the word 'right'?

SOCRATES: I will explain. If a man knew the way to Larisa, or 275 anywhere else, and went to the place and led others thither, would he not be a right and good guide?

MENO: Certainly.

SOCRATES: And a person who had a right opinion about the way, but had never been and did not know, might be a good guide also, 280 might he not?

MENO: Certainly.

SOCRATES: And while he has true opinion about that which the other knows, he will be just as good a guide if he thinks the truth, as he who knows the truth?

285 MENO: Exactly.

SOCRATES: Then true opinion is as good a guide to correct action as knowledge; and that was the point which we omitted in our speculation about the nature of virtue, when we said that knowledge only is the guide of right action; whereas there is also right opinion.

290 MENO: True.

SOCRATES: Then right opinion is not less useful than knowledge?

MENO: The difference, Socrates, is only that he who has knowledge will always be right; but he who has right opinion will sometimes be right, and sometimes not.

295 SOCRATES: What do you mean? Can he be wrong who has right opinion, so long as he has right opinion?

> *[T]rue opinion is as good a guide to correct action as knowledge…*

MENO: I admit the cogency of your argument, and therefore, Socrates, I wonder that knowledge should be preferred to right opinion—or why they should ever differ....

300 SOCRATES: That knowledge differs from true opinion is no matter of conjecture with me. There are not many things which I profess to know, but this is most certainly one of them.

MENO: Yes, Socrates; and you are quite right in saying so.

SOCRATES: And am I not also right in saying that true opinion leading the way perfects action quite as well as knowledge?

MENO: There again, Socrates, I think you are right.

SOCRATES: Then right opinion is not inferior to knowledge, or less useful in action; nor is the man who has right opinion inferior to him who has knowledge?

310 MENO: True.

SOCRATES: And surely the good man has been acknowledged by us to be useful?

MENO: Yes.

SOCRATES: Seeing then that men become good and useful to states, not only because they have knowledge, but because they have right opinion, and that neither knowledge nor right opinion is given to man by nature or acquired by him … Then if they are not given by nature, neither are the good by nature good?

MENO: Certainly not.

320 SOCRATES: And nature being excluded, then came the question whether virtue is acquired by teaching?

MENO: Yes.

SOCRATES: If virtue was wisdom (or knowledge), then, as we thought, it was taught?

325 MENO: Yes.

SOCRATES: And if it was taught it was wisdom?

MENO: Certainly.

SOCRATES: And if there were teachers, it might be taught; and if there were no teachers, not?

330 MENO: True.

SOCRATES: But surely we acknowledged that there were no teachers of virtue?

MENO: Yes.

SOCRATES: Then we acknowledged that it was not taught, and was not wisdom?

MENO: Certainly.

SOCRATES: And yet we admitted that it was a good?

MENO: Yes.

SOCRATES: And the right guide is useful and good?

340 MENO: Certainly.

SOCRATES: And the only right guides are knowledge and true opinion—these are the guides of man; for things which happen by chance are not under the guidance of man: but the guides of man are true opinion and knowledge.

345 MENO: I think so too.

SOCRATES: But if virtue is not taught, neither is virtue knowledge.

MENO: Clearly not.

CHAPTER 2

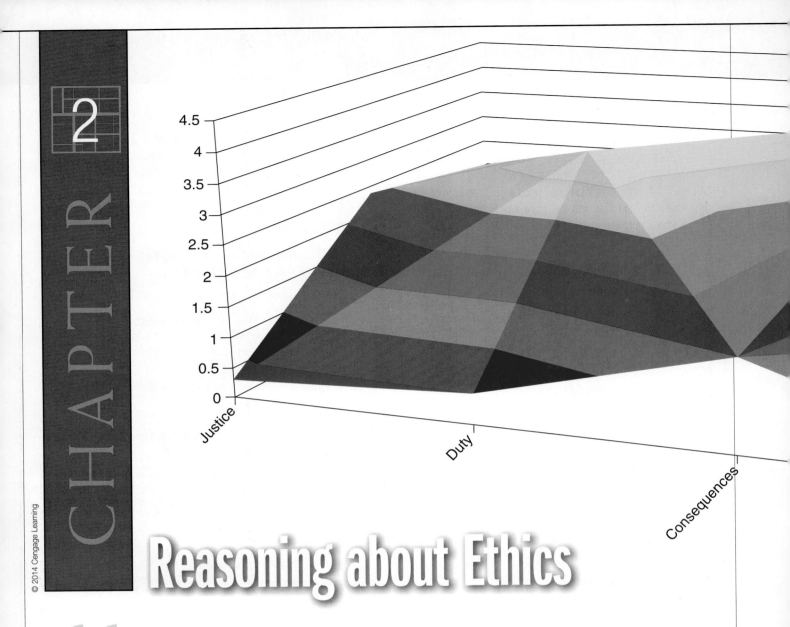

Reasoning about Ethics

"Power, riches, honor, even health, and the general well-being and contentment with one's condition which is called happiness, inspire pride, and often presumption, if there is not a good will to correct the influence of these on the mind, and with this also to rectify the whole principle of acting and adapt it to its end."

Immanuel Kant, *Fundamental Principles of the Metaphysics of Morals* (1785)

"The creed which accepts as the foundation of morals, Utility, or the Greatest Happiness Principle, holds that actions are right in proportion as they tend to promote happiness, wrong as they tend to produce the reverse of happiness."

John Stuart Mill, *Utilitarianism* (1863)

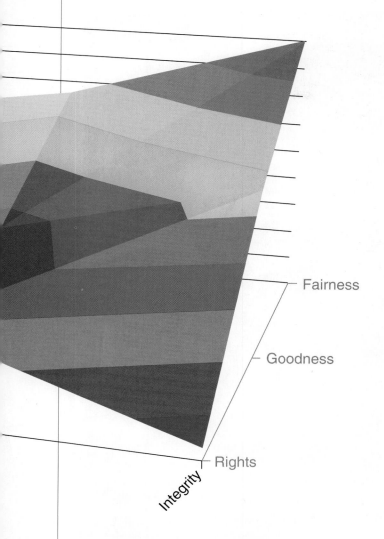

Fairness

Goodness

Rights

Integrity

Can ethics be put into a chart?

We all have gut reactions to ethical challenges. No doubt we have all participated in endless discussions on a variety of controversies from capital punishment to stem cell research to environmental ethics. Nobody needs to go to college to learn how to do this. What we hope to accomplish here in this chapter and the later ones is to help you learn how to reason more effectively and convincingly about these pressing ethical issues. In philosophy, we study what great philosophers of the past and present have to say—not because we consider them authorities who are necessarily correct. Rather, we study them for ideas and guidance on how to reason through these challenging issues so we can develop strong reasoning skills of our own.

Overview

In this chapter, we will consider the nature of moral reasoning, including the important distinction between facts and values. We will look at the appropriate and inappropriate uses of statistics in ethics, as well as common informal fallacies to avoid in our own ethical reasoning. The difference between ethical relativism on the one hand and open-mindedness and tolerance on the other will be explored. We also will survey several of the major theories in ethics that we will use later in this book when we consider specific applied issues, including Kantianism, utilitarianism, and other ethical perspectives.

What do you think?

As all ethics is relative, we can never agree on any objectively valid principles.

Strongly Disagree						Strongly Agree
1	2	3	4	5	6	7

Finally, we examine excerpts from foundational writings by Immanuel Kant and John Stuart Mill.

2-1 MORAL REASONING AND ITS APPLICATION

We considered in Chapter 1 the wide range of significant ethical issues we all confront throughout our lives. Much of this course will examine reasoning about those issues so that you will be better equipped to examine them yourselves, not just in this course but in later life as you encounter ethical dilemmas not even imaginable today. The skills of good reasoning are paramount in addressing these issues.

2-1a Apply Clarity, Precision, and Consistency

Good reasoning emphasizes clarity and precision in the use of key terms and premises. Merely looking up a term in the dictionary is a start, but it is not good enough for serious critical thinking. For central terms such as *justice*, *goodness*, *discrimination*, or *euthanasia*, or any of the many other terms at the center of our discussions, we want to look very closely at nuances, shadings of meaning, different ways we use the terms, and the importance of precision in how we use them in our analysis.

Good reasoning also demands consistency in applying principles to reach conclusions. For example, in the ongoing debates about the cost of health care, it was easy for many to tell pollsters that we should not waste money on old people who do not have long to live anyway and cost the nation a lot of money in the final months of life. But how would you react when the person in need of serious health care is your own grandfather? Would you insist that no expense should be spared to save his life? We need to examine our positions on the ethical use of scarce medical resources, so we think consistently across different situations. Consistency also applies to how we use a term. If in an argument you use the term *just*, to mean "fair" as opposed to "lawful," you need to make sure that you do not abruptly start using it in the second sense. Indeed, some things may be fair, in a moral sense, but unlawful. For example, in the United States, it used to be unlawful for blacks to use "whites-only" facilities, but it does not mean that it was fair for this nation to enforce this institutionalized segregation.

2-1b Build Premises and Clarify Assumptions

Once you have clarified what central terms and concepts will be at the core of your argument, you need to build the premises that will be the foundation of your reasoning.

Building an argument is analogous to building a brick wall: for the argument to be strong, every premise, like every brick, must support the next.

Start by laying out statements in short and clear sentences that explain step by step how you get from your first premise to your next one and finally to your conclusion.

Then, look carefully over each statement to find any in which certain facts or beliefs may be taken for granted. Reveal and explain any assumptions. For example, consider the following argument opposing segregation, "If a group of persons is singled out for different treatment in a society, then that group's individuals are deprived of the same rights as the members of the larger society; so, segregation is wrong." You might make clear that you make the important assumption that "persons" refers to any human being, regardless of gender, race, or other identifying characteristic.

2-1c Test Your Premises

Consider again your argument, "If a group of persons is singled out for different treatment in a society, then that group's individuals are deprived of the same rights as the

age fotostock/SuperStock

Is the different treatment of a group of persons always wrong? Is providing ramps for individuals in wheelchairs not a way to help them achieve rights available to the larger social group and therefore positive and necessary?

members of the larger society; so, segregation is wrong." Do you really believe that different treatment is always wrong? What of providing ramps for persons in wheelchairs? Or sign-language interpreters for the deaf? In those cases, providing different treatment seems to enable those persons to achieve rights of education and employment available to others, rather than denying those rights. Or different treatment might include affirmative action policies to compensate for past injustices. Again, those policies might actually be beneficial in enabling some groups to attain rights already held by others to education and employment. You may decide that you need to reformulate your argument so that it cannot be used to oppose policies you actually support. In our example, the word "different" is ambiguous. Therefore, it could be restated as: If a group of persons is singled out for pernicious and inferior treatment, then that group's individuals are deprived of the same rights as the members of the larger society; so, segregation is wrong.

2-1d Draw Logical Conclusions and Avoid Fallacies

Now that you have reframed your premises, consider again whether you can appropriately reach the conclusion that segregation is wrong. Or do you need to go back and add

another premise that all segregation is not necessarily wrong? For instance, if some women wished to form a discussion group to candidly address women's health issues, such a group would segregate itself, by gender. Would that necessarily be wrong? In other words, keep working through your premise or premises to reach a conclusion that you are satisfied follows appropriately from the premises and cannot be countered.

Good reasoning is rigorous in avoiding fallacies of all kinds that distort thinking. In this chapter, we will consider some of the most common informal fallacies that often slip into our everyday thinking.

In this chapter, we will also learn about a variety of ethical principles that have been proposed over the centuries by great thinkers. These are not introduced because they are necessarily "true," "accurate," or "right," but because they demonstrate a variety of ways in which ethical problems have been tackled over the years. It will be our job here to sift through the principles that best explain our ethical reasoning and provide the best techniques for addressing new challenges.

⌈**[E]thical principles ... proposed over the centuries by great thinkers ... demonstrate a variety of ways in which ethical problems have been tackled over the years.**⌋

2-2 FACTS VERSUS VALUES

Facts tell us the way the world "is," whereas values tell us the way the world "ought to be." Both the natural and social sciences focus on identifying accurate factual descriptions of our world, and many disciplines of the humanities, especially philosophy, focus on the "ought" questions. Another way to mark this distinction is to note that facts are "descriptive," that is, facts *describe* what exists, what "is," whereas values are "normative," that is, they propose norms that should be adhered to. Although we want to reach our ethical value conclusions based on accurate information about the world in which we live, those facts alone do not dictate any particular conclusion about our ethical principles.

To see the importance of keeping these facts and values distinct in our reasoning, consider the impact of rapidly developing technologies on our value decision making. An issue we will take up in Chapter 3 is the morality of euthanasia and assisted suicide. These challenges have become ever more urgent as medical technology has advanced in its ability to keep patients

The atomic bomb: Was it wrong to invent it? Was it wrong to use it?

SuperStock/Age Fotostock

2-3 STATISTICS IN ETHICAL REASONING

Many areas of the social sciences focus on gathering statistics of all sorts that seem relevant to our ethical decision making, but the use of statistics should be approached with caution. One of the most obvious mistakes is to assume that if a majority of people believe something, it must be true. Throughout history, we have learned that the opinions of even a huge majority of people can turn out to be wrong. So we need to distinguish between what is right or ethical and what is believed by many, even most people. In 1967, in a decision called *Loving v. Virginia*, the U.S. Supreme Court held that laws in many states prohibiting interracial marriage violated the basic human right to marry. Yet it was not until the 1980s that at least half of the U.S. population approved of interracial marriage. The Supreme Court knew that a clear majority of Americans disapproved of interracial marriage when it announced its decision, but the larger consideration of human rights prevailed over majority sentiment.

In other situations, though, shifting public opinion seems to drive our evolving ethical and legal views. In 2002, the U.S. Supreme Court in *Atkins v. Virginia* prohibited execution of the mentally retarded. To justify its conclusions, the court cited evolving public standards of decency, including the fact that thirty states had already banned such executions.

alive—even though it often comes at tremendous cost and frequently fails to produce an acceptable quality of life for the patient. Medical science can tell us what *is* possible now in keeping somebody alive, but that does not mean we necessarily *should* or *would want to* take advantage of all those technologies, especially when patients request not to be kept on life support. In other words, facts do not dictate values in this domain of reasoning. J. Robert Oppenheimer, one of the inventors of the atomic bomb during World War II, famously said that it is the job of scientists to discover facts, the way the laws of nature work, but that it is the responsibility of the U.S. people and their elected government to determine how those discoveries—such as nuclear fission—should be used.

> **Facts … are often relevant in working through ethical reasoning.**

Once again, knowing how to build a bomb does not imply knowing how to draw the proper ethical conclusion about whether or how that bomb should be used.

Even so, rapid growth in our factual knowledge seems to have some relevance in our ethical reasoning. As we learn more about the biological bases of mental illnesses and no longer just assume that such people are possessed by the devil or behaving badly of their own free will, we need to revise our conclusions about moral and legal responsibility for that behavior. Factual scientific information about the origins of homosexuality as triggered by genetic and perhaps environmental factors seems to challenge views that it is simply a choice of lifestyle. If it is not a genuine choice, should we reach different conclusions about the rights of homosexuals?

Facts do not dictate a particular set of values, but they are often relevant in working through ethical reasoning.

Legal reasoning is not identical with ethical reasoning, but the two overlap. For almost all of the issues in this book, we will see that the courts in our legal system have had to grapple with the same issues. More striking from the perspective of philosophy is that the reasoning of those courts so often sounds like philosophical reasoning. So we will frequently take a look at some of those important decisions. In part, this is to examine legal reasoning for its own sake, just as we want to learn more about philosophical reasoning. But looking at these decisions also helps us connect what might seem like theoretical musings with the real-world issues that impact daily life. And as many philosophy students have already figured out, if you are thinking about pursuing law school or a law-related career, developing your skills in philosophical reasoning will help immensely in the pursuit of a legal career.

Although the beliefs of a majority of people do not necessarily make something "right," those evolving sentiments do seem relevant in taking a fresh look at ethical standards today. One consequence is that any citation of statistics in our reasoning will require a close look to determine the relevancy of that data. We need to look, for example, at what factors seem to be driving the evolution of public opinion.

Nowhere is this evolution more clear today than the changing views of homosexuality and marriage equality. The approval of these practices seems to vary considerably depending on the age of the persons asked. If 70 percent of a younger age group and 30 percent of an elderly age group approves, as many recent polls seem to suggest, what conclusions should we draw about the ethical status of same-sex marriage? The numbers alone tell us nothing with-out careful examination of many other factors.

Interracial marriage once was frowned upon. Does the fact that it is no longer taboo affect your views regarding homosexual marriage?

Stephen Coburn/Shutterstock.com

2-4 INFORMAL FALLACIES

Fallacies are unreliable ways of arguing; that is, they are techniques that do not provide sound reasons for accepting a conclusion. If you study formal logic, you will encounter "formal fallacies," which are invalid logical rules. In a critical thinking course, you will encounter "informal fallacies," which are common in both everyday discourse and more sophisticated argumentation. These informal fallacies include a wide range of suspicious argumentation. Typically, they will not be so blatant that they are immediately obvious in your debates, but are more subtly woven into otherwise convincing discussions. Several of the most common informal fallacies are listed in Feature 2.1.

Now that you have familiarized yourself with the essentials of ethical reasoning, review the first of the recurring tools that will guide you through the basic steps of sound argumentation, Critical Thinking Table 2.1. In Chapters 3 through 13, you will have a chance to watch the process "in action" for different ethical claims.

In CourseMate, watch a video and take the quiz.

Feature 2.1: Informal Fallacies

ad hominem (to the person): an irrelevant attack on the person making the argument, rather than the argument itself

For example, "Sally's argument that capital punishment is ethical is obviously incorrect, as Sally is an airhead." The attack here is on Sally, rather than on Sally's argument.

faulty analogy: misusing reasoning by analogy to exploit irrelevant similarities

For example, "Bicycle riding and swimming in deep lakes are both dangerous for children. So we should require children to wear bicycle helmets when they are swimming to protect them." Both of these activities do present dangers to children, but they differ in many respects as well, making the conclusion about helmets silly.

begging the question: assuming the conclusion that you set out to prove

For example, "Anybody who criticizes President Obama must be a racist. Why? Because only people who are racist would criticize the nation's first African American President." This assumes exactly what the person sets out to prove.

equivocation: relying implicitly on different meanings of a key term to reach a conclusion

For example, "I appreciate people with discriminating taste in art, food, and wine, so how dare the government make discrimination illegal?" *Discrimination* is being used in different senses here; the latter use refers to certain types of discrimination by race, gender, and national origin, not discriminating taste.

hasty generalization: rushing to a general conclusion from a very small or biased sample size

For example, "My neighbor has a Volkswagen that's a lemon and my brother has a Volkswagen that's a lemon, so that must mean that all Volkswagens are lemons and I shouldn't buy one." Generalizing based on only two instances to reach a conclusion about tens of thousands of cars is not justified.

appeal to ignorance: claiming something is true because we have no evidence that it is false, or vice versa

For example, "Climate change is a major threat because nobody has proved that it isn't." The absence of proof that something is false does not prove it is true.

(Continued)

Feature 2.1: *(Continued)*

post hoc, ergo propter hoc **("after this, therefore because of this"):** claiming that one thing caused another because they occurred in sequence of time

For example, "Whenever there is an eclipse of the sun, I always do my special dance to make sure the sun comes out again." This person falsely believes that the special dance caused the sun to come out after the eclipse.

red herring: an irrelevant claim introduced to distract focus from the real issue at stake

For example, "I just can't get too upset about those starving children in Somalia because it was Somalians who killed U.S. soldiers the last time we tried to provide food aid." The murders of U.S. soldiers by Somalians many years ago are irrelevant to the children starving today in that country.

slippery slope: claiming that some small steps in a certain direction will inevitably lead to other, major consequences

For example, "If we allow terminally ill patients to choose assisted suicide, before you know it we'll be euthanizing the mentally ill just like Hitler." Carefully regulated assisted suicide laws in a few states do not inevitably lead to the atrocious violations of human rights of the Nazis.

A slippery slope: No one can stop the vertiginous fall of any object put at the top of the slope.

straw man: distorting your opponent's position and then attacking the distortion

For example, "Medical review boards to recommend effective treatments are really just death panels aiming to kill people they don't like." Recommendations for good medical treatments for society at large are not recommendations for whom to kill or not to kill.

Table 2.1 Critical Thinking Steps and Their Application in an Example

"If we truly support 'justice for all,' then we should insist that nonhuman animals have equal rights with humans."

Critical Thinking Steps	Application
1. Examine and clarify key terms and concepts. 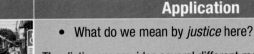 • Look words up in a dictionary as a start if necessary. • Unravel or unpack the complexities and nuances of a central term, such as *justice*, *right*, or *good*.	• What do we mean by *justice* here? The dictionary provides several different meanings. Which one applies to our statement? Are we referring to the application of punishment or reward, as in "justice was served"? Are we referring to the concept of the application of fair and equitable treatment? Are we referring to the objective application of laws? • What do we mean by *equal rights*? What do we mean by *equal*? And what are *rights*? What types of rights should we consider?
2. Work through the meaning of the key terms and concepts to make sure you will use them consistently. • Consider the ways the term can be used by including it in different sentences and contexts to zero in on the particular meaning you are after.	Does justice in this context mean a treatment that is identical or comparable? Although *identical* would suggest "exactly the same," *comparable* would convey "equivalence." Because of the many differences between humans and nonhumans, we ought to use *comparable*. • How do we measure comparable treatment?

Critical Thinking Steps	Application
• Ask yourself what words are potential synonyms for the concept. Do those capture everything you want to understand about that term?	• Should the rights granted nonhuman animals be exactly the same? If so, would, for example, the right to vote be granted to nonhuman animals? Or do we mean that nonhuman animals should be granted only certain rights as sentient beings? If so, does this mean those who can feel pain? Who are conscious of their existence? Who can use language? (Moving up the cognitive scale, we might recognize some but not others.) • Do we believe that nonhuman animals understand moral concepts in the "same" way as humans?
3. Build premises and bring any assumptions to light.  Stephen Coburn/Shutterstock.com • Put together short and clear sentences to build each of your premises. • Think through what you may be taking for granted in your reasoning. What assumptions are you making? • Once you have identified assumptions, articulate them in your premise, so that your audience has the same understanding of a term or a concept as you.	The premises of the argument could be constructed as follows: (i) All should have justice. (ii) "All" includes both human and nonhuman animals. (iii) *Justice* includes, at least, "having equal rights." CONCLUSION: Nonhuman animals should have equal rights with human animals. The implicit assumptions in the original statement include: (a) Justice is the *kind* of right that can be held by all animals, both human and nonhuman. (b) Justice *is* a right possessed by all animals, both human and nonhuman. (c) If human animals possess a right such as justice, then nonhuman animals should have that same right. (d) *Justice* means, at least, "having equal rights."
4. Test/Verify your premises. • Now that you have stated your premises explicitly, do you want to stick with them? • Are you relying on premises drawn from unsubstantiated sources or from questionable authorities? • Are you consistent in your premises? Or are you appealing to different and inconsistent foundations in your reasoning? • Reformulate your premises if they have proven to be faulty.	Each of the following premises and implicit assumptions can be challenged: • Justice is the kind of right that both human and nonhuman animals possess. • Even human animals have a right to justice. • *Justice* strictly means "having equal rights" and does not include other things. If you are not persuaded of those premises and assumptions, you will disagree in varying degrees with the original statement. If you are persuaded, then you will agree with it.
5. Confirm that the conclusions you draw are logical. Check for reliance on fallacies and correct any premise that you identify as relying on a fallacy. Teich/Caro/Alamy	Work through these various questions and reformulations to see if you can reach a persuasive conclusion, one you are able to defend convincingly. Are there any fallacies here, now that you see the arguments broken out explicitly? For example, does the original statement rely on the fallacy of equivocation in the meaning of *all* and *justice*?

2-5 ETHICAL RELATIVISM

Our society places a higher value on tolerance and open-mindedness today than it used to, leading some to conclude that all ethical principles are relative and that there are no objective principles that apply to everyone. With instantaneous global communication, we are increasingly aware of the divergent lifestyles and cultures on planet Earth, further encouraging many to assume that all values are relative and nothing is universal.

Yet simply making a factual observation, as a social scientist would, that there are many different value systems around the world, does not necessarily lead to the conclusion that there are no universal principles that somehow apply to all of us. Is it possible to reconcile tolerance and open-mindedness with adherence to at least some universal principles?

As a first step, we need to get clear on what relativism is. Although terminology sometimes varies, let us use **cultural relativism** here as a way to describe the simple fact that (people and) cultures disagree on their ethical views. This is only a factual description of the way the world is and it is hard to deny. As we look around, we see that different people in different cultures do in fact disagree on all sorts of ethical views. Some cultures believe, for example, that women should have equal rights to education and others do not share that belief. Some cultures believe that polygamy is ethical and others do not. But just because cultures disagree on all sorts of things like this does not mean that is the end of the matter. We do not have to conclude that they are all "right" or that we have to tolerate all of them.

Now, let us use **ethical relativism** for the much more stringent claim that there *are* no universal ethical principles that apply to all. A common mistake is to assume that the *descriptive* cultural relativism forces us to accept the *normative* ethical relativism. Here is another example to see the difference: Society X believes that infanticide (child murder) is ethically permissible. Society Y believes that infanticide is not ethically permissible. So far, we have only given a description of something existing in the facts of the world, namely, the inconsistent beliefs of two different societies. That is all cultural relativism is saying. Ethical relativism claims something more, namely, that there is no way to resolve these differences, that we must tolerate all such views, and there are no overarching principles we could appeal to that would conclude that one society is right in its views and the other society is wrong in its views.

Ethical relativism is a very strong theoretical claim. But an effective way to challenge ethical relativism is to consider the unacceptable consequences of such a position. If there are no universal ethical principles that apply to all people at all times, then how could we today criticize Adolf Hitler's conduct? He seems to have violated a host of human rights during World War II, but a consistent ethical relativist would have to conclude that we have no basis for criticizing him ethically and taking appropriate steps to stop him.

We disagree on many issues of human rights, but it seems there are at least a few areas where we now find agreement. Was the global community right in challenging apartheid, the legal segregation of the races in South Africa, now abolished? Not if we are truly ethical relativists.

We can disagree—and certainly do—on what universal ethical principles apply and what reasoning gets us to those conclusions. But if we insist that there are universal principles that apply to all, then we are not ethical relativists, but absolutists.

We can still be flexible in our applications of those principles and tolerant of variations that do not violate the bedrock universal principles. But we need not give up our search for universal principles.

2-6 KANTIANISM AND UTILITARIANISM

In contemporary ethics, two approaches are still dominant, centuries after the earliest proponents set forth their ethical ideas. Although we will see many other approaches to ethical reasoning, these give us an understandable framework within which to test out ethical ideas.

Kantianism is an objectivist approach to ethics because it holds that there are universal principles that apply to all rational beings. Note that the term *absolutism* is sometimes used to refer to what we are here calling *objectivism*. The Kantian approach was developed by the great German philosopher Immanuel Kant and has been enormously influential to this day. Kant recognized that our actions have consequences, but considered those irrelevant in determining what is right and wrong. Rather, he emphasized the intrinsic value of our actions, regardless of consequences in particular circumstances. His central principle is called his categorical imperative. First, a **categorical imperative** is a requirement that we follow no matter what. By contrast, Kant explains, a hypothetical imperative is a requirement we would follow only if we wanted a certain outcome. If we want to become a physician, then we must go to medical school; this is a hypothetical imperative, but it is not an imperative for everyone, because we do not all want to become physicians.

Kant presents three versions or "formulations" of his categorical imperative, two of which we consider here. In one of those versions of the categorical imperative Kant says that we should follow those maxims (or ethical rules) and only those maxims that we would want all persons to follow. This sounds a bit like the "Golden Rule," but it is intended as a test for universalizing, that is, for applying universally. We might ask ourselves: should I follow a rule (a maxim) that I should never lie? Kant's categorical imperative tells us to test this rule by asking if we would want to universalize that rule. So, would we want everybody to follow a rule that they should never lie? This exercise is meant as a mental undertaking, not a social science experiment. Universal promise-breaking contradicts itself, whereas universal truth-telling does not, so we should follow the maxim to keep promises. Kant places great confidence in our ability to reason through all of these ethical issues using his categorical imperative as the testing tool. We might wonder if every person, regardless of their educational and cultural backgrounds, would arrive at the same

conclusion. But universalization is a thought experiment to identify rational action; we do not actually require that every person employ it in practice for it to work.

A second version or "formulation" of Kant's categorical imperative is sometimes called the formula of the end in itself or the **practical imperative**. It says that we should never treat other persons solely as a means to an end, but only as ends in themselves. This says that we should always treat all other persons with dignity and respect in themselves and not as a mere thing to use for our own advantage. Owning slaves would be an extreme example of failing to treat persons as ends in themselves but only as a means to our own ends.

Utilitarianism has been proposed and developed by many philosophers, but is perhaps most associated with the English philosopher, John Stuart Mill. Like Kant, he is also an objectivist, as he believes that there is a fundamental and universal ethical principle that applies to everyone. But he disagrees with Kant as to what that principle is. For Mill, the fundamental principle of morality is the principle of utility, that is, "actions are right in proportion as they tend to promote happiness, wrong as they tend to produce the reverse of happiness." The rightness and wrongness of actions depends entirely on their consequences. Specifically, he wants us to consider the happiness generated by our choices and do the thing that would create the greatest happiness for the greatest number of people. If all of our options would create unhappiness, then we should do the thing that creates the least unhappiness for the greatest number.

This is a consequentialist position because it determines rightness and wrongness of actions solely in terms of consequences. But utilitarians consider the consequences for all persons, including themselves. In contrast, as we have seen in Chapter 1, altruists consider only consequences for others, never themselves, and egoists consider consequences only for themselves, never others.

Like Kant, Mill is proposing a mental exercise to test out proposed actions with ethical consequences. He is not telling us to actually conduct a social science experiment to measure happiness. But we might wonder how accurate this reasoning tool could be in

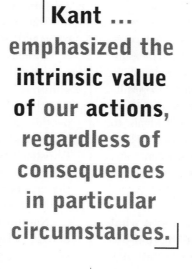

> Kant ... emphasized the intrinsic value of our actions, regardless of consequences in particular circumstances.

akiyoko/Shutterstock

What are the true costs of burning fossil fuels that pollute our environment?

practice. Do we really have a good sense of all the possible consequences of our actions? How should we weigh the good to people now versus the good to people in future generations?

Burning fossil fuels now might create happiness through cheap energy and jobs for people today, but at the likely cost of air pollution and climate change for both current and future generations. How are we supposed to measure with precision these trade-offs in our ethical reasoning? Does Mill's methodology leave too much to manipulation by individuals to rationalize their actions? These questions highlight what are some of the major challenges for utilitarian reasoning.

In CourseMate, apply what you've learned to the real-life scenarios in the simulations.

2-7 ALTERNATIVE APPROACHES TO ETHICAL REASONING

Although Kant and Mill contribute enormously important ethical theories, many other approaches have been proposed over the years, and we are not able to do justice to them here. A few of you might pursue these ideas in an advanced course in ethical theory, but for now some brief summaries will give you a sense of the alternative approaches that have received support.

Aristotle, the student of Plato in ancient Greece, is well known for proposing **virtue ethics**, which stressed the development of character in all persons and the "Golden Mean" suggesting that we find a moderate middle ground in our pursuit of ethical behavior. Examples of virtues, for Aristotle, are courage, justice, and temperance. Note that these are traits or states of being, not specific actions that we would assess as right or wrong.

Thomas Aquinas in the middle ages developed what we now call **natural law**. He claimed that an eternal and universal law from God was manifest in this world. This is a theological version of natural law because it relies on this assumption about God as the source of ethics and provides much of the foundation for contemporary Christianity. But in contemporary philosophy, natural law has also evolved to refer to a nontheological approach that insists that certain basic rights are embedded in the nature of all human beings.

Natural law continues to be a matter of extensive debate today. It holds that ethical standards exist universally, whether or not we recognize them, just as the law of gravity exists independently of us, whether or not we recognize it. The contrast to natural law is the view that all ethical rules are merely stipulated or constructed by human beings and thus could presumably be stipulated differently. For example, natural law theory would say that killing another person is wrong, whether or not we recognize that law or state it in our own terms. Those who reject natural law would say that we have agreed to stipulate an ethical rule that killing another person is wrong, but we could have stipulated something different.

John Locke, another English philosopher, is best known for developing, in the seventeenth century, a **social contract** approach to ethics, in which we all enter into agreements, implicit or otherwise, for treating each other in ethical ways to improve the lot of all of us. It appears that the Founding Fathers who wrote the U.S. Constitution were heavily influenced by Locke's reasoning. Contemporary social contract theory is

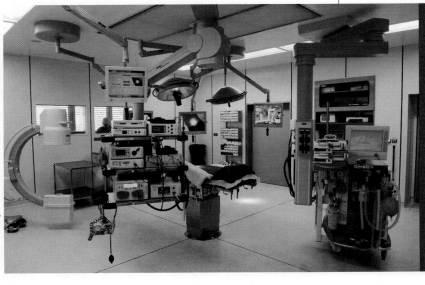

Technology now seems to have the power to prolong life indefinitely. How has this fact changed the discourse on euthanasia and living wills, among other things?

Teich/Caro/Alamy

one of the most influential of ethical theories, especially as articulated by John Rawls, in his *A Theory of Justice.*

Care ethics emerged first in the work of psychologists and has been developed in more rigorous detail by such philosophers as Virginia Held. **Care ethics** focuses on the ethical principles in the family, especially the rights and obligations of parents, to extend ethical reasoning to a greater community.

Look at Timeline 2.1 to learn about some philosophers you may not know about or review a brief historical survey of contributors to the field of philosophy.

In CourseMate, listen to the audio summary of the chapter.

In CourseMate, practice what you learned by taking the chapter quiz.

2-8 YOUR PERSONAL GOALS

As Chapter 1 suggested, you will now be asked to identify an ethical issue that is important to you at the moment and that you are comfortable discussing in class.

1. In a journal that you will complete through this course, articulate the issue as succinctly, but as precisely, as you can.

2. Now in your journal, identify goals that will help you address this issue. These goals should be as specific and quantifiable as possible.

3. In the book's modules, you will be given opportunities to address steps you can take to reach these goals.

Example 1:

The most important ethical issue I am facing at the moment is whether to tell my brother that I wonder if his treatment of his girlfriend is too casual and sometimes disrespectful.

The goals that I would like to reach to help come up with a resolution of this issue are: (1) Figuring out whether I should speak up or whether I should just mind my own business; (2) confirming with my friends the best ways to convey my opinions to my brother so that he hears me and doesn't get defensive.

Example 2:

The most important ethical issue I am facing at the moment is helping my parents make a decision regarding whether to take my mother's father off life support.

The goals that I would like to reach to help come up with a resolution of this issue are: (1) finding out whether all of us as a family can feel comfortable with the medical team's assessment of the quality of life for my grandfather and (2) identifying what would constitute, for all of us as a family, "reasonable" conditions to reach the conclusion that he should be taken off life support.

Immanuel Kant

The German philosopher Immanuel Kant is one of the most influential thinkers in the western world, and he continues to have enormous impact on many areas of philosophy. Although his work can be difficult to read and understand, he introduced several key ideas that are foundational in much of our thinking today in ethics.

For instance, he synthesized a range of different approaches to philosophy in his day, from the rationalists who emphasized human reasoning and logic (such as Descartes, Leibniz, and Spinoza) to the empiricists who emphasized experience and sense perception (such as Locke, Berkeley, and Hume). Kant proposed that our mind structures our experiences recognizing both human rationality and sense experiences.

In ethics, he believed our rationality could think through the laws of ethics we should follow. His approach to "personhood" remains central in our contemporary considerations of issues as diverse as abortion, euthanasia, and capital punishment. Kant recognized the autonomous dignity of every person and our capacity for rational thought to work through ethical choices between right and wrong.

Among the many contemporary Kantian philosophers are John Rawls, who taught until his death at Harvard University, and Barbara Herman, who teaches at UCLA.

Immanuel Kant (1724–1804)

Lebrecht Music and Arts Photo Library/Alamy

Timeline 2.1 Famous Philosophers in History

World events and leaders, prominent philosophers

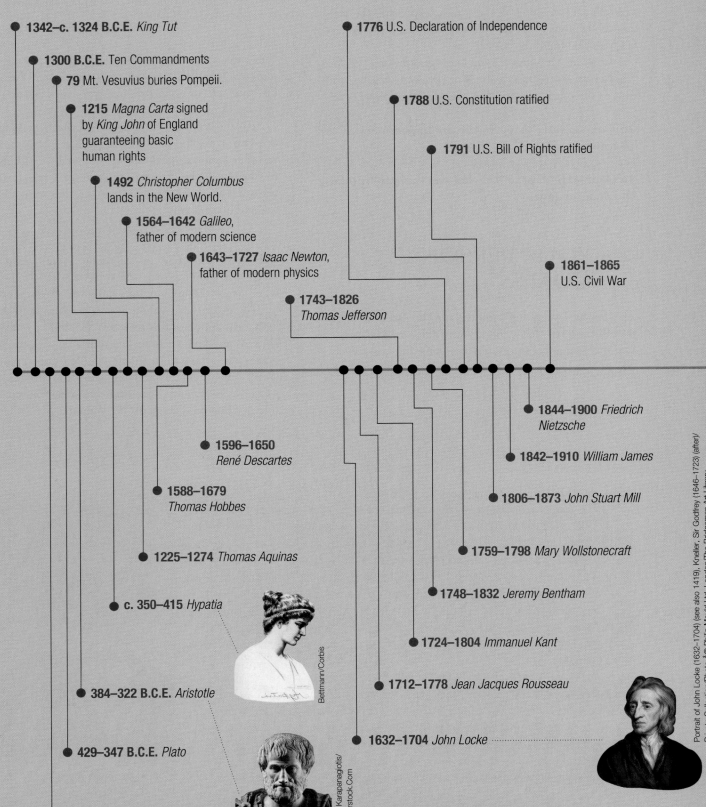

- **1342–c. 1324 B.C.E.** *King Tut*
- **1300 B.C.E.** Ten Commandments
- **79** Mt. Vesuvius buries Pompeii.
- **1215** *Magna Carta* signed by *King John* of England guaranteeing basic human rights
- **1492** *Christopher Columbus* lands in the New World.
- **1564–1642** *Galileo*, father of modern science
- **1643–1727** *Isaac Newton*, father of modern physics
- **1596–1650** *René Descartes*
- **1588–1679** *Thomas Hobbes*
- **1225–1274** *Thomas Aquinas*
- **c. 350–415** *Hypatia*
- **384–322 B.C.E.** *Aristotle*
- **429–347 B.C.E.** *Plato*
- **551–479 B.C.E.** *Confucius*

- **1776** U.S. Declaration of Independence
- **1788** U.S. Constitution ratified
- **1791** U.S. Bill of Rights ratified
- **1861–1865** U.S. Civil War
- **1743–1826** *Thomas Jefferson*
- **1844–1900** *Friedrich Nietzsche*
- **1842–1910** *William James*
- **1806–1873** *John Stuart Mill*
- **1759–1798** *Mary Wollstonecraft*
- **1748–1832** *Jeremy Bentham*
- **1724–1804** *Immanuel Kant*
- **1712–1778** *Jean Jacques Rousseau*
- **1632–1704** *John Locke*

Bettmann/Corbis

Panos Karapanagiotis/ Shutterstock.Com

Portrait of John Locke (1632–1704) (see also 1419), Kneller, Sir Godfrey (1646–1723) (after)/ Private Collection/Photo Â© Philip Mould Ltd, London/The Bridgeman Art Library

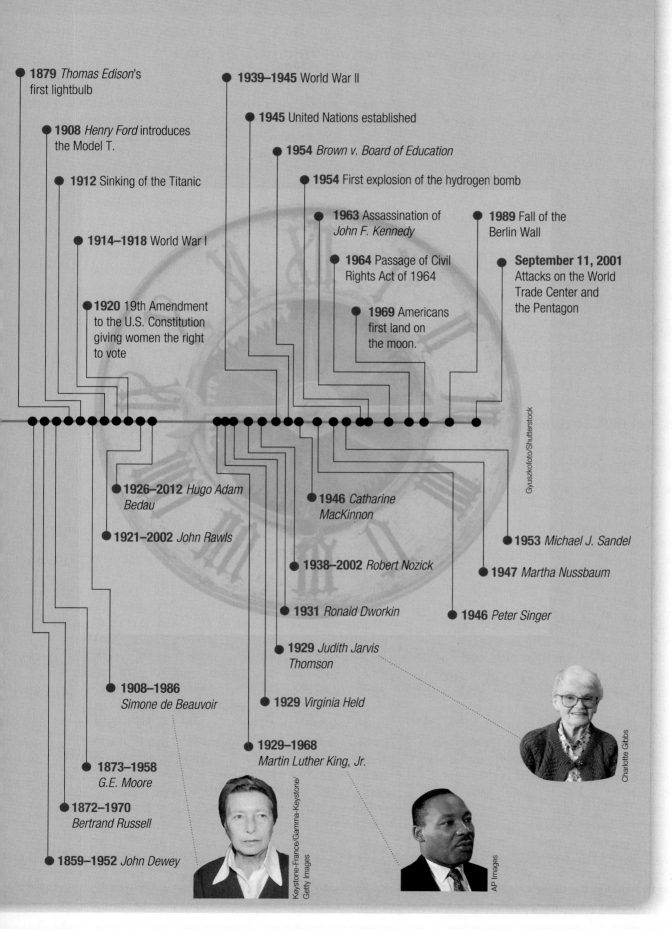

1879 *Thomas Edison*'s first lightbulb

1908 *Henry Ford* introduces the Model T.

1912 Sinking of the Titanic

1914–1918 World War I

1920 19th Amendment to the U.S. Constitution giving women the right to vote

1939–1945 World War II

1945 United Nations established

1954 *Brown v. Board of Education*

1954 First explosion of the hydrogen bomb

1963 Assassination of *John F. Kennedy*

1964 Passage of Civil Rights Act of 1964

1969 Americans first land on the moon.

1989 Fall of the Berlin Wall

September 11, 2001 Attacks on the World Trade Center and the Pentagon

1926–2012 *Hugo Adam Bedau*

1921–2002 *John Rawls*

1946 *Catharine MacKinnon*

1953 *Michael J. Sandel*

1938–2002 *Robert Nozick*

1947 *Martha Nussbaum*

1931 *Ronald Dworkin*

1946 *Peter Singer*

1929 *Judith Jarvis Thomson*

1908–1986 *Simone de Beauvoir*

1929 *Virginia Held*

1873–1958 *G.E. Moore*

1929–1968 *Martin Luther King, Jr.*

1872–1970 *Bertrand Russell*

1859–1952 *John Dewey*

Gyuszkofoto/Shutterstock

Charlotte Gibbs

Keystone-France/Gamma-Keystone/ Getty Images

AP Images

Reading Excerpt: Immanuel Kant, *Fundamental Principles of the Metaphysics of Morals* (1785)

INTRODUCTION

In these brief excerpts from Kant's work on ethics, he develops his principle of respect for persons. He explains his concepts of hypothetical imperative and categorical imperative. The latter is the

Kant argued, "[N]ever act in such a way that I could not also will that my maxim should be a universal law." Just as the law of gravitation applies to all objects across the universe, Kant's law would require a principle to apply across the human universe.

Marvin Dembinsky Photo Associates/Alamy

ultimate command for ethical behavior, a command that applies to all rational beings in all circumstances. He then introduces three formulations of this categorical imperative. The first says "[N]ever act in such a way that I could not also will that my maxim should be a universal law." A maxim for Kant is a rule or principle that determines how I should act. The second formulation addresses personhood: "Act so that you treat humanity, whether in your own person or in that of another, as an end and never as a means only." The third formulation, although not stated as an imperative, recognizes the capacity of each of us to rationally develop ethical conduct: "the idea of the will of every rational being as making universal law."

This excerpt from Kant's *Fundamental Principles of the Metaphysics of Morals* is based on a translation by Thomas Kingsmill Abbott.

QUESTIONS FOR REFLECTION

1. What is "good will" for Kant? Why is it good without qualification? How does it differ from other good things?

2. What is a hypothetical imperative? A categorical imperative? How do categorical imperatives get their authority?

3. What is the importance of human autonomy for ethics? How can we be subject to a law of our own will? How does that make us autonomous?

4. What is Kant's "kingdom" or "realm" of ends? What role does that play in his ethics?

READING

A Good Will

Nothing can possibly be conceived in the world, or even out of it, which can be called good, without qualification, except a good will. Intelligence, wit, judgment, and the other talents of the mind, how-
5 ever they may be named, or courage, resolution, perseverance, as qualities of temperament, are undoubtedly good and desirable in many respects; but these gifts of nature may also become extremely bad and mischievous if the will which is to make use of them, and which, therefore, constitutes what is called character,
10 is not good. It is the same with the gifts of fortune. Power, riches, honor, even health, and the general well-being and contentment with one's condition which is called happiness, inspire pride, and often presumption, if there is not a good will to correct the influence of these on the mind, and with this also to rectify the
15 whole principle of acting and adapt it to its end. The sight of a being who is not adorned with a single feature of a pure and good

will, enjoying unbroken prosperity, can never give pleasure to an impartial rational spectator. Thus a good will appears to constitute the indispensable condition even of being worthy of happiness....
20 A good will is good not because of what it performs or effects, not by its aptness for the attainment of some proposed end, but simply by virtue of the volition; that is, it is good in itself, and considered by itself is to be esteemed much higher than all that can be brought about by it in favor of any inclination, nay even of the
25 sum total of all inclinations. Even if it should happen that, owing to special disfavor of fortune, or the stingy provision of a step-motherly nature, this will should wholly lack power to accomplish its purpose, if with its greatest efforts it should yet achieve nothing, and there should remain only the good will (not, to be sure, a mere
30 wish, but the summoning of all means in our power), then, like a jewel, it would still shine by its own light, as a thing which has its whole value in itself. Its usefulness or fruitlessness can neither add

nor take away anything from this value. It would be, as it were, only the setting to enable us to handle it the more conveniently in common commerce, or to attract to it the attention of those who are not yet connoisseurs, but not to recommend it to true connoisseurs, or to determine its value....

Thus the moral worth of an action does not lie in the effect expected from it, nor in any principle of action which requires to borrow its motive from this expected effect. For all these effects—agreeableness of one's condition and even the promotion of the happiness of others—could have been also brought about by other causes, so that for this there would have been no need of the will of a rational being; whereas it is in this alone that the supreme and unconditional good can be found. The pre-eminent good which we call moral can therefore consist in nothing else than the conception of law in itself, which certainly is only possible in a rational being, in so far as this conception, and not the expected effect, determines the will. This is a good which is already present in the person who acts accordingly, and we have not to wait for it to appear first in the result.

But what sort of law can that be, the conception of which must determine the will, even without paying any regard to the effect expected from it, in order that this will may be called good absolutely and without qualification? As I have deprived the will of every impulse which could arise to it from obedience to any law, there remains nothing but the universal conformity of its actions to law in general, which alone is to serve the will as a principle, i.e., I am never to act otherwise than so that I could also will that my maxim should become a universal law. Here, now, it is the simple conformity to law in general, without assuming any particular law applicable to certain actions, that serves the will as its principle and must so serve it, if duty is not to be a vain delusion and a chimerical notion. The common reason of men in its practical judgements perfectly coincides with this and always has in view the principle here suggested. Let the question be, for example: May I when in distress make a promise with the intention not to keep it? I readily distinguish here between the two significations which the question may have: Whether it is prudent, or whether it is right, to make a false promise? The former may undoubtedly of be the case. I see clearly indeed that it is not enough to extricate myself from a present difficulty by means of this subterfuge, but it must be well considered whether there may not hereafter spring from this lie much greater inconvenience than that from which I now free myself, and as, with all my supposed cunning, the consequences cannot be so easily foreseen but that credit once lost may be much more injurious to me than any mischief which I seek to avoid at present, it should be considered whether it would not be more prudent to act herein according to a universal maxim and to make it a habit to promise nothing except with the intention of keeping it. But it is soon clear to me that such a maxim will still only be based on the fear of consequences.

> **"[I]t should be considered … more prudent to act … according to a universal maxim and to make it a habit to promise nothing except with the intention of keeping it."**

Acting from Duty

Now it is a wholly different thing to be truthful from duty and to be so from apprehension of injurious consequences. In the first case, the very notion of the action already implies a law for me; in the second case, I must first look about elsewhere to see what results may be combined with it which would affect myself. For to deviate from the principle of duty is beyond all doubt wicked; but to be unfaithful to my maxim of prudence may often be very advantageous to me, although to abide by it is certainly safer. The shortest way, however, and an unerring one, to discover the answer to this question whether a lying promise is consistent with duty, is to ask myself, "Should I be content that my maxim (to extricate myself from difficulty by a false promise) should hold good as a universal law, for myself as well as for others?" and should I be able to say to myself, "Every one may make a deceitful promise when he finds himself in a difficulty from which he cannot otherwise extricate himself?" Then I presently become aware that while I can will the lie, I can by no means will that lying should be a universal law. For with such a law there would be no promises at all, since it would be in vain to allege my intention in regard to my future actions to those who would not believe this allegation, or if they over hastily did so would pay me back in my own coin. Hence my maxim, as soon as it should be made a universal law, would necessarily destroy itself.

Universal Laws

I do not, therefore, need any far-reaching penetration to discern what I have to do in order that my will may be morally good. Inexperienced in the course of the world, incapable of being prepared for all its contingencies, I only ask myself: Canst thou also will that thy maxim should be a universal law? If not, then it must be rejected, and that not because of a disadvantage accruing from it to myself or even to others, but because it cannot enter as a principle into a possible universal legislation, and reason extorts from me immediate respect for such legislation. I do not indeed as yet discern on what this respect is based (this the philosopher may inquire), but at least I understand this, that it is an estimation of the worth which far outweighs all worth of what is recommended by inclination, and that the necessity of acting from pure respect 120 for the practical law is what constitutes duty, to which every other motive must give place, because it is the condition of a will being good in itself, and the worth of such a will is above everything…

…Everything in nature works according to laws. Rational beings alone have the faculty of acting according to the concep-125 tion of laws, that is according to principles, i.e., have a will. Since the deduction of actions from principles requires reason, the will is nothing but practical reason.…

Imperatives

The conception of an objective principle, in so far as it is obligatory 130 for a will, is called a command (of reason), and the formula of the command is called an imperative.

All imperatives are expressed by the word ought, and thereby indicate the relation of an objective law of reason to a will, which from its subjective constitution is not necessarily determined by 135 it (an obligation). They say that something would be good to do or to forbear, but they say it to a will which does not always do a thing because it is conceived to be good to do it. That is practically good, however, which determines the will by means of the concep-tions of reason, and consequently not from subjective causes, but 140 objectively, that is on principles which are valid for every rational being as such. It is distinguished from the pleasant, as that which influences the will only by means of sensation from merely subjec-tive causes, valid only for the sense of this or that one, and not as a principle of reason, which holds for every one.…

145 Now all imperatives command either hypothetically or cat-egorically. The former represent the practical necessity of a pos-sible action as means to something else that is willed (or at least which one might possibly will). The categorical imperative would be that which represented an action as necessary of itself without 150 reference to another end, i.e., as objectively necessary.

Because every practical law represents a possible action as good and, on this account, for a subject who is practically deter-minable by reason, necessary, all imperatives are formulas deter-mining an action which is necessary according to the principle of 155 a will good in some respects. If now the action is good only as a means to something else, then the imperative is hypothetical; if it is conceived as good in itself and consequently as being neces-sarily the principle of a will which of itself conforms to reason, then it is categorical.…

160 **The Imperative of Morality**

Finally, there is an imperative which commands a certain conduct immediately, without having as its condition any other purpose to be attained by it. This imperative is categorical. It concerns not the matter of the action, or its intended result, but 165 its form and the principle of which it is itself a result; and what is essentially good in it consists in the mental disposition, let the consequence be what it may. This imperative may be called that of morality.…

> " *[T]here is an imperative which … concerns not the matter of the action, or its intended result, but its form and the principle of which it is itself a result … and … may be called that of morality… .]* "

Supposing, however, that there were something whose exis-170 tence has in itself an absolute worth, something which, being an end in itself, could be a source of definite laws; then in this and this alone would lie the source of a possible categorical imperative, i.e., a practical law.

Now I say: man and generally any rational being exists as 175 an end in himself, not merely as a means to be arbitrarily used by this or that will, but in all his actions, whether they concern himself or other rational beings, must be always regarded at the same time as an end. All objects of the inclinations have only a conditional worth, for if the inclinations and the wants founded 180 on them did not exist, then their object would be without value. But the inclinations, themselves being sources of want, are so far from having an absolute worth for which they should be desired that on the contrary it must be the universal wish of every rational being to be wholly free from them. Thus the worth 185 of any object which is to be acquired by our action is always conditional. Beings whose existence depends not on our will but on nature's, have nevertheless, if they are irrational beings, only a relative value as means, and are therefore called things; rational beings, on the contrary, are called persons, because 190 their very nature points them out as ends in themselves, that is as something which must not be used merely as means, and so far therefore restricts freedom of action (and is an object of respect). These, therefore, are not merely subjective ends whose existence has a worth for us as an effect of our action, but 195 objective ends, that is, things whose existence is an end in itself;

The slaves brought over from Africa to the United States were not considered beings "whose existence is an end in itself." As property, they were thought of and treated as objects, as means for others to enrich themselves, for example.

an end moreover for which no other can be substituted, which they should subserve merely as means, for otherwise nothing whatever would possess absolute worth; but if all worth were conditioned and therefore contingent, then there would be no
200 supreme practical principle of reason whatever.

The Practical Imperative

If then there is a supreme practical principle or, in respect of the human will, a categorical imperative, it must be one which, being drawn from the conception of that which is necessarily an end for
205 everyone because it is an end in itself, constitutes an objective principle of will, and can therefore serve as a universal practical law. The foundation of this principle is: rational nature exists as an end in itself. Man necessarily conceives his own existence as being so; so far then this is a subjective principle of human

210 actions. But every other rational being regards its existence similarly, just on the same rational principle that holds for me: so that it is at the same time an objective principle, from which as a supreme practical law all laws of the will must be capable of being deduced. Accordingly the practical imperative will be as
215 follows: So act as to treat humanity, whether in thine own person or in that of any other, in every case as an end withal, never as means only. . . .

Looking back now on all previous attempts to discover the principle of morality, we need not wonder why they all failed. It
220 was seen that man was bound to laws by duty, but it was not observed that the laws to which he is subject are only those of his own giving, though at the same time they are universal, and that he is only bound to act in conformity with his own will; a will, however, which is designed by nature to give universal
225 laws. For when one has conceived man only as subject to a law (no matter what), then this law required some interest, either by way of attraction or constraint, since it did not originate as a law from his own will, but this will was according to a law obliged by something else to act in a certain manner. Now by this necessary
230 consequence all the labor spent in finding a supreme principle of duty was irrevocably lost. For men never elicited duty, but only a necessity of acting from a certain interest. Whether this interest was private or otherwise, in any case the imperative must be conditional and could not by any means be capable of being a
235 moral command. I will therefore call this the principle of autonomy of the will, in contrast with every other which I accordingly reckon as heteronomy.

The Kingdom of Ends

The conception of the will of every rational being as one which
240 must consider itself as giving in all the maxims of its will universal laws, so as to judge itself and its actions from this point of view— this conception leads to another which depends on it and is very fruitful, namely that of a kingdom of ends.

By a kingdom I understand the union of different rational
245 beings in a system by common laws. Now since it is by laws that ends are determined as regards their universal validity, hence, if we abstract from the personal differences of rational beings and likewise from all the content of their private ends, we shall be able to conceive all ends combined in a systematic whole (including
250 both rational beings as ends in themselves, and also the special ends which each may propose to himself), that is to say, we can conceive a kingdom of ends, which on the preceding principles is possible.

For all rational beings come under the law that each of them
255 must treat itself and all others never merely as means, but in every case at the same time as ends in themselves. Hence results a systematic union of rational being by common objective laws, i.e.,

a kingdom which may be called a kingdom of ends, since what these laws have in view is just the relation of these beings to one another as ends and means. It is certainly only an ideal.

A rational being belongs as a member to the kingdom of ends when, although giving universal laws in it, he is also himself subject to these laws. He belongs to it as sovereign when, while giving laws, he is not subject to the will of any other.

A rational being must always regard himself as giving laws either as member or as sovereign in a kingdom of ends which is rendered possible by the freedom of will. He cannot, however, maintain the latter position merely by the maxims of his will, but only in case he is a completely independent being without wants and with unrestricted power adequate to his will.

Morality consists then in the reference of all action to the legislation which alone can render a kingdom of ends possible. This legislation must be capable of existing in every rational being and of emanating from his will, so that the principle of this will is never to act on any maxim which could not without contradiction be also a universal law and, accordingly, always so to act that the will could at the same time regard itself as giving in its maxims universal laws. If now the maxims of rational beings are not by their own nature coincident with this objective principle, then the necessity of acting on it is called practical necessitation, i.e., duty. Duty does not apply to the sovereign in the kingdom of ends, but it does to every member of it and to all in the same degree.

The Dignity of Rational Beings

The practical necessity of acting on this principle, i.e., duty, does not rest at all on feelings, impulses, or inclinations, but solely on the relation of rational beings to one another, a relation in which the will of a rational being must always be regarded as legislative, since otherwise it could not be conceived as an end in itself. Reason then refers every maxim of the will, regarding it as legislating universally, to every other will and also to every action towards oneself; and this not on account of any other practical motive or any future advantage, but from the idea of the dignity of a rational being, obeying no law but that which he himself also gives.

In the kingdom of ends everything has either value or dignity. Whatever has a value can be replaced by something else which is equivalent; whatever, on the other hand, is above all value, and therefore admits of no equivalent, has a dignity.

Whatever has reference to the general inclinations and wants of mankind has a market value; whatever, without presupposing a want, corresponds to a certain taste, that is to a satisfaction in the mere purposeless play of our faculties, has a fancy value; but that which constitutes the condition under which alone anything can be an end in itself, this has not merely a relative worth, i.e., value, but an intrinsic worth, that is, dignity.

Now morality is the condition under which alone a rational being can be an end in himself, since by this alone is it possible that he should be a legislating member in the kingdom of ends. Thus morality, and humanity as capable of it, is that which alone has dignity. Skill and diligence in labor have a market value; wit, lively imagination, and humor, have fancy value; on the other hand, fidelity to promises, benevolence from principle (not from instinct), have an intrinsic worth. Neither nature nor art contains anything which in default of these it could put in their place, for their worth consists not in the effects which spring from them, not in the use and advantage which they secure, but in the disposition of mind, that is, the maxims of the will which are ready to manifest themselves in such actions, even though they should not have the desired effect. These actions also need no recommendation from any subjective taste or sentiment, that they may be looked on with immediate favor and satisfaction: they need no immediate propension or feeling for them; they exhibit the will that performs them as an object of an immediate respect, and nothing but reason is required to impose them on the will; not to flatter it into them, which, in the case of duties, would be a contradiction. This estimation therefore shows that the worth of such a disposition is dignity, and places it infinitely above all value, with which it cannot for a moment be brought into comparison or competition without as it were violating its sanctity.

What then is it which justifies virtue or the morally good disposition, in making such lofty claims? It is nothing less than the privilege it secures to the rational being of participating in the giving of universal laws, by which it qualifies him to be a member of a possible kingdom of ends, a privilege to which he was already destined by his own nature as being an end in himself and, on that account, legislating in the kingdom of ends; free as regards all laws of physical nature, and obeying those only which he himself gives, and by which his maxims can belong to a system of universal law, to which at the same time he submits himself. For nothing has any worth except what the law assigns it. Now the legislation itself which assigns the worth of everything must for that very reason possess dignity, that is an unconditional incomparable worth; and the word respect alone supplies a becoming expression for the esteem which a rational being must have for it. Autonomy then is the basis of the dignity of human and of every rational nature....

Autonomy then is the basis of the dignity of human and of every rational nature....

Reading Excerpt: John Stuart Mill, *Utilitarianism* (1863)

INTRODUCTION

The British philosopher John Stuart Mill was not the first philosopher to propose the ethical theory of utilitarianism. (Jeremy Bentham is usually given that credit.) But Mill is recognized as enormously influential in working out details of this approach to ethics, which today remains one of the most significant approaches to moral reasoning. In these excerpts from his book *Utilitarianism*, he explains his Principle of Utility. This single principle says simply that we

John Stuart Mill

should choose as right action that which will promote the greatest happiness for the greatest number of people. Mill believes this ethical principle applies universally, making him an absolutist, even though he recognizes wide variation in what constitutes happiness for different people. Because he assesses rightness and wrongness of actions in terms of consequences, he is a consequentialist, rejecting intrinsic value.

Mill defines happiness as "pleasure and the absence of pain," which also makes him a hedonist. But his concept of pleasure includes the intellectual and "higher" pleasures, not mere bodily pleasures. In this excerpt he answers a variety of criticisms of utilitarianism as a way of defending his position.

This excerpt from John Stuart Mill's *Utilitarianism* was originally published in English in 1863 and is in the public domain.

QUESTIONS FOR REFLECTION

1. Mill distinguishes between higher and lower pleasures. How does he do this? Is his proposal credible?

2. How does Mill respond to the criticism that utilitarianism is "a doctrine worthy only of swine"? Is this an effective response?

3. Is it unrealistic to expect people to always act in the interests of all people? Is this what any ethical theory should accomplish? How does Mill respond to this criticism?

4. How do Mill's ethical proposals differ from Kant's? Do they have anything in common?

READING

The Greatest Happiness Principle

The creed which accepts as the foundation of morals, Utility, or the Greatest Happiness Principle, holds that actions are right in proportion as they tend to promote happiness, wrong as they tend
5 to produce the reverse of happiness. By happiness is intended pleasure, and the absence of pain; by unhappiness, pain, and the privation of pleasure. To give a clear view of the moral standard set up by the theory, much more requires to be said; in particular, what things it includes in the ideas of pain and pleasure; and to
10 what extent this is left an open question. But these supplementary explanations do not affect the theory of life on which this theory of morality is grounded—namely, that pleasure, and freedom from pain, are the only things desirable as ends; and that all desirable things (which are as numerous in the utilitarian as in
15 any other scheme) are desirable either for the pleasure inherent in themselves, or as means to the promotion of pleasure and the prevention of pain.

A Doctrine Worthy of Swine?

Now, such a theory of life excites in many minds, and among them
20 in some of the most estimable in feeling and purpose, inveterate dislike. To suppose that life has (as they express it) no higher end than pleasure—no better and nobler object of desire and pursuit—they designate as utterly mean and grovelling; as a doctrine worthy only of swine, to whom the followers of Epicurus were, at
25 a very early period, contemptuously likened; and modern holders of the doctrine are occasionally made the subject of equally polite comparisons by its German, French, and English assailants.

When thus attacked, the Epicureans have always answered, that it is not they, but their accusers, who represent human nature
30 in a degrading light; since the accusation supposes human beings to be capable of no pleasures except those of which swine are capable. If this supposition were true, the charge could not be gainsaid, but would then be no longer an imputation; for if the sources of pleasure were precisely the same to human beings and

to swine, the rule of life which is good enough for the one would be good enough for the other. The comparison of the Epicurean life to that of beasts is felt as degrading, precisely because a beast's pleasures do not satisfy a human being's conceptions of happiness. Human beings have faculties more elevated than the animal appetites, and when once made conscious of them, do not regard anything as happiness which does not include their gratification. I do not, indeed, consider the Epicureans to have been by any means faultless in drawing out their scheme of consequences from the utilitarian principle. To do this in any sufficient manner, many Stoic, as well as Christian elements require to be included. But there is no known Epicurean theory of life which does not assign to the pleasures of the intellect; of the feelings and imagination, and of the moral sentiments, a much higher value as pleasures than to those of mere sensation. It must be admitted, however, that utilitarian writers in general have placed the superiority of mental over bodily pleasures chiefly in the greater permanency, safety, uncostliness, etc., of the former—that is, in their circumstantial advantages rather than in their intrinsic nature. And on all these points utilitarians have fully proved their case; but they might have taken the other, and, as it may be called, higher ground, with entire consistency. It is quite compatible with the principle of utility to recognise the fact, that some *kinds* of pleasure are more desirable and more valuable than others. It would be absurd that while, in estimating all other things, quality is considered as well as quantity, the estimation of pleasures should be supposed to depend on quantity alone.

Different Qualities of Pleasures

If I am asked, what I mean by difference of quality in pleasures, or what makes one pleasure more valuable than another, merely as a pleasure, except its being greater in amount, there is but one possible answer. Of two pleasures, if there be one to which all or almost all who have experience of both give a decided preference, irrespective of any feeling of moral obligation to prefer it, that is the more desirable pleasure. If one of the two is, by those who are competently acquainted with both, placed so far above the other that they prefer it, even though knowing it to be attended with a greater amount of discontent, and would not resign it for any quantity of the other pleasure which their nature is capable of, we are justified in ascribing to the preferred enjoyment a superiority in quality, so far outweighing quantity as to render it, in comparison, of small account.

Now it is an unquestionable fact that those who are equally acquainted with, and equally capable of appreciating and enjoying, both, do give a most marked preference to the manner of existence which employs their higher faculties. Few human creatures would consent to be changed into any of the lower animals, for a promise of the fullest allowance of a beast's pleasures; no

intelligent human being would consent to be a fool, no instructed person would be an ignoramus, no person of feeling and conscience would be selfish and base, even though they should be persuaded that the fool, the dunce, or the rascal is better satisfied with his lot than they are with theirs. They would not resign what they possess more than he, for the most complete satisfaction of all the desires which they have in common with him. . . .

> **" [N]o intelligent human being would consent to be a fool … "**

The Happiness of All

I must again repeat, what the assailants of utilitarianism seldom have the justice to acknowledge, that the happiness which forms the utilitarian standard of what is right in conduct, is not the agent's own happiness, but that of all concerned. As between his own happiness and that of others, utilitarianism requires him to be as strictly impartial as a disinterested and benevolent spectator. In the golden rule of Jesus of Nazareth, we read the complete spirit of the ethics of utility. To do as one would be done by, and to love one's neighbor as oneself, constitute the ideal perfection of utilitarian morality. As the means of making the nearest approach to this ideal, utility would enjoin, first, that laws and social arrangements should place the happiness, or (as speaking practically it may be called) the interest, of every individual, as nearly as possible in harmony with the interest of the whole; and secondly, that education and opinion, which have so vast a power over human character, should so use that power as to establish in the mind of every individual an indissoluble association between his own happiness and the good of the whole; especially between his own happiness and the practice of such modes of conduct, negative and positive, as regard for the universal happiness prescribes: so that not only he may be unable to conceive the possibility of happiness to himself, consistently with conduct opposed to the general good, but also that a direct impulse to promote the general good may be in every individual one of the habitual motives of action, and the sentiments connected therewith may fill a large and prominent place in every human being's sentient existence. If the impugners of the utilitarian morality represented it to their own minds in this its true character, I know not what recommendation possessed by any other morality they could possibly affirm to be wanting to it: what more beautiful or more exalted developments of human nature any other ethical system can be supposed to foster, or what springs of action, not accessible to the utilitarian, such systems rely on for giving effect to their mandates.

Jubilist/Dreamstime.com

According to Mill: "In the golden rule of Jesus of Nazareth, we read the complete spirit of the ethics of utility. To do as one would be done by, and to love one's neighbor as oneself, constitute the ideal perfection of utilitarian morality."

Too High a Standard?

125 The objectors to utilitarianism cannot always be charged with representing it in a discreditable light. On the contrary, those among them who entertain anything like a just idea of its disinterested character, sometimes find fault with its standard as being too high for humanity. They say it is exacting too much 130 to require that people shall always act from the inducement of promoting the general interests of society. But this is to mistake the very meaning of a standard of morals, and to confound the rule of action with the motive of it. It is the business of ethics to tell us what are our duties, or by what test we may know 135 them; but no system of ethics requires that the sole motive of all we do shall be a feeling of duty; on the contrary, ninety-nine hundredths of all our actions are done from other motives, and rightly so done, if the rule of duty does not condemn them. It is the more unjust to utilitarianism that this particular misappre- 140 hension should be made a ground of objection to it, inasmuch as utilitarian moralists have gone beyond almost all others in affirming that the motive has nothing to do with the morality of the action, though much with the worth of the agent. He who saves a fellow creature from drowning does what is morally 145 right, whether his motive be duty, or the hope of being paid for his trouble: he who betrays the friend that trusts him, is guilty of a crime, even if his object be to serve another friend to whom he is under greater obligations. But to speak only of actions done from the motive of duty, and in direct obedience to principle: it is

150 a misapprehension of the utilitarian mode of thought, to conceive it as implying that people should fix their minds upon so wide a generality as the world, or society at large. The great majority of good actions are intended, not for the benefit of the world, but for that of individuals, of which the good of the world is made 155 up; and the thoughts of the most virtuous man need not on these occasions travel beyond the particular persons concerned, except so far as is necessary to assure himself that in benefiting them he is not violating the rights—that is, the legitimate and authorized expectations—of anyone else. The multiplication 160 of happiness is, according to the utilitarian ethics, the object of virtue: the occasions on which any person (except one in a thousand) has it in his power to do this on an extended scale, in other words, to be a public benefactor, are but exceptional; and on these occasions alone is he called on to consider public util- 165 ity; in every other case, private utility, the interest or happiness of some few persons, is all he has to attend to. Those alone the influence of whose actions extends to society in general, need concern themselves habitually about so large an object. In the case of abstinences indeed—of things which people forbear to 170 do, from moral considerations, though the consequences in the particular case might be beneficial—it would be unworthy of an intelligent agent not to be consciously aware that the action is of a class which, if practised generally, would be generally injurious, and that this is the ground of the obligation to abstain from 175 it. The amount of regard for the public interest implied in this

recognition, is no greater than is demanded by every system of morals; for they all enjoin to abstain from whatever is manifestly pernicious to society....

A Doctrine of Mere Expediency?

180 Again, Utility is often summarily stigmatized as an immoral doctrine by giving it the name of Expediency, and taking advantage of the popular use of that term to contrast it with Principle. But the Expedient, in the sense in which it is opposed to the Right, generally means that which is expedient for the particular interest of 185 the agent himself: as when a minister sacrifices the interest of his country to keep himself in place. When it means anything better than this, it means that which is expedient for some immediate object, some temporary purpose, but which violates a rule whose observance is expedient in a much higher degree. The expedient, 190 in this sense, instead of being the same thing with the useful, is a branch of the hurtful.

Thus, it would often be expedient, for the purpose of getting over some momentary embarrassment, or attaining some object immediately useful to ourselves or others, to tell a lie. But inas-195 much as the cultivation in ourselves of a sensitive feeling on the subject of veracity, is one of the most useful, and the enfeeblement of that feeling one of the most hurtful, things to which our conduct can be instrumental; and inasmuch as any, even unintentional, deviation from truth, does that much towards weakening the 200 trustworthiness of human assertion, which is not only the principal support of all present social well-being, but the insufficiency of which does more than any one thing that can be named to keep back civilization, virtue, everything on which human happiness on the largest scale depends; we feel that the violation, for a present 205 advantage, of a rule of such transcendent expediency, is not expedient, and that he who, for the sake of a convenience to himself or to some other individual, does what depends on him to deprive mankind of the good, and inflict upon them the evil, involved in the greater or less reliance which they can place in each other's word, 210 acts the part of one of their worst enemies.

Yet that even this rule, sacred as it is, admits of possible exceptions, is acknowledged by all moralists; the chief of which is when the withholding of some fact (as of information from a male-factor, or of bad news from a person dangerously ill) would 215 preserve some one (especially a person other than oneself) from great and unmerited evil, and when the withholding can only be effected by denial. But in order that the exception may not extend itself beyond the need, and may have the least possible effect in weakening reliance on veracity, it ought to be recognized, and, if 220 possible, its limits defined; and if the principle of utility is good for anything, it must be good for weighing these conflicting utilities against one another, and marking out the region within which one or the other preponderates.

Time to Decide

225 Again, defenders of utility often find themselves called upon to reply to such objections as this—that there is not time, previous to action, for calculating and weighing the effects of any line of conduct on the general happiness. This is exactly as if any one were to say that it is impossible to guide our conduct by Christianity, 230 because there is not time, on every occasion on which anything has to be done, to read through the Old and New Testaments. The answer to the objection is, that there has been ample time, namely, the whole past duration of the human species. During all that time mankind have been learning by experience the tendencies of 235 actions; on which experience all the prudence, as well as all the morality of life, is dependent. People talk as if the commencement of this course of experience had hitherto been put off, and as if, at the moment when some man feels tempted to meddle with the property or life of another, he had to begin considering for the first 240 time whether murder and theft are injurious to human happiness. Even then I do not think that he would find the question very puzzling; but, at all events, the matter is now done to his hand. It is truly a whimsical supposition, that if mankind were agreed in considering utility to be the test of morality, they would remain without 245 any agreement as to what is useful, and would take no measures for having their notions on the subject taught to the young, and enforced by law and opinion. There is no difficulty in proving any ethical standard whatever to work ill, if we suppose universal idiocy to be conjoined with it, but on any hypothesis short of that, 250 mankind must by this time have acquired positive beliefs as to the effects of some actions on their happiness; and the beliefs which have thus come down are the rules of morality for the multitude, and for the philosopher until he has succeeded in finding better.

> " [D]efenders of utility often find themselves called upon to reply to … objections … that there is not time, previous to action, for calculating and weighing the effects of any line of conduct on the general happiness. "

That philosophers might easily do this, even now, on many 255 subjects; that the received code of ethics is by no means of divine right; and that mankind have still much to learn as to the effects of actions on the general happiness, I admit, or rather, earnestly maintain. The corollaries from the principle of utility, like the precepts of every practical art, admit of indefinite improvement, and, in a progressive state of the human mind, their improvement is perpetually going on. But to consider the rules of morality as improvable, is one thing; to pass over the intermediate generalizations entirely, and endeavor to test each individual action directly by the first principle, is another. It is a strange notion that the acknowledgment of a first principle is inconsistent with the admission of secondary ones. To inform a traveller respecting the place of his ultimate destination, is not to forbid the use of landmarks and direction-posts on the way. The proposition that happiness is the end and aim of morality, does not mean that no road ought to be laid down to that goal, or that persons going thither should not be advised to take one direction rather than another. Men really ought to leave off talking a kind of nonsense on this subject, which they would neither talk nor listen to on other matters of practical concernment. Nobody argues that the art of navigation is not founded on astronomy, because sailors cannot wait to calculate the Nautical Almanack. Being rational creatures, they go to sea with it ready calculated; and all rational creatures go out upon the sea of life with their minds made up on the common questions of right and wrong, as well as on many of the far more difficult questions of wise and foolish. And this, as long as foresight is a human quality, it is to be presumed they will continue to do. Whatever we adopt as the fundamental principle of morality, we require subordinate principles to apply it by: the impossibility of doing without them, being common to all systems, can afford no argument against any one in particular: but gravely to argue as if no such secondary principles could be had, and as if mankind had remained till now, and always must remain, without drawing any general conclusions from the experience of human life, is as high a pitch, I think, as absurdity has ever reached in philosophical controversy.

Dealing with Conflict

The remainder of the stock arguments against utilitarianism mostly consist in laying to its charge the common infirmities of human nature, and the general difficulties which embarrass conscientious persons in shaping their course through life. We are told that an utilitarian will be apt to make his own particular case an exception to moral rules, and, when under temptation, will see an utility in the breach of a rule, greater than he will see in its observance. But is utility the only creed which is able to furnish us with excuses for evil doing, and means of cheating our own conscience? They are afforded in abundance by all doctrines which recognise as a fact in morals the existence of conflicting considerations; which all doctrines do, that have been believed by sane persons. It is not the fault of any creed, but of the complicated nature of human affairs, that rules of conduct cannot be so framed as to require no exceptions, and that hardly any kind of action can safely be laid down as either always obligatory or always condemnable. There is no ethical creed which does not temper the rigidity of its laws, by giving a certain latitude, under the moral responsibility of the agent, for accommodation to peculiarities of circumstances; and under every creed, at the opening thus made, self-deception and dishonest casuistry get in. There exists no moral system under which there do not arise unequivocal cases of conflicting obligation. These are the real difficulties, the knotty points both in the theory of ethics, and in the conscientious guidance of personal conduct. They are overcome practically with greater or with less success according to the intellect and virtue of the individual; but it can hardly be pretended that any one will be the less qualified for dealing with them, from possessing an ultimate standard to which conflicting rights and duties can be referred. If utility is the ultimate source of moral obligations, utility may be invoked to decide between them when their demands are incompatible. Though the application of the standard may be difficult, it is better than none at all: while in other systems, the moral laws all claiming independent authority, there is no common umpire entitled to interfere between them; their claims to precedence one over another rest on little better than sophistry, and unless determined, as they generally are, by the unacknowledged influence of considerations of utility, afford a free scope for the action of personal desires and partialities. We must remember that only in these cases of conflict between secondary principles is it requisite that first principles should be appealed to. There is no case of moral obligation in which some secondary principle is not involved; and if only one, there can seldom be any real doubt which one it is, in the mind of any person by whom the principle itself is recognized.

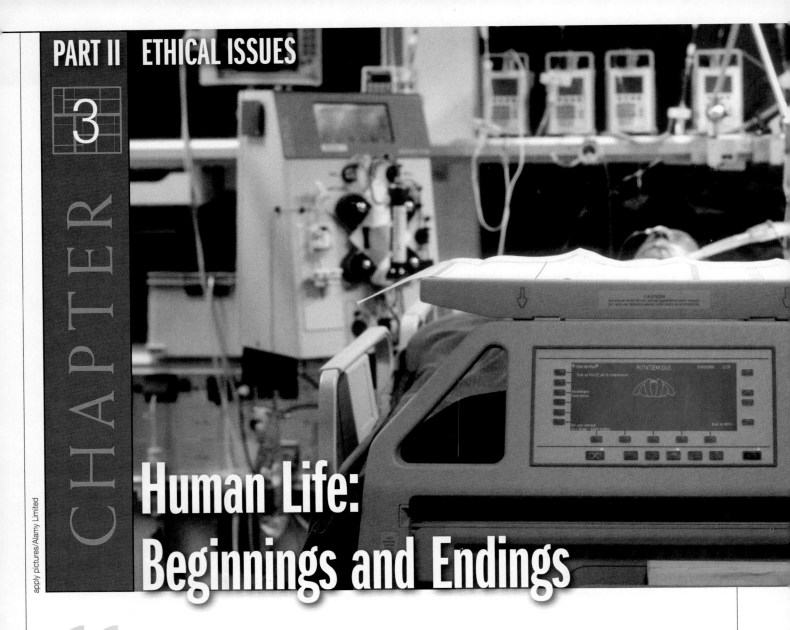

apply pictures/Alamy Limited

CHAPTER 3

Human Life: Beginnings and Endings

Rational suicide represents one of the fullest forms of expression of one's autonomy. It is the right of people to shape the ends of their lives.

Margaret P. Battin,
Professor of Philosophy,
University of Utah

Anyone who is not mentally ill and chooses the irrationality of committing suicide has done something morally wrong.

Daniel P. Sulmasy,
Professor of Medicine and Ethics,
University of Chicago

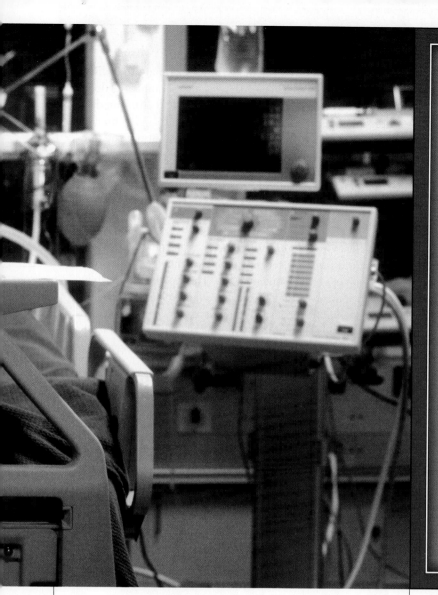

ebates about the creation and the termination of life are among the most contentious in today's culture. The ethics of abortion are as hotly contested as ever in this country, four decades after the U.S. Supreme Court decision in *Roe v. Wade*. The termination of life through assisted suicide or euthanasia increases in urgency as medical technology advances the possibilities for keeping people alive on machines even while medical costs skyrocket. Other biotechnologies allow for artificial creation of life through genetic engineering and research on embryonic stem cells, both of which were once only the domain of science fiction. The legality of these procedures does not resolve the ethical dilemmas faced by individual people. Evolving philosophical understanding of the ethical issues, such as the concept of a *person*, continues to have an effect on broader policy debates, including the legal reasoning of legislatures and courts.

Overview

This chapter tackles some of today's thorniest ethical questions. All are interrelated by their reliance on concepts of the person and how this highly contested concept of a person matters in making decisions about the beginning and end of life, from abortion and stem cell research to euthanasia and assisted suicide. The types of ethical reasoning

What do **you** think?

It is unethical to terminate human life, whether it is a single embryonic cell at the beginning of life or a full human body at the end of life.

Strongly Disagree						Strongly Agree
1	2	3	4	5	6	7

that can be used to work through these issues are looked at. The similarities and differences in this ethical reasoning and legal court decisions on the same set of issues will also be considered. Finally, we will look back at classical philosophical views on suicide, which precede many of the contemporary debates on the end of life, especially whether we have a right to end our own lives. An excerpt presents the observations of St. Thomas Aquinas and the other those of David Hume.

3-1 ISSUES

Clear reasoning on the ethics of these controversial practices begins with clarity on what is being discussed. As in so many areas of disagreement, it is important to be sure that we are debating the same thing and are not using fallacious reasoning and injecting "straw men" or ambiguous terminology. For example, is it euthanasia when an elderly patient refuses extraordinary measures to continue his or her life? Or is the term *euthanasia* limited to something narrower, such as the overt killing of a terminally ill patient at his or her request? Working definitions can themselves be subject to discussion, but they are necessary to provide a starting point to consider these issues.

3-1a Abortion

At least in current discussion in North America, **abortion** typically refers to the human-induced termination of a fetus before what would have been the natural birth of that fetus. Early terminations that occur naturally are usually referred to as *miscarriages*.

3-1b Suicide

When a person decides to terminate his or her own life by himself or herself, the action is referred to as **suicide**. To literally count as a suicide, it must be the result of an intentional decision by the person to die and not the result of an accidental death.

3-1c Assisted Suicide

In **assisted suicide**, people wish to terminate their lives, making this "suicide," but they need assistance in doing so, such as a lethal dose of drugs obtained from medical personnel. Even so, the "agent of death"—the final or proximate cause of the death—is the patient not the doctor. Where assisted suicide is permitted (e.g., Oregon), the patient must be terminally ill and not merely depressed or unhappy for the procedure to be legally acceptable.

3-1d Euthanasia

In ancient Greek, **euthanasia** meant "good death." The main difference from assisted suicide is that the agent of death is not the patient but someone else. This opens the possibility that the person causing the death could be charged with murder. Conditions for justifying euthanasia, when it is acceptable, include clear consent from the patient, terminal illness with no chance of recovery, and certainty of the diagnosis.

3-1e Genetic Engineering

The use of DNA technology to modify any life form, including plant life, nonhuman animals, and now also humans, is called **genetic engineering**.

Dr. Jack Kevorkian (1928–2011). This physician believed that helping patients who were terminally ill and wanted to put an end to their own lives was more important than taking any measure to keep them alive. Do you believe that helping patients to die is consistent with a medical practitioner's goals?

DFree/Shutterstock.com

3-1f Stem Cell Research

Research can be conducted with embryonic **stem cells** and also with adult stem cells; this is called *stem cell research*. Stem cells are undifferentiated cells that have the potential to develop in many ways and can thus be used to study and endeavor to treat many diseases. The main controversy today is over the use of embryonic stem cells, including those from fertilized eggs created for the in vitro fertilization (IVF) process.

3-2 "PERSONHOOD" AND EVOLVING MEDICAL TECHNOLOGIES

A *person* is construed as something more than what the biological category *Homo sapiens* describes. In addition to biological properties, personhood is often seen to involve consciousness, rationality, and the capacities for communication and moral judgment; however, personhood is not denied to someone who is in a coma or suffers from severe disabilities with regard to communication. Personhood has an ethical status on one hand and a legal status on the other hand, which both recognize these broader characteristics (other than simple biological traits) and is a central issue in the debates at both the beginning and the end of life.

In recent decades, with advancements of medical technologies, the definition of death (i.e., the time at which we cease to be a person) has had to be reconsidered. No longer is death merely the cessation of a beating heart. This is most obvious now that such techniques as CPR, defibrillation, and epinephrine injections either prevent death or resuscitate individuals and that artificial hearts are available and transplants possible. Instead, almost all states have now adopted a standard definition of death as either (1) irreversible cessation of circulatory and respiratory functions or (2) irreversible cessation of all functions of the entire brain, including the brain stem.

This definition of death is critical in the best-known cases of euthanasia: Karen Ann Quinlan, Nancy Cruzan, and Terri Schiavo. All three women were in a persistent, vegetative state, with some brainwave activity. Thus, they were not legally dead, even though there was no hope for their recovery to anything resembling a normal cognitive life. If they had been legally

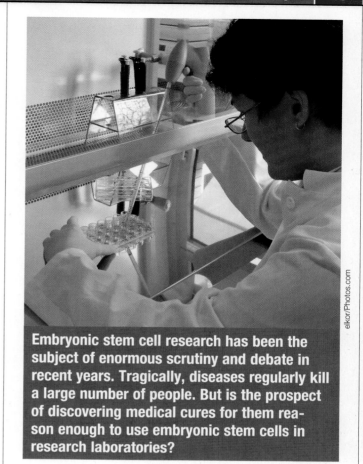

Embryonic stem cell research has been the subject of enormous scrutiny and debate in recent years. Tragically, diseases regularly kill a large number of people. But is the prospect of discovering medical cures for them reason enough to use embryonic stem cells in research laboratories?

elkor/Photos.com

> [P]ersonhood is often seen to involve consciousness, rationality, and the capacities for communication and moral judgment ...

dead, there would have been no controversy over removing their artificial respirators or nourishment.

At the beginning of life, much controversy surrounds the point at which we become persons. Is it at the moment of conception, the position held by many opposed to all abortions? Or is it at the point when we have a functioning brain, paralleling one of the now-accepted definitions of death, a position that makes abortion allowable until that point? Or is it the point in time when the fetus is viable for living on its own outside the womb?

Personhood also is critical in the debate over embryonic stem cell research. If the fertilized embryo is a person, with all the rights of persons, then experimentation on that stem cell is arguably unethical. But if that fertilized egg does not yet have the status of person, then use in medical research would not be unethical, at least on those grounds.

In CourseMate, watch a video and take the quiz.

3-3 APPLYING KANTIAN AND UTILITARIAN REASONING

3-3a Kantian Reasoning

In this context, Kantian reasoning centers on the concept of a *person*, which Immanuel Kant did so much to develop and refine. Once a being is recognized as a person, that entity would seem to have important rights to continued life. Remember that according to Kant's "practical imperative," we should always treat other persons as ends in themselves and never merely as a means to an end. So, all other persons should always be treated with dignity and respect. Thus, based on Kant's argument, *when* a fertilized egg becomes a person, it ought to be treated with dignity and respect, which would seem to include being given an unalienable right to life. If a fertilized egg, that is, a single cell that contains the genetic material of both the female and male parents, becomes a person at conception, then any termination of that life would deny that person its fundamental right to life, and thus, this termination would be unethical. Conversely, if the status of person is achieved when a functioning brain has developed, Kant's imperative would not apply any time before that point; thus, ethically, there would be no person to consider, and any decision made about this entity would be ethically acceptable.

But as Judith Jarvis Thomson argued in 1971, *even if* we are persons from the moment of conception (a hypothesis Thomson does not accept, except for the sake of argument), there are several ethical arguments that could justify the termination of that person anyway. In other contexts, for example, a right of self-defense is recognized; thus, if a pregnancy threatens the life of the mother, then she would have a self-defense right against that fetus, *even if* it is a person.

The concept of person is also central in the analysis of assisted suicide and euthanasia. The first issue is whether persons have a right to terminate their own life, a matter of considerable disagreement (see the readings from Aquinas and Hume at the end of this chapter). If a person has a right to suicide, then the next issue is whether the criteria are met for making assisted suicide or euthanasia ethical. But ultimately, these debates also rest on the nature of persons and their rights.

The debate over research on embryonic stem cells also centers on the nature of persons. If we are persons

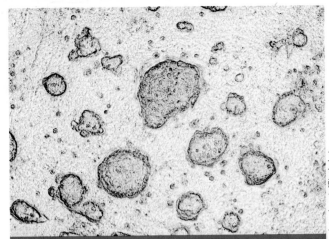

Most embryonic stem cells come from embryos developed from eggs that have been fertilized in vitro and then donated for research purposes with informed consent from the donors. Does the fact that cells are developed in vitro (i.e., outside of a human womb) make the case against their use in experiments more or less compelling?

dra_schwartz/iStockphoto.com

> **[B]ased on Kant's argument,** *when* **a fertilized egg becomes a person, it ought to be treated with dignity and respect ...**

from the moment of conception, then experimentation on the stem cells would seem to violate the rights of those persons not to be the subject of scientific experiments and not to be destroyed. But even here, there might be situations in which those rights could be overridden by other ethical claims, as seen with abortion.

Genetic engineering debates again look to the nature of a person and the rights that person possesses. Do parents have a right to alter the genetic makeup of their offspring by making judgments about which traits are desirable and which are not? Again, any genetic-altering action taken on the entity growing in a womb, if that entity is a person, would be unethical according to the Kantian approach.

In this discussion, Kant's "formula of the end itself," which is also sometimes called the "practical imperative," has been the main focus. These ethical issues can also be considered from another formulation of his "categorical imperative," that is, whether these practices could be universalized without contradiction. When these practices are engaged in, could we coherently will a world in which everyone followed these practices? For example, if a fetus is a person, then, no, we could not coherently will as a rule to kill innocent people.

3-3b Utilitarian Reasoning

Utilitarianism focuses on consequences, and specifically, which of several possible actions will bring about the greatest happiness for the greatest number. This approach also is commonly used to support arguments in these debates.

Abortion debates sometimes ask about the well-being of the fetus, the other children in the family, and the mother. For instance, for a family in poverty, the addition of another child might result in extreme hardship. The consequence of this new arrival could mean that such basic necessities as shelter, food, and clothing would be denied to the existing family members and the family would find itself homeless and without resources. The downside of this type of utilitarian reasoning is that the same arguments might also be used to justify infanticide, which is the intentional killing of infants and is almost universally viewed as unethical.

The assisted suicide and euthanasia debates also often rely on utilitarian reasoning. Elderly patients sometimes worry that they have become a burden on their families, especially a financial burden. Viewed from this perspective, one of the consequences of euthanasia would be to eliminate such a burden and thus, to some, might mean that euthanasia is an appropriate choice and ethically acceptable. But this type of reasoning also has a serious downside because members of an elderly patient's family themselves may put undue pressure on the elderly to avoid lingering on in life and thus costing the family more money.

Stem cell research and genetic engineering also lend themselves to utilitarian reasoning. The benefits from research for many persons suffering from serious illnesses would seem to be a major consequence that might justify this research. But for those who believe that these embryonic cells are persons with all the rights associated with this status, those benefits do not override those rights.

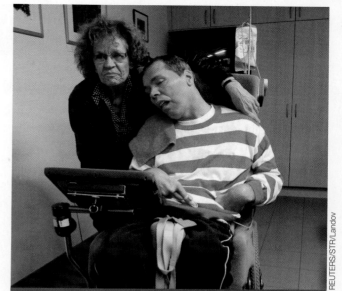

REUTERS/STR/Landov

Recent cases of persons found to be conscious after being believed to be in a coma further complicate issues concerning the definition of death. Rom Houben was diagnosed as being in a coma for twenty-three years, until new high-tech scans showed his brain was still functioning almost completely normally. The validity of statements he made via guided communication regarding his long ordeal is in dispute. But this type of case further demonstrates the difficulties inherent in defining such conditions as comas and vegetative states.

Now, equipped with the knowledge you acquired in the overview of two types of reasoning applied to the topics discussed, review Critical Thinking Table 3.1 to follow the examination of an ethical claim on a related topic.

Table 3.1 Critical Thinking Steps and Their Application in an Example

{ "Stem cell research should be banned because it is nothing less than murder." }

Critical Thinking Steps	Application
1. **Examine and clarify key terms and concepts.** • Look words up in a dictionary, if necessary. • Unravel or unpack the complexities and nuances of a central term, such as *justice*, *right*, or *good*.	• What do we mean by *stem cell* here? Are we including both adult stem cell research, which uses the adult patient's own cells, and embryonic stem cell research, which uses cells from another living thing? • What counts as a *ban* here? Does the ban mean merely voicing disapproval? Or does it mean criminal prohibition?

elkor/Photos.com

(Continued)

Table 3.1 Continued

Critical Thinking Steps	Application
2. Work through the meaning of the key terms and concepts to make sure you will use them consistently. • Consider the ways the term can be used by including it in different sentences and contexts to zero in on the particular meaning you are after. • Ask yourself what words are potential synonyms for the concept. Do those capture everything you want to understand about that term?	• If it has been determined that stem cell refers specifically to embryonic stem cell research in the statement, should the term *embryonic* be examined carefully? That is, how are embryos defined? For example, are they persons with the full rights of persons? • If it is believed that embryos are persons with the full rights of persons, is an understanding of "full rights of persons" needed? • Is a prohibition through the criminal justice system being considered by *ban*? Is a more limited ban the focus (e.g., as to federal funding of such research)? Is this only about moral disapproval? • Is "murder" meant literally, in the criminal justice sense? Or in the ethical prohibitions outside that criminal justice system? Or is it being used metaphorically for effect (i.e., as a way of expressing outrage)? If so, does the statement need to be rephrased? • Because there are sometimes justifications for "murder," even in the criminal justice system (e.g., self-defense), should exceptions to punishment in this context be entertained?
3. Build premises and bring any assumptions to light. GerritdeHeus/ANP/ age fotostock • Put together short and clear sentences to build each of your premises. • Think through what you may be taking for granted in your reasoning. What assumptions are you making? • Once you have identified assumptions, articulate them in your premise, so that your audience has the same understanding of a term or a concept as you.	The premises of the argument could be constructed as follows, using these clarifications of terminology: (i) Embryonic stem cells are persons. (ii) Embryonic stem cell research requires the destruction of a human being. (iii) The destruction of a human being is always murder. (iv) All forms of murder should be prohibited by the criminal law. CONCLUSION: All embryonic stem cell research should be prohibited by the criminal justice system.
4. Test/Verify your premises. • Now that you have stated your premises explicitly, do you want to stick with them? • Are you relying on premises drawn from unsubstantiated sources or from questionable authorities? • Are you consistent in your premises? Or are you appealing to different and inconsistent foundations in your reasoning?	Each of these premises can be challenged. (i) If you believe that we are persons from the moment of conception, then these cells are persons, but many people do not accept that belief. (ii) It does appear, from what is known of these research techniques, that the stem cell is at least altered and further development into a person is halted. (iii) In broader contexts, situations in which murder is justified are recognized (e.g., self-defense or war), so the question here is whether this research situation should also be recognized as an exception.

Critical Thinking Steps	Application
• Reformulate your premises if they have proven to be faulty.	(iv) This is a valid premise only if one recognizes no situations in which murder is considered justifiable in the criminal law. If you do not accept all of these premises, then you will not accept the conclusion either. But if you do accept all of them, then you would find the conclusion valid and justified.
5. Confirm that the conclusions you draw are logical. Check for reliance on fallacies and correct any premise that you identify as relying on a fallacy.	• The fallacy of equivocation is an issue, especially for the controversial terms *person* and *murder*. In this type of fallacy, key terms are used in different ways in the argument, clouding the validity of the final conclusion. For example, by *person*, some mean a fertilized egg from the moment of conception, whereas the moment of birth and a functioning brain are defining criteria for others. But if you are persuaded that they are used in the same way throughout and are consistent with your other usage in general, then you would find the conclusion valid and justified.

dra_schwartz/ iStockphoto.com

In CourseMate, apply what you've learned to the real-life scenario in the simulation.

In CourseMate, practice what you learned by taking the chapter quiz.

3-4 ETHICAL REASONING APPLIED TO THE LAW

Court decisions on all of these issues evolve frequently. Much of the court's reasoning sounds much like the reasoning in philosophical arguments, especially in this legal domain. Courts regularly appeal to the "dignity of persons," just as Kantian reasoning does. However, to date, the U.S. Supreme Court has avoided trying to define *person*, at least regarding whether it begins at conception or later. Courts also often appeal to utilitarian consequences in support of their conclusions.

In addition to this philosophy-based reasoning, courts rely on precedent (i.e., the case law that went before and established principles followed by later courts). In legal terminology, this is known as *stare decisis* ("stay the decision") or in other words, "let the decision stand." Courts also appeal to the Constitution (i.e., whether the U.S. Constitution or, in state courts, the state constitutions); factors which are not considered in philosophical reasoning.

> **Courts regularly appeal to ... Kantian reasoning ...[and] also often to utilitarian consequences in support of their conclusions.**

With regard to abortion, *Roe v. Wade* (1973) has never been overturned. The 1992 decision *Planned Parenthood of Southeastern Pennsylvania v. Casey* affirmed the central holding that women have a liberty right to abortion, but it shifted the "dividing line" for this right to "viability." After that point, even through the third trimester, abortion is permitted if continued pregnancy would threaten a women's life or health. The 1973 *Roe* decision relied on the concept of a Constitutional "privacy" right, which is controversial because the word *privacy* appears nowhere in the Constitution itself. The rationale was that the right to privacy is implied by other rights within the Constitution. This right is within the Constitution's "penumbra," which is a shadow created by a source of light. In other words, it exists within perimeters delineated by other rights defined in the Constitution—See Feature 3.1 for more detail. However, in the 1992 *Casey* decision, the court shifted away from the concept of a privacy right to that of a "liberty right," which is less controversial, especially because the word *liberty* does appear in the Constitution. For a quick overview of some important court cases that have tackled issues of privacy and liberty, review Time line 3.1.

Feature 3.1: Is There a Right to "Privacy"?

The word *privacy* does not appear in the U.S. Constitution, even though it is explicitly listed as a right in the constitutions of several states. The first known legal recognition of a right to privacy appeared in an article in 1890 in the *Harvard Law Review*, written by Samuel D. Warren and Louis D. Brandeis. Both were attorneys in Boston when they wrote the article; Brandeis was later appointed to the U.S. Supreme Court in 1916 by President Woodrow Wilson.

Among philosophers, recognition of a private sphere of life in home and family in contrast with public political life can be found as far back as the writings of Aristotle. But this recognized merely the *existence* of a private sphere without recognizing privacy as a *right*. Several contemporary philosophers, including Judith Jarvis Thomson and Ronald Dworkin, have pursued a more developed sense of privacy as a right.

The right of privacy has been recognized by numerous justices of the U.S. Supreme Court in the twentieth century as included in the penumbra of the Constitution. What is this penumbra? Several provisions of the Constitution are typically cited as supporting this right to privacy. In the 1965 decision *Griswold v. Connecticut*, Justice William O. Douglas explained this concept of a penumbra of rights:

> ... specific guarantees in the Bill of Rights have penumbras, formed by emanations from those guarantees that help give them life and substance. Various guarantees create zones of privacy. The right of association contained in the penumbra of the First Amendment is one, as we have seen. The Third Amendment in its prohibition against the quartering of soldiers 'in any house' in time of peace without the consent of the owner is another facet of that privacy. The Fourth Amendment explicitly affirms the 'right of the people to be secure in their persons, houses, papers, and effects, against unreasonable searches and seizures.' The Fifth Amendment in its Self-Incrimination Clause enables the citizen to create

Timeline 3.1 Privacy and Liberty in the Courts

A series of important court cases has addressed issues of privacy and liberty under the U.S. Constitution over a period of more than a century. Although the word *privacy* does not appear in the Constitution, the right has been recognized by numerous courts.

1923 *Meyer v. Nebraska:* Parents may decide whether their children can study a foreign language because of a fundamental liberty right in the family.

1925 *Pierce v. Society of Sisters:* Parents may send their children to private school and cannot be forced to send them to public schools, again because of a fundamental liberty right in the family.

1942 *Skinner v. Oklahoma:* A law in Oklahoma providing for sterilization of "habitual criminals" is struck down on the grounds that all people have a fundamental right to choices about marriage and procreation.

1965 *Griswold v. Connecticut:* Laws prohibiting the sale and distribution of contraception to married couples are struck down on the grounds of a privacy right within marriage.

a zone of privacy which government may not force him to surrender to his detriment. The Ninth Amendment provides: 'The enumeration in the Constitution, of certain rights, shall not be construed to deny or disparage others retained by the people.' The Fourth and Fifth Amendments were described ... as protection against all governmental invasions 'of the sanctity of a man's home and the privacies of life.'

Even if there is a legal and moral right of privacy, the question still remains as to what you get for this right. A right to use contraception? To have an abortion? To choose assisted suicide? To sell one's bodily organs for profit? One can consistently recognize the right and yet argue persuasively that not all of those rights follow from a right of privacy. It is important in considering the issues in this chapter that *even if* people have a right to privacy (whether ethically or legally), that right does not necessarily guarantee any particular result in these ethical debates.

The right of the people against unreasonable searches and seizures: how important is this right? If you are a law-abiding citizen, is this right liable to be an important one to have or do you believe that only those who break the law are grateful for such a Fourth Amendment right?

1973 *Roe v. Wade:* Women have a right to choose abortion through the second trimester based on a right to privacy.

1990 *Cruzan v. Director, Missouri Dept. of Health:* The U.S. Supreme Court recognized a liberty right to decline unwanted medical treatment.

1998–2004 *Bush v. Schiavo (numerous decisions):* The Supreme Court of Florida recognized a liberty right to decline medical treatment, following *Cruzan*.

1976 *In the Matter of Karen Quinlan:* The Supreme Court of New Jersey, following the reasoning in *Roe v. Wade*, recognized a privacy right to decline medical treatment and be allowed to die.

1997 *Washington v. Glucksberg and Vacco v. Quill:* The U.S. Supreme Court rejected the claims of a constitutional liberty right to assisted suicide.

The U.S. Supreme Court held in 1990 that consenting adults have a right to refuse medical treatment in *Cruzan v. Director, Missouri Dept. of Health*, but that states can insist on clear and convincing evidence of this consent. This can be considered a passive euthanasia, allowing a patient to die, but the Court, to date, has never approved of an active euthanasia.

The question of assisted suicide came before the U.S. Supreme Court in two cases in 1997, *Washington v. Glucksberg* and *Vacco v. Quill*. The patients's attorneys argued that they should have a liberty or privacy right to assisted suicide, a claim rejected by the court. But the court also said that experiments in the states on permitting assisted suicide, such as Oregon's, were acceptable.

In other words, although patients do not have a right under the Constitution to assisted suicide, neither does the Constitution prohibit assisted suicide if a state government elects to provide for it.

The U.S. Supreme Court has not to date addressed the issues of stem cell research or genetic engineering. Congress has passed legislation permitting this research, and federal agencies have issued regulations to implement these laws. A major concern for all is to ensure careful ethical guidelines for this type of research.

In CourseMate, listen to the audio summary of the chapter.

Judith Jarvis Thomson

Judith Jarvis Thomson is Professor Emerita in the Department of Linguistics and Philosophy at the Massachusetts Institute of Technology in Cambridge, Massachusetts, where, before retiring, she had taught since 1964. She grew up in New York and received her B.A. from Barnard College, a B.A. and M.A. from Cambridge University in England, and a Ph.D. from Columbia University. She is perhaps best known for her much-reprinted essay, "A Defense of Abortion," first published in 1971, two years before the *Roe v. Wade* decision by the U.S. Supreme Court. She presents arguments about the moral justifiability of abortion in many circumstances, although she does not believe it is morally justified in all situations. In a famous analogy, she asks us to imagine waking up and discovering that a world-famous violinist needs to be attached to you for a rare blood transfusion for nine months. As with her use of imaginary hypotheticals in other work, this is a tool for thinking through your obligations, if any, to this violinist and then reasoning by analogy to your obligations to an unborn fetus. She also has published influential work on physician-assisted suicide.

Thomson has published numerous books and articles on ethics, philosophy of law, and metaphysics. She works in a rigorous analytic method, applied to this wide range of philosophical issues. Honors accorded to her work include fellowships from the Guggenheim Memorial Foundation, the National Endowment for the Humanities, and the Fulbright program. She was President of the American Philosophical Association, Eastern Division, in 1992–1993.

J-Elgaard/iStockphoto

Judith Jarvis Thomson (1929-)

CHAPTER 3 Case Study

The End of Life

After Hurricane Katrina in New Orleans in 2005, personnel at Memorial Medical Center found themselves stranded for several days with no electrical power; dwindling medical supplies, food, and water; more than 200 patients; no air conditioning; temperatures higher than 100 degrees; and little help for evacuation. Many patients had been on electrical ventilators and required that medical personnel operate bagged valve masks by hand. Life support monitors quickly exhausted the back-up batteries. Oxygen supplies ran out. Critically ill patients had to be moved down five flights of stairwells

Memorial Medical Center in New Orleans, LA

A view of the Carlyle Group's facilities after Hurricane Katrina hit New Orleans in 2005, showing the devastation sustained in the building. The LifeCare unit inside Memorial Medical Center lost twenty-four patients during their five-day wait for rescue.

on stretchers when elevators failed. Coast Guard helicopters were in short supply for rescue, and there were no clear prospects as to when sufficient help might come.

Two days after the hurricane, more than one hundred patients were stranded, with communication coming only from rescue efforts on airboats through the flooded streets. Eventually some patients were evacuated by airports and Coast Guard helicopters, but dozens more remained on high floors of the hospital.

In investigations conducted by the state attorney general and the city coroner of more than forty suspicious patient deaths, evidence was found that many had been injected with unusually high doses of morphine before their deaths. Several outside experts concluded that this constituted homicide caused by human intervention. More than a year later, one of the doctors, Anna Pou, was charged with four counts of murder. At a news conference the next day, the attorney general claimed, "This is not euthanasia. This is plain and simple homicide." When Pou was interviewed on the television show *60 Minutes*, she insisted, "I am not a murderer. I do not believe in euthanasia." In 2007 the Grand Jury in New Orleans declined to indict Pou on any of the charges of murder sought by the district attorney's office.

Today, several civil suits brought by family members are pending against Pou for wrongful death. After Katrina, the Committee for Disaster Medicine Reform was established in Louisiana. Working with Pou, it has successfully gained passage of laws in Louisiana that provide immunity from most civil lawsuits for medical personnel working in future disasters.

1. Euthanasia typically requires (at a minimum) consent by the patient, along with medical review by two independent physicians and a hospital ethics board. Should this procedure be streamlined in an emergency of the magnitude of Katrina? What should be required to justify euthanasia in these situations?

2. Morphine is a "double-effect" drug which both alleviates pain and also can slow breathing so much that it causes death. Whether administering morphine constitutes alleviation of pain or murder depends on the intent of the physician administering the drug. Does this ambiguity make it easier for doctors to commit euthanasia and escape prosecution for murder? Is this a loophole that should be permitted, as least in an emergency situation such as Katrina?

3. None of the patients had signed a living will requesting termination of life-support equipment, although many had signed Do Not Resuscitate (DNR) orders. A DNR means that patients do not want efforts to be made to revive them if their heart or breathing stops. Is this essentially a passive euthanasia? Does the existence of a DNR order justify administering a lethal dose of morphine in the extreme emergency conditions of Katrina? Should passively allowing someone to die be treated the same ethically as actively bringing about their death with morphine?

4. Should medical personnel be exempt from liability in these emergencies, as sought by the Committee for Disaster Medicine Reform? In what situations should they be held accountable?

For additional case studies, please see the CourseMate for this text.

itsmejust/Shutterstock

A bag valve mask

Reading Excerpt: St. Thomas Aquinas, *Summa Theologica* (1265–1274)

INTRODUCTION

St. Thomas Aquinas,
1225–1274

Centuries before contemporary debates about assisted suicide and euthanasia, philosophers considered whether persons have a right to commit suicide. If there is no right to suicide, then there is no right to assisted suicide or euthanasia, even among consenting adults. To consider this underlying question, it is worth considering the arguments against suicide by the medieval philosopher St. Thomas Aquinas.

Aquinas addressed a wide range of moral questions in his *Summa Theologica*, always using the same structure to lay out his answer and reasoning.

To answer the question of whether suicide can be moral, he states his own position in the passage that follows, beginning with "I answer that … ," followed by his list of three reasons. His own position is framed or bookended by first, a series of objections some might raise to his position, and finally, answers to those objections. Thus, in addition to providing his own reasoning, he bolsters his position by anticipating and answering objections, a reasoning technique still used today.

In addition to this pure reasoning, Aquinas typically cites passages from the Bible and also from the writings of Aristotle, referred to as "The Philosopher" and the author of *Nichomachean Ethics*, and Augustine, a fourth-century Bishop and philosopher who sought to merge the thought of ancient Greece and Judeo-Christian theology. We generally shun conclusions based on a simple appeal to authority, but Aquinas uses a reasoning structure that seems to stand on its own without these appeals.

QUESTIONS FOR REFLECTION

1. What reasoning, which does *not* depend on appeals to Biblical or philosophical authority, does Aquinas provide to support his position that suicide is unethical? Is this persuasive reasoning by today's standards? What additional reasons might you add to support his positions?

2. Has Aquinas anticipated all plausible objections to his position in his opening list of five objections? Do any seem to be missing?

3. Has Aquinas provided satisfactory answers to the objections he has identified?

4. If Aquinas has shown that suicide is wrong, then it would seem he has also shown that assisted suicide is wrong. Are you persuaded or are there additional considerations that you would take into account today?

READING

Question 64: Suicide: Whether it is lawful to kill oneself?

Objection 1. It would seem lawful for a man to kill himself. For murder is a sin in so far as it is contrary to justice. But no man can
5 do an injustice to himself, as is proved in Ethic. v, 11. Therefore no man sins by killing himself.

Objection 2. Further, it is lawful, for one who exercises public authority, to kill evil-doers. Now he who exercises public authority is sometimes an evil-doer. Therefore he may lawfully kill himself.

10 **Objection 3.** Further, it is lawful for a man to suffer spontaneously a lesser danger that he may avoid a greater: thus it is lawful for a man to cut off a decayed limb even from himself, that he may save his whole body. Now sometimes a man, by killing himself, avoids a greater evil, for example an unhappy life, or the shame of sin.
15 Therefore a man may kill himself.

Objection 4. Further, Samson killed himself, as related in Judges 16, and yet he is numbered among the saints (Hebrews 11). Therefore it is lawful for a man to kill himself.

Objection 5. Further, it is related (2 Maccabees 14:42) that a
20 certain Razias killed himself, "choosing to die nobly rather than to fall into the hands of the wicked, and to suffer abuses unbecoming his noble birth." Now nothing that is done nobly and bravely is unlawful. Therefore suicide is not unlawful.

On the contrary, Augustine says (De Civ. Dei i, 20): "Hence it
25 follows that the words 'Thou shalt not kill' refer to the killing of a

man—not another man; therefore, not even thyself. For he who kills himself, kills nothing else than a man."

I answer that, It is altogether unlawful to kill oneself, for three reasons. First, because everything naturally loves itself, the result being that everything naturally keeps itself in being, and resists corruptions so far as it can. Wherefore suicide is contrary to the inclination of nature, and to charity whereby every man should love himself. Hence suicide is always a mortal sin, as being contrary to the natural law and to charity. Secondly, because every part, as such, belongs to the whole. Now every man is part of the community, and so, as such, he belongs to the community. Hence by killing himself he injures the community, as the Philosopher declares (Ethic. v, 11). Thirdly, because life is God's gift to man, and is subject to His power, Who kills and makes to live. Hence whoever takes his own life, sins against God, even as he who kills another's slave, sins against that slave's master, and as he who usurps to himself judgment of a matter not entrusted to him. For it belongs to God alone to pronounce sentence of death and life, according to Deuteronomy 32:39, "I will kill and I will make to live."

Reply to Objection 1. Murder is a sin, not only because it is contrary to justice, but also because it is opposed to charity which a man should have towards himself: in this respect suicide is a sin in relation to oneself. On relation to the community and to God, it is sinful, by reason also of its opposition to justice.

Reply to Objection 2. One who exercises public authority may lawfully put to death an evil-doer, since he can pass judgment on him. But no man is judge of himself. Wherefore it is not lawful for one who exercises public authority to put himself to death for any sin whatever: although he may lawfully commit himself to the judgment of others.

Reply to Objection 3. Man is made master of himself through his free-will: wherefore he can lawfully dispose of himself as to those matters which pertain to this life which is ruled by man's free-will. But the passage from this life to another and happier one is subject not to man's free-will but to the power of God. Hence it is not lawful for man to take his own life that he may pass to a happier life, nor that he may escape any unhappiness whatsoever of the present life, because the ultimate and most fearsome evil of this life is death, as the Philosopher states (Ethic. iii, 6). Therefore to bring death upon oneself in order to escape the other afflictions of this life, is to adopt a greater evil in order to avoid a lesser. On like manner it is unlawful to take one's own life on account of one's having committed a sin, both because by so doing one does oneself a very great injury, by depriving oneself of the time needful for repentance, and because it is not lawful to slay an evildoer except by the sentence of the public authority. Again it is unlawful for a woman to kill herself lest she be violated, because she ought not to commit on herself the very great sin of suicide, to avoid the lesser sin of another. For she commits no sin in being violated by force, provided she does not consent, since "without consent of the mind there is no stain on the body," as the Blessed Lucy declared. Now it is evident that fornication and adultery are less grievous sins than taking a man's, especially one's own, life: since the latter is most grievous, because one injures oneself, to whom one owes the greatest love. Moreover it is most dangerous since no time is left wherein to expiate it by repentance. Again it is not lawful for anyone to take his own life for fear he should consent to sin, because "evil must not be done that good may come" (Romans 3:8) or that evil may be avoided especially if the evil be of small account and an uncertain event, for it is uncertain whether one will at some future time consent to a sin, since God is able to deliver man from sin under any temptation whatever.

GerritdeHeus/ANP/age fotostock

If prisoners facing dire conditions, such as indefinite solitary confinement or torture, wished to end their suffering and had an opportunity to kill themselves, would they be justified in taking their own lives, according to St. Thomas Aquinas?

> *Again it is not lawful for anyone to take his own life for fear he should consent to sin ...*

Reply to Objection 4. As Augustine says (De Civ. Dei i, 21), "not even Samson is to be excused that he crushed himself together with his enemies under the ruins of the house, except the Holy Ghost, Who had wrought many wonders through him, had secretly commanded him to do this." He assigns the same reason in the case of certain holy women, who at the time of persecution took their own lives, and who are commemorated by the Church.

95 **Reply to Objection 5.** It belongs to fortitude that a man does not shrink from being slain by another, for the sake of the good of virtue, and that he may avoid sin. But that a man take his own life in order to avoid penal evils has indeed an appearance of fortitude (for which reason some, among whom was Razias, have killed 100 themselves thinking to act from fortitude), yet it is not true fortitude, but rather a weakness of soul unable to bear penal evils, as the Philosopher (Ethic. iii, 7) and Augustine (De Civ. Dei 22,23) declare.

Reading Excerpt: David Hume, Essay on Suicide (c. 1755?)

INTRODUCTION

David Hume, 1711–1776

After his death in 1776, several essays by the Scottish philosopher David Hume were published, including versions of an essay on suicide. The essay in fact was printed during Hume's life, but early reviewers found it so controversial that they pressured Hume's publisher to physically remove the essay from all printed copies. Stray copies of the essay circulated, and after his death they appeared in print without his prior authorization. The version of his essay that we have today is based on an annotated copy that was among Hume's private papers.

Hume systematically rejects each of the arguments we saw in Aquinas against suicide, even though Aquinas's name is never mentioned in this essay, and he may not have even had Aquinas specifically in mind. Hume does believe suicide is justifiable in some circumstances.

QUESTIONS FOR REFLECTION

1. Although Aquinas's name does not appear in this essay, Hume responds to each of Aquinas's three arguments against suicide in various passages throughout this essay. Identify where each of Aquinas's arguments appears and how Hume responds to them.

2. Hume believes suicide is justifiable in many different circumstances. Look for the various passages in this essay where he gives examples of times when suicide might be justifiable. Do you agree with all of his examples? What objections can be raised to those examples?

3. We should use human reason and experience, not superstition, to make moral decisions, including the decision whether or not to commit suicide, according to Hume. In which passages does he make this point and is he persuasive?

4. Many of Aquinas's arguments that suicide is always wrong depend on the existence of God. Hume never denies the existence of God in this essay, but concludes, in sharp contrast with Aquinas, that suicide is often justifiable. How does Hume make his arguments with regard to the nature of God to support suicide?

READING

… Let us here endeavor to restore men to their native liberty, by examining all the common arguments against Suicide, and showing that that action may be free from every imputation of guilt or blame, according to the sentiments of all the ancient philosophers.

5 **Our duty to God**

If Suicide be criminal, it must be a transgression of our duty either to God, our neighbor, or ourselves. — To prove that suicide is no transgression of our duty to God, the following considerations may perhaps suffice. In order to govern the material world, the 10 almighty Creator has established general and immutable laws, by which all bodies, from the greatest planet to the smallest particle of matter, are maintained in their proper sphere and function. To govern the animal world, he has endowed all living creatures with bodily and mental powers; with senses, passions, appetites, 15 memory, and judgment, by which they are impelled or regulated in that course of life to which they are destined. These two distinct principles of the material and animal world, continually encroach upon each other, and mutually retard or forward each other's operation. The powers of men and of all other animals are restrained and directed by the nature and qualities of the surrounding bodies, and the modifications and actions of these bodies are incessantly altered by the operation of all animals. Man is stopped by rivers in his passage over the surface of the earth; and rivers, when properly directed, lend their force to the motion of machines, which serve to the use of man. But though the provinces of the material and animal powers are not kept entirely separate, there results from this no discord or disorder in the creation; on the contrary, from the mixture, union, and contrast of all the various powers of inanimate bodies and living creatures, arises that sympathy, harmony, and proportion, which affords the surest argument of supreme wisdom.

The providence of the Deity appears not immediately in any operation, but governs everything by those general and immutable laws, which have been established from the beginning of time. All events, in one sense, may be pronounced the action of the Almighty, they all proceed from those powers with which he has endowed his creatures. A house which falls by its own weight, is not brought to ruin by his providence, more than one destroyed by the hands of men; nor are the human faculties less his workmanship, than the laws of motion and gravitation. When the passions play, when the judgment dictates, when the limbs obey; this is all the operation of God, and upon these animate principles, as well as upon the inanimate, has he established the government of the universe. Every event is alike important in the eyes of that infinite being, who takes in at one glance the most distant regions of space, and remotest periods of time. There is no event, however important to us, which he has exempted from the general laws that govern the universe, or which he has peculiarly reserved for his own immediate action and operation. The revolution of states and empires depends upon the smallest caprice or passion of single men; and the lives of men are shortened or extended by the smallest accident of air or dies, sunshine or tempest. Nature still continues her progress and operation; and if general laws be ever broke by particular volitions of the Deity, it is after a manner which entirely escapes human observation.

> **❝** *All events, in one sense, may be pronounced the action of the Almighty …* **❞**

As on the one hand, the elements and other inanimate parts of the creation carry on their action without regard to the particular interest and situation of men; so men are entrusted to their own

judgment and discretion in the various shocks of matter, and may employ every faculty with which they are endowed, in order to provide for their ease, happiness, or preservation. What is the meaning then of that principle, that a man who tired of life, and hunted by pain and misery, bravely overcomes all the natural terrors of death, and makes his escape from this cruel scene: that such a man I say, has incurred the indignation of his Creator by encroaching on the office of divine providence, and disturbing the order of the universe? Shall we assert that the Almighty has reserved to himself in any peculiar manner the disposal of the lives of men, and has not submitted that event, in common with others, to the general laws by which the universe is governed? This is plainly false; the lives of men depend upon the same laws as the lives of all other animals; and these are subjected to the general laws of matter and motion. The fall of a tower, or the infusion of a poison, will destroy a man equally with the meanest creature; an inundation sweeps away everything without distinction that comes within the reach of its fury. Since therefore the lives of men are forever dependant on the general laws of matter and motion, is a man's disposing of his life criminal, because in every case it is criminal to encroach upon these laws, or disturb their operation? But this seems absurd; all animals are entrusted to their own prudence and skill for their conduct in the world, and have full authority as far as their power extends, to alter all the operations of nature. Without the exercise of this authority they could not subsist a moment; every action, every motion of a man, innovates on the order of some parts of matter, and diverts from their ordinary course the general laws of motion.

The General Laws of the Universe
Putting together, therefore, these conclusions, we find that human life depends upon the general laws of matter and motion, and that it is no encroachment on the office of providence to disturb or alter these general laws: Has not every one, of consequence, the free disposal of his own life? And may he not lawfully employ that power with which nature has endowed him? In order to destroy the evidence of this conclusion, we must show a reason why this particular cafe is excepted; is it because human life is of such great importance, that it is a presumption for human prudence to dispose of it? But the life of a man is of no greater importance to the universe than that of an oyster. And were it of ever so great importance, the order of human nature has actually submitted it to human prudence, and reduced us to a necessity, in every incident, of determining concerning it. — Were the disposal of human life so much reserved as the peculiar province of the Almighty, that it were an encroachment on his right, for men to dispose of their own lives; it would be equally criminal to act for the preservation of life as for its destruction. If I turn aside a stone which is falling upon my head, I disturb the course of nature, and I invade

the peculiar province of the Almighty, by lengthening out my life beyond the period which by the general laws of matter and motion he had assigned it.

110   A hair, a fly, an insect is able to destroy this mighty being whose life is of such importance. Is it an absurdity to suppose that human prudence may lawfully dispose of what depends on such insignificant causes? It would be no crime in me to divert the *Nile* or *Danube* from its course, were I able to effect such purposes.

115 Where then is the crime of turning a few ounces of blood from their natural channel? — Do you imagine that I complain at Providence or curse my creation, because I go out of life, and put a period to a being, which, were it to continue, would render me miserable? Far be such sentiments from me; I am only convinced

120 of a matter of fact, which you yourself acknowledge possible, that human life may be unhappy, and that my existence, if further prolonged, would become ineligible; but I thank Providence, both for the good which I have already enjoyed, and for the power with which I am endowed of escaping the ill that threatens me. To you

125 it belongs to complain at providence, who foolishly imagine that you have no such power, and who must still prolong a hated life, though loaded with pain and sickness, with shame and poverty — Do not you teach, that when any ill happens to me, though by the malice of my enemies, I ought to be resigned to providence,

130 and that the actions of men are the operations of the Almighty as much as the actions of inanimate beings? When I fall upon my own sword, therefore, I receive my death equally from the hands of the Deity as if it had proceeded from a lion, a precipice, or a fever. The submission which you require to providence, in every calamity that

135 happens to me, excludes not human skill and industry, if possible by their means I can avoid or escape the calamity: And why may I not employ one remedy as well as another?

> **When I fall upon my own sword, therefore, I receive my death equally from the hands of the Deity as if it had proceeded from a lion, a precipice, or a fever.**

    If my life be not my own, it were criminal for me to put it in danger, as well as to dispose of it; nor could one man deserve

140 the appellation of *hero*, whom glory or friendship transports into the greatest dangers, and another merit the reproach of *wretch* or *miscreant* who puts a period to his life, from the same or like motives. — There is no being, which possesses any power or faculty, that it receives not from its Creator, nor is there any one,

145 which by ever so irregular an action can encroach upon the plan of his providence, or disorder the universe. Its operations are his works equally with that chain of events which it invades, and which ever principle prevails, we may for that very reason conclude it to be most favored by him. Be it animate, or inanimate, rational,

150 or irrational, it is all a case: its power is still derived from the supreme Creator, and is alike comprehended in the order of his providence. When the horror of pain prevails over the love of life; when a voluntary action anticipates the effects of blind causes, it is only in consequence of those powers and principles which he

155 has implanted in his creatures. Divine providence is still inviolate, and placed far beyond the reach of human injuries.

    It is impious says the old Roman superstition to divert rivers from their course, or invade the prerogatives of nature. It is impious says the French superstition to inoculate for the small-

160 pox, or usurp the business of providence by voluntarily producing distempers and maladies. It is impious says the modern *European* superstition, to put a period to our own life, and thereby rebel against our Creator; and why not impious, say I, to build houses, cultivate the ground, or sail upon the ocean? In all these actions

165 we employ our powers of mind and body, to produce some innovation in the course of nature; and in none of them do we any more. They are all of them therefore equally innocent, or equally criminal. *But you are placed by providence, like a centinal, in a particular station, and when you desert it without being recalled, you are*

170 *equally guilty of rebellion against your almighty sovereign, and have incurred his displeasure.* — I ask, why do you conclude that providence has placed me in this station? For my part I find that I owe my birth to a long chain of causes, of which many depended upon voluntary actions of men. *But providence guided all these*

175 *causes, and nothing happens in the universe without its consent and co-operation.* If so, then neither does my death, however voluntary, happen without its consent; and whenever pain or sorrow so far overcome my patience, as to make me tired of life, I may conclude that I am recalled from my station in the clearest and

180 most express terms. It is providence surely that has placed me at this present in this chamber: But may I not leave it when I think proper, without being liable to the imputation of having deserted my post or station? When I shall be dead, the principles of which I am composed will still perform their part in the universe, and will

185 be equally useful in the grand fabric, as when they composed this individual creature. The difference to the whole will be no greater than between my being in a chamber and in the open air. The one change is of more importance to me than the other; but not more so to the universe.

190   It is a kind of blasphemy to imagine that any created being can disturb the order of the world, or invade the business of Providence! It supposes, that that being possesses powers and faculties, which it received not from its creator, and which are not subordinate to his government and authority. A man may

PhilAugustavo/iStockphoto

What is Hume arguing by asking the question, " ...why not impious, say I, to build houses, cultivate the ground, or sail upon the ocean?" Does our power in these earthly spheres justify exercising dominion over our own lives by committing suicide?

195 disturb society no doubt, and thereby incur the displeasure of the Almighty: But the government of the world is placed far beyond his reach and violence. And how does it appear that the Almighty is displeased with those actions that disturb society? By the principles which he has implanted in human nature, and which inspire
200 us with a sentiment of remorse if we ourselves have been guilty of such actions, and with that of blame and disapprobation, if we ever observe them in others: — Let us now examine, according to the method proposed, whether Suicide be of this kind of actions, and be a breach of our duty to our *neighbor* and to *society*.

205 **Our Duty to Our Neighbors**
A man who retires from life does no harm to society: He only ceases to do good; which, if it is an injury, is of the lowest kind. — All our obligations to do good to society seem to imply something reciprocal. I receive the benefits of society, and therefore ought to promote
210 its interests; but when I withdraw myself altogether from society, can I be bound any longer? But allowing that our obligations to do good were perpetual, they have certainly some bounds; I am not obliged to do a small good to society at the expense of a great harm to myself; why then should I prolong a miserable existence, because
215 of some frivolous advantage which the public may perhaps receive from me? If upon account of age and infirmities, I may lawfully resign any office, and employ my time altogether in fencing against these calamities, and alleviating, as much as possible, the miseries of my future life: why may I not cut short these miseries at once
220 by an action which is no more prejudicial to society? But suppose that it is no longer in my power to promote the interest of society, suppose that I am a burden to it, suppose that my life hinders some person from being much more useful to society. In such cases, my resignation of life must not only be innocent, but laudable. And most
225 people who lie under any temptation to abandon existence, are in some such situation; those who have health, or power, or authority, have commonly better reason to be in humor with the world.

A man who is engaged in a conspiracy for the public interest; is seized upon suspicion; is threatened with the rack; and
230 knows from his own weakness that the secret will be extorted from him: Could such a one consult the public interest better than by putting a quick period to a miserable life? This was the case of the famous and brave *Strozi* of *Florence*. — Again, suppose a malefactor is justly condemned to a shameful death,
235 can any reason be imagined, why he may not anticipate his punishment, and save himself all the anguish of thinking on its dreadful approaches? He invades the business of providence no more than the magistrate did, who ordered his execution; and his voluntary death is equally advantageous to society, by ridding it
240 of a pernicious member.

Our Duty to Ourselves
That Suicide may often be consistent with interest and with our duty to ourselves, no one can question, who allows that age, sickness, or misfortune, may render life a burden, and make it worse even
245 than annihilation. I believe that no man ever threw away life, while it was worth keeping. For such is our natural horror of death, that small motives will never be able to reconcile us to it; and though perhaps the situation of a man's health or fortune did not seem to require this remedy, we may at least be assured that anyone
250 who, without apparent reason, has had recourse to it, was cursed with such an incurable depravity or gloominess of temper as must poison all enjoyment, and render him equally miserable as if he had been loaded with the most grievous misfortunes. — If suicide be supposed a crime, it is only cowardice can impel us to it. If it
255 be no crime, both prudence and courage should engage us to rid ourselves at once of existence, when it becomes a burden. It is the only way that we can then be useful to society, by setting an example, which if imitated, would preserve to everyone his chance for happiness in life, and would effectually free him from all danger
260 of misery.

INTRODUCTION: THINKING IT THROUGH 1–6

Thinking It Through 1 Through 6 guides you through some of the essential steps to begin to develop the reasoning needed in an ethical inquiry. Following these steps will help you to clarify the complexities and implications of such an inquiry. It will also show you how to start applying the soundest methods to examine and attempt to resolve an ethical issue. This process follows the five-step progression illustrated in the critical thinking tables in the chapters in Part II.

{ Instructors:

For options on how to use these modules in or outside of class, consult the *Instructor's Manual*. **}**

In Chapter 2, you were asked to identify a specific ethical issue to examine throughout this course. **Thinking It Through 1** prepares the foundation of your investigation by inviting you to assess whether it is spelled out the way an ethical inquiry needs to be. The sections that follow outline a process that can help you accomplish this important task. Examples throughout demonstrate the do's and doesn't.

Elnur/Shutterstock

THINKING IT THROUGH 1

1. Overview

What Does Ethics Do? Go back to your formulation of this issue. Reread it carefully to make sure that this issue is indeed one that warrants an ethical inquiry. Remember that ethics asks questions in the hope of finding answers about what is good or bad or right or wrong. Ethics endeavors to answer the question: How should we decide which actions are right or wrong? To establish whether you formulated an issue that offers an ethical challenge, check whether this issue as expressed can be turned into a question of right and wrong or of good and bad. If, for example, your issue as formulated is a statement that does not involve a choice between at least two options, and specifically two *moral* options, it might very well not be adequate as the object of an ethical inquiry.

Propose a Choice. A quick study of the following example can help illustrate how to evaluate whether you need to revise the formulation of the issue you picked: "Should high school students in this country own a laptop, so that the U.S. workforce can be more competitive?" A choice is expressed in this statement: high school students should own laptops or high school students should not own laptops.

A Moral Dilemma. However, does this choice involve right or wrong actions? Could you say that owning a laptop or not is an action that can be viewed as right or wrong in a moral sense? You might say that it is good to own a laptop. But *good* in this instance means *beneficial*. *Good* here, you might say, expresses a resolvable quality. You could ask: on a scale from 1 to 10, grade how good it is to own a laptop. But this is not the type of *goodness* we are asking about here. Could we judge whether ownership of a laptop is good the way ownership of a responsibility is? We could not. We could not assign a value judgment to ownership of a laptop.

{ STRATEGY:

Determine whether an issue involves right and wrong. **}**

{ ASK YOURSELF: Does the ethical claim I made pass the first test by involving right and wrong, that is, a moral choice? }

2. Specifics

Assess. Is the formulation of the issue as succinct and as precise as it can be? Try rewording it in a different way, and if at all possible, in a briefer way. Revise it so that it says the same thing in fewer words and conveys the issue more accurately. Keep things simple and sentences short. If you do not feel like you can do so, working through the next **Thinking It Through** modules might show ways in which words or concepts can be reconsidered and lead you to reformulate your issue more effectively. For example, an issue is initially written out as:

> I enjoy gambling sometimes, and I am not happy that I have to travel long distances to do it. I don't need to gamble all the time, but I like it enough that I want to be able to go to a casino without driving for hours.

Apply the First Test. This issue as worded does not pass the first test: it does not pose an ethical challenge, nor does it involve a moral choice or right and wrong options. The formulation is also unclear because it is not certain what specific question the issue raises. Is the question whether you should be able to go to a casino without driving for hours? If it is, it does not pass the first test. Driving for hours is not about right or wrong, but of practical importance related to material conditions, such as whether you own a car, have the means to keep it running, and have the time to drive for hours. It does not have to do with values. Or is the preceding question whether you should be able to go to a casino that is close to where you live, which means that casinos ought to be more accessible? In this case, again, the question is not one involving ethical options. Your own preference in lifestyle is at issue.

Reevaluate. This issue is neither precisely nor clearly articulated. You need to reexamine the wording to get at ethical choices first, and a readily identifiable question second. Phrasing an ethical issue as a question will help you easily recognize the positions that are yielded by this issue. So, you might reframe the preceding issue as

> **STRATEGY:**
> - Reformulate the issue.
> - Condense the formulation as much as possible.

> **STRATEGY:**
> - Review the formulation to eliminate irrelevant elements.
> - Phrase the issue as a question.

"Should casino gambling be permissible?" Or you might wish to explore the question, "Should casino gambling be widely accessible?"

> **ASK YOURSELF:** What in my ethical claim is most important, and is anything unneeded or superfluous? Can my ethical claim be phrased as a question?

3. Goals

Review. Finally, you were also asked to identify goals that would help you address this issue. Review your goals to make sure that they are as specific and resolvable as possible. Chapter 2 provided the following example: "Should I tell my brother that I wonder if his treatment of his girlfriend might be too casual and sometimes disrespectful?" The first goal of figuring out whether to share your concern with your brother or not is easily "resolvable"; your reflections will lead you toward one resolution: speaking up or not.

Resolvable Focus. Finding out whether your own sense that your brother's treatment of his girlfriend is inappropriate is not as easily resolvable. The concern you express is in part an opinion and thus subjective. You could consult with trusted friends and family to confirm whether your assessment of his treatment toward his girlfriend seems accurate. But this goal would be more difficult to achieve and perhaps not as clear-cut. The parties you survey would need to be as intimately familiar with your brother and his relationship with his girlfriend as you are. If you are unsure whether your stated goals are clearly achievable, you might think of other goals or you might proceed with your inquiry and gauge as you progress whether they are.

> **ASK YOURSELF:** What is my goal? Will I be able to clearly determine when I have reached it?

The ultimate goal for this assignment is to state your position on this issue by building an argument that will lead to a logical conclusion. In the next module, you will be shown how to start the process by carefully examining the key words and concepts that make up your inquiry's formulation.

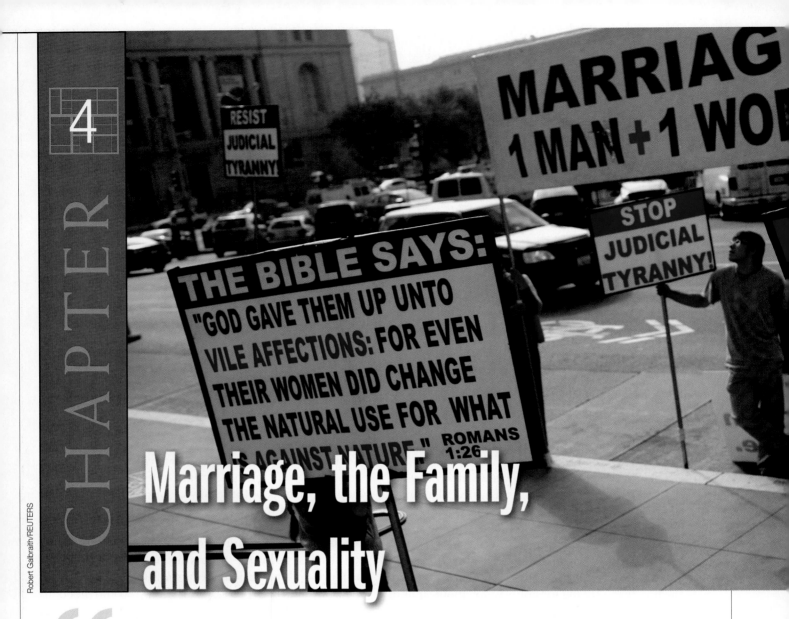

Robert Galbraith/REUTERS

CHAPTER 4

Marriage, the Family, and Sexuality

"[A]ccording to the objective moral order, homosexual relations are acts which lack an essential and indispensable finality... . homosexual acts are intrinsically disordered and can in no case be approved of."

Pope Paul VI, "Declaration on Certain Questions Concerning Sexual Ethics," 1975

"The petitioners [homosexual consenting adults] are entitled to respect for their private lives. The State cannot demean their existence or control their destiny by making their private sexual conduct a crime. Their right to liberty under the Due Process Clause gives them the full right to engage in their conduct without intervention of the government."

Justice Anthony Kennedy, *Lawrence v. Texas* (majority opinion), 2003.

LEARNING OUTCOMES

After you complete this unit, you should be able to:

4-1 Identify areas of family life in which our rights to privacy and liberty are central.

4-2 Demonstrate use of central philosophical reasoning tools to address the rights of privacy and liberty in the context of families (e.g., marriage, children, and education of children).

4-3 Explain how ethical reasoning is applied in legal reasoning on these issues.

rivacy is central in the often-heated debates about the beginning and end of life that we considered in Chapter 3 on abortion, contraception, assisted suicide, and euthanasia. But privacy is also a central concept in a variety of other activities throughout our lives. How much freedom do we have in the education of our children? Should we be free to marry anybody we want, regardless of their race, gender, or sexual orientation or to marry several spouses at once? Should we be allowed to enter into a contract to hire somebody to carry a child for us during pregnancy?

Overview

In this chapter, we extend our consideration of privacy to realms of great current interest, namely, privacy in our family life. We consider what relationships should be allowed among consenting adults. Should interracial marriage be allowed? Should a right to marry extend to same-sex couples? Next we consider reproduction within that family relationship. Should we be allowed to pursue new technology, such as in vitro fertilization, to reproduce? Should we be allowed to hire somebody to carry a child for us? We then consider another central element of family privacy: the education of children and the rights and obligations of parents to determine what that

What do you think?

People should be able to marry whomever they want and raise their children however they want.

Strongly Disagree   Strongly Agree
1   2   3   4   5   6   7

education should be. These basic questions have challenged philosophers for hundreds, even thousands, of years. To address them, we will use the tools we have developed so far for good critical-thinking and appropriate philosophical approaches, especially Kantian appeals to human dignity and autonomy and utilitarian analysis of right and wrong action. Finally, we study an excerpt from Plato and both the majority opinion and the dissenting opinion of the U.S. Supreme Court case *Lawrence v. Texas.*

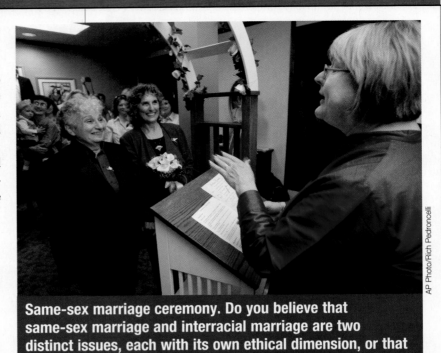

Same-sex marriage ceremony. Do you believe that same-sex marriage and interracial marriage are two distinct issues, each with its own ethical dimension, or that they are ethically comparable?

4-1 FAMILY LIFE AND PRIVACY AND LIBERTY

Although contemporary public dialogue often focuses on privacy and liberty rights with regard to life and death (see Chapter 3), those rights also shape many other aspects of our lives. In particular, these rights are relevant to certain activities and relationships in our own family life. If we adopt a philosophical approach, which stresses a systematic, orderly consideration of a problem, we should start by identifying the areas of concern.

Initially, we should focus on the precise relationships within that family. Traditionally, a family consisted of a married heterosexual couple of the same race. But in the not so distant past, acceptance of interracial marriage has resulted in increased numbers of these unions. About one in seven marriages in 2008 was interracial or interethnic, according to a 2010 Pew Research Center report. In the more recent past, we have started considering whether same-sex marriage should be recognized. Homosexuality itself has been more widely accepted in recent decades and that has strengthened the movement to challenge this institution's tradition and legalize same-sex marriage. Some wonder if we also now should consider polygamous marriage, as is accepted in other parts of the world or whether that ban should continue. Nearly fifty countries, mostly Muslim and African, recognize polygamous marriages. There is a wide range of acceptance of the practice; although no country requires polygamy, some countries permit and recognize it, and others permit and recognize some forms of polygamous marriage.

> **[I]n the not so distant past, acceptance of interracial marriage has resulted in increased numbers of these unions.**

Another focus within that family has to be on the children. Changing recognition of what constitutes a family and advancements in technology raise new issues. Should couples unable to conceive be permitted to hire a woman to carry a child for them? Should in vitro fertilization (IVF) be permitted? Should homosexual couples be permitted to adopt a child?

A third area of continuing concern is the education of those children. What obligations and rights do parents have in the education of their children? To what extent should the state intervene to protect the interests of the child, if parents are not handling their education? Should education even be institutionalized—that is, should there be a nationwide system, including standards for instruction and curricula? Traditionally, state governments have been responsible for overseeing educational standards. Regulation at the national level (such as "No Child Left Behind") has been fraught with controversy and is in flux. But regardless of which level of government is setting standards, the question for us is the extent to which the rights and obligations of parents should be balanced against the rights and obligations of governments to intervene to protect the children.

In CourseMate, watch a video and take the quiz.

4-2 REASONING TOOLS AND PRIVACY AND LIBERTY IN FAMILIES

The philosophical reasoning tools we have developed so far will help us once again sift through these issues in family life, as well as issues in the future that we cannot yet anticipate. Kantian reasoning emphasizes the role of human autonomy and dignity. For all of these issues, we can ask whether the persons in the family are being accorded that human dignity. Consequentialist reasoning considers the happiness that results for different persons from various possible actions. The utilitarian says that we should choose as right action the option that creates the greatest happiness for the greatest number.

Are interracial marriages fully accepted nowadays? What reasons do those opposed to such unions give in support of their position?

Brian Chase/iStockphoto

4-2a Marriage

If an interracial couple wishes to marry, are we denying them basic human autonomy and liberty by denying them that choice? Someone opposed to interracial marriage might argue that marrying outside of one's race is degrading and society should pressure individuals not to enter into such a union.

Utilitarian reasoning might support interracial marriage by noting the good results that derive from the stability that marriage confers to a couple. Along with that stability comes a social recognition of the relationship that contributes to helping the couple integrate into their community. Opponents of interracial marriage might also use utilitarian reasoning to argue that allowing interracial marriage has harmful effects on the greater community because it embraces and condones a union that goes against tradition.

It was only in 1967 that the U.S. Supreme Court held in a case called *Loving v. Virginia* that many states' laws banning interracial marriage were unconstitutional because they violated the basic right to privacy and liberty in choosing a marriage partner. Although, as we saw previously, the rates of interracial marriages have increased a great deal, public sentiment has taken much longer to accept the idea of marrying across races. According to a Pew Research Center report, in 2008, only about 60 percent of Americans consider interracial marriage acceptable, four decades after the Supreme Court decision.

In the past decade, the debate over same-sex marriage has taken center stage. Many insist that the traditional conception of marriage as only between a man and a woman is imperative to a stable society. That stability amounts to a consequence that would be relevant in consequentialist reasoning. Supporters of marriage equality insist that marriage is a civil right with many legal consequences and benefits, and no one should be denied this right because of sexual orientation. The rights include visitation rights in hospitals, favorable treatment under tax laws, and inheritance rights. These marriage-equality proponents are insisting that everyone be treated with dignity as persons, regardless of orientation. Supporters also point to the good consequences of stability and commitment in any relationship, regardless of sexual orientation. Supporters often appeal to the *Loving* decision and the country's growing acceptance of interracial marriage as a highly relevant precedent, not just for the technical legal issues but also for the moral grounds of respecting the privacy and liberty of individuals to marry. The recognition of marriage equality seems to be moving very quickly in the public opinion sphere, but as of 2011 six states (Connecticut, Iowa, Massachusetts, New Hampshire, New York, and Vermont) and the District of Columbia recognize same-sex marriage; four (Hawaii, Illinois, New Jersey, and Rhode Island) recognize civil unions; and six (California, Maine, Nevada, Oregon, Washington, and Wisconsin) provide registered domestic partnership which provides some or all legal rights of married couples.

4-2b Children in the Family

With growing recognition of marriage equality and advancements in medical technology, the rights concerning children in families are also receiving close attention.

IVF can be considered from a Kantian perspective. Should couples have the autonomy to decide to conceive using new technologies such as this one? But IVF also encounters concerns about the status of a "person," and whether it is ethical to create a person in nontraditional ways. Utilitarians might consider results of all kinds from permitting IVF. With the planet getting overcrowded, for example, is it ethical to make it easier to produce even more children? The resulting overpopulation might be perceived as a negative consequence that would outweigh the potential happiness for the couple of producing a biological child of their own. And what should we do with the leftover fertilized eggs typically created during the IVF process, especially if they are considered persons in their own right, as some believe?

Another strategy for childless couples who wish to have children is to hire a woman—a surrogate mother—to carry a child through pregnancy for them. Critics charge, in Kantian terms, that we are denying the autonomy and dignity of the womb-for-hire, especially because she is likely to be someone in need of money and is risking her own health and well-being to carry out this contract. Another criticism, also in Kantian terms, charges that the baby is being treated as property that can be bought and sold, rather than as a person. But the consequentialist might reach different conclusions. If the woman carrying the child for hire needs the money and the childless couple is to enjoy the biological child of their own that they so desire, is happiness not secured all around? So long as everyone is treated fairly and with respect (per Kantian principles), why should the state intervene to prohibit such contracts?

Another issue currently debated is adoption of children. Should we favor same-race adoption, if available? What of adoption by same-sex couples, especially for children difficult to place, such as older children or children with AIDS or drug addictions resulting from their addicted mother's pregnancy? Two states, Utah and Mississippi, prohibit adoption by same-sex couples, but only eighteen states and the District of Columbia expressly permit such adoptions and the situation is unclear in many others.

To systematically consider adoption issues, we need to consider the privacy and liberty of the children as well as the would-be adoptive parents. If same-sex couples want the experience of raising children in a loving home, why should they not have the liberty and freedom to do this? If an older child, difficult to place, has a choice between a foster home or a more stable adoption by a same-sex couple, should the child have that freedom to choose? The utilitarian approach also needs to consider the possible happiness and unhappiness of each person involved, especially for difficult-to-place children, such as AIDS babies, crack babies, or children with disabilities. Are those children more likely to find happiness in an adoptive family, even if they are a same-sex couple, rather than an institution or foster care? If the adoptive parents benefit from the satisfaction of raising these children, why should they be denied that positive consequence?

> **Should couples have the autonomy to decide to conceive using new technologies such as [in vitro fertilization]?**

Reflections on Education 4.1

What do leading philosophers say about education?

Jean-Jacques Rousseau (1712–1778) says: "Our true study is that of the human condition. Those who can best endure the good and evil of life are in my view the best educated. Hence it follows that true education consists less in precept than in practice. We begin to learn when we begin to live; our education begins with ourselves. Our first teacher is our nurse. Moreover this word "education" had with the ancients another meaning that we no longer give it—it meant 'nurture.' ... Thus, education, discipline, and instruction are three things as different in their purpose as the nurse, the preceptor, and the master. But these distinctions are undesirable and the child should only follow one guide."

—**Jean-Jacques Rousseau,** *Emile*, **1762**

4-2c Education of Children

Should parents have autonomy in how they raise their children, including their choices for the education of their children? Should the rights of parents to this autonomy also be balanced against the rights of children to their future lives? If we allow parents to deny a minimally decent education to the children, are we hurting the future autonomy of the children to pursue careers of their own choosing as adults?

Philosophers have had a great deal to say about appropriate education for children—as an example shows in Reflections on Education 4.1.

But who should impose those standards, the parents or the state or the community? As a culture, we have moved away from older ideas that children were the property of their parents and that the state should not get involved to a notion that there are times when the state must intervene to remove children from harmful settings. Yet even today, many believe that the state should never intervene in the decisions of parents on how to raise and educate their children. This is demonstrated in the increase in homeschooling across the nation.

From a Kantian perspective, consider the autonomy and dignity of all the persons involved, including the children, now and in their future lives. Parents want the liberty to raise their children according to their own beliefs, including their beliefs on religion, education, and morality. But the children seem to have rights to be prepared for independent living as adults, which might require adaptation of society standards for education and morality—see Reflections on Education 4.2 for such a perspective.

From a utilitarian perspective, think of the different results from the choices available for education and rearing of children. Parents might derive considerable satisfaction homeschooling their children because they can teach what they believe is important. Children might be seen as benefitting from the substantial companionship, individualized attention, and presence of their parents providing homeschooling. But others might note the positive benefits of socializing in a diverse public school setting, which prepares children for the realities of the adult world—Reflections on Education 4.3 offers a famous philosopher's relevant view. Negative consequences might also be identified for public school education, such as overcrowding, teaching divergent from parental beliefs, and bullying.

In CourseMate, apply what you've learned to the real-life scenario in the simulation.

In CourseMate, practice what you learned by taking the chapter quiz.

4-3 ETHICAL REASONING APPLIED TO THE LAW

Theoretical philosophical reasoning can be applied effectively to a wide range of public policy issues we face in our daily lives. Yet another application of those philosophical ideas can be seen in the legal environment, where so many important court decisions on these issues directly

---

Reflections on Education 4.2
What do leading philosophers say about education?

John Dewey (1859–1952) says: "I believe that the school is primarily a social institution. Education being a social process, the school is simply that form of community life in which all those agencies are concentrated that will be most effective in bringing the child to share in the inherited resources of the race, and to use his own powers for social ends. I believe that education, therefore, is a process of living and not a preparation for future living."

—John Dewey, *My Pedagogic Creed*, 1897

---

impact our fundamental rights and liberties. We have noted previously some important legal benchmarks that have changed the direction of our actions, if not our thinking, on these issues.

Although philosophical and legal reasoning extensively overlap, they are not identical. Still, in these legal conflicts, appeals to what sounds like Kantian and utilitarian reasoning are common in court decisions. In decisions on abortion, homosexual rights, surrogate motherhood, euthanasia, and a host of other hot-button issues, courts typically appeal to the dignity and autonomy of persons, in language that tracks remarkably the language and reasoning of Kantian ethics. In addition, courts typically review consequences, good and bad, of possible decisions, using reasoning that sounds like the utilitarian philosophical reasoning we have considered. In discussing surrogate motherhood, for example, some courts entertain utilitarian reasoning in discussing the economic benefit to the

CEFutcher/iStockphoto.com

Does the larger community have an interest in ensuring that all children are given the kind of education that will prepare them to live healthy and productive lives according to that community's standards?

surrogate mother, as well as the exploitation of those surrogates; this also echoes Kant's imperative to never use others as a means to an end.

These philosophical applications to legal realities are important for another reason. It is all well and good to conclude philosophically that we should have an ethical right to marriage equality, regardless of gender orientation, for example. But if the laws of your state prohibit that type of marriage, you are not able to act on those rights. So, knowing the current state of the law on these issues matters, when we consider them philosophically. And knowing that situation puts us in a better position to try to influence the broader legal environment to actually achieve those rights. Many philosophers have been central in shifting arguments in

a legal context by appealing to philosophical reasoning in "friends of the court" briefs on these topics.

We reviewed historically important recognition in the legal system of privacy rights in Chapter 3. In addition to those, a few additional decisions need to be mentioned. With regard to who can marry, *Loving v. Virginia* (1967) established a right of interracial marriage. This case is now cited in support of arguments that same-sex marriage also should be recognized in our legal system, and some courts have found just that right. The first to recognize a right of civil union was the Vermont decision in 1999, *Baker v. Vermont*. In response, the Vermont legislature legalized civil unions, but it has now recently adopted same-sex marriage equality. The first state to recognize same-sex marriage through its courts was Massachusetts, in a decision called *Goodridge v. Dept. of Public Health* (2003). The U.S. Supreme Court has not to date taken up the issue of same-sex marriage, but they have recognized homosexual privacy rights in the *Lawrence v. Texas* decision (2003), which is excerpted in this chapter. Many think this will be a strong basis, along with the *Loving* decision, for eventually recognizing a national right of same-sex marriage. Of special interest to us in a philosophy course are the similarities with philosophical reasoning. If *Loving* provides a basis for recognizing same-sex marriage, it will be essentially reasoning by analogy, which we use regularly in philosophical reasoning, and which can also be a trap

> ⌐ **Some states ... permit [surrogacy] ... with strict conditions ...** ⌐

of the fallacy of faulty analogies. That is, the cases might have some things in common (as they deal with mixed marriage), but are not sufficiently similar to draw the same conclusion (that both types of mixed marriage should be a right). *Lawrence* and *Loving* appealed specifically to human liberty and autonomy, Kantian ideals, so our understanding of those philosophical principles helps us understand the broader public policy applications.

Some worry that if same-sex marriage is recognized in this country, we will be on a slippery slope—another type of fallacy presented earlier in this book—toward being forced to recognize polygamy. President Abraham Lincoln signed legislation in 1862 that banned bigamy in the territories, including the territory of Utah. This law was challenged in the courts as a violation of religious freedom, but was upheld by the U.S. Supreme Court in 1879 in *Reynolds* v. *United States*, a decision that has never been overturned and represents the most recent decision by the Supreme Court on polygamy. The reasoning in *Reynolds* appealed to principles of human dignity and autonomy for the women and children in these relationships, calling them "innocent victims." In other words, the Supreme Court used a Kantian appeal to human dignity and autonomy (for the women and children in these relationships) in concluding that there is no right to polygamy. Utah eventually achieved statehood in 1896 after adding a ban on polygamy to its state constitution and after the Mormon Church changed its policy on polygamy to say that it was no longer advocated.

With regard to children in the family, the issue of same-sex adoption has been considered in several cases in the states, but not in the U.S. Supreme Court. Another issue we have considered in this chapter, surrogacy, is also in flux in state legislatures and courts.

A well-publicized case of contracting with a surrogate mother was *In the Matter of Baby M* in New Jersey (1988), which concluded that surrogacy contracts were against public policy and amounted to baby-selling. The reasoning in this case appealed to the consequences of exploitation of the surrogate mother who needed the money, as well as her dignity and autonomy as a person who decided she wanted to keep the baby. Since then, other states have struggled to address this issue. Some states ban it outright. Others permit it, but only with strict conditions to ensure that the surrogate mother is not exploited and the contract does not amount to "baby-selling."

The education of children has received a great deal of attention in the courts, including the Nebraska privacy cases over a century ago. A recent decision in California is included in the Case Study for this chapter. It concerns how much flexibility parents should have in educating their children consistently with their religious views, while still meeting the entrance requirements for the University of California. The legal reasoning in the range of these cases strongly parallels the philosophical approaches we have studied, especially respect for the autonomy and dignity of persons and recognition of privacy and liberty rights of parents in the ways their children are raised. Reflections on Education 4.4 offers a final perspective on education from a philosopher of note.

Now that you have studied how various types of reasoning apply to the topics discussed previously, review Critical Thinking Table 4.1 to follow the process of examining an ethical claim on a related topic.

In CourseMate, listen to the audio summary of the chapter.

Ronald M. Dworkin

One of the most distinguished philosophical and legal scholars of our day, Ronald M. Dworkin, earned degrees from Harvard College, Harvard Law School, Oxford University, and Yale University. He has held joint appointments in philosophy and in law at New York University, Oxford University, and University College London. Dworkin has published numerous books and articles on a wide range of issues addressed in this volume, including assisted suicide, legal and moral rights, discrimination, pornography, and abortion. Many lengthy articles of his can be found in *The New York Review of Books,* in which he publishes regularly.

His approach to legal philosophy stresses what some would call a pragmatic approach, although he also appeals to a nontheological sense of natural human rights in which there are absolute truths about right and wrong. Everyone from scholars to artists to judges engages in a process of "interpretation" that draws on the past traditions and reinvests them in present-day terms. Regardless of the issue, he emphasizes the centrality of human dignity and self-respect.

Ronald M. Dworkin (1931–)

Table 4.1 Critical Thinking Steps and Their Application in an Example

{ "Marriage equality for homosexuals should be recognized as a human right, as homosexuals are people, too." }

Critical Thinking Steps	Application
1. Examine and clarify key terms and concepts.  • Look words up in a dictionary as a start if necessary. • Unravel or unpack the complexities and nuances of a central term, such as *justice*, *right*, or *good*.	• What do we mean by *marriage* here? Are we speaking of both religious marriage, as recognized by a religious group, and civil marriage, as recognized by a governmental entity? • By *recognition*, do we mean ethical recognition by society? Legal recognition by the government? Or do we intend both senses? • What do we mean by *human right*? • By *people* do we mean more precisely adult persons, as defined by the law?
2. Work through the meaning of the key terms and concepts to make sure you will use them consistently. • Consider the ways the term can be used by including it in different sentences and contexts to zero in on the particular meaning you are after. • Ask yourself what words are potential synonyms for the concept. Do those capture everything you want to understand about that term?	• If we include religious marriage in our understanding of marriage, will we encounter problems reconciling marriage equality with religious freedom? Does that suggest that we should restrict our consideration to governmental civil marriage? • Is civil marriage synonymous with civil union? If not, what are the similarities and differences? • Do we need to think through what recognition in either an ethical or legal meaning would result in? For example, if ethical recognition does not result in giving rights accorded to spouses, like that of being allowed to visit a family member in a hospital, is it too restrictive and insufficient a concept to have any value? • Are human rights here those granted solely by the Constitution? If we are only interested in ethical issues, what is the alternative basis for those human rights
3. Build premises and bring any assumptions to light. 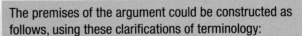 • Put together short and clear sentences to build each of your premises. • Think through what you may be taking for granted in your reasoning. What assumptions are you making? • Once you have identified assumptions, articulate them in your premise, so that your audience has the same understanding of a term or a concept as you.	The premises of the argument could be constructed as follows, using these clarifications of terminology: (i) All adult persons should have the same human rights. (ii) Those human rights include the ethical right to civil marriage. (iii) Homosexuals are persons. CONCLUSION: Homosexuals should have the ethical right to civil marriage.

Critical Thinking Steps	Application
4. Test/Verify your premises. Brian Chase/iStockphoto • Now that you have stated your premises explicitly, do you want to stick with them? • Are you relying on premises drawn from unsubstantiated sources or from questionable authorities? • Are you consistent in your premises? Or are you appealing to different and inconsistent foundations in your reasoning? • Reformulate your premises if they have proven to be faulty.	Each of the premises should be examined. (i) Human rights are explained and justified in different ways (whether from natural law, from human stipulations, or other theoretical vantage points), but the explanations seem to converge on this conclusion, namely, that the rights should be universal rights. (ii) *Which* human rights we possess is much more controversial. Do we have a human right to guaranteed health care? A college education? Decent housing? An abortion? This premise needs much more extensive justification to pass muster. (iii) It seems uncontroversial to state that homosexuals are persons. If you do not accept all of these premises, then you will not accept the conclusion either. But if you do accept all of them, then you would find the conclusion valid and justified.
5. Confirm that the conclusions you draw are logical. Check for reliance on fallacies and correct any premise that you identify as relying on a fallacy.	The fallacy of begging the question seems to be at play in the second premise, namely, which human rights we all have. Whether the same human rights all adults should have include the ethical right to civil marriage is debatable and may not be universally accepted as a human right. If we assume that human rights include a right to marriage, the conclusion follows easily. This assumption could be challenged as easily as our statement could be.

CHAPTER **4** Case Study

Educating Children

Philosophers such as Jean-Jacques Rousseau, Mary Wollstonecraft, and John Dewey have addressed ideal forms of education and the *obligations* of parents regarding the education of their children, but they did not focus on the issue of parental *rights* in determining that education. More than a century ago, the privacy right of parents to educate their children was recognized in the United States in two U.S. Supreme Court cases. One struck down a law in Nebraska prohibiting the teaching of German, and the other recognized the right of parents to send their children to private schools. More recently, in 1972, another Supreme Court case recognized the right of Amish parents to educate their children consistently with their religious views. The reasoning in these court cases has drawn extensively on familiar philosophical concepts of individual autonomy and privacy. Essentially, these parents insisted on the liberty of educating their children consistently with their own religious views, but that education clashed with the demands of the state education authorities' standards for educating children.

(Continued)

James Marshall/CORBIS

Were you homeschooled or do you know anyone who was? If not, what do you know about this practice? Do parents homeschooling their children have any obligations toward the authorities of the state where they live or of the federal government? Does the government have any ethical obligation to the children to ensure they receive an adequate education to prepare them for adult life?

In 2005, a lawsuit was filed against the University of California by the Association of Christian Schools International, the Calvary Chapel Christian School, and six students from Calvary Chapel. The University of California is the most prestigious public university system in the state. It sets requirements for courses that must be completed in high school to be considered for admission. The university refused to recognize four of the courses taught by the Calvary Chapel Christian School as meeting those entrance requirements, which meant that these students were not eligible even to be considered for admission. The four courses were in government, history, literature, and science. All these courses, as taught by the Calvary School, the university explained, insisted that all truth in these fields be measured against the absolute truth of the Bible, including creationism in science. The Christian schools claimed that their freedom of religion and freedom of expression were violated by the university's policy. The university said the entrance requirements "are intended to ensure that incoming students are conversant with substantive content and methods of inquiry at the level required for UC students." The Court sided with the university.

1. Attending the University of California, the most prestigious of the public universities in the state, is an important entrée to a successful career for many students. By refusing to recognize high school coursework in creationism as meeting the entrance requirements in science, is the university discriminating against the religious freedom of those students, not only in their education but also in their future career prospects? If so, explain how or how not. Should the conflict be resolved by requiring science courses only for applicants who wish to pursue careers in science, engineering, medicine, and technology? Or would such a requirement undercut the university's goal of having all students conversant in basic science to function effectively in contemporary society?

2. If these students had not pursued admission to the university, do you believe they should be free in their high school education or in homeschooling to study only creationism and receive a high school diploma recognized by the state? What restrictions would be appropriate for the state to apply in setting standards for these alternative formats for high school education?

3. Are there ways to study religious topics in school without promoting a particular theology or supporting a particular viewpoint, especially in a publicly funded setting? Have you studied religious topics in your high school or college studies? How have you learned about a variety of religious views in those settings? Is there value to studying the religious views of many world religions? Should these studies be restricted to private family or religious settings and not be taught in publicly funded schools?

For additional case studies, please see the CourseMate for this text.

Reading Excerpt: Plato, *The Symposium*

INTRODUCTION

Plato explores different types of love in these excerpts, including homosexual relationships, although the Greeks did not have a word comparable to *homosexuality*. Although not widely accepted in ancient Greece, relationships between men were common, especially among the elite. Plato seems to argue, through the statements of Aristophanes in the dialogue, that homosexual attractions are not immoral but are motivated by courage, manliness, and masculinity. This dialogue is often cited in contemporary discussions as the earliest justification of homosexual relationships in the West. This excerpt from *The Symposium* was translated by Benjamin Jowett.

This mosaic was found among the Pompeii artifacts buried by the explosion of Mount Vesuvius in 79 A.D. It is commonly thought to depict Plato's Academy.

Vanni/Art Resource, NY

QUESTIONS FOR REFLECTION

1. Part of Plato's defense of homosexual relationships centers on the intellectual superiority of men over women, as perceived in that age. He also never mentions relationships between women. Given these differences with contemporary life, can his defense be considered relevant to today's debates about the morality of homosexuality?

2. Many of the relationships Plato describes are between "boys" and men, although he says nothing about the specific ages of these partners. Given our contemporary insistence on consent between adults for private relationships, does Plato's acceptance of these relationships invalidate his defense of homosexuality in general?

3. Even given these many differences between Plato's time and culture and our own, are there elements of his reasoning that can be applied to today's ethical issues?

READING

… Aristophanes professed to open another vein of discourse; he had a mind to praise Love in another way, unlike that either of Pausanias or Eryximachus. Mankind; he said, judging by their neglect of him, have never, as I think, at all understood the power
5 of Love. For if they had understood him they would surely have built noble temples and altars, and offered solemn sacrifices in his honor; but this is not done, and most certainly ought to be done: since of all the gods he is the best friend of men, the helper and the healer of the ills which are the great impediment to the
10 happiness of the race. I will try to describe his power to you, and you shall teach the rest of the world what I am teaching you.

In the first place, let me treat of the nature of man and what has happened to it; for the original human nature was not like the present, but different. The sexes were not two as they are now, but
15 originally three in number; there was man, woman, and the union of the two, having a name corresponding to this double nature, which had once a real existence, but is now lost, and the word "Androgynous" is only preserved as a term of reproach. In the

second place, the primeval man was round, his
20 back and sides forming a circle; and he had four
hands and four feet, one head with two faces,
looking opposite ways, set on a round neck
and precisely alike; also four ears, two privy
members, and the remainder to correspond. He
25 could walk upright as men now do, backwards
or forwards as he pleased, and he could also roll
over and over at a great pace, turning on his four
hands and four feet, eight in all, like tumblers
going over and over with their legs in the air;
30 this was when he wanted to run fast. Now the
sexes were three, and such as I have described
them; because the sun, moon, and earth are
three;—and the man was originally the child of
the sun, the woman of the earth, and the man-
35 woman of the moon, which is made up of sun
and earth, and they were all round and moved
round and round: like their parents. Terrible was
their might and strength, and the thoughts of
their hearts were great, and they made an attack
40 upon the gods; of them is told the tale of Otys
and Ephialtes who, as Homer says, dared to
scale heaven, and would have laid hands upon
the gods. Doubt reigned in the celestial councils.
Should they kill them and annihilate the race
45 with thunderbolts, as they had done the giants,
then there would be an end of the sacrifices
and worship which men offered to them; but, on
the other hand, the gods could not suffer their
insolence to be unrestrained.

> " *[M]en shall
> continue to exist,
> but I will cut them
> in two . . .* "

This excerpt describes the third sex as the union of man and woman. Throughout history, androgyny, or the condition of having both masculine and feminine characteristics, has been depicted in art pieces such as this one. This late 17th century miniature from a German manuscript shows the Hermetic Androgyne.

50 Zeus's Plan

At last, after a good deal of reflection, Zeus discovered a way.
He said: "I think I have a plan which will humble their pride and
improve their manners; men shall continue to exist, but I will
cut them in two and then they will be diminished in strength
55 and increased in numbers; this will have the advantage of making them more profitable to us. They shall walk upright on two
legs, and if they continue insolent and will not be quiet, I will
split them again and they shall hop about on a single leg." He
spoke and cut men in two, like a sorb-apple which is halved for
60 pickling, or as you might divide an egg with a hair; and as he
cut them one after another, he bade Apollo give the face and the
half of the neck a turn in order that the man might contemplate
the section of himself: he would thus learn a lesson of humility.
Apollo was also instructed to heal their wounds and compose
65 their forms. So he gave a turn to the face and pulled the skin
from the sides all over that which in our language is called the
belly, like the purses which draw in, and he made one mouth

at the centre, which he fastened in a knot (the same which is called the navel); he also molded the breast and took out most
70 of the wrinkles, much as a shoemaker might smooth leather upon a last; he left a few, however, in the region of the belly and navel, as a memorial of the primeval state. After the division the two parts of man, each desiring his other half, came together, and throwing their arms about one another, entwined
75 in mutual embraces, longing to grow into one, they were on the point of dying from hunger and self-neglect, because they did not like to do anything apart; and when one of the halves died and the other survived, the survivor sought another mate, man or woman as we call them, being the sections of entire men or
80 women, and clung to that.

They were being destroyed, when Zeus in pity of them invented a new plan: he turned the parts of generation round to the front, for this had not been always their position and they sowed the seed no longer as hitherto like grasshoppers in the ground,
85 but in one another; and after the transposition the male generated in the female in order that by the mutual embraces of man and woman they might breed, and the race might continue; or if man came to man they might be satisfied, and rest, and go their ways to the business of life: so ancient is the desire of one another
90 which is implanted in us, reuniting our original nature, making one of two, and healing the state of man.

Each of us when separated, having one side only, like a flat fish, is but the indenture of a man, and he is always looking for his other half. Men who are a section of that double nature
95 which was once called Androgynous are lovers of women; adulterers are generally of this breed, and also adulterous women who lust after men: the women who are a section of the woman do not care for men, but have female attachments; the female companions are of this sort. But they who are a section of the
100 male follow the male, and while they are young, being slices of the original man, they hang about men and embrace them, and they are themselves the best of boys and youths, because they have the most manly nature. Some indeed assert that they are shameless, but this is not true; for they do not act thus from
105 any want of shame, but because they are valiant and manly, and have a manly countenance, and they embrace that which is like them. And these when they grow up become our statesmen, and these only, which is a great proof of the truth of what I am saving. When they reach manhood they are loves of youth, and
110 are not naturally inclined to marry or beget children, —if at all, they do so only in obedience to the law; but they are satisfied if they may be allowed to live with one another unwedded; and such a nature is prone to love and ready to return love, always embracing that which is akin to him. And when one of them
115 meets with his other half, the actual half of himself, whether he be a lover of youth or a lover of another sort, the pair are lost in an amazement of love and friendship and intimacy, and would not be out of the other's sight, as I may say, even for a moment: these are the people who pass their whole lives together; yet
120 they could not explain what they desire of one another. For the intense yearning which each of them has towards the other does not appear to be the desire of lover's intercourse, but of something else which the soul of either evidently desires and cannot tell, and of which she has only a dark and doubtful
125 presentiment.

The Pursuit of the Whole

Suppose Hephaestus, with his instruments, to come to the pair who are lying side, by side and to say to them, "What do you people want of one another?" they would be unable to explain.
130 And suppose further, that when he saw their perplexity he said: "Do you desire to be wholly one; always day and night to be in one another's company? for if this is what you desire, I am ready to melt you into one and let you grow together, so that being two you shall become one, and while you live a common life as if you were
135 a single man, and after your death in the world below still be one departed soul instead of two—I ask whether this is what you lovingly desire, and whether you are satisfied to attain this?"—there is not a man of them who when he heard the proposal would deny or would not acknowledge that this meeting and melting into one
140 another, this becoming one instead of two, was the very expression of his ancient need. And the reason is that human nature was originally one and we were a whole, and the desire and pursuit of the whole is called love. There was a time, I say, when we were one, but now because of the wickedness of mankind God has
145 dispersed us, as the Arcadians were dispersed into villages by the Lacedaemonians. And if we are not obedient to the gods, there is a danger that we shall be split up again and go about in basso-relievo, like the profile figures having only half a nose which are sculptured on monuments, and that we shall be like tallies.

> " *[H]uman nature was originally one and we were a whole, and the desire and pursuit of the whole is called love.* "

150 Wherefore let us exhort all men to piety, that we may avoid evil, and obtain the good, of which Love is to us the lord and minister; and let no one oppose him—he is the enemy of the gods who oppose him. For if we are friends of the God and at peace with him we shall find our own true loves, which rarely happens in
155 this world at present....

Reading Excerpt: Justice Anthony Kennedy, *Lawrence v. Texas* (majority opinion) and Justice Antonin Scalia (dissenting opinion) (2003)

INTRODUCTION

The *Lawrence v. Texas* 2003 U.S. Supreme Court decision overturned the 1986 decision, *Bowers v. Hardwick*, which had held that private homosexual conduct among consenting adults was not protected under the U.S. Constitution. In other words, if a state like Georgia wants to make such conduct illegal, it could do so and it would not violate the constitutional rights of Georgia's citizens.

Jim Young/Reuters

Justice Anthony Kennedy

The *Lawrence* decision, though, stipulated that states could no longer outlaw such behavior. This reversal resulted in public outcry from some who believed that homosexual conduct was immoral. They complained that the law no longer took morality into account and that citizens should be allowed to pass laws that reflected their moral views.

A careful reading of the actual language, excerpted here, shows that the majority opinion relies extensively on the ethical reasoning of Kant, especially the appeal to human dignity and autonomy. Justice Kennedy was relying on moral reasoning, but it was not the specific religious morality preferred by his critics. In other words, rather than rejecting moral reasoning, Justice Kennedy and the majority are just changing the particular ethical standards to which they appeal.

The majority opinion in the *Lawrence* decision also claims that it sets no precedent for same-sex marriage, a claim strenuously disputed in the Scalia dissent. In recent public debates, *Lawrence* is emerging as strong support for marriage equality, especially when considered along with the *Loving* decision that recognized a right of interracial marriage. Whether this basis will prevail will depend on the use of analogical reasoning from *Lawrence* and *Loving* to the new issues of same-sex marriage.

QUESTIONS FOR REFLECTION

1. Has the majority opinion struck the right balance between the appropriate roles of the law and of private morality? Is there any immoral sexual behavior that should still be illegal, even if society's concerns found their source in moral prohibitions?

2. Under the reasoning of the majority opinion here, should the criminal laws on fornication, bigamy, adultery, adult incest, bestiality, and obscenity also be struck down? If not, what considerations can you cite to support the continuation of those laws?

3. Does Justice Scalia engage in "slippery slope" reasoning. If so, how? If not, why not?

4. Does the majority opinion provide a compelling basis for eventually holding that homosexual marriage is a constitutional right, despite the court's insistence that it does not? Is Justice Scalia right to be concerned that the reasoning of the majority makes it inevitable that homosexual marriage will eventually be found to be a constitutional right?

READING

Justice Anthony Kennedy's Opinion for the Majority

Liberty protects the person from unwarranted government intrusions into a dwelling or other private places. In our tradi-
5 tion the State is not omnipresent in the home. And there are other spheres of our lives and existence, outside the home, where the State should not be a dominant presence. Freedom extends beyond spatial bounds. Liberty presumes an autonomy of self that includes freedom of thought, belief, expression,
10 and certain intimate conduct. The instant case involves liberty of the person both in its spatial and more transcendent dimensions.

Anthony Kennedy, majority opinion, excerpt, Lawrence v. Texas (2003).

The question before the Court is the validity of a Texas statute making it a crime for two persons of the same sex to engage in
15 certain intimate sexual conduct....

We conclude the case should be resolved by determining whether the petitioners were free as adults to engage in the private conduct in the exercise of their liberty under the Due Process Clause of the Fourteenth Amendment to the Constitution. For this
20 inquiry we deem it necessary to reconsider the Court's holding in *Bowers.*

... The Court began its substantive discussion in *Bowers* as follows: The issue presented is whether the Federal Constitution confers a fundamental right upon homosexuals to engage in
25 sodomy and hence invalidates the laws of the many States that still make such conduct illegal and have done so for a very long time.... That statement, we now conclude, discloses the Court's own failure to appreciate the extent of the liberty at stake. To say that the issue in *Bowers* was simply the right to engage in certain
30 sexual conduct demeans the claim the individual put forward, just as it would demean a married couple were it to be said marriage is simply about the right to have sexual intercourse. The laws involved in *Bowers* and here are, to be sure, statutes that purport to do no more than prohibit a particular sexual act. Their penalties
35 and purposes, though, have more far-reaching consequences, touching upon the most private human conduct, sexual behavior, and in the most private of places, the home. The statutes do seek to control a personal relationship that, whether or not entitled to formal recognition in the law, is within the liberty of persons to
40 choose without being punished as criminals.

> " *The statutes do seek to control a personal relationship that . . . is within the liberty of persons to choose without being punished as criminals.* "

This, as a general rule, should counsel against attempts by the State, or a court, to define the meaning of the relationship or to set its boundaries absent injury to a person or abuse of an institution the law protects. It suffices for us to acknowledge that
45 adults may choose to enter upon this relationship in the confines of their homes and their own private lives and still retain their dignity as free persons. When sexuality finds overt expression in intimate conduct with another person, the conduct can be but one element in a personal bond that is more enduring. The liberty
50 protected by the Constitution allows homosexual persons the right to make this choice.

John Lawrence, right, and Tyron Garner at a rally at Houston City Hall following the U.S. Supreme Court decision that overturned the Texas sodomy law on Thursday, June 26, 2003.

... It must be acknowledged, of course, that the Court in *Bowers* was making the broader point that for centuries there have been powerful voices to condemn homosexual conduct as immoral. The condemnation has been shaped by religious beliefs, conceptions of right and acceptable behavior, and respect for the traditional family. For many persons these are not trivial concerns but profound and deep convictions accepted as ethical and moral principles to which they aspire and which thus determine the course of their lives. These considerations do not answer the question before us, however. The issue is whether the majority may use the power of the State to enforce these views on the whole society through operation of the criminal law....

> ❝ *It is clear ... that the Court has taken sides in the culture war.* ❞

... Equality of treatment and the due process right to demand respect for conduct protected by the substantive guarantee of liberty are linked in important respects, and a decision on the latter point advances both interests. If protected conduct is made criminal and the law which does so remains unexamined for its substantive validity, its stigma might remain even if it were not enforceable as drawn for equal protection reasons. When homosexual conduct is made criminal by the law of the State, that declaration in and of itself is an invitation to subject homosexual persons to discrimination both in the public and in the private spheres. The central holding of *Bowers* has been brought in question by this case, and it should be addressed. Its continuance as precedent demeans the lives of homosexual persons....

... *Bowers* was not correct when it was decided, and it is not correct today. It ought not to remain binding precedent. *Bowers v. Hardwick* should be and now is overruled.

The present case does not involve minors. It does not involve persons who might be injured or coerced or who are situated in relationships where consent might not easily be refused. It does not involve public conduct or prostitution. It does not involve whether the government must give formal recognition to any relationship that homosexual persons seek to enter. The case does involve two adults who, with full and mutual consent from each other, engaged in sexual practices common to a homosexual lifestyle. The petitioners are entitled to respect for their private lives. The State cannot demean their existence or control their destiny by making their private sexual conduct a crime. Their right to liberty under the Due Process Clause gives them the full right to engage in their conduct without intervention of the government.... The Texas statute furthers no legitimate state interest which can justify its intrusion into the personal and private life of the individual.

Had those who drew and ratified the Due Process Clauses of the Fifth Amendment or the Fourteenth Amendment known the components of liberty in its manifold possibilities, they might have been more specific. They did not presume to have this insight. They knew times can blind us to certain truths and later generations can see that laws once thought necessary and proper in fact serve only to oppress. As the Constitution endures, persons in every generation can invoke its principles in their own search for greater freedom....

Justice Scalia, Dissenting

...The Texas statute undeniably seeks to further the belief of its citizens that certain forms of sexual behavior are immoral and unacceptable,... the same interest furthered by criminal laws against fornication, bigamy, adultery, adult incest, bestiality, and obscenity. *Bowers* held that this was a legitimate state interest. The Court today reaches the opposite conclusion. The Texas statute, it says, "furthers no legitimate state interest which can justify its intrusion into the personal and private life of the individual,...." The Court

Justice Antonin Scalia

UPI/Gary Fabiano/POOL/Landov

Antonin Scalia, dissenting opinion, excerpt, Lawrence v. Texas (2003).

embraces instead Justice Stevens's declaration in his *Bowers* dissent, that "the fact that the governing majority in a State has traditionally viewed a particular practice as immoral is not a sufficient reason for upholding a law prohibiting the practice,...." This effectively decrees the end of all morals legislation. If, as the Court asserts, the promotion of majoritarian sexual morality is not even a legitimate state interest, none of the above-mentioned laws can survive rational-basis review....

One of the most revealing statements in today's opinion is the Court's grim warning that the criminalization of homosexual conduct is "an invitation to subject homosexual persons to discrimination both in the public and in the private spheres...." It is clear from this that the Court has taken sides in the culture war, departing from its role of assuring, as neutral observer, that the democratic rules of engagement are observed. Many Americans do not want persons who openly engage in homosexual conduct as partners in their business, as scoutmasters for their children, as teachers in their children's schools, or as boarders in their home. They view this as protecting themselves and their families from a lifestyle that they believe to be immoral and destructive. The Court views it as discrimination which it is the function of our judgments to deter....

One of the benefits of leaving regulation of this matter to the people rather than to the courts is that the people, unlike judges, need not carry things to their logical conclusion. The people may feel that their disapproval of homosexual conduct is strong enough to disallow homosexual marriage, but not strong enough to criminalize private homosexual acts and may legislate accordingly. The Court today pretends that it possesses a similar freedom of action, so that we need not fear judicial imposition of homosexual marriage, as has recently occurred in Canada (in a decision that the Canadian Government has chosen not to appeal)....

At the end of its opinion—after having laid waste the foundations of our rational-basis jurisprudence—the Court says that the present case "does not involve whether the government must give formal recognition to any relationship that homosexual persons seek to enter...." Do not believe it.... Today's opinion dismantles the structure of constitutional law that has permitted a distinction to be made between heterosexual and homosexual unions, insofar as formal recognition in marriage is concerned. If moral disapprobation of homosexual conduct is "no legitimate state interest" for purposes of proscribing that conduct,...; and if, as the Court coos (casting aside all pretense of neutrality), [w]hen sexuality finds overt expression in intimate conduct with another person, the conduct can be but one element in a personal bond that is more enduring,...; what justification could there possibly be for denying the benefits of marriage to homosexual couples exercising [t]he liberty protected by the Constitution,...Surely not the encouragement of procreation, since the sterile and the elderly are allowed to marry. This case does not involve the issue of homosexual marriage only if one entertains the belief that principle and logic have nothing to do with the decisions of this Court. Many will hope that, as the Court comfortingly assures us, this is so....

CHAPTER 5

George Doyle/Stockbyte/Jupiter Images

Personal Freedoms

"[S]ociety is not something that is kept together physically; it is held by the invisible bonds of common thought. If the bonds were too far relaxed the members would drift apart. A common morality is part of the bondage. The bondage is part of the price of society; and mankind, which needs society, must pay its price. . . . [I]t is not possible to set theoretical limits to the power of the state to legislate against immorality."

Patrick Devlin, *The Enforcement of Morals*, 1965

"The only freedom which deserves the name, is that of pursuing our own good in our own way, so long as we do not attempt to deprive others of theirs, or impede their efforts to obtain it. Each is the proper guardian of his own health, whether bodily, or mental or spiritual. Mankind are greater gainers by suffering each other to live as seems good to themselves, than by compelling each to live as seems good to the rest."

John Stuart Mill, *On Liberty*, 1859

L iberty is a treasured right in much of the world and sought after in much of the rest of it. But precisely what liberty should we expect if we want to live in an ordered society? What limits on that liberty are acceptable and with what justification? Philosophers have proposed many approaches to determining just what liberty should be unrestricted and when we need to put some limits on our freedom.

Overview

In this chapter, we will first address the challenge of identifying activities that many hold should be free of any government interference or regulation and are sometimes called "victimless crimes." We will then review several of the major philosophical approaches to explaining and justifying government restrictions on some of those liberties, including the "harm principle,"

paternalism, and legal moralism. We also will apply those theories to some of the most discussed victimless crimes today. We will read and reflect on excerpts by two leading philosophers who have addressed personal liberty, John Stuart Mill and Bertrand Russell.

What do you think?

Adults should be free to do anything they want, so long as they do not hurt other people in doing so, even if they harm themselves.

Strongly Disagree						Strongly Agree
1	2	3	4	5	6	7

5-1 PERSONAL FREEDOMS

The term *victimless crime* is popular for identifying activities in which no one supposedly is harmed except the actor himself or herself. That term itself can be used in somewhat different ways, so we need to be more precise in spelling out the activities about which we are concerned in this chapter.

We first try focusing on the *actor* who carries out the activities. We should limit the scope of our concern to consenting adults who can make well-informed choices for themselves about what to do. Children who do not have well-developed decision-making capacities or persons limited in their ability to reason seem to deserve protection by adults who know more about the likely consequences of their actions. Adults who are ignorant of possible consequences, for whatever reason, also seem outside the scope of this analysis of personal freedoms.

A second issue is identification of the *activities* in question. Are we concerned mainly with activities that plausibly might harm no one other than the actor? Then we need to give some thought to what we mean by *harm*. This might be physical harm or economic harm, but it might also include psychological or emotional harm that might be caused to another person who knows about the activities.

Activities typically referred to as victimless crimes include gambling, prostitution, drug use, riding a motorcycle without a helmet, driving a car without wearing a seat belt, suicide, smoking cigarettes, drinking alcohol, and overeating to the point of obesity. For example, those who consider gambling a victimless crime argue that, in choosing to wager their own money, people do not ordinarily cause immediate harm to anyone. Their actions do not normally affect others, whether they are close family members, neighbors, or members of the larger community. Prostitution is also viewed as a victimless crime because, it is argued, prostitutes choose to engage in this activity. They should have the freedom to do with their bodies as they please. Again, close family members or neighbors are not directly harmed by the prostitute's activities. The other activities follow this pattern. Riding a motorcycle without a helmet might result

Should the notion that gambling might have negative consequences on the larger human community trump an individual's freedom to engage in an activity that does not immediately seem to harm anyone?

Monkey Business Images/Shutterstock.com

in severe brain injury or death to the rider, but no one else is harmed. Cigarette smoking, it is claimed, might harm the health and life expectancy of the smoker, but not harm anyone else. Drinking alcohol might result in health problems or even death for the drinker without causing harm to others. Overeating to the point of obesity probably creates health problems and a shortened life for the overeater but does not affect others. In all cases, the claim is that no harm results for anyone else from these activities. In practice, even these radical libertarians, as we might call them, are likely to argue a somewhat modified position, namely, that ordinarily their actions cause no or insignificant harm to others. Even so, their assertion is put to the test in each case by further probing into how, directly or indirectly, these activities may or do exact a price on others. What additional activities do you believe might plausibly be considered as victimless crimes?

In CourseMate, watch a video and take the quiz.

> ┌ We ... limit the scope of our concern to consenting adults.... ┐

5-2 PHILOSOPHICAL METHODS

To develop good reasoning that supports, or rejects, the right to pursue these activities, we can draw on several well-established philosophical approaches that have been proposed and then examine whether those approaches are themselves justifiable.

5-2a The Harm Principle

One of the best-known proposals comes from the English philosopher John Stuart Mill. An excerpt from his writing in *On Liberty* is included in this chapter. He urged that we adopt what is typically referred to as the **harm principle** for deciding when it is appropriate for the government to restrict our liberty. We might refer to this alternatively as Mill's "liberty principle."

> . . . the only purpose for which power can be rightfully exercised over any member of a civilized community, against his will, is to prevent harm to others. His own good, either physical or moral, is not a sufficient warrant.

Examples of activities that clearly cause harm to others include murder or rape or theft of property. By Mill's principle, these activities would appropriately be the subject of restriction by the government, typically through the criminal justice system. But what of our examples of victimless crimes? If they do not cause harm to others, then the government should stay out of those affairs and let us do what we want, according to this harm principle. Some contemporary writers, such as Joel Feinberg, have extended Mill's reasoning approach by adding what they call an **offense principle**. Under this approach, along with clear harm, the government is justified in regulating or prohibiting activities which cause severe offense to others. The challenge is to define just how serious that offense must be to warrant government intervention.

Mill's harm principle has been an enormously popular way of drawing lines about when government intervention is appropriate and when it is not. As the Supreme Court Justice Oliver Wendell Holmes once said, "Your right to swing your fist ends where the end of my nose begins." In trying to preserve as much individual liberty as possible, while still recognizing the need for some government regulation to promote civil society, the harm principle seems to work well.

John Stuart Mill, On Liberty, 1859

But many have challenged this harm principle. First, carefully examine what constitutes harm. How narrowly should this be understood in terms of physical or economic harm? Suicide causes enormous emotional suffering by the family members and friends who remain; is that not a form of harm that should be considered? Alcoholism, obesity, riding a bike without a helmet, and many other supposed victimless crimes do seem to have serious consequences for others. If people are no longer able to support their family members, who will provide economic support for them? If people end up in emergency rooms or hospitals, who will pay the bill? Are there truly any victimless crimes that do not cause any harm at all to other people?

5-2b Paternalism

This second approach to restriction of personal freedoms has gained considerable credence in the twentieth century. According to this view, the government should act as a

KEY TERMS

harm principle: the philosophical theory that government intervention and restriction of individual liberties is justified only when the action in question would result in harm to another person, and not when the only person harmed is the actor himself or herself

offense principle: the philosophical theory that government intervention and restriction of individual liberties is justified when the action in question causes serious offense to others

Has wearing seat belts become so accepted that no one would dare defy what seems to be a widely supported government imposition and campaign to get seat belt regulations reversed?

Comstock/Photos.com

paternalism: the philosophical theory that government intervention and restriction of individual liberties is justified when the action in question would harm somebody, whether the actor himself or herself or another person, because the role of government is to act as a parent protecting us from ourselves

legal moralism: the philosophical theory that government intervention and restriction of individual liberties is justified by the necessity of enforcing society's overall moral codes in the most effective way possible, namely, through the power of government and the criminal justice system

parent in protecting us from ourselves. The theory of **paternalism** would accept all the government restrictions that Mill proposes (namely, those that would prevent actions that harm others). But this view goes further by justifying restrictions to prevent us from harming ourselves.

Consider the example of current seat belt requirements. Automobile makers started including seat belts as an option in the late 1940s, but laws requiring the wearing of seat belts did not appear until the 1970s in industrialized nations and not until 1983 in the United States. Opponents of these laws say that drivers should be free to put themselves at risk of serious injury if they choose. But the requirement is appreciated by many who are glad that they no longer have to make excuses for buckling up when they know it is the safest way to ride in a car. A paternalistic approach to government regulation supports mandatory seat belt rules. But even without paternalism, would Mill's harm principle support abandoning these requirements? In other words, if a driver or passenger is severely injured because a seat belt was not buckled, is it true that no one else is harmed? What about the cost incurred by society to treat the injured?

Paternalism also justifies such rules as wearing a helmet while riding a motorcycle or prohibiting certain drug use. Should paternalism also be used to prohibit the sale and use of tobacco products? Of alcohol? Or foods containing high quantities of fat, salt, or calories? One challenge for paternalistic approaches is figuring out where to draw the line on government intervention. Do we really want the government to act as a parent for every behavior that might cause us harm?

5-2c Legal Moralism

Another and more extreme approach to government restrictions on personal freedoms, **legal moralism**, espouses all the restrictions of Mill and the paternalists but claims to justify even more. The position of the legal moralist is that the government has not only the right but also the obligation to enforce public morality using the full power of the government, regardless of whether anybody is harmed by the actions in question. So, for example, if the society's moral code holds that adults looking at pornography in the privacy of their own homes is immoral,

then the government should prohibit such practices. As with paternalism, one challenge is figuring out where to draw the line on government intervention. If the majority's moral code in society holds that playing a card game like bridge is a waste of time that should be spent in prayer, should the government regulate that behavior?

5-2d General Considerations

All three approaches to analyzing appropriate government restrictions on our personal liberty are problematic. All turn on definitions of critical terms (such as *harm* and *morality*) that are in great dispute. Arguably, each approach can be criticized for not going far enough or going too far.

Note also that all of these approaches are consequentialist, in that they examine the results of actions in deciding which action is right. These results include harm to oneself, harm to others, and harm to society at large. These theories disagree on which results matter in decision making, but all mainly take into account results or consequences. Another approach entirely would consider the more Kantian appeal to human autonomy and dignity. Could that provide a more promising approach in deciding when government interference with liberty is appropriate? Do we best respect human dignity and autonomy by giving people free rein to do what they want? Or by protecting them from their worst instincts to harm themselves? If you treat yourself with dignity, then you will have a range of duties to yourself, such as your duty to cultivate your mind and avoid harming your body. For Kant, just as society can enforce our important duties to others, such as by prohibiting theft, so too can it enforce our important duties to oneself, such as by requiring seat belt use. Some degree of government paternalism, then, would be justified.

In CourseMate, apply what you've learned to the real-life scenario in the simulation.

In CourseMate, practice what you learned by taking the chapter quiz.

5-3 APPLYING PHILOSOPHICAL APPROACHES

The previous sections include several examples showing how to analyze appropriate governmental restrictions on our liberties. To continue our analysis, we apply the three approaches detailed previously to additional examples to find whether these approaches yield justifiable results, that is, help us come to conclusions we feel are acceptable and defensible.

Prostitution, an activity sometimes considered a victimless crime, is illegal in most states and countries. The state of Nevada and the country of the Netherlands are notable examples of areas where it is legal, but even there the activities of prostitution are regulated. Interestingly, some feminist philosophers have urged that women should be free to earn a living as "sex workers," if they choose. In Canada, these arguments were successful in a lawsuit by sex workers in 2010, and the laws prohibiting prostitution-related activities were struck down as unconstitutional. Let us see how different philosophical approaches would consider prostitution.

Mill's harm principle might seem to support legalization of prostitution, on the grounds that it harms no one but the actors. Legalization would entail that only consenting adults who voluntarily undertake this activity could practice it. The restrictions imposed by the law would exclude minors and any person forcibly required to engage in prostitution. Is it true that the only harm, if any, would come to the prostitute and her or his clients? Does a prostitution enterprise necessarily trigger criminal activities and violence that society justifiably wants to prohibit? Or are criminal activities and violence the result of their illegal status, which forces participants to go underground to support their enterprise.

> **But do we want the government regulating all activities that a parent might want to discourage or only some things?**

A paternalist would need to argue that, just as no parent would want their child to enter the profession of prostitution, so the government should prohibit it, even if no one were harmed in carrying out the activity but the prostitute and the clients. But do we want the government regulating all activities that a parent might want to discourage or only some things? Almost all of the examples we have been considering are contentious. Although most might want to keep prostitution illegal, some think government should not regulate it. Although many want to keep hard drugs like heroin illegal, some think it would be better for the government to legalize drugs, regulate their sale (as we do for alcohol and tobacco), and make money from taxation imposed on the sales. But although a few think pornography should be prohibited by the government because of the corrupting effect they claim it has on individuals, most agree that it should remain legal for adults to "consume." Note that societal expectations also seem to be evolving on areas of possible regulation. The attitudes on marijuana use, for example, seem to be growing more and more in favor of legalization.

The legal moralist would need to argue that society's moral code dictates that prostitution is immoral, and therefore, the government should prohibit it for the good of society. But does everybody agree that prostitution

xyno/iStockphoto.com

The sale of liquor is regulated by each state in the United States. The consumption of alcohol can lead to major problems for some people. The intent of Prohibition, from 1919 to 1933, was to reduce alcohol consumption. Was it a successful endeavor in the end?

A medical marijuana clinic. Marijuana sale and consumption is illegal under U.S. federal law, but sixteen states and the District of Columbia have passed laws, as of 2011, legalizing the use of marijuana for medicinal purposes.

is immoral? Should this be determined by a vote of the majority? Is there any room for minority views in the legal moralist position? If, by society's moral code everybody should find a way to support themselves, could legalized prostitution by consenting adults arguably be justified as a way to meet that requirement?

You can see how complicated these analyses are. Try working through the different approaches with other victimless crimes to see whether they can be used for satisfactory accounts, that is, provide ethical reasoning foundations that help us make decisions in today's society.

Now that you have studied how various types of reasoning apply to the topics discussed, review Critical Thinking Table 5.1 to follow the process of examining an ethical claim on a related topic.

In CourseMate, listen to the audio summary of the chapter.

John Stuart Mill

John Stuart Mill was one of the most distinguished and influential philosophers in England in the nineteenth century, and his ideas are enormously influential even today throughout the English-speaking world. His views often have been cited by the United States courts in discussing their decisions. Mill addressed a wide range of issues from women's rights and capital punishment to what today are sometimes called victimless crimes. His philosophical theory in ethics is called utilitarianism, which was introduced in Chapter 2 of this book.

Mill is well known in political philosophy for the harm principle, which he proposed and defended in his book *On Liberty* (1859). In his *Autobiography* (1873), Mill describes the active role that his wife Harriet Taylor played in authoring this work with him:

> During the two years which immediately preceded the cessation of my official life, my wife and I were working together at the "Liberty." I had first planned and written it as a short essay in 1854. It was in mounting the steps of the Capitol, in January, 1855, that the thought first arose of converting it into a volume. None of my writings have been either so carefully composed, or so sedulously corrected as this. After it had been written as usual twice over, we kept it by us, bringing it out from time to time, and going through it *de novo* [from the beginning, anew], reading, weighing, and criticizing every sentence.

John Stuart Mill (1806–1873) and Helen Taylor, Harriet Taylor's daughter from a first marriage.

He argued that governments should restrict our liberty only in those situations where we would cause real harm to other persons. Governments should not interfere when the only harm we cause is to ourselves, the so-called victimless crimes. And he insisted that the only harm to others that would justify government intervention was *real* harm, either to a person or to property. For example, merely saying something upsetting or offensive to someone would not be considered real harm, and thus should not be restricted by the government. This simple but enormously important principle provides a rationale for removing government restrictions on liberty in a wide variety of situations, including freedom of expression, which we take up in the next chapter.

Along with his wife Harriet, and after her death, with her daughter Helen, Mill was a committed supporter of equal opportunity for women, including the right to vote and equal educational opportunities. His 1869 essay on *The Subjection of Women* reflected deeply engrained biases of that era concerning employment opportunities for women and responsibilities for domestic chores, but Mill was far ahead of his time in urging that women receive the right to vote. In the United States, women did not get that right until 1920. In England, it was not until 1928 that all adults older than age twenty-one received the right to vote.

John Stuart Mill, On Liberty, 1859, excerpts.

Table 5.1 Critical Thinking Steps and Their Application in an Example

{"Marijuana use should be legal, as it is less harmful than alcohol."}

Critical Thinking Steps	Application
1. Examine and clarify key terms and concepts. 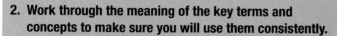 Wendy Connett/ Alamy • Look words up in a dictionary as a start if necessary. • Unravel or unpack the complexities and nuances of a central term, such as *justice*, *right*, or *good*.	• One key term here is *harmful*. The term obviously means "that causes harm." Are we referring only to physical harm? Or to emotional harm as well? • *Use* is obviously referring to the consumption of a substance.
2. Work through the meaning of the key terms and concepts to make sure you will use them consistently. • Consider the ways the term can be used by including it in different sentences and contexts to zero in on the particular meaning you are after. • Ask yourself what words are potential synonyms for the concept. Do those capture everything you want to understand about that term?	In this case, the key terms are likely not to derail any attempt at clarity in our reasoning. However, the concepts they are connected to are worth exploring. • How do we know whether something or some action is harmful? Who or what determines that? • Are there degrees of harmfulness? • Should we consider potential harm or harm that has been caused or both? For instance, should we contemplate the potentially harmful results of marijuana use on others, such as impaired driving? • What use is at issue here? Do we implicitly mean only use by competent adults? Is use limited to private places, not public areas? Is use restricted to medical or generalized use? • Should we consider occasional and light use versus frequent and heavy use of a substance? Or do the consequences of the use of a substance matter beyond anything else?
3. Build premises and bring any assumptions to light.  xyno/iStockphoto. com • Put together short and clear sentences to build each of your premises. • Think through what you may be taking for granted in your reasoning. What assumptions are you making? • Once you have identified assumptions, articulate them in your premise, so that your audience has the same understanding of a term or a concept as you.	The premises of the argument could be constructed as follows, using these clarifications of terminology: (i) If X is less harmful than Y, and use of Y is legal, then X should be legal. (ii) Marijuana use is less harmful than use of alcohol. (iii) Use of alcohol is legal. CONCLUSION: Use of marijuana should be legal.

(Continued)

Table 5.1 Continued

Critical Thinking Steps	Application
4. Test/Verify your premises. • Now that you have stated your premises explicitly, do you want to stick with them? • Are you relying on premises drawn from unsubstantiated sources or from questionable authorities? • Are you consistent in your premises? Or are you appealing to different and inconsistent foundations in your reasoning? • Reformulate your premises if they have proven to be faulty.	Each of these premises should be examined. (i) When stated as a generalized principle, is this claim still as attractive? Are there counterexamples for X and Y that make this less self-evident? Is harm the only factor relevant to legalization? (ii) This states an empirical claim about which health scientists still disagree. How do we measure, say, harm to one's lungs and harm to one's liver and compare them quantitatively? How do we measure impact on life expectancy? How extensively should we consider harm? Only physical harm to the user? Should harm to others be included? How should we compare impaired driving while using marijuana to use of alcohol? (iii) Alcohol use is actually restricted in many ways. Only adults may consume alcohol legally. Some restrictions on place of consumption can be found in many cities. Dry towns and counties, where sale of alcohol is entirely banned, still exist. If you do not accept all of these premises, then you will not accept the conclusion either. But if you do accept all of them, then you would find the conclusion valid and justified.
5. Confirm that the conclusions you draw are logical. Check for reliance on fallacies and correct any premise that you identify as relying on a fallacy. 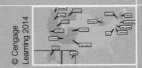 © Cengage Learning 2014	The problem of ambiguity in language is significant here, especially for key terms such as *use* and the level of use that should be considered and *harm*, and the level and kind of harm specifically that is defined.

CHAPTER 5 Case Study

Legalizing Marijuana

More than a dozen states in the United States have legalized medical marijuana in recent years, mainly on the humanitarian grounds that this limited use eases severe pain and the nausea caused by some medical treatments. To date, however, no state has fully legalized all marijuana use. A recent effort at legalization occurred in California in November 2010, Proposition 19, but it was defeated by the voters. Supporters of the proposition claim that low turnout in the mid-term election by younger voters led to the defeat, even though polls showed overwhelming support for legalization by these younger voters.

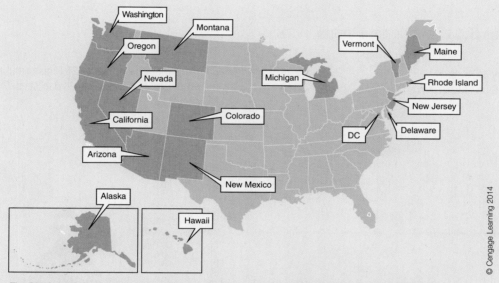

The District of Columbia and sixteen states in the United States have legalized the use of marijuana for medicinal purposes. Considering the dangers using this drug presents according to some, what do you think of this legalization?

In Canada, in spring 2011, a judge struck down the nation's law banning marijuana use, on the grounds that it prohibited humanitarian use of medical marijuana. The Canadian parliament must now decide whether to revise laws or let this decision stand.

In other areas of the world, marijuana use is illegal in almost all countries, although enforcement is lax in many. In the Netherlands, well-known for "cannabis" cafes, marijuana use is legal, although some restrictions are imposed on visitors to the country, outdoor use, and use near schools.

1. Supporters of legalization often cite a range of consequentialist arguments, such as a reduction in the cost of enforcing the existing laws, increased government revenues from taxing legal marijuana, and reduction in drug gang violence. Are there additional beneficial consequences that support legalization? Are there negative consequences that outweigh the positive ones?

2. Is marijuana use truly a victimless crime? What consequences for other people argue against legalization? Do these consequences apply to other victimless crimes, such as alcohol and cigarette consumption? Should they all be treated the same, that is, either all should be legalized or all should be banned? If there are consequences for other people, can reasonable regulations limit that impact?

3. Opponents of legalization sometimes cite the slippery slope argument. What is that argument precisely in this context? Is it persuasive?

For additional case studies, please see the CourseMate for this text.

Reading Excerpt: John Stuart Mill, *On Liberty* (1859)

INTRODUCTION

First published in 1859 (Timeline 5.1 provides an overview of major events that year), Mill's *On Liberty* spells out a theory of human liberty that remains enormously influential even today. He articulates what is known as the harm principle, sometimes called the liberty principle, as a central guideline for when it is appropriate to restrict human freedom. The Chapter II excerpts here extend this principle to freedom of speech, which we will consider separately in the next chapter in this book.

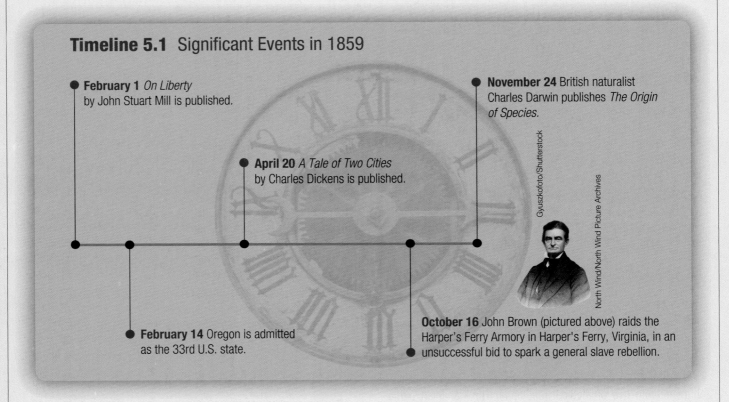

Timeline 5.1 Significant Events in 1859

February 1 *On Liberty* by John Stuart Mill is published.

April 20 *A Tale of Two Cities* by Charles Dickens is published.

February 14 Oregon is admitted as the 33rd U.S. state.

November 24 British naturalist Charles Darwin publishes *The Origin of Species.*

October 16 John Brown (pictured above) raids the Harper's Ferry Armory in Harper's Ferry, Virginia, in an unsuccessful bid to spark a general slave rebellion.

Gyuszkofoto/Shutterstock

North Wind/North Wind Picture Archives

QUESTIONS FOR REFLECTION

1. What does Mill mean by "compulsion and control" of the individual? In what different ways is this principle applied?

2. Explain in your own words what Mill means by a "harm" principle. What language does he use to explain harm, and what does he seem to mean by it? Does it capture everything you understand by harm?

3. What does Mill understand as "the appropriate region of human liberty"? What are the specific three areas he identifies? How do you understand those areas?

4. In extending the harm principle to liberty of thought and discussion, Mill provides several additional reasons why we should promote free speech. Explain those in your own words and consider whether they are persuasive today with modern forms of communication.

READING

Chapter I: Introductory

The subject of this Essay is…the nature and limits of the power which can be legitimately exercised by society over the individual.…There is, in fact, no recognized principle by which the
5 propriety or impropriety of government interference is customarily tested.…And it seems to me that, in consequence of this absence of rule or principle, one side is at present as often wrong as the other; the interference of government is, with about equal frequency, improperly invoked and improperly condemned.
10   The object of this Essay is to assert one very simple principle, as entitled to govern absolutely the dealings of society with the individual in the way of compulsion and control, whether the means used be physical force in the form of legal penalties, or the moral coercion of public opinion. That principle is, that the sole end for
15 which mankind are warranted, individually or collectively in interfering with the liberty of action of any of their number, is self-protection. That the only purpose for which power can be rightfully exercised over any member of a civilized community, against his will, is to prevent harm to others. His own good, either physical or moral, is not a
20 sufficient warrant. He cannot rightfully be compelled to do or forbear because it will be better for him to do so, because it will make him happier, because, in the opinions of others, to do so would be wise, or even right. These are good reasons for remonstrating with him, or reasoning with him, or persuading him, or entreating him, but not for
25 compelling him, or visiting him with any evil, in case he do otherwise. To justify that, the conduct from which it is desired to deter him must be calculated to produce evil to someone else. The only part of the conduct of any one, for which he is amenable to society, is that which concerns others. In the part which merely concerns himself,
30 his independence is, of right, absolute. Over himself, over his own body and mind, the individual is sovereign.

It is, perhaps, hardly necessary to say that this doctrine is meant to apply only to human beings in the maturity of their faculties. We are not speaking of children, or of young persons below the age which
35 the law may fix as that of manhood or womanhood. Those who are still in a state to require being taken care of by others, must be protected against their own actions as well as against external injury …

But there is a sphere of action in which society, as distinguished from the individual, has, if any, only an indirect interest;
40 comprehending all that portion of a person's life and conduct which affects only himself, or, if it also affects others, only with their free, voluntary, and undeceived consent and participation. When I say only himself, I mean directly, and in the first instance: for whatever affects himself, may affect others through himself;
45 and the objection which may be grounded on this contingency, will receive consideration in the sequel. This, then, is the appropriate region of human liberty. It comprises, first, the inward domain of consciousness; demanding liberty of conscience, in the most comprehensive sense; liberty of thought and feeling;
50 absolute freedom of opinion and sentiment on all subjects, practical or speculative, scientific, moral, or theological. The liberty of expressing and publishing opinions may seem to fall under a different principle, since it belongs to that part of the conduct of an individual which concerns other people; but, being almost of
55 as much importance as the liberty of thought itself, and resting in great part on the same reasons, is practically inseparable from it. Secondly, the principle requires liberty of tastes and pursuits; of framing the plan of our life to suit our own character; of doing as we like, subject to such consequences as may follow; without
60 impediment from our fellow-creatures, so long as what we do does not harm them even though they should think our conduct foolish, perverse, or wrong. Thirdly, from this liberty of each individual, follows the liberty, within the same limits, of combination among individuals; freedom to unite, for any purpose not involving
65 harm to others: the persons combining being supposed to be of full age, and not forced or deceived.

> *The liberty of expressing and publishing opinions …belongs to that part of the conduct of an individual which concerns other people …*

No society in which these liberties are not, on the whole, respected, is free, whatever may be its form of government; and none is completely free in which they do not exist absolute and
70 unqualified. The only freedom which deserves the name, is that of pursuing our own good in our own way, so long as we do not attempt to deprive others of theirs, or impede their efforts to obtain it. Each is the proper guardian of his own health, whether bodily, or mental or spiritual. Mankind are greater gainers by suffering each
75 other to live as seems good to themselves, than by compelling each to live as seems good to the rest.

It will be convenient for the argument, if, instead of at once entering upon the general thesis, we confine ourselves in the first instance to a single branch of it, . . . the Liberty of Thought: from
80 which it is impossible to separate the cognate liberty of speaking and of writing. Although these liberties, to some considerable amount, form part of the political morality of all countries which

profess religious toleration and free institutions, the grounds, both philosophical and practical, on which they rest, are perhaps not
85 so familiar to the general mind, nor so thoroughly appreciated by many even of the leaders of opinion, as might have been expected. Those grounds, when rightly understood, are of much wider application than to only one division of the subject, and a thorough consideration of this part of the question will be found the best
90 introduction to the remainder. . . .

Chapter II: Of the Liberty of Thought and Discussion

The time, it is to be hoped, is gone by when any defense would be necessary of the "liberty of the press" as one of the securities
95 against corrupt or tyrannical government. No argument, we may suppose, can now be needed, against permitting a legislature or an executive, not identified in interest with the people, to prescribe opinions to them, and determine what doctrines or what arguments they shall be allowed to hear. This aspect of the question,
100 besides, has been so often and so triumphantly enforced by preceding writers, that it needs not be specially insisted on in this place. . . . Were an opinion a personal possession of no value except to the owner; if to be obstructed in the enjoyment of it were simply a private injury, it would make some difference whether
105 the injury was inflicted only on a few persons or on many. But the peculiar evil of silencing the expression of an opinion is, that it is robbing the human race; posterity as well as the existing generation; those who dissent from the opinion, still more than those who hold it. If the opinion is right, they are deprived of the opportunity
110 of exchanging error for truth: if wrong, they lose, what is almost as great a benefit, the clearer perception and livelier impression of truth, produced by its collision with error. . . .

> **❝** *The time, it is to be hoped, is gone by when any defense would be necessary of the "liberty of the press" as one of the securities against corrupt or tyrannical government.* **❞**

First: the opinion which it is attempted to suppress by authority may possibly be true. Those who desire to suppress it, of course
115 deny its truth; but they are not infallible. They have no authority to decide the question for all mankind, and exclude every other person from the means of judging. To refuse a hearing to an opinion, because they are sure that it is false, is to assume that their certainty is the same thing as absolute certainty. All silencing of
120 discussion is an assumption of infallibility. Its condemnation may be allowed to rest on this common argument, not the worse for being common. . . .

. . . There is the greatest difference between presuming an opinion to be true, because, with every opportunity for contesting
125 it, it has not been refuted, and assuming its truth for the purpose of not permitting its refutation. Complete liberty of contradicting and disproving our opinion, is the very condition which justifies us in assuming its truth for purposes of action; and on no other terms can a being with human faculties have any rational assurance of
130 being right. . . .

Charles Dickens's *A Tale of Two Cities* was first published in the periodical, *All the Year Round*, April 30, 1859. This illustration in a book edition of the novel depicts a scene from the narrative: Lucie saying goodbye to Carton.

It still remains to speak of one of the principal causes which make diversity of opinion advantageous, and will continue to do so until mankind shall have entered a stage of intellectual advancement which at present seems at an incalculable dis-
135 tance. We have hitherto considered only two possibilities: that the received opinion may be false, and some other opinion, consequently, true; or that, the received opinion being true, a conflict with the opposite error is essential to a clear apprehension and deep feeling of its truth. But there is a commoner case than either
140 of these; when the conflicting doctrines, instead of being one true and the other false, share the truth between them; and the nonconforming opinion is needed to supply the remainder of the truth, of which the received doctrine embodies only a part. Popular opinions, on subjects not palpable to sense, are often true, but seldom
145 or never the whole truth. They are a part of the truth; sometimes a greater, sometimes a smaller part, but exaggerated, distorted, and disjoined from the truths by which they ought to be accompanied and limited. Heretical opinions, on the other hand, are generally some of these suppressed and neglected truths, bursting the
150 bonds which kept them down, and either seeking reconciliation with the truth contained in the common opinion, or fronting it as enemies, and setting themselves up, with similar exclusiveness, as the whole truth. The latter case is hitherto the most frequent, as, in the human mind, one-sidedness has always been the rule, and
155 many-sidedness the exception.

> **" *Popular opinions…*
> *are often true, but*
> *seldom or never the*
> *whole truth.* "**

Hence, even in revolutions of opinion, one part of the truth usually sets while another rises. Even progress, which ought to superadd, for the most part only substitutes one partial and incomplete truth for another; improvement consisting chiefly in
160 this, that the new fragment of truth is more wanted, more adapted to the needs of the time, than that which it displaces. Such being the partial character of prevailing opinions, even when resting on a true foundation; every opinion which embodies somewhat of the portion of truth which the common opinion omits, ought to be
165 considered precious, with whatever amount of error and confusion that truth may be blended. No sober judge of human affairs will feel bound to be indignant because those who force on our notice truths which we should otherwise have overlooked, overlook some of those which we see. Rather, he will think that so long as
170 popular truth is one-sided, it is more desirable than otherwise that

unpopular truth should have one-sided asserters too; such being usually the most energetic, and the most likely to compel reluctant attention to the fragment of wisdom which they proclaim as if it were the whole. . . .
175 I do not pretend that the most unlimited use of the freedom of enunciating all possible opinions would put an end to the evils of religious or philosophical sectarianism. Every truth which men of narrow capacity are in earnest about, is sure to be asserted, inculcated, and in many ways even acted on, as if no other truth existed
180 in the world, or at all events none that could limit or qualify the first. I acknowledge that the tendency of all opinions to become sectarian is not cured by the freest discussion, but is often heightened and exacerbated thereby; the truth which ought to have been, but was not, seen, being rejected all the more violently because proclaimed
185 by persons regarded as opponents. But it is not on the impassioned partisan, it is on the calmer and more disinterested bystander, that this collision of opinions works its salutary effect. Not the violent conflict between parts of the truth, but the quiet suppression of half of it, is the formidable evil: there is always hope when people are
190 forced to listen to both sides; it is when they attend only to one that errors harden into prejudices, and truth itself ceases to have the effect of truth, by being exaggerated into falsehood. And since there are few mental attributes more rare than that judicial faculty which can sit in intelligent judgment between two sides of a question, of
195 which only one is represented by an advocate before it, truth has no chance but in proportion as every side of it, every opinion which embodies any fraction of the truth, not only finds advocates, but is so advocated as to be listened to.

We have now recognized the necessity to the mental well-
200 being of mankind (on which all their other well-being depends) of freedom of opinion, and freedom of the expression of opinion, on four distinct grounds; which we will now briefly recapitulate.

First, if any opinion is compelled to silence, that opinion may, for aught we can certainly know, be true. To deny this is to assume
205 our own infallibility.

Secondly, though the silenced opinion be an error, it may, and very commonly does, contain a portion of truth; and since the general or prevailing opinion on any object is rarely or never the whole truth, it is only by the collision of adverse opinions that the
215 remainder of the truth has any chance of being supplied.

Thirdly, even if the received opinion be not only true, but the whole truth; unless it is suffered to be, and actually is, vigorously and earnestly contested, it will, by most of those who receive it, be held in the manner of a prejudice, with little comprehension
220 or feeling of its rational grounds. And not only this, but, fourthly, the meaning of the doctrine itself will be in danger of being lost, or enfeebled, and deprived of its vital effect on the character and conduct: the dogma becoming a mere formal profession, inefficacious for good, but cumbering the ground, and preventing

225 the growth of any real and heartfelt conviction, from reason or personal experience.

Before quitting the subject of freedom of opinion, it is fit to take notice of those who say, that the free expression of all opinions should be permitted, on condition that the manner be
230 temperate, and do not pass the bounds of fair discussion. Much might be said on the impossibility of fixing where these supposed bounds are to be placed; for if the test be offense to those whose opinion is attacked, I think experience testifies that this offense is given whenever the attack is telling and powerful, and that every
235 opponent who pushes them hard, and whom they find it difficult to answer, appears to them, if he shows any strong feeling on the subject, an intemperate opponent. But this, though an important consideration in a practical point of view, merges in a more fundamental objection. Undoubtedly the manner of asserting an
240 opinion, even though it be a true one, may be very objectionable, and may justly incur severe censure. But the principal offenses of the kind are such as it is mostly impossible, unless by accidental self-betrayal, to bring home to conviction. The gravest of them is, to argue sophistically, to suppress facts or arguments, to misstate
245 the elements of the case, or misrepresent the opposite opinion. But all this, even to the most aggravated degree, is so continually done in perfect good faith, by persons who are not considered, and in many other respects may not deserve to be considered, ignorant or incompetent, that it is rarely possible on adequate
250 grounds conscientiously to stamp the misrepresentation as morally culpable; and still less could law presume to interfere with this kind of controversial misconduct.

With regard to what is commonly meant by intemperate discussion, namely, invective, sarcasm, personality, and the like, the
255 denunciation of these weapons would deserve more sympathy if it were ever proposed to interdict them equally to both sides; but it is only desired to restrain the employment of them against the prevailing opinion: against the unprevailing they may not only be used without general disapproval, but will be likely to obtain for him who
260 uses them the praise of honest zeal and righteous indignation. Yet whatever mischief arises from their use, is greatest when they are employed against the comparatively defenseless; and whatever unfair advantage can be derived by any opinion from this mode of asserting it, accrues almost exclusively to received opinions. The
265 worst offense of this kind which can be committed by a polemic, is to stigmatize those who hold the contrary opinion as bad and immoral men. To calumny of this sort, those who hold any unpopular opinion are peculiarly exposed, because they are in general few

and uninfluential, and nobody but themselves feels much interest
270 in seeing justice done them; but this weapon is, from the nature of the case, denied to those who attack a prevailing opinion: they can neither use it with safety to themselves, nor if they could, would it do anything but recoil on their own cause.

In general, opinions contrary to those commonly received can
275 only obtain a hearing by studied moderation of language, and the most cautious avoidance of unnecessary offense, from which they hardly ever deviate even in a slight degree without losing ground: while unmeasured vituperation employed on the side of the prevailing opinion, really does deter people from professing contrary
280 opinions, and from listening to those who profess them. For the interest, therefore, of truth and justice, it is far more important to restrain this employment of vituperative language than the other; and, for example, if it were necessary to choose, there would be much more need to discourage offensive attacks on infidelity, than
285 on religion. It is, however, obvious that law and authority have no business with restraining either, while opinion ought, in every instance, to determine its verdict by the circumstances of the individual case; condemning every one, on whichever side of the argument he places himself, in whose mode of advocacy either
290 want of candor, or malignity, bigotry or intolerance of feeling manifest themselves, but not inferring these vices from the side which a person takes, though it be the contrary side of the question to our own; and giving merited honor to everyone, whatever opinion he may hold, who has calmness to see and honesty to state what
295 his opponents and their opinions really are, exaggerating nothing to their discredit, keeping nothing back which tells, or can be supposed to tell, in their favor. This is the real morality of public discussion; and if often violated, I am happy to think that there are many controversialists who to a great extent observe it, and a still
300 greater number who conscientiously strive towards it.

> *In general, opinions contrary to those commonly received can only obtain a hearing by studied moderation of language . . .*

Reading Excerpt: Bertrand Russell, *Proposed Roads to Freedom* (1918)

INTRODUCTION

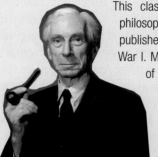

This classic text by the great British philosopher Bertrand Russell was first published in 1918, at the end of World War I. Much of the book was a critique of three then-popular approaches to political theory (socialism, anarchism, and syndicalism), which have been superseded in current political thinking. But Russell also offers his own ideas on personal freedoms and the circumstances when government is justified in restricting those freedoms; the latter are included in the brief excerpts following.

Bertrand Russell, 1872–1970

QUESTIONS FOR REFLECTION

1. What does Russell understand as "freedom" and "liberty"? How does his understanding compare with that of Mill's?

2. What factors does Russell believe most interfere with human freedom? Has he identified all the factors you consider most important?

3. What principles does he spell out for limiting the power of the state to protect human freedom and liberty?

4. Russell mentions in passing some examples of what might now be considered victimless crimes. Does he recognize them as appropriate matters of government restriction?

READING

. . . Government and Law, in their very essence, consist of restrictions on freedom, and freedom is the greatest of political goods.[1] A hasty reasoner might conclude without further ado that Law and government are evils which must be abolished if freedom is our
5 goal. But this consequence, true or false, cannot be proved so simply. In this chapter we shall examine the arguments . . . against law and the State. We shall proceed on the assumption that freedom is the supreme aim of a good social system. . . .

Respect for the liberty of others is not a natural impulse with
10 most men: envy and love of power lead ordinary human nature to find pleasure in interferences with the lives of others. If all men's actions were wholly unchecked by external authority, we should not obtain a world in which all men would be free. The strong would oppress the weak, or the majority would oppress the minority, or
15 the lovers of violence would oppress the more peaceable people.

I fear it cannot be said that these bad impulses are WHOLLY due to a bad social system, though it must be conceded that the present competitive organization of society does a great deal to foster the worst elements in human nature. The love of power is an impulse
20 which, though innate in very ambitious men, is chiefly promoted as a rule by the actual experience of power. In a world where none could acquire much power, the desire to tyrannize would be much less strong than it is at present. Nevertheless, I cannot think that it would be wholly absent, and those in whom it would exist would often be
25 men of unusual energy and executive capacity. Such men, if they are not restrained by the organized will of the community, may either succeed in establishing a despotism, or, at any rate, make such a vigorous attempt as can only be defeated through a period of prolonged disturbance. And apart from the love of political power, there
30 is the love of power over individuals. If threats and terrorism were not prevented by law, it can hardly be doubted that cruelty would be rife in the relations of men and women, and of parents and children.

It is true that the habits of a community can make such cruelty rare, but these habits, I fear, are only to be produced through the
35 prolonged reign of law. Experience of backwoods communities,

---

[1] I do not say freedom is the greatest of ALL goods: the best things come from within—they are such things as creative art, and love, and thought. Such things can be helped or hindered by political conditions, but not actually produced by them; and freedom is, both in itself and in its relation to these other goods the best thing that political and economic conditions can secure.

Bertrand Russell, *Proposed Roads to Freedom,* excerpts, 1918.

mining camps and other such places seems to show that under new conditions men easily revert to a more barbarous attitude and practice. It would seem, therefore, that, while human nature remains as it is, there will be more liberty for all in a community
40 where some acts of tyranny by individuals are forbidden, than in a community where the law leaves each individual free to follow his every impulse. But, although the necessity of some form of government and law must for the present be conceded, it is important to remember that all law and government is in itself in
45 some degree an evil, only justifiable when it prevents other and greater evils. Every use of the power of the State needs, therefore, to be very closely scrutinized, and every possibility of diminishing its power is to be welcomed provided it does not lead to a reign of private tyranny. . . .

50 If we admit, however reluctantly, that a criminal law is necessary and that the force of the community must be brought to bear to prevent certain kinds of actions, a further question arises: How is crime to be treated? What is the greatest measure of humanity and respect for freedom that is compatible with the recognition
55 of such a thing as crime? The first thing to recognize is that the whole conception of guilt or sin should be utterly swept away. At present, the criminal is visited with the displeasure of the community: the sole method applied to prevent the occurrence of crime is the infliction of pain upon the criminal. Everything possible is
60 done to break his spirit and destroy his self-respect. Even those pleasures which would be most likely to have a civilizing effect are forbidden to him, merely on the ground that they are pleasures, while much of the suffering inflicted is of a kind which can only brutalize and degrade still further. I am not speaking, of course,
65 of those few penal institutions which have made a serious study of reforming the criminal. Such institutions, especially in America, have been proved capable of achieving the most remarkable results, but they remain everywhere exceptional. The broad rule is still that the criminal is made to feel the displeasure of society. He
70 must emerge from such a treatment either defiant and hostile, or submissive and cringing, with a broken spirit and a loss of self-respect. Neither of these results is anything but evil. Nor can any good result be achieved by a method of treatment which embodies reprobation.

75 When a man is suffering from an infectious disease he is a danger to the community, and it is necessary to restrict his liberty of movement. But no one associates any idea of guilt with such a situation. On the contrary, he is an object of commiseration to his friends. Such steps as science recommends are taken to cure
80 him of his disease, and he submits as a rule without reluctance to the curtailment of liberty involved meanwhile. The same method in spirit ought to be shown in the treatment of what is called "crime." It is supposed, of course, that the criminal is actuated by calculations of self-interest, and that the fear of punishment, by supplying
85 a contrary motive of self-interest affords the best deterrent,

The dog, to gain some private end,

Went mad and bit the man.

This is the popular view of crime; yet no dog goes mad from choice, and probably the same is true of the great majority of
90 criminals, certainly in the case of crimes of passion. Even in cases where self-interest is the motive, the important thing is to prevent the crime, not to make the criminal suffer. Any suffering which may be entailed by the process of prevention ought to be regarded as regrettable, like the pain involved in a surgical operation. The man
95 who commits a crime from an impulse to violence ought to be subjected to a scientific psychological treatment, designed to elicit more beneficial impulses. The man who commits a crime from calculations of self-interest ought to be made to feel that self-interest itself, when it is fully understood, can be better served by a life which
100 is useful to the community than by one which is harmful. For this purpose it is chiefly necessary to widen his outlook and increase the scope of his desires. At present, when a man suffers from insufficient love for his fellow-creatures, the method of curing him which is commonly adopted seems scarcely designed to succeed, being,
105 indeed, in essentials, the same as his attitude toward them. The object of the prison administration is to save trouble, not to study the individual case. He is kept in captivity in a cell from which all sight of the earth is shut out: he is subjected to harshness by warders, who have too often become brutalized by their occupation. He is solemnly
110 denounced as an enemy to society. He is compelled to perform mechanical tasks, chosen for their wearisomeness. He is given no education and no incentive to self-improvement. Is it to be wondered at if, at the end of such a course of treatment, his feelings toward the community are no more friendly than they were at the beginning?

115 Severity of punishment arose through vindictiveness and fear in an age when many criminals escaped justice altogether, and it was hoped that savage sentences would outweigh the chance of escape in the mind of the criminal. At present a very large part of the criminal law is concerned in safeguarding the rights of property, that is to
120 say—as things are now—the unjust privileges of the rich. . . . Many of the actions by which men have become rich are far more harmful to the community than the obscure crimes of poor men, yet they go unpunished because they do not interfere with the existing order.

> "Even in cases where self-interest is the motive, the important thing is to prevent the crime, not to make the criminal suffer."

Bettmann/Corbis

British troops during World War I, 1914–1918. Does Bertrand Russell suggest that government is entirely bad? What does he say about what necessary functions it seems the state should assume?

125 If the power of the community is to be brought to bear to prevent certain classes of actions through the agency of the criminal law, it is as necessary that these actions should really be those which are harmful to the community, as it is that the treatment of "criminals" should be freed from the conception of guilt and inspired by the same spirit as is shown in the treatment of disease. But, if these two
130 conditions were fulfilled, I cannot help thinking that a society which preserved the existence of law would be preferable. . . .

The State . . . seems a necessary institution for certain purposes. Peace and war, tariffs, regulation of sanitary conditions and of the sale of noxious drugs, the preservation of a just system of
135 distribution: these, among others, are functions which could hardly be performed in a community in which there was no central government. Take, for example, the liquor traffic, or the opium traffic in China. If alcohol could be obtained at cost price without taxation, still more if it could be obtained for nothing, . . . can we believe
140 that there would not be a great and disastrous increase of drunkenness? China was brought to the verge of ruin by opium, and every patriotic Chinaman desired to see the traffic in opium restricted. In such matters freedom is not a panacea, and some degree of legal restriction seems imperative for the national health.

145 But granting that the State, in some form, must continue, we must also grant, I think, that its powers ought to be very strictly limited to what is absolutely necessary. There is no way of limiting its powers except by means of groups which are jealous of their privileges and determined to preserve their autonomy, even if
150 this should involve resistance to laws decreed by the State, when these laws interfere in the internal affairs of a group in ways not warranted by the public interest. The glorification of the State, and the doctrine that it is every citizen's duty to serve the State, are radically against progress and against liberty.

155 The State, though at present a source of much evil, is also a means to certain good things, and will be needed so long as violent and destructive impulses remain common. But it is MERELY a means, and a means which needs to be very carefully and sparingly used if it is not to do more harm than good. It is not the State, but the com-
160 munity, the worldwide community of all human beings present and future, that we ought to serve. And a good community does not spring from the glory of the State, but from the unfettered development of individuals: from happiness in daily life, from congenial work giving opportunity for whatever constructiveness each man or woman may
165 possess, from free personal relations embodying love and taking away the roots of envy in thwarted capacity from affection, and above all from the joy of life and its expression in the spontaneous creations of art and science. It is these things that make an age or a nation worthy of existence, and these things are not to be secured by bowing down
170 before the State. It is the individual in whom all that is good must be realized, and the free growth of the individual must be the supreme end of a political system which is to re-fashion the world. . . .

The World as It Could Be Made

From the point of view of liberty, what system would be the best?
175 In what direction should we wish the forces of progress to move?
. . . The only human relations that have value are those that are rooted in mutual freedom, where there is no domination and no slavery, no tie except affection, no economic or conventional necessity to preserve the external show when the inner life is dead. One of
180 the most horrible things about commercialism is the way in which it poisons the relations of men and women. The evils of prostitution are generally recognized, but, great as they are, the effect of economic conditions on marriage seems to me even worse. There is not infrequently, in marriage, a suggestion of purchase, of acquiring a woman
185 on condition of keeping her in a certain standard of material comfort. Often and often, a marriage hardly differs from prostitution except by being harder to escape from. The whole basis of these evils is economic. Economic causes make marriage a matter of bargain and contract, in which affection is quite secondary, and its absence
190 constitutes no recognized reason for liberation. Marriage should be a free, spontaneous meeting of mutual instinct, filled with happiness not unmixed with a feeling akin to awe: it should involve that degree of respect of each for the other that makes even the most trifling interference with liberty an utter impossibility, and a common life
195 enforced by one against the will of the other an unthinkable thing of deep horror. It is not so that marriage is conceived by lawyers who make settlements, or by priests who give the name of "sacrament" to an institution which pretends to find something sanctifiable in the brutal lusts or drunken cruelties of a legal husband. It is not in a spirit
200 of freedom that marriage is conceived by most men and women at present: the law makes it an opportunity for indulgence of the desire to interfere, where each submits to some loss of his or her own liberty, for the pleasure of curtailing the liberty of the other. . . .

THINKING IT THROUGH

In this first step in critical thinking, as outlined in Chapters 3 through 13, we undertake the task of examining and clarifying the key terms and concepts included in the formulation of your inquiry. With this and the rest of the **Thinking It Through** modules, we follow each of the steps defined in the chapters' critical thinking tables. For all of the modules, we will work through a single ethical claim, to show you step by step the process to apply from beginning to end. Let's use a claim that seems to be relevant to students' lives:

Cheating: Among the many questions one can ask about doing it, one can ponder: Does *everybody* really do it? And, if so, does that make it right?

Step I. Examine and clarify key terms and concepts.

- Look words up in a dictionary as a start, if necessary.
- Unravel or unpack the complexities and nuances of a central term, such as *justice*, *right*, or *good*.

"Cheating in college is acceptable, so long as you don't get caught because everybody does it and good grades are necessary to get a good job after graduation."

1. Look words up in a dictionary

First, make sure you identify all of the key words and concepts that will matter. You might identify a first set of key words and concepts that are most important in your statement. You might also identify "secondary" words and concepts that will play a less critical role in the formulation but that may nonetheless have an impact on its overall meaning.

For our sentence, let's focus on the following primary key words and concepts: *cheating*, *acceptable*, and *caught*. Secondary words and concepts to keep in mind are *everybody* and *necessary*.

ASK YOURSELF: Have I identified all of the key terms in my ethical claim?

Dictionary definitions might not seem necessary for this sentence. The words all seem straightforward and are used regularly in ordinary language. But sometimes those dictionary definitions can give you ideas about complexities in the terminology that will be useful later. You might be surprised

---

STRATEGY:
Take a careful look at all possible meanings given by a dictionary for a key term.

---

at alternative meanings you find that will help you dig more deeply into the meaning of the key sentence at issue. We will see in the next **Thinking It Through** modules how these meaning variations can affect and even transform your reasoning. For now, let's start with examining the dictionary definitions.

- **Cheating:** Dictionary definitions include "fraud or swindle," which remind us that the word has connotations that suggest dishonesty.
- **Acceptable:** Dictionary definitions include "satisfactory or adequate," which suggest a positive attribute, although not on an overly praiseworthy level.
- **Caught:** This is the past tense for "catch," which is defined as "capture or seize," and also as "taking by trapping or snaring." The implication in this word is that a loss of freedom is at stake.

For the secondary terms, we might try to highlight important connotations liable to be applicable to our claim.

- **Everybody:** According to dictionary definitions, this term refers to "all, or each person." In this context, "everybody" would mean every single student.
- **Necessary:** This word's definitions include "required or essential; inevitable or inescapable." Does the term suggest more than the adjective "needed," and perhaps a notion of "absolute need"?

{ **ASK YOURSELF: How do the definitions I found shed light on the ethical claim I made?** }

2. Unravel or unpack the complexities and nuances of a central term, such as *justice*, *right*, or *good*.

We now need to try and identify the range of meanings a term might comprise, its nuances and connotations. Connotations will reveal what a term implies beyond its direct meaning and identifying them may help either zero in on a more specific meaning of the term or prevent using a meaning that is either inappropriate or misleading. Let's go back to each of the key terms.

- **Cheating:** The term can be used in many different situations, but we need to focus on the term as it is used in a college setting. In this context, the term's meaning might include submitting a paper that you bought from a term paper mill or that you paid a friend to write for you. It might also suggest asking a friend to sign your name on an attendance sheet when you were not really present in class. It involves hiding a crib sheet inside your sleeve to

If an individual cheats in college, what happens once that person is in the professional world? What if information that was not learned because of cheating is necessary to accomplish one's job?

Alastair Balderstone/Alamy

glance at during an exam. It would include forging a doctor's note to delay taking an exam.

These are all ways in which a student might defraud the professor in the pursuit of an academic credit or grade. Also, cheating may occur outside the classroom, perhaps in pursuit of an office of student government, a parking place in the student lots, or a coveted place on a student athletic team.

- **Acceptable:** Although a positive judgment of conduct, this qualifier does not constitute high praise. It connotes getting by or just making the grade somehow. Whose acceptability is at issue: your peers,

{ **STRATEGY:** In digging further into the meaning of a term, consider as wide a range of situations and contexts as possible. }

your parents, future employers, or professors? Does acceptability matter for all who might make a judgment of you someday or just your closest friends? Does this low grade of a positive assessment suggest that it is problematic in some way, that you know it does not pass a significant test?

- **Caught:** People are found out in many different ways when they are cheating. It might be a classmate who worries about the class curve or a former friend eager to get revenge for something in the past. It might be an electronic scanning tool that many colleges use to identify plagiarism in student writing. It might be an observant professor or teaching assistant during an exam.

As the definitions suggest, a loss of freedom is implied in the term. Outside of an educational setting, it might be the loss of freedom to keep your insurance premiums down, if you were "caught" by the police running a red light. It might be the loss of freedom to pursue important relationships, if you were "caught" by your roommate stealing gas money from his or her wallet. In the end, the connotations in those other settings suggest something akin to a crime or at least a clear wrongdoing, with consequences coming into effect.

{ **ASK YOURSELF: What particular meanings of key terms are likely to be most important? What particular meanings of key words are not relevant?** }

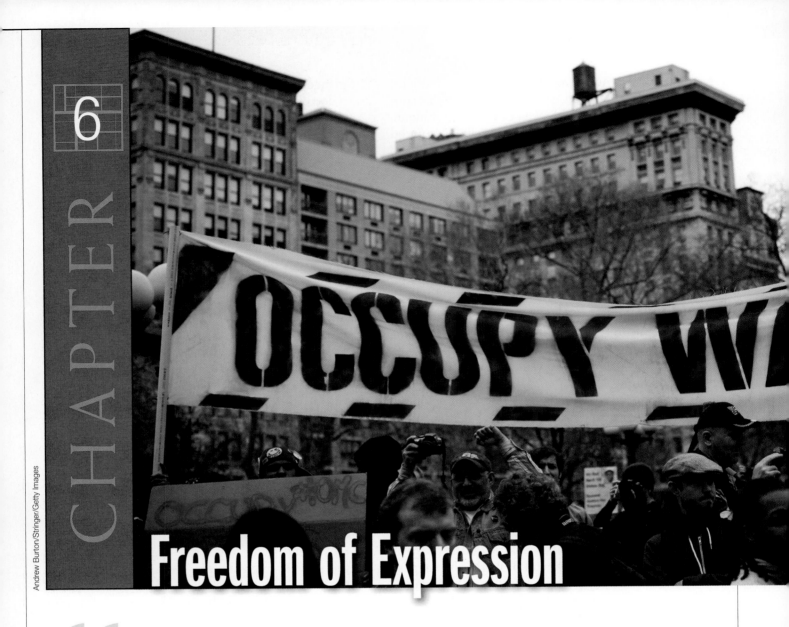

Freedom of Expression

> " I disapprove of what you say, but I will defend to the death your right to say it. "
>
> Evelyn Beatrice Hall, *Friends of Voltaire* (1906),
> paraphrasing Voltaire's view of free speech

> " No picture shall be produced that will lower the moral standards of those who see it. Hence the sympathy of the audience should never be thrown to the side of crime, wrongdoing, evil or sin. "
>
> Motion Picture Production Code of 1930 (Hays Code)

Andrew Burton/Stringer/Getty Images

LEARNING OUTCOMES

After you complete this unit, you should be able to:

6-1 Identify a range of examples of freedom of expression at issue today.

6-2 Explain major philosophical approaches for analyzing the right to freedom of expression.

6-3 Apply philosophical approaches to important issues in freedom of expression today.

6-4 Identify possible exceptions to a right of freedom of expression and the justification for making those exceptions.

"**W**here they burn books, they will ultimately also burn people." This famous quote is often cited with regard to the book-burning by Nazis in Berlin in 1933. In fact, it originated in an 1821 play, *Almansor*, by the German poet Heinrich Hein. Hein was referring to the burning of the Muslim *Qur'an* during the Spanish Inquisition. The continued relevance of this quote demonstrates how important freedom of expression is, even in modern political systems. These examples also point to another crucial observation: Free speech protections are not needed for views held by the majority of the population. They are most urgently needed to protect unpopular speech and the speech of minorities, whether Muslims during the Inquisition or Jews during the Nazi regime.

Overview

In this chapter, we will consider the range of freedom of expression issues subject to debate today. We will then look at ways in which different philosophical approaches to reasoning can help us sort out these issues. Finally, we will study excerpts from two classic statements about the importance of free speech, one by the French political philosopher Montesquieu and one by the great English writer John Milton.

What do **you** think?

Our right of free speech should be completely unrestricted.

Strongly Disagree   Strongly Agree
1   2   3   4   5   6   7

6-1 FREEDOM OF EXPRESSION EXAMPLES

The most obvious example of freedom of expression is the spoken and written word, from spoken lectures to print books and newspapers. But *expression* extends far more broadly to include symbolic speech, such as artistic expression in paintings, poetry, and the performing arts of theater, music, and dance. In this context, we will treat *speech* and *expression* as synonymous when considering the ethical issues.

However, the freedom of some specific types of expression has been contested through time and many cultures and nations. These kinds of communication include political speech that is critical of governments and their leaders. Other common areas of controversy center on criticism of dominant religions or blasphemy. Censorship of sexually explicit material, such as obscenity or pornography, is common in history.

In contemporary times, what we now call hate speech, directed against minority groups (especially about race, religion, or sexual orientation), is an area of controversy.

> [W]hat we now call **hate speech** ...is an area of controversy.

Should we be free to express our hatred of these groups, as long as we are not physically harming them?

We also seem more tolerant recently of censorship of speech that is purported to threaten national security interests. Censorship in this case, it is argued, is tolerable because releasing such information might result in harm to citizens.

The public's fear of terrorism since 9/11 seems to have shifted to tolerance of more suppression of civil liberties, including freedom of speech. How should we draw the line on this type of censorship?

Timeline 6.1 offers an overview of major historical developments that led to the recognition of the right of freedom of expression.

6-2 MAJOR PHILOSOPHICAL APPROACHES

As with other issues we have considered in this volume, good reasoning that supports (or rejects) censorship of specific types of expression or communication can draw on several well-established philosophical approaches.

Timeline 6.1 Recognition of the Right of Freedom of Expression

1644 John Milton published *Areopagitica,* urging the importance of publication free from censorship by the government.

Photos.com/Thinkstock

1748 The Baron de Montesquieu published *The Spirit of Laws,* spelling out his principles of liberty and free speech.

1690 John Locke published his *Second Treatise of Civil Government,* urging freedom of the press along with other human freedoms.

1766 The Freedom of the Press Act is introduced in Sweden, the first such act worldwide.

© Cengage Learning 2014

6-2a The Harm Principle

In Chapter 5, we considered the work of English philosopher John Stuart Mill, especially his writing in *On Liberty*. Take another look at the excerpts from his Chapter II, "Of the Liberty of Thought and Discussion," in that chapter. He uses what is typically called his "harm principle," or alternatively, his "principle of liberty," extended specifically to speech, to determine when it is appropriate for governments to restrict speech. Only when those expressions would result in real harm (not merely psychological discomfort) would a government be justified in censorship, according to this principle. Note that he does not use as a standard government restrictions that apply to what is "false" because the process of determining what is true and false requires a free and open exchange of ideas in the public forum. Mill did not trust governments to make that determination of truth and falsity. Writing by the great English poet John Milton centuries earlier holds similar beliefs about the importance of free and open exchange of ideas; the French political philosopher Montesquieu shared these ideas, and excerpts from their work are included at the end of this chapter.

As before, we can question the precise meaning of *harm* as used in this harm principle. We can ask whether speech that causes someone severe psychological distress ought to be censored. If pornography, as one of many forms of expression, encourages some men to commit rape, is that sufficient to censor all pornography? Note that the proposal to censor all pornography on this basis has been made by legal philosopher Catherine MacKinnon, but it is highly contested by both male and female experts in philosophy and the law. We can also consider whether the possibility that hate speech causes so much emotional

How difficult is it to define hate speech? How difficult is it to prove a causal connection between the pronouncement of hate speech and a violent action?

Richard Levine/Alamy

1791 The First Amendment to the U.S. Constitution is ratified, including prohibition on the government from "abridging the freedom of speech, or of the press."

1948 The United Nations established the Universal Declaration of Human Rights, including the right to "freedom of opinion and expression."

S. Greg Panosian/ iStockphoto.com

1859 John Stuart Mill published *On Liberty*, urging the freedom of expression and thought.

Gyuszkofoto/Shutterstock

KEY TERMS

defamation: words that make false claims of fact that harm the reputation of a person

libel: defamation in the form of written words

slander: defamation in the form of spoken words

distress that some people feel compelled to commit suicide is sufficient to censor all hate speech. Furthermore, we can question how we even prove that the specific hate speech is indeed the direct cause of the suicide.

6-2b Paternalism

In this other approach to analyzing freedom of expression, as discussed in Chapter 5, the government acts like a parent to protect us from ourselves. But this is a more tenuous argument with regard to speech than with other behaviors that might cause us to harm ourselves. What criteria should the government use to establish what kind of harm different types of expression cause? How does the government evaluate whether these kinds of harm warrant regulation or prohibition? Would our parents prohibit us from looking at violent movies or video games because those might motivate us to engage in violence? Should the government thus censor all expressions of violence?

6-2c Legal Moralism

Legal moralism also can be invoked to provide a theoretical framework. As discussed in Chapter 5, according to legal moralism, the government is justified in intervening in and regulating all of our expressions if doing so helps enforce an overall moral code for the society. Again, how is the moral code established and what constituencies shape the moral code? Who should decide what we should read and not read in this sort of framework?

In CourseMate, watch a video and take the quiz.

6-3 APPLYING PHILOSOPHICAL APPROACHES

The harm principle is a good starting point for analysis of specific free speech issues, and it appears to have been a factor in the analysis of free speech rights in U.S. courts. If we are following a principle of limited government restriction on our liberties, and as freedom of expression is one type of human action that governments might want to restrict, extending Mill's harm principle

> Mill's harm principle would argue that blasphemy is wrong if it causes real harm to other persons.

is a promising way to determine when it is appropriate for the government to restrict our liberty of free speech. But another approach we might use in analyzing specific examples is Kantian respect for the dignity and autonomy of all persons.

Hate speech is a good example of a contemporary issue in which good intentions play an important role. On the one hand, we want to encourage civility and respect to all other persons (a Kantian approach to respecting others), and hate speech seems to run afoul of that civility. On the other, we want humans to all have autonomy in the way we live our lives, which might include speech that others would find offensive. How should we balance these apparently conflicting results?

Another contemporary issue is blasphemy toward religion. Whatever principle we reach, it should apply consistently to all religions. If we accept criticism of Christianity as a right protected by free speech, should we also not accept criticism of Islam, Mormonism, or Judaism? We can ask what harm, if any, results from criticism of religion and whether that is the sort of harm that justifies censorship. Here, Mill's harm principle would argue that blasphemy is wrong if it causes real harm to other persons. Does verbal criticism of a particular religion harm persons? It might be offensive or upsetting to many, but is that what we mean by "real" harm? We can also ask about how we show respect for the autonomy and dignity of individuals, regardless of their religious views. Here we would be using a Kantian approach to focus on the autonomy and dignity of practitioners of various religions. Are we denying that autonomy if we criticize their religion? Do we really want to extend that view to all religions and say none can ever be criticized?

Violence in movies and video games is yet another contemporary issue. Should the violence displayed in these media be censored if we can prove that it causes those who watch this violence to cause violence themselves? What sort of causal proof would we demand to enact this form of censorship—that is, can it be demonstrated that the violence seen in a specific movie is the only or the most direct and immediate cause of a violent act? Do we require to be shown a clear, demonstrable, irrefutable connection between cause and effect? Past and current factual research has yet to show a clear correlation between watching violence and perpetrating acts of violence. These inconclusive studies do not prove that there are no causal effects. To claim otherwise would be to commit the informal

The series *Mad Men* depicts the business world of the 1960s in the United States. How would someone today characterize the type of speech used with and about women in this show? If used today, would any of it constitute sexual harassment in the workplace?

fallacy of the appeal to ignorance. It is possible that future studies could finally demonstrate such causal effects. If we decide to censor such expressed violence, can this censorship be justified as a violation of the harm principle? As a violation of our respect for human autonomy and dignity?

Another approach to consider, along with governmental censorship, is societal disapproval and scorn, outside the purview of government. This form of "shunning" can also be a powerful tool to silence speech, for good or ill. If other students make clear that they will not be friends with students who engage in hate speech, would that be a powerful deterrent to bullying, independently of school rules? If parents make clear that they will not spend their money on violent video games, will that be effective in helping interest in these games decline, independently of government efforts to restrict access to minors? If coworkers make clear that they will not tolerate offensive and harassing language to other people in their workplace, will that be an effective means of reducing that language in the workplace, quite independently of laws and regulations against sexual harassment?

In CourseMate, apply what you've learned to the real-life scenario in the simulation.

In CourseMate, practice what you learned by taking the chapter quiz.

6-4 EXCEPTIONS TO THE RIGHT OF FREEDOM OF EXPRESSION

No human right is absolute, especially when those rights conflict with other rights, and free speech is no exception. We consider some familiar types of controversial speech that many think should be censored to establish whether these exceptions are justifiable.

a. Causing Panic: If you scream *fire* in a crowded theater when there is no fire and start a stampede for the exits in which people are injured, should you be accountable for the harm you have caused? When Orson Welles aired the *War of the Worlds* on radio and sent listeners scrambling on the highways in their cars to escape the supposed invasion of extraterrestrials, should Welles have been held accountable for the accidents resulting on the highways that he triggered among listeners trying to drive away to safety? Sometimes words can cause panic in a crowd, resulting in real harm. In analyzing these exercises of speech, we also need to look at the causal relationship between our speech and the supposed harm and ask whether it is a direct causation. We also need to consider where we draw the line on protecting free speech and censoring speech that causes real harm. For speech that causes panic, government intervention consists in laws that provide punishment of some kind; this threat of punishment is expected to be a discouragement or deterrence to such speech in the future.

b. **Defamation:** Words that make false claims of fact that harm the reputation of a person constitute defamation. **Libel** is a written defamation, and **slander** is spoken defamation. Sometimes harming a reputation can cause real economic harm, which Mill would recognize as the type of harm that justifies government's prohibition of, or punishment for, such speech. The government's laws allow for damages for such defamation; therefore the threat of potential punishment can be considered censorship of this speech. Note that defamation only pertains to claims of facts, not mere opinions.

c. Incitement to crime: Words that encourage others to break the law and thus cause harm can themselves be the object of the government's punishment. But what should count as *incitement*? Again, as with causing panic, the causal relationship between the words and a third-party's actions would have to be proven for a punishment to be inflicted. If someone merely writes something inflammatory in a book that someone reads, is that incitement? In the absence of a direct, incontrovertible causal link between inflammatory language in a book and harmful actions committed by someone who read that language, is it possible to lay the blame for the actions on the book? Similarly, if a video game designer includes violence in the game, does that incite the players to commit violence themselves?

d. Sedition: Language that advocates the violent overthrow of the government would appear to be a clear case of incitement to crime. In U.S. courts, laws that prohibit such language have been upheld as not violating rights of free speech. The harm at issue does seem to be real (violent overthrow of the government), but how much of a causal connection should we demand before we censor this speech through criminal punishments?

e. Obscenity: This is perhaps the most controversial of proposed censored speech. Mill did not think that it caused real harm and thus should not be censored. Legal moralists would likely want obscenity to be censored as part of the overall imposition of their version of "morality." The U.S. Supreme Court has held consistently that obscenity is not protected by the Bill of Rights because that was not the intent of the Founding Fathers—as the claim is routinely made. The justices look for and discern the Founding Fathers's intent in their letters, speeches, and other documents from the period when the Bill of Rights was written. Even defining *obscenity* is difficult. The courts themselves have struggled to come up with a precise definition of it. Then, one has to consider whether obscenity causes real harm sufficient to support government prohibition.

Now that you have studied how various types of reasoning apply to the topics discussed, review Critical Thinking Table 6.1 to follow the process of examining an ethical claim on a related topic.

In CourseMate, listen to the audio summary of the chapter.

What does it mean in everyday life for you, wherever you are from, to have freedom of expression? When have you wanted to exercise that right and what did it mean for you? If you feel like you never have exercised that right, can you think of any occasion when you might feel the need to voice your opinion in a public forum?

Alex Wong/Getty Images News/Getty Images

Joel Feinberg

A philosopher of ethics, social, and legal philosophy, Joel Feinberg worked in the general framework laid out by John Stuart Mill regarding what is typically called Mill's harm principle or alternatively, his principle of liberty, to explain the justifiability of some government restrictions on liberty. But Feinberg argued that Mill's approach did not go far enough in justifying our actual practices in restricting some extreme conduct, especially some forms of expression that cannot be avoided (such as icky noises people might make on a public bus), violent pornography, and hate speech. He proposed an "offense principle" to analyze these additional restrictions. With this principle, Feinberg is trying to justify government censorship that goes farther than Mill's harm principle would permit. Offense is not real harm, at least not in the strict sense Mill used, but it is sufficiently serious that Feinberg believes the government is justified in suppressing that speech. For Feinberg, the offense must be profound, not just trivial or a mere nuisance.

Feinberg's most important contribution was the four-volume work called *The Moral Limits of the Criminal Law*, including *Harm to Others* (1984), *Offense to Others* (1985), *Harm to Self* (1986), and *Harmless Wrongdoing* (1988). He also published numerous books and articles on wide-ranging subjects, from abortion and children's rights to environmental pollution and pornography.

Feinberg received his education in philosophy at the University of Michigan and taught at several universities before settling at the University of Arizona, where he taught until his retirement. He was honored during his lifetime by many organizations and served as President of the American Philosophical Association.

Joel Feinberg (1926–2004)

Betty Feinberg

Table 6.1 Critical Thinking Steps and Their Application in an Example

{ "Hate speech should be censored because it is harmful to vulnerable people." }

Critical Thinking Steps	Application
1. Examine and clarify key terms and concepts. 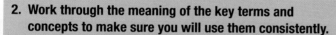 • Look words up in a dictionary as a start if necessary. • Unravel or unpack the complexities and nuances of a central term, such as *justice*, or *right*, or *good*.	• What is *hate speech*? Is this term found in contemporary dictionaries? What is my common sense understanding of the term? • *Harm* has a common dictionary meaning, but is this enough for the claim being made here? • *Vulnerable* suggests a certain sort of sensitivity to being harmed.
2. Work through the meaning of the key terms and concepts to make sure you will use them consistently. • Consider the ways the term can be used by including it in different sentences and contexts to zero in on the particular meaning you are after. • Ask yourself what words are potential synonyms for the concept. Do those capture everything you want to understand about that term?	• What counts as hate speech here? Is this all speech that might be offensive to somebody somewhere? Can this be narrowed to be more precise? Should we limit this to language considered severe to a reasonable or ordinary person? • What kind of harm is of concern here? Is being annoyed enough to count as harm? Should it be so severe that it causes a mental breakdown? Is there a middle ground that works? • Who counts as vulnerable here? Are we only concerned with overly sensitive people? Average people? Thick-skinned people?
3. Build premises and bring any assumptions to light. • Put together short and clear sentences to build each of your premises. • Think through what you may be taking for granted in your reasoning. What assumptions are you making? • Once you have identified assumptions, articulate them in your premise, so that your audience has the same understanding of a term or a concept as you.	The premises of the argument could be constructed as follows, using these clarifications of terminology: (i) Anything that is harmful to vulnerable people should be censored. (ii) Hate speech is harmful to vulnerable people. CONCLUSION: Hate speech should be censored.
4. Test/Verify your premises. • Now that you have stated your premises explicitly, do you want to stick with them? • Are you relying on premises drawn from unsubstantiated sources or from questionable authorities? • Are you consistent in your premises? Or are you appealing to different and inconsistent foundations in your reasoning?	Each of these premises should be examined. (i) "Anything" is very sweeping. "Harmful" is vague and broad. "Vulnerable people" also seems vague and excessively broad. Accepting this premise would require being satisfied with all of these issues. (ii) What evidence is there of the supposed harm of hate speech to vulnerable people? Is this just anecdotal? Have medical and social scientists studied this in persuasive ways?

Richard Levine/Alamy

AF archive/Alamy

(Continued)

Table 6.1 Continued

Critical Thinking Steps	Application
• Reformulate your premises if they have proven to be faulty.	If you do not accept all of these premises, then you will not accept the conclusion either. But if you do accept all of them, then you would find the conclusion valid and justified.
5. Confirm that the conclusions you draw are logical. Check for reliance on fallacies and correct any premise that you identify as relying on a fallacy.	This argument is especially vulnerable to criticism that it relies on the fallacy of equivocation, especially regarding the word *harmful*—that is, the word *harmful* is being used in different ways in the argument.

Alex Wong/ Getty Images News/Getty Images

CHAPTER 6 Case Study

Free Speech for neo-Nazis?

In 1977, the neo-Nazi "National Socialist Party" wanted to march through Skokie, Illinois, a town inhabited by elderly Jewish residents, many of whom were Holocaust survivors. Although the town initially denied the permit, the courts ordered that the Nazis be allowed to conduct their march through town on grounds of freedom of expression, as protected by the First Amendment to the U.S. Constitution. Many other Nazi parades continue to take place, and Nazi uniforms and swastikas are displayed to this day, because they are protected by the First Amendment. The rationale for this approach to free speech is that "sunlight is the best disinfectant," in the words of Justice Louis Brandeis a century ago. By allowing the free and open exchange of ideas, people can reach their own decisions about good and evil, truth and falsity.

In most European countries today, the public display of Nazi symbols and the sale and distribution of the writings of Adolf Hitler are prohibited by law. Examples abound of this censorship in recent years in these countries. For example, in France, laws prohibiting the sale or display of anything that incites racism were used to ban the online auctions of neo-Nazi memorabilia in 2000. The French judge said the Nazi memorabilia "offended the collective memory of the country." Germany insisted that Amazon .com stop selling copies of Hitler's writings to German residents. Denying that the Holocaust occurred is also illegal in most of these European countries. Such an example of speech is protected under the First Amendment in the United States. In Amsterdam in 2010, a Dutch Muslim group was fined $3,200 for publishing a cartoon

Dutch court

denying the Holocaust. The court said that, despite the importance of freedom of speech, the European Court of Human Rights "makes an exception for the denial or trivialization of the Holocaust."

1. What seems to be the best approach to address the resurgence of neo-Nazi hatred, the unfettered free speech of the United States or the censorship of contemporary European nations?

2. European nations experienced invasions and occupations by the Nazis during World War II more than sixty-five years ago. Europeans today subscribe to the Charter of Fundamental Rights of the European Union, proclaiming that "Everyone has the right to freedom of expression" (Article 11). How can the contradiction between the latter fact and the examples of imposed censorship cited be justified, if at all? Americans allow neo-Nazi speech on the grounds of the First Amendment in the Bill of rights. Is the U.S. tolerance of neo-Nazi speech justified?

3. Hate speech can take many forms. The Ku Klux Klan in the United States enjoys the free speech rights of the neo-Nazis. Should that speech be censored if it advocates violence?

4. Campus speech policies against bullying seem to be an example of censorship of the language of hatred. Should that speech be protected under the First Amendment?

For additional case studies, please see the CourseMate for this text.

Reading Excerpt: Charles de Secondat, Baron de Montesquieu, *The Spirit of Laws* (1748)

INTRODUCTION

The French political philosopher usually referred to simply as Montesquieu spelled out principles of liberty and free speech in this book, first published in 1748. He was one of the most influential philosophers of the eighteenth century and his ideas were reflected in the writing of the Founding Fathers of the U.S. Constitution. The translation of this work of his into English by Thomas Nugent was first published in 1750.

Charles de Secondat, Baron de Montesquieu (1689–1755)

De Agostini/Getty Images

QUESTIONS FOR REFLECTION

1. What does Montesquieu seem to understand as the difference between "philosophic liberty" and "political liberty"?

2. Why does he urge freedom of thought? How is thought different from action?

3. What is his complaint against using speech as proof of treason?

4. What is the difference between "words" and "overt acts"? Is the government ever justified in punishing words?

5. Should satire be protected speech? What is the danger of satire to governments, if any?

READING

Book XII. Of the Laws That Form Political Liberty, in Relation to the Subject

... **Of the Liberty of the Subject**. Philosophic liberty consists in the free exercise of the will; or at least, if we must speak agreeably
5 to all systems, in an opinion that we have the free exercise of our will. Political liberty consists in security, or, at least, in the opinion that we enjoy security.

This security is never more dangerously attacked than in public or private accusations. It is, therefore, on the goodness of
10 criminal laws that the liberty of the subject principally depends...

Of Thoughts. Marsyas [a mythological figure in ancient Greece] dreamed that he had cut Dionysius's [a Greek god's] throat. Dionysius put him to death, pretending that he would never have dreamed of such a thing by night if he had not thought of it by day.
15 This was a most tyrannical action: for though it had been the subject of his thoughts, yet he had made no attempt towards it. The laws do not take upon them to punish any other than overt acts.

Of indiscreet Speeches. Nothing renders the crime of high treason more arbitrary than declaring people guilty of it for indiscreet
20 speeches. Speech is so subject to interpretation; there is so great a difference between indiscretion and malice; and frequently so little is there of the latter in the freedom of expression, that the law can hardly subject people to a capital punishment for words unless it expressly declares what words they are.
25 Words do not constitute an overt act; they remain only in idea. When considered by themselves, they have generally no determinate signification; for this depends on the tone in which they are uttered. It often happens that in repeating the same words they have not the same meaning; this depends on their connection with
30 other things, and sometimes more is signified by silence than by any expression whatever. Since there can be nothing so equivocal and ambiguous as all this, how is it possible to convert it into a crime of high treason? Wherever this law is established, there is an end not only of liberty, but even of its very shadow....

> *Words do not constitute an overt act; they remain only in idea.*

35 Not that I pretend to diminish the just indignation of the public against those who presume to stain the glory of their sovereign; what I mean is that, if despotic princes are willing to moderate their power, a milder chastisement

40 would be more proper on those occasions than the charge of high treason—a thing always terrible even to innocence itself.

Overt acts do not happen every day; they are exposed to the eye of the public; and a

45 false charge with regard to matters of fact may be easily detected. Words carried into action assume the nature of that action. Thus a man who goes into a public market-place to incite the subject to revolt incurs the guilt of high treason,

50 because the words are joined to the action, and partake of its nature. It is not the words that are punished, but an action in which words are employed. They do not become criminal, but when they are annexed to a criminal action:

55 everything is confounded if words are construed into a capital crime, instead of considering them only as a mark of that crime....

Of Writings. In writings there is something more permanent than in words, but when they

60 are in no way preparative to high treason they cannot amount to that charge....

Satirical writings are hardly known in despotic governments, where dejection of mind on the one hand, and ignorance on

65 the other, afford neither abilities nor will to write. In democracies they are not hindered, for the very same reason which causes them to be prohibited in monarchies; being generally leveled against men of power and authority, they

70 flatter the malignancy of the people, who are the governing party. In monarchies they are forbidden, but rather as a subject of civil animadversion than as a capital crime. They may amuse the general malevolence, please the malcontents, diminish the envy against public employments, give

75 the people patience to suffer, and make them laugh at their sufferings.

Montesquieu, an aristocrat, was born when Louis XV ruled France. At first beloved, the king, by his actions, ended up weakening the nation. His grandson, Louis XVI, succeeded him in 1774. Fifteen years later, the French revolution started, putting an end to absolute monarchy in the country.

But no government is so averse to satirical writings as the aristocratic. There the magistrates are petty sovereigns, but not great enough to despise affronts. If in a monarchy a satirical stroke

80 is designed against the prince, he is placed on such an eminence that it does not reach him; but an aristocratic lord is pierced to the very heart. Hence the decemvirs [the group of ten magistrates in ancient Rome], who formed an aristocracy, punished satirical writings with death....

Reading Excerpt: John Milton, *Areopagitica: For the Liberty of unlicenc'd Printing* (1644)

INTRODUCTION

This letter to the English Parliament in 1644 is the first major published plea for freedom of expression. Milton objected to a new regulation by Parliament that nothing could be published until it had been approved and licensed by the government, an extreme form of censorship. Although Milton's letter did not change the minds of Parliament, it became influential in many later writings on free speech, even including the Bill of Rights to the U.S. Constitution. The name *Areopagitica* is derived from a term that means "Hill of Ares," the site of the high court of Athens in ancient Greece, which practiced censorship. Milton urges that the free exchange of ideas is essential to ethical growth, in an argument very similar to one used by John Stuart Mill centuries later (see the excerpts from *Make On Liberty* in Chapter 5 of this text). Milton's spelling in the seventeenth century was often different from contemporary standards and has been changed to modern spellings here.

John Milton (1608–1674)

QUESTIONS FOR REFLECTION

1. What is the benefit of the freedom to read books, according to Milton? How does that freedom improve our knowledge?

2. Why does he reject concerns that reading books promoting vice will harm us irretrievably?

3. What is the best way to pursue truth and virtue? Does wide freedom in reading books really promote this, as Milton claims?

4. In any licensing or censoring system, who should make the decision as to what is to be censored? Is Milton right in worrying about who will fill that role? Who is best qualified to do this censoring, in your opinion?

5. Do you agree with Milton that free access to books for teachers is enormously important? Should teachers have the freedom to teach anything they wish?

READING

This is true Liberty when free born men
Having to advise the public may speak free,
Which he who can, and will, deserves high praise,
Who neither can nor will, may hold his peace;
5 *What can be more just in a State then this?*

Euripedes Hicetid.

… I know not what should withhold me from presenting you with an appropriate instance to show both that love of truth which you eminently profess, and that uprightness of your judgment which is 10 not partial to your selves; by judging again that Order which you have ordained *to regulate Printing, That no Book, pamphlet, or paper shall be Printed,* unless *it is first* approved *and* licensed … [W]hat is to be thought in general of reading, whatever sort the Books be; and that this Order does nothing to suppress scandal-15 ous, seditious, and libelous Books, which were mainly intended to be suppressed. Last, that it will primarily discourage all learning, and the stop of Truth, not only by blunting our abilities in what we know already, but by hindering and restricting the discovery that might be yet further made both in religious and civil Wisdom.

> " *[T]his Order … will primarily discourage all learning, and the stop of Truth …* "

20 … what is to be thought in general of reading Books, whatever sort they be, and whether be more the benefit, or the harm that proceeds from them? … Since therefore the knowledge and survey of vice is in this world so necessary to the constituting of human virtue, and the scanning of error to the confirmation of truth, how 25 can we more safely, and with less danger explore into the regions of sin and falsity then by reading all manner of books, and hearing

A Greek philosopher, Epicurus, 341–270 B.C.E., is most known for his belief that human beings should seek to attain a life free of pain and enjoy peace and freedom from fear. Epicurus postulated that nothing should be believed, except what was tested through direct observation and logical deduction.

all manner of reason? And this is the benefit which may be had of books promiscuously read. But of the harm that may result from this reading, three kinds are usually recognized. First, is feared the
30 infection that may spread; but then all human learning and controversy in religious points must remove out of the world, even the Bible itself; for that often relates blasphemy not nicely, it describes the carnal sense of wicked men not unelegantly, it brings in holiest men passionately murmuring against providence through all the
35 arguments of *Epicurus*: in other great disputes it answers dubiously and darkly to the common reader....

And again if it be true, that a wise man like a good refiner can gather gold out of the worst volume, and that a fool will be a fool with the best book, or without book, there is no reason that we
40 should deprive a wise man of any advantage to his wisdom, while we seek to restrain from a fool, that which being restrained will be no hindrance to his folly.... It is next alleged we must not expose ourselves to temptations without necessity, and next to that, not use our time in worthless things. To both these objections one
45 answer will serve, out of the grounds already laid, that to all men such books are not temptations, nor vanities; but useful drugs and materials with which to temper and compose effective and strong medicines, which man's life cannot want.... See the ingenuity of Truth, who when she gets a free and willing hand, opens herself
50 faster than the pace of method and discourse can overtake her. It was the task which I began with, To show that no Nation, or well instituted State, if they valued books at all, did ever use this way of licensing; and it might be answered, that this is a piece of prudence recently discovered. To which I return, that as it was a thing
55 slight and obvious to think about, if it had been difficult to find out, they would have suggested this long ago; but instead they leave us a pattern of their judgment, that it was not the not knowing, but the not approving, which was the cause of their not using it.

... Lastly, who shall forbid and separate all idle resort, all evil
60 company?... If every action which is good, or evil in man at ripe years, were to be under pittance, and prescription, and compulsion, what is virtue but a name, what praise could be then due to well-doing, what incentive to be sober, just or continent? Many complain of divine Providence for suffering *Adam* to transgress,
65 foolish tongues! When God gave him reason, he gave him freedom to choose, for reason is but choosing;... This justifies the high providence of God, who though he command us temperance, justice, continence, yet powers out before us even to a profusion of all desirable things, and gives us minds that can wander beyond all
70 limit and satisfaction. Why should we then affect a rigor contrary to the manner of God and of nature, by abridging or shortening those means, which books freely permitted are, both to the trial of virtue and the exercise of truth....

Another reason, whereby to make it plain that this order will
75 miss the end it seeks, consider by the quality which ought to be in every licenser. It cannot be denied but that he who is made judge to sit upon the birth, or death of books whether they may be brought into this world, or not, must be a man above the common measure, both studious, learned, and judicious; there may be
80 else no mean mistakes in the censure of what is passable or not; which is also no mean injury. If he be of such worth, there cannot be a more tedious and unpleasing job, a greater loss of time levied upon his head, then to be made the perpetual reader of unchosen books and pamphlets, often huge volumes. There is no book that is
85 acceptable unless at certain seasons; but to be enjoyed the reading of that at all times, and in a hand barely legible, of three pages would not down at any time in the fairest Print, is an imposition I cannot believe how he that values time, and his own studies, or is

but of a sensible nostril should be able to endure. In this one thing I crave leave of the present licensers to be pardoned for so thinking: who doubtless took this office up, looking on it through their obedience to the Parliament, whose command perhaps made all

> **[H]e who is made judge to sit upon the birth, or death of books … must be a man above the common measure, both studious, learned, and judicious.**

things seem easy to them; but that this short trial has worn them out already, their own expressions and excuses to them who make so many journeys to solicit their license, are testimony enough. Seeing therefore those who now possess the employment, by all evident signs wish themselves well rid of it, and that no man of worth, none that is not a plain waster of his own hours is ever likely to succeed them, except he mean to put himself to the salary of a Press-corrector, we may easily foresee what kind of licensers we are to expect from now on, either ignorant, imperious, and remiss, or basely pecuniary. This is what I had to show, wherein this order cannot result in that end, whereof it bears the intention.

I lastly proceed from the no good it can do, to the manifest hurt it causes, in being first the greatest discouragement and affront, that can be offered to learning and to learned men…. And how can a man teach with authority, which is the life of teaching, how can he be a Doctor in his book as he ought to be, or else had better be silent, when as all he teaches, all he delivers, is but under the restriction, under the correction of his patriarchal licenser to blot or alter what precisely is inconsistent with the hidebound humor which he calls his judgment. When every acute reader upon the first sight of a license, will be ready with these words to ding the book a long distance from him, I hate a pupil teacher, I endure not an instructor that comes to me under the control of an overseeing fist. I know nothing of the licenser, but that I have his own hand here for his arrogance; who shall warrant me his judgment?…

CHAPTER 7

Religious Freedom

"Leave the matter of religion to the family altar, the church, and the private school, supported entirely by private contributions. Keep the church and state forever separate.

Ulysses S. Grant,
Eighteenth President of the United States

"Far from being rivals or enemies, religion and law are twin sisters, friends, and mutual assistants. Indeed, these two sciences run into each other. The divine law, as discovered by reason and the moral sense, forms an essential part of both.

James Wilson,
Signer of the Constitution

LEARNING OUTCOMES

After you complete this unit, you should be able to:

7-1 Identify examples of religious freedom at issue today.

7-2 Explain major philosophical approaches for analyzing the right to freedom of religion.

7-3 Apply philosophical approaches to important issues in freedom of religion today.

7-4 Identify possible exceptions to a right of freedom of religion and the justification for making those exceptions.

Alfred Smith and Galen Black were fired from their jobs at a private drug rehabilitation organization in Oregon because they had used peyote during a religious ceremony at their Native American Church. Peyote is a hallucinogenic drug banned under the state's controlled substance law. They were then denied unemployment benefits on the grounds that they had been fired for work-related "misconduct." Smith and Black sued to get the benefits, arguing that their freedom of religion, guaranteed under the First Amendment to the U.S. Constitution, took precedence over the state's drug laws. The U.S. Supreme Court sided with the state of Oregon in concluding that the drug laws took priority over this exercise of religious freedom. Balancing religious freedoms with other important rights is enormously complicated as this example shows. The relationship of religious codes with moral standards is also challenging.

A major focus of this chapter is developing an understanding of how to reconcile religious freedom with the diverse and often inconsistent views held by those religions on the one hand and secular society on the other. Further complicating these relationships between ethics and religious diversity is the role of government in setting laws that often mirror ethical rules.

These challenges are important in several areas of philosophy, especially ethics but also political philosophy, and we will touch on both in this chapter.

What do **you** think?

Freedom of religion should be absolute, with no exceptions.

Strongly Disagree						Strongly Agree
1	2	3	4	5	6	7

Overview

We will review various examples of religious freedom at issue today. We will then consider again how the major philosophical approaches we have studied can be used to analyze those controversies. Exceptions to the right of freedom of religion will be examined. The writings of two major philosophers, John Locke and Alexis de Tocqueville, on freedom of religion are examined and their implications for issues today identified.

7-1 RELIGIOUS FREEDOMS TODAY

7-1a Legal Protection and Intolerance

Religion is intertwined with morality in many ways. Some people's religious views are the same as their ethical views. Other individuals view their secular ethical perspectives as separate from their religious views. Many secular ethical and legal rules in the broader culture overlap and are sometimes aligned with religious ethical strictures. For example, it is illegal to murder. It is also unethical to kill, and killing violates the religious tenets of most (perhaps all) religions. But although the rules might seem the same in these religious, ethical, and governmental contexts, the justification or rationale for following those rules typically differ. The threatened punishments or consequences also are likely to vary. Even among different religions, the basis for a rule not to kill varies.

In contemporary societies, freedom of religion is protected. It is a tenet of the United Nations statement of human rights, and it can now be found in the constitutions of most advanced nations. Some nations still have state-imposed religions, but the pressure to recognize religious diversity is enormous and growing.

In most industrialized nations, freedom of religion is taken for granted. People feel free to worship at the church, temple, synagogue, or other religious site of their choice. But continuing news reports suggest stresses in these old assumptions. Many in the United States and elsewhere have protested the presence of mosques or

AP Photo/Ng Han Guan

Chinese military forces in Tibet. China's sovereignty over Tibet was formalized in 1951. Tibetans have long complained about China's attempts to erode their freedoms. In recent years, reports of self-immolation by Tibetan monks have drawn attention again to the Tibetans's struggles to maintain their cultural and religious identity.

sites where Muslims congregate in their communities; rejection of those of the Jewish faith (anti-Semitism) persists in many nations. In some areas of the world, different sects of Islam challenge each other. Even in nations that guarantee religious freedom by law, tensions continue over the very practices of some religious groups. So, freedom of religion may be the law of the land in some nations, but true and peaceful acceptance of all religions may not be, and often is not, achieved.

> [F]reedom of religion may be the law of the land in some nations, but true and peaceful acceptance of all religions may not be ... achieved.

7-1b Religious Belief and Practice

A second area of contention is in recognizing the rights of religious people to exercise or act upon certain practices in which they believe. Polygamy continues to be a matter of debate. Although the Mormon Church banned the practice in the late nineteenth century, break-away sects continue to insist on a right to engage in polygamy. Immigrants from cultures in which polygamy is accepted ask that Western nations recognize their right to that religious practice. A right to wear certain types of clothing dictated by religious views is another current controversy. In France, a recent law banning the wearing of veils and other items of clothing that hide the identity of women is drawing criticism from practitioners of some in the Islamic faith. In some American Indian religions, the consumption of peyote, an illegal drug, is part of religious ceremonies.

A key distinction is typically made between the right to hold a belief and to speak about that belief, which is protected in most countries by freedom of speech, and on the other hand, a right to *act* on those beliefs, which is not necessarily protected by religious freedom. However, religious practitioners might question how they can have the right to hold a belief but not that of acting on or practicing that belief. They would see this distinction as hollowing out their rights and leaving them with only the useless right to believe something, but never put it into action.

7-1c Freedom of Religion and Separation of Church and State

A third area of contention is a special problem in the United States, where the First Amendment to the Constitution also bans the establishment of a state religion. The separation of church and state forbids all governmental institutions from sponsoring any religion or religious practice. One of the earliest and clearest statements of the importance of this separation can be found in the treatise, "A Plea for Religious Liberty," by Roger Williams, who founded what is now the state of Rhode Island in 1636. He also founded the first Baptist church in the U.S. colonies. His insistence on the separation of church and state grew out of his dismay at what he considered the corruption

President Thomas Jefferson owned an English translation of the *Koran*. It is now in the Rare Books Collection of the Library of Congress. Jefferson was well versed in world religions and was a strong supporter of the separation of church and state.

of the Church of England, in which he had grown up. Another staunch supporter of the separation of church and state was Thomas Jefferson, the third U.S. President. A deeply religious man, he believed that religion was a personal matter.

This prohibition seems to clash with the freedom of religion also found in this amendment. For example, some students might wish to assert their freedom of religion within a public, taxpayer-supported school. They might wish to say prayers in the classroom, on a football field, or at a commencement service. However, a public school is an institution that may not establish or favor a religion or religious practice of any kind. If state and church are to be separate, and public entities and institutions must reflect secular views, some might wonder why the Pledge of Allegiance includes the phrase "under God" (added in the 1950s). Other similar challenges include questioning why the U.S. currency includes the words "in God we trust," and whether a government judge who wants to post the Judeo-Christian Ten Commandments in his courtroom is sponsoring a particular religion, which is prohibited, or exercising his freedom of religion, which is protected.

All of these issues, and many more, should be considered not solely from a religious or legal perspective, but also from an ethical perspective, which we will endeavor to do in this chapter.

7-2 MAJOR PHILOSOPHICAL APPROACHES

Good reasoning that supports, or rejects, freedom of religion can draw on several well-established philosophical approaches, regardless of the particular country and legal system in which we reside.

Utilitarian analysis of this freedom can be fruitful. We need to evaluate consequences and their impact on maximization of happiness for most or all when freedom of religion is present versus when it is not. The utilitarian approach will mean examining the benefits and disadvantages provided by freedom of religion versus the lack of it. We will seek evidence and support to demonstrate what these specific benefits and drawbacks are. One positive benefit of this freedom is a healthier functioning democracy, as observed by Alexis de Tocqueville in the reading excerpt at the end of this chapter. Some religious views might result in more socially responsible and ethical conduct by their adherents, and this would represent a benefit to all in that nation or culture.

These benefits to religious freedom can be compared with the benefits of restricting religious freedom. For persons convinced that there is one and only one correct religion (whatever that might be), then they might plausibly believe that requiring all persons to accept that religion would be beneficial to everyone. This position would require rejecting all other religious beliefs and practices. This in turn would negate the very freedom that would allow the imposition of a single creed—thus, under such a view, freedom of religion itself would be impossible.

Mill's harm principle can also be helpful. If the exercise of religious freedom causes real harm to others, then the government should restrict that exercise of freedom, according to this principle. This approach provides guidance on why some religious practices should be allowed, whereas others should be banned. If polygamy causes harm to women and children, then this harm would be a justification for banning the practice. What if overwhelming evidence could be assembled that banning the practice resulted in harm to women who had no other means of supporting themselves than to be in a polygamous union? Even if one might question the validity of a system that would lead to women not being given the opportunity to support themselves, in such a system, women left unable to provide for themselves would face the horrible conditions brought about by destitution. Would such dire circumstances be worth an outright ban?

Kantian reasoning would focus on human rights and the dignity of persons. Does tolerating and indeed encouraging religious freedom show the respect for persons that Kant would urge? Would his categorical imperative lead us to conclude that we should follow those ethical rules that we could imagine universalizing when religious diversity is tolerated?

In CourseMate, watch a video and take the quiz.

7-3 APPLYING PHILOSOPHICAL APPROACHES

We have identified some of the main religious freedom issues in contention today. You no doubt have thought of others of concern to you. Try to systematically use the philosophical approaches we have examined to analyze them.

A photo of the proposed site for an Islamic community center in New York City: this building is located two blocks away from Ground Zero. What ethical arguments would you use to make a case for or against the building of this Islamic facility at this site?

TIMOTHY A. CLARY/AFP/Getty Images/Newscom

Here is an example of a recent controversy and how this application could be helpful. In lower Manhattan, a few blocks from the site of the World Trade Center towers destroyed on 9/11, a group of Muslim U.S. citizens wanted to renovate an abandoned building and turn it into an Islamic community center. According to the utilitarian approach, the consequences of the proposed creation of this community center would be central in examining this issue. How would this project affect the desired result for a utilitarian of achieving the greatest happiness for the greatest number of members of the larger community? What consequences are relevant here? The social environment for the local Muslim community? The emotional distress of some family members of 9/11 victims? The economic benefit to merchants on what had been a decaying city block in need of revitalization?

This issue can also be considered from a Kantian perspective, with competing rights of the many individuals and groups with a stake in the outcome. Should we show respect and dignity to the families of survivors? To the larger community that seeks tolerance and fairness? To the Muslim practitioners who want to create this community? What other considerations should we take into account?

In CourseMate, apply what you've learned to the real-life scenario in the simulation.

In CourseMate, practice what you learned by taking the chapter quiz.

7-4 EXCEPTIONS TO THE RIGHT OF RELIGIOUS FREEDOM

As we have already observed, religious freedom by necessity must have limits—for example, to avoid the imposition of one specific belief on all members of a community without their consent.

Thus, the right of religious freedom cannot be absolute, whether from an ethical, religious, or legal perspective. The challenge is to articulate principles that explain and justify consistently when the exercise of religious freedom should be curtailed and when it should not.

Such principles might rely on Mill's harm principle. Curtailing the exercise of freedom of religion would be justified, under this principle, if exercising that freedom were to cause real harm to others. Courts of law sometimes appeal to "public policy" or "prevailing community standards" in supporting a conclusion that limits freedoms. The U.S. Supreme Court used this approach in the nineteenth century in holding that the religious practice of polygamy in the Mormon religion was not a protected religious freedom.

Scrutiny might be justified for other specific religious freedoms. For example, should the practice of animal sacrifice, as in the Santería religion practiced

> ⌐**[R]eligious freedom by necessity must have limits ...**⌐

in Florida, be banned, even though it is part of their religious beliefs and does not harm humans? The people in the City of Hialeah tried to ban this animal sacrifice, claiming that the practice created public health and safety risks for their citizens. If that were true, then these negative consequences would provide utilitarian support for banning the practice of animal sacrifice. But the city was inconsistent in continuing to allow a wide range of animal slaughtering and hunting, exposing their bias against Santería on religious grounds and their hypocrisy on public health and safety. When the U.S. Supreme Court considered this case, they sided with the Santería religion in permitting their religious practice of animal sacrifice.

Should the teaching of the religious doctrine of creationism be banned in taxpayer-supported public schools, even if it is part of the religious views of many students in that classroom? Such teaching would seem to violate the prohibition on establishment of a state religion. Those students who voluntarily wanted to attend church classes outside of school could study creationism as part of their exercise of freedom of religion. Imposing one and only one religion on others using the power of the state seems clearly to deny religious freedom.

Should the requirement for a photo ID on a driver's license be waived if the person seeking the license says that photographs of her without a veil violate her religious beliefs? Before 9/11, several states were flexible and waived this requirement, letting religious freedom prevail in an environment in which other residents did not seem to be at much risk. But after 9/11, states shifted their reasoning to put the potential harm to residents from masked terrorists first and foremost over this particular religious freedom. This is an example of the use of utilitarian reasoning to conclude that the potential unhappiness of all citizens from terrorists outweighs the unhappiness of the applicant denied the religious freedom to wear a veil in a driver's license photo ID.

In an age when many fear terrorism, the balancing of religious freedom for all with other human concerns is especially challenging, but the tools we have developed for other issues help with clarifying our reasoning.

Now that you have studied how various types of reasoning apply to the topics discussed, review Critical Thinking Table 7.1 to follow the process of examining an ethical claim on a related topic.

In CourseMate, listen to the audio summary of the chapter.

Matt Slocum/AP Images

Santería is practiced in much of the Caribbean, including Puerto Rico and parts of Florida. It originated with the Yoruba people of Africa, in what is known today as Nigeria. It is rich in symbolism and rituals.

Table 7.1 Critical Thinking Steps and Their Application in an Example

{ "Freedom of religion means that people should be allowed to say or do anything that is advocated by their religion." }

Critical Thinking Steps	Application
1. **Examine and clarify key terms and concepts.** AP Photo/Ng Han Guan • Look words up in a dictionary as a start if necessary. • Unravel or unpack the complexities and nuances of a central term, such as *justice*, *right*, or *good*.	• What counts as "religion" here? Should we only consider established religious sects or should we include anything that a person claims is his or her religion? If the latter, do we need to draw some boundaries for what should count as religion? • Is the term *advocated* sufficiently broad or too much so?
2. **Work through the meaning of the key terms and concepts to make sure you will use them consistently.** • Consider the ways the term can be used by including it in different sentences and contexts to zero in on the particular meaning you are after. • Ask yourself what words are potential synonyms for the concept. Do those capture everything you want to understand about that term?	• Would the terms *encouraged* and *required*, which are close in meaning to *advocated,* be more helpful in our argument? • What do we mean by "anything that is advocated"? Should this "anything" be limited to beliefs pertaining to reality and morality, whether or not recognized by an established religious group? Should this be limited to formal doctrines codified by that religious group? • Who is doing the allowing here? Are we only concerned with the power of the government? Do we also mean to include the power of social pressure or censure?
3. **Build premises and bring any assumptions to light.**  TIMOTHY A. CLARY/AFP/Getty Images/Newscom • Put together short and clear sentences to build each of your premises. • Think through what you may be taking for granted in your reasoning. What assumptions are you making? • Once you have identified assumptions, articulate them in your premise, so that your audience has the same understanding of a term or a concept as you.	The premises of the argument could be constructed as follows: (i) Freedom means being allowed to say or do anything one wants to say or do. (ii) Freedom should be absolute with regard to one's religious beliefs. CONCLUSION: Freedom of religion means that people should be allowed to say or do anything that is advocated by their religion.
4. **Test/Verify your premises.** • Now that you have stated your premises explicitly, do you want to stick with them? • Are you relying on premises drawn from unsubstantiated sources or from questionable authorities? • Are you consistent in your premises? Or are you appealing to different and inconsistent foundations in your reasoning? • Reformulate your premises if they have proven to be faulty.	Each of these premises should be examined. (i) "Anything" is very sweeping. Is this what we understand by "freedom"? Do we as a culture or a government put some restrictions on freedoms? Accepting this premise would require being satisfied with all of these issues. (ii) Do we ever permit absolute freedom, no matter what? If you do not accept all of these premises, then you will not accept the conclusion either. But if you do accept all of them, then you would find the conclusion valid and justified.

Critical Thinking Steps	Application
5. Confirm that the conclusions you draw are logical. Check for reliance on fallacies and correct any premise that you identify as relying on a fallacy.	This argument is especially vulnerable to criticism that it uses the fallacy of equivocation—that is, a key term is used in several different ways during an argument. In this case, equivocation applies especially regarding the words *freedom* and *religion*.

William James

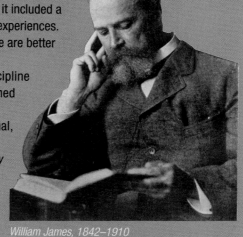

One of the United States's most distinguished philosophers, William James, taught for most of his career at Harvard University. He is known as a "pragmatist" who wrote widely on many issues. Pragmatism defies easy definition, but for James it included a belief in American practicality, especially that the truth is what works in our life experiences. James does not claim that pragmatism proves the existence of God, but that "we are better off" if we believe in those eternal claims.

His book *The Principles of Psychology* led to the development of the discipline of psychology in the twentieth century. For much of his career, James examined religion from a variety of perspectives. He sometimes thought religion should move in a scientific direction, but at other times he recognized a more spiritual, supernatural dimension to religion. His pragmatic views on religion can be found in his books *The Will to Believe and Other Essays in Popular Philosophy* (1897), *The Varieties of Religious Experience* (1902), and *Pragmatism* (1907). He rejected an absolutist version of the existence of God, but believed instead that religion was "pluralistic," depending on our individual experiences, which, of course, vary considerably. In turn, this recognition of pluralism necessitated tolerance of the religious views of others. James writes, "for each man to stay in his own [religious] experience, whate'er it be, and for others to tolerate him there, is surely best" (*Varieties*, Ch. 20).

William James, 1842–1910

CHAPTER 7 Case Study

Polygamy and Religious Freedom

When the territory of Utah sought to gain admission as a state to the United States, polygamy was widely practiced by members of the Mormon religion, formally known as the Church of Jesus Christ of Latter-day Saints. Indeed, church doctrine in the nineteenth century claimed that it was "the duty of male members" of the church to practice polygamy. However, Utah was required to ban this practice to become part of the United States.

President Abraham Lincoln signed into law a ban on bigamy in the territories in 1862, a law that was upheld by the U.S. Supreme Court in 1879 in *Reynolds v. United States*. The right to religious freedom, the Court said, did not extend to a right to engage in bigamy because it had long been considered "odious" in the Western world. The Court said the "innocent victims" of polygamy are "pure-minded women" and "innocent children" who are the "sufferers" of this practice.

(Continued)

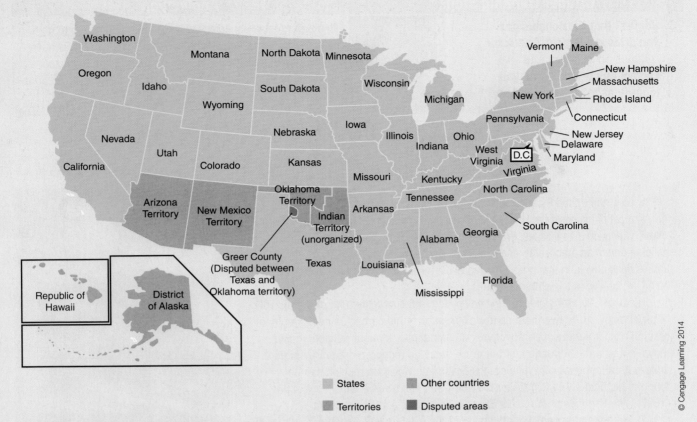

A map of the United States of America in 1896, after Utah was admitted into the Union.

Utah finally attained statehood in 1896 after including a ban on polygamy in the state constitution and after the Mormon Church enacted a policy change that it no longer advocated polygamy.

1. In the nineteenth century, the Mormons claimed polygamy to be an expression of their religious freedom, protected by the First Amendment to the U.S. Constitution. How does this claim by the Mormons support or not support the argument that all expressions of religious freedom should be protected? In your answer, consider the case of a religion that might hold that human sacrifice or peyote consumption is essential to its religious rituals. You might ponder whether these particular beliefs should be protected. You might then question whether every religion has a right to act on all of its beliefs, and if not, how you would distinguish among those beliefs that would be permissible.

2. Justice Antonin Scalia wrote in his dissent in the 2003 decision, *Lawrence v. Texas*, that striking down state laws restricting private sexual conduct between consenting adult homosexuals would likely lead to challenges to long-standing bans on polygamy. Does this seem like appropriate analogical reasoning? If homosexual conduct is protected as a private liberty right, should polygamy also be recognized as a right, quite independently of its religious elements?

3. In the nineteenth century, Mormon religious beliefs held that polygamy was an obligation to be met by male members of the church. If we objected to the particular requirement that this obligation was to be met by males specifically, would we no longer object if the requirement was that this obligation be met by both males and females?

4. Some legal immigrants to the United States come from countries in other parts of the world where polygamy is recognized and allowed as part of their religious beliefs. Should those immigrants be allowed to practice their religion with regard to polygamy once they immigrate?

For additional case studies, please see the CourseMate for this text.

Reading Excerpt: John Locke, *A Letter Concerning Toleration* (1689)

INTRODUCTION

The English philosopher John Locke urged the separation of church and state; in this and many other ways, Locke heavily influenced the Founding Fathers in the United States in drafting the U.S. Constitution. For Locke, the government has a defined realm of responsibility in protecting life, liberty, health, and property, but the government cannot force anyone to adopt any particular religious belief, at least not effectively. A major element of his argument for religious toleration is his view that no religion has the means to prove that it is "right" or "correct." It is not clear which religious views Locke followed in his own life, although he appears to have adopted some version of Protestantism as an adult. This excerpt, written in 1689, was translated from the Latin by William Popple.

John Locke, 1632–1704

Fine Art Images/SuperStock

QUESTIONS FOR REFLECTION

1. What is the goal of civil government, according to Locke? What are "civil interests"? What is the duty of the civil magistrate in that government? Are Locke's conclusions consistent with your own views of the role of government?

2. The power of civil government does not extend to the salvation of souls, Locke claims. What are his three reasons in support of this conclusion? Do you find each reason persuasive?

3. How does religion gain its power over people? Do you agree with Locke that civil government cannot effectively impose this power of religion on all its citizens?

4. What does Locke understand by a "church"? What is the most effective way to tie people to a certain religion?

READING

… The commonwealth seems to me to be a society of men constituted only for the procuring, preserving, and advancing of their own civil interests. Civil interests I call life, liberty, health, and indolency of body; and the possession of outward things, such as
5 money, lands, houses, furniture, and the like.

It is the duty of the civil magistrate, by the impartial execution of equal laws, to secure unto all the people in general and to every one of his subjects in particular the just possession of these things belonging to this life. If anyone presume to violate the laws of public
10 justice and equity, established for the preservation of those things, his presumption is to be checked by the fear of punishment, consisting of the deprivation or diminution of those civil interests, or goods, which otherwise he might and ought to enjoy. But seeing no man does willingly suffer himself to be punished by the deprivation of any
15 part of his goods, and much less of his liberty or life, therefore, is the magistrate armed with the force and strength of all his subjects, in order to the punishment of those that violate any other man's rights.

Now that the whole jurisdiction of the magistrate reaches only to these civil concernments, and that all civil power, right and
20 dominion, is bounded and confined to the only care of promoting these things; and that it neither can nor ought in any manner to be extended to the salvation of souls, these following considerations seem unto me abundantly to demonstrate.

First, because the care of souls is not committed to the civil
25 magistrate, any more than to other men. It is not committed unto him, I say, by God; because it appears not that God has ever given any such authority to one man over another as to compel anyone to his religion. Nor can any such power be vested in the magistrate by the consent of the people, because no man can so far abandon
30 the care of his own salvation as blindly to leave to the choice of any other, whether prince or subject, to prescribe to him what faith or worship he shall embrace. For no man can, if he would, conform his faith to the dictates of another. All the life and power of true religion consist in the inward and full persuasion of the mind; and faith is
35 not faith without believing. Whatever profession we make, to whatever outward worship we conform, if we are not fully satisfied in our own mind that the one is true and the other well pleasing unto God, such profession and such practice, far from being any furtherance, are indeed great obstacles to our salvation. For in this manner,
40 instead of expiating other sins by the exercise of religion, I say, in offering thus unto God Almighty such a worship as we esteem to be displeasing unto Him, we add unto the number of our other sins those also of hypocrisy and contempt of His Divine Majesty.

In the second place, the care of souls cannot belong to the
45 civil magistrate, because his power consists only in outward force; but true and saving religion consists in the inward persuasion of

In 1647 Locke went to Westminster School, in London. He was a King's Scholar—that is, part of a small group of boys who had the privilege of living in the school.

Roberto Herrett/Age Fotostock

the mind, without which nothing can be acceptable to God. And such is the nature of the understanding, that it cannot be compelled to the belief of anything by outward force. Confiscation of
50 estate, imprisonment, torments, nothing of that nature can have any such efficacy as to make men change the inward judgment that they have framed of things.

It may indeed be alleged that the magistrate may make use of arguments, and, thereby; draw the heterodox into the way of truth,
55 and procure their salvation. I grant it; but this is common to him with other men. In teaching, instructing, and redressing the erroneous by reason, he may certainly do what becomes any good man to do. Magistracy does not oblige him to put off either humanity or Christianity; but it is one thing to persuade, another to command;
60 one thing to press with arguments, another with penalties. This civil power alone has a right to do; to the other, goodwill is authority enough. Every man has commission to admonish, exhort, convince another of error, and, by reasoning, to draw him into truth; but to give laws, receive obedience, and compel with the sword, belongs
65 to none but the magistrate. And, upon this ground, I affirm that the magistrate's power extends not to the establishing of any articles of faith, or forms of worship, by the force of his laws. For laws are of no force at all without penalties, and penalties in this case are absolutely impertinent, because they are not proper to convince the
70 mind. Neither the profession of any articles of faith, nor the conformity to any outward form of worship (as has been already said), can be available to the salvation of souls, unless the truth of the one and the acceptableness of the other unto God be thoroughly believed by those that so profess and practice. But penalties are no way
75 capable to produce such belief. It is only light and evidence that can work a change in men's opinions; which light can in no manner proceed from corporal sufferings, or any other outward penalties.

In the third place, the care of the salvation of men's souls cannot belong to the magistrate; because, though the rigor of laws and
80 the force of penalties were capable to convince and change men's minds, yet would not that help at all to the salvation of their souls. For there being but one truth, one way to heaven, what hope is there that more men would be led into it if they had no rule but the religion of the court and were put under the necessity to quit the light of their
85 own reason, and oppose the dictates of their own consciences, and blindly to resign themselves up to the will of their governors and to the religion which either ignorance, ambition, or superstition had chanced to establish in the countries where they were born? In the variety and contradiction of opinions in religion, wherein the princes of the world
90 are as much divided as in their secular interests, the narrow way would be much straitened; one country alone would be in the right, and all the rest of the world put under an obligation of following their princes in the ways that lead to destruction; and that which heightens the absurdity, and very ill suits the notion of a Deity, men would owe
95 their eternal happiness or misery to the places of their nativity.

> " [T]he care of the salvation of men's souls cannot belong to the magistrate ... "

These considerations, to omit many others that might have been urged to the same purpose, seem unto me sufficient to conclude that all the power of civil government relates only to men's civil interests, is confined to the care of the things of this world,
100 and hath nothing to do with the world to come.

Let us now consider what a church is. A church, then, I take to be a voluntary society of men, joining themselves together of their own accord in order to make possible the public worshipping of God in such manner as they judge acceptable to Him, and
105 effectual to the salvation of their souls.

I say it is a free and voluntary society. Nobody is born a member of any church; otherwise the religion of parents would descend unto children by the same right of inheritance as their temporal estates, and everyone would hold his faith by the same tenure he does his
110 lands, than which nothing can be imagined more absurd. Thus, therefore, that matter stands. No man by nature is bound unto any particular church or sect, but everyone joins himself voluntarily to that society in which he believes he has found that profession and worship which is truly acceptable to God. The hope of salvation, as
115 it was the only cause of his entrance into that communion, so it can be the only reason of his stay there. For if afterwards he discover anything either erroneous in the doctrine or incongruous in the worship of that society to which he has joined himself, why should it not be as free for him to go out as it was to enter? No member of a
120 religious society can be tied with any other bonds but what proceed from the certain expectation of eternal life. A church, then, is a society of members voluntarily uniting to that end…

Reading Excerpt: Alexis de Tocqueville, *Democracy in America* (1835)

INTRODUCTION

Alexis de Tocqueville was a French aristocrat who traveled extensively in the United States in the 1830s as a young man and wrote about his observations in the well-known book *Democracy in America*. To this day, de Tocqueville's writing impresses political philosophers and historians, particularly because of the author's astute reflections on the then-young nation and the conditions that would later lead to the Civil War and other developments. When he visited, the First Amendment protecting the freedom of religion, as well as the prohibition on the establishment of a state religion, was included in the Bill of Rights, ratified decades earlier. These selections are from Ch. 17, "Principal Causes Maintaining the Democratic Republic." Originally published in 1835, they were translated from the French in 1899 by Henry Reeve.

Alexis de Tocqueville
(1805–1859)

Chasseriau, Theodore (1819–56)/The Art Gallery Collection/Alamy

QUESTIONS FOR REFLECTION

1. How are the "spirit of religion" and "spirit of freedom" united in the United States?

2. What is the importance of the separation of church and state, according to de Tocqueville? What role does it seem to play in the United States?

3. How does religion succeed in gaining its power? Over what areas of life is it most effective in exercising power? Over what areas of life do you believe it should exercise power?

READING

… Upon my arrival in the United States, the religious aspect of the country was the first thing that struck my attention; and the longer I stayed there the more did I perceive the great political consequences resulting from this state of things, to which I was
5 unaccustomed. In France I had almost always seen the spirit of religion and the spirit of freedom pursuing courses diametrically opposed to each other; but in America I found that they were intimately united, and that they reigned in common over the same country. My desire to discover the causes of this phenomenon
10 increased from day to day. In order to satisfy it I questioned the members of all the different sects; and I more especially sought the society of the clergy, who are the depositaries of the different persuasions, and who are more especially interested in their duration. As a member of the Roman Catholic Church I was
15 more particularly brought into contact with several of its priests, with whom I became intimately acquainted. To each of these men I expressed my astonishment and I explained my doubts; I found that they differed upon matters of detail alone; and that they mainly attributed the peaceful dominion of religion in their
20 country to the separation of Church and State. I do not hesitate to affirm that during my stay in America I did not meet with a single individual, of the clergy or of the laity, who was not of the same opinion upon this point.

The Central Synagogue in New York City.

Kord.com/Age Fotostock

Alexis de Tocqueville, *Democracy in America,* 1835, excerpts, adapted from English translation by Henry Reeve, 1899.

... Man alone, of all created beings, displays a natural contempt of existence, and yet a boundless desire to exist; he scorns life, but he dreads annihilation. These different feelings incessantly urge his soul to the contemplation of a future state, and religion directs his musings thither. Religion, then, is simply another form of hope; and it is no less natural to the human heart than hope itself. Men cannot abandon their religious faith without a kind of aberration of intellect, and a sort of violent distortion of their true natures; but they are invincibly brought back to more pious sentiments; for unbelief is an accident, and faith is the only permanent state of mankind. If we only consider religious institutions in a purely human point of view, they may be said to derive an inexhaustible element of strength from man himself, since they belong to one of the constituent principles of human nature.

I am aware that at certain times religion may strengthen this influence, which originates in itself, by the artificial power of the laws, and by the support of those temporal institutions which direct society. Religions, intimately united to the governments of the earth, have been known to exercise a sovereign authority derived from the twofold source of terror and of faith; but when a religion contracts an alliance of this nature, I do not hesitate to affirm that it commits the same error as a man who should sacrifice his future to his present welfare; and in obtaining a power to which it has no claim, it risks that authority which is rightfully its own. When a religion founds its empire upon the desire of immortality which lives in every human heart, it may aspire to universal dominion; but when it connects itself with a government, it must necessarily adopt maxims which are only applicable to certain nations. Thus, in forming an alliance with a political power, religion augments its authority over a few, and forfeits the hope of reigning over all.

As long as a religion rests upon those sentiments which are the consolation of all affliction, it may attract the affections of mankind. But if it be mixed up with the bitter passions of the world, it may be constrained to defend allies whom its interests, and not the principle of love, have given to it; or to repel as antagonists men who are still attached to its own spirit, however opposed they may be to the powers to which it is allied. The Church cannot share the temporal power of the State without being the object of a portion of that animosity which the latter excites.

The King Fahad mosque in Culver City in Los Angeles County.

EuroStyle Graphics/Alamy

The political powers which seem to be most firmly established have frequently no better guarantee for their duration than the opinions of a generation, the interests of the time, or the life of an individual. A law may modify the social condition which
70 seems to be most fixed and determinate; and with the social condition everything else must change. The powers of society are more or less fugitive, like the years which we spend upon the earth; they succeed each other with rapidity, like the fleeting cares of life; and no government has ever yet been founded
75 upon an invariable disposition of the human heart, or upon an imperishable interest.

As long as a religion is sustained by those feelings, propensities, and passions which are found to occur under the same forms, at all the different periods of history, it may defy the efforts
80 of time; or at least it can only be destroyed by another religion. But when religion clings to the interests of the world, it becomes almost as fragile a thing as the powers of earth. It is the only one of them all which can hope for immortality; but if it be connected with their ephemeral authority, it shares their fortunes, and may
85 fall with those transient passions which supported them for a day. The alliance which religion contracts with political powers must be onerous to itself; since it does not require their assistance to live, and by giving them its assistance to live, and by giving them its assistance it may be exposed to decay.
90 The danger which I have just pointed out always exists, but it is not always equally visible. In some ages governments seem to be imperishable; in others, the existence of society appears to be more precarious than the life of man. Some constitutions plunge the citizens into a lethargic somnolence, and others
95 rouse them to feverish excitement. When governments appear to be so strong, and laws so stable, men do not perceive the dangers which may accrue from a union of Church and State. When governments display so much weakness, and laws so much inconstancy, the danger is self-evident, but it is no longer
100 possible to avoid it; to be effectual, measures must be taken to discover its approach.

In proportion as a nation assumes a democratic condition of society, and as communities display democratic propensities, it becomes more and more dangerous to connect religion with
105 political institutions; for the time is coming when authority will be bandied from hand to hand, when political theories will succeed each other, and when men, laws, and constitutions will disappear, or be modified from day to day, and this, not for a season only, but unceasingly. Agitation and mutability are inherent in the nature of
110 democratic republics, just as stagnation and inertness are the law of absolute monarchies.

If the Americans, who change the head of the Government once in four years, who elect new legislators every two years, and renew the provincial officers every twelvemonth; if the Americans,
115 who have abandoned the political world to the attempts of innovators, had not placed religion beyond their reach, where could it abide in the ebb and flow of human opinions? where would that respect which belongs to it be paid, amidst the struggles of faction? And what would become of its immortality, in the midst of
120 perpetual decay? The American clergy were the first to perceive this truth, and to act in conformity with it. They saw that they must renounce their religious influence, if they were to strive for political power; and they chose to give up the support of the State, rather than to share its vicissitudes.
125 In America, religion is perhaps less powerful than it has been at certain periods in the history of certain peoples; but its influence is more lasting. It restricts itself to its own resources, but of those none can deprive it: its circle is limited to certain principles, but those principles are entirely its own, and under its undisputed
130 control.

… [I]f the unbeliever does not admit religion to be true, he still considers it useful. Regarding religious institutions in a human point of view, he acknowledges their influence upon manners and legislation. He admits that they may serve to make
135 men live in peace with one another, and to prepare them gently for the hour of death. He regrets the faith which he has lost; and as he is deprived of a treasure which he has learned to estimate at its full value, he scruples to take it from those who still possess it.

> **[I]f the unbeliever does not admit religion to be true, he still considers it useful.**

140 On the other hand, those who continue to believe are not afraid openly to avow their faith. They look upon those who do not share their persuasion as more worthy of pity than of opposition; and they are aware that to acquire the esteem of the unbelieving, they are not obliged to follow their example. They are hostile to no
145 one in the world; and as they do not consider the society in which they live as an arena in which religion is bound to face its thousand deadly foes, they love their contemporaries, whilst they condemn their weaknesses and lament their errors.…

USE THE TOOLS.

- Rip out the Review Cards in the back of your book to study.

Or Visit CourseMate to:

- Read, search, highlight, and take notes in the Interactive eBook
- Review Flashcards (Print or Online) to master key terms
- Test yourself with Auto-Graded Quizzes
- Bring concepts to life with Games, Videos, and Animations!

Go to CourseMate for (**ETHICS**) to begin using these tools. Access at **www.cengagebrain.com**

Complete the Speak Up survey in CourseMate at **www.cengagebrain.com**

f Follow us at **www.facebook.com/4ltrpress**

THINKING IT THROUGH 3

What constitutes cheating?

Precision in reasoning to reach justifiable conclusions requires us to pursue in more depth and detail the meanings of the terms we identified in the **Thinking It Through 2** module. The process outlined here shows why this focus on the meaning of key terms is the foundation of good reasoning. To attain clarity and make a persuasive argument, we must rely on clear and definite notions of what we are talking about.

> **Step II. Work through the meaning of the key terms and concepts to make sure you will use them consistently.**
>
> • Consider the ways the term can be used by including it in different sentences and contexts to zero in on the particular meaning you are after.
>
> • Ask yourself what words are potential synonyms for the concept. Do those capture everything you want to understand about that term?

1. Consider the ways the term can be used by including it in different sentences and contexts to zero in on the particular meaning you are after.

For each term given, think of the many different ways you might use it in ordinary conversations.

1a. Cheating.

• **"She broke up with him because he was cheating on her."**
We might assume here that a girlfriend broke up with her boyfriend because he engaged romantically with someone else. Dishonesty or fraud is involved if they had a commitment to be exclusive. Fraud is an element of our original claim concerning cheating in school. But the evidence showing cheating took place or what constitutes proof of cheating would be different here from the evidence for cheating in college.

• **"She didn't lose any weight on that fad diet because she cheated constantly."**
According to this statement, a commitment to staying on a diet is broken by failing to adhere to its requirements. But cheating does not seem as much

like fraud here as it does in the case of school cheating because the consequences involve the self, whereas they involve other people when cheating takes place in college. In an educational setting, we enter a classroom with an unspoken commitment to play by the rules of the college and perform our own work as required—for example, to write our own papers and to respond to test questions on the strength of our studies. Thus, the unspoken assumption is that we do this work without cheating. This example uncovers a new element, namely, the breaking of agreements to play by the rules.

• **"He cheated death by surviving many years, despite a diagnosis of terminal cancer and a prediction that he would only live a few more months."**
Here, he seems to be cheating a thing, death.

The fraud or trickery involved seems to be violating the prediction of that death in a few months—a fraud accomplished by living many years. But cheating here means breaking or violating an expectation that a nonfeeling entity, "death," had, and thus perhaps does not amount so clearly to a fraud as in the other examples. But an expectation from a professional—the doctor who made the diagnosis and prediction of

> **STRATEGY:**
> Do not limit yourself to a specific context. For example, here social interactions and personal life are considered, instead of just the college studies framework.

life expectancy—is violated. In the field of education, instructors prepare for class diligently to impart learning to their students and aim to grade fairly by comparing the work and merit of all the class's students. Thus, they expect that all students will do their best and play by the rules, and cheating violates those expectations.

1b. Acceptable

- **"His work for me as a mason was acceptable, but I would not hire him again."**
  This use seems to share the meaning we found previously: "satisfactory or adequate, but not particularly praiseworthy." In this statement, it is understood that adequacy alone meant the mason would not be hired again, specifically because our expectations are higher. In our case, is acceptable conduct in college good enough or will professors and future employers want something more than that?

What could result from cheating when building the walls of a house?

- **"She opted for the pass-fail option for that course, in which a 'pass' means that her work was acceptable and that was good enough for her to graduate."**
  We again seem to have a set of standards or measures for assessing quality. "Acceptable" is better than failing and good enough, but not the same as an A in that course. So this shares the sense, identified in our original ethical claim, of being just slightly better than neutral but still not very good.

- **"It is no longer acceptable to discuss women's rights as separate from human rights."**
  In her pronouncement at a conference on human rights in China, Hillary Rodham Clinton does not seem to be appealing to a measuring rule of degrees, but a standard of either–or. Either something is acceptable or it is not, and she is claiming that the separate discussion is no longer acceptable. This applies to cheating: it is an either–or question. Either it is okay or it is not. There should be no shadings of ethical standards in the case of cheating.

1c. Caught

- **"He was caught red-handed stealing the watch by the security cameras."**
  Catching someone does not necessarily require physically incapacitating them. The camera captured an image that constituted proof of the theft. For cheating, getting caught does not require physical contact. A professor or student sees a student use a crib sheet for instance. Or a software program detects plagiarism sources in a term paper.

- **"She was caught in a web of deceit that destroyed her career."**
  This person seems like a victim of the wrongful, dishonest actions of others, the passive recipient of these deeds. In a way, are students who cheat in their studies passive victims? This usage does not seem to fit this situation. The examination of this term helps highlight the fact that in our ethical claim the person cheating is behaving consciously, purposefully, and actively.

{ **ASK YOURSELF:** Are there other uses worth exploring? How do these different sentence uses help clarify my thoughts? How do they help me zero in on shades of meaning that matter? }

Getting "caught" in the real world can have dire consequences.

2. Ask yourself what words are potential synonyms for the concept. Do those capture everything you want to understand about that term?

Looking for synonyms further helps to peel back the layers of meaning of these central concepts. A synonym is a word that is equivalent to another in meaning and that could be substituted in a sentence without altering that meaning. Note that an antonym is a word that is the opposite of the term in question.

A standard reference work for identifying possible synonyms is called a thesaurus. The most famous is Roget's *International Thesaurus*. Start by looking up the term in question in the index in the back of the book; this will refer you to several sections in the main body of the text and a wide range of possible synonyms. Some word-processing programs include a thesaurus. These are a good starting point for identifying synonyms, but consider whether you can find additional synonyms from your own usage.

The following examples show what a search for synonyms can yield.

- **Cheating.** Synonyms that seem to apply here include faking, falsifying, counterfeiting, forging, defrauding, chiseling, pretending, and bluffing. All seem to include the negative connotation of claiming to be something one is not. All denote sneakiness or a need to hide. If we want to make sure people continue trusting us, if we care about our reputations, we would want to distance ourselves from actions that could be qualified as these terms suggest. These synonyms capture elements of cheating that add further nuance to our key term.

STRATEGY:

- Compare and contrast various meanings. Cast out those that do not appear to fit.

- In searching for synonyms, take a careful look at antonyms. They might help clarify subtleties.

- **Acceptable.** Some synonyms, such as pleasing, agreeable, attractive, worthy, desirable, and enviable, seem to include a dimension of praiseworthiness. But, as we came to recognize in our preceding investigation, the sense of this word as understood in our claim indicates a lukewarm assessment, as captured by the following other synonyms: not objectionable, eligible, admissible, tolerable, satisfactory, and qualified.

- **Caught.** Such synonyms as wedged, stranded, and stuck do not capture the sense meant in our central ethical statement because they suggest an innocent passivity by the person caught. Synonyms that seem to make sense here include held and trapped because they suggest that another person succeeded in identifying wrongdoing and holding the wrongdoer in custody. In the context of our claim, although cheaters in college may not find themselves in jail, they would likely suffer consequences that would curtail their freedom in different ways.

ASK YOURSELF: How do these different synonyms shed light on the ethical claim I am examining? Which are most relevant to that claim?

Dictionaries and thesauruses offer a wealth of information to their users. They open windows into worlds of knowledge previously unknown to us.

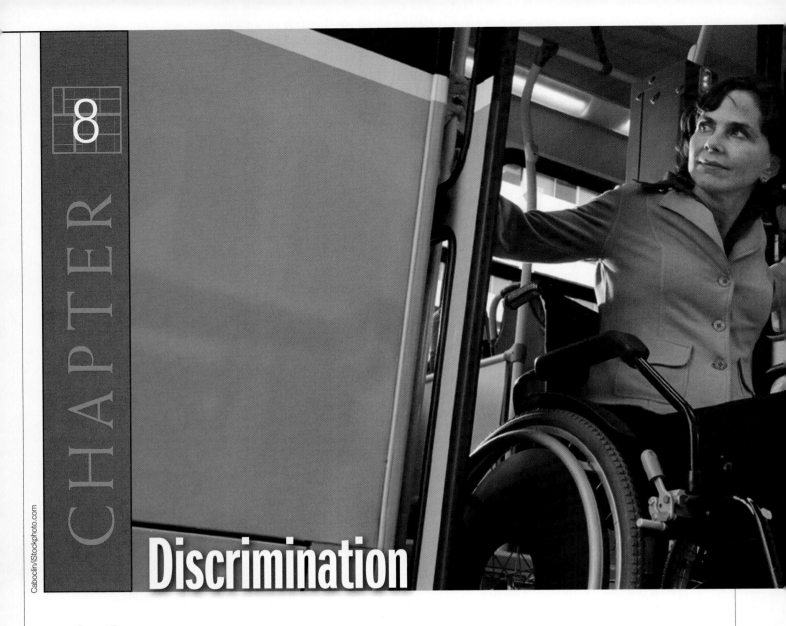

CHAPTER 8

Discrimination

"I have a dream that one day this nation will rise up and live out the true meaning of its creed: 'We hold these truths to be self-evident: that all men are created equal.'"

—Martin Luther King, Jr.,
August 28, 1963

"Prejudice, not being founded on reason, cannot be removed by argument."

—attributed to Samuel Johnson,
eighteenth century

Not all discrimination is wrong. That might seem shocking to say, but if we consider the broad nature of the term *discrimination*, it makes sense. We praise people with "discriminating taste." We make distinctions all the time in all areas of life that are quite ethical and legitimate. This is because discrimination is really just about identifying differences in things. We might distinguish good wine from poor wine, a good car from a lemon, or a well-built home from a shoddily constructed one.

So when we talk about unethical discrimination or illegal discrimination, we are concerned with a certain type of discrimination based on irrelevant or inappropriate criteria for making decisions. Our focus in this chapter will be these unethical forms of discrimination and how we should go about examining and analyzing them. You might then make your own decisions about things to do in response to some forms of unethical discrimination, but it is beyond the scope of this chapter to dictate what those things should be.

Overview

In this chapter, we will consider different forms of discrimination, especially concerning race, gender, disability, and sexual orientation. We will once again use major philosophical frameworks to consider how those reasoning tools help us work through these contentious issues. Work by two major writers, Mary Wollstonecraft and Frederick Douglass, will be examined for their early insights on the importance of respecting the rights of all people, regardless of gender or race.

What do you think?

All discrimination is wrong, regardless of the motives or goals.

Strongly Disagree						Strongly Agree
1	2	3	4	5	6	7

8-1 THE NATURE OF DISCRIMINATION

Issues related to discrimination typically arise when decisions are being made in educational or employment settings, where so much is at stake in every person's life and their ability to pursue their dreams and earn a good living.

If a prestigious university were to announce that every applicant whose parents donated a million dollars to the building fund would be admitted, regardless of their grades and test scores, the university is making a distinction between the wealthy and the not-wealthy in its admissions decisions. If the university announced that the children of its own graduates would be admitted, regardless of their grades and test scores, the university is again making a distinction between types of applicants based on factors other than sheer merit, at least as measured by grades and test scores. And yet many universities, especially private schools, acknowledge that they follow these practices in their admission decisions. Is this fair? Should it be illegal? Or does this policy result in providing the institution with sufficient funding to extend its services to candidates with modest means but high grades?

Continuing debates about discrimination typically center on what some perceive as unfair distinctions and favoritism based on race or gender, and that is our main focus in this chapter. In the philosophical, legal, and public policy debates, we can identify specific ways of framing the issue.

8-1a Education

First, we can ask how to distinguish between relevant characteristics in applying for educational institutions and irrelevant ones. Characteristics typically recognized as relevant in education admissions are merit, as measured by test scores, school grades, and demonstrated aptitudes for success. But controversy swirls around each of these. Standardized tests (such as the Scholastic Aptitude Test or the American College Test) have long been accused of bias that favors certain races and classes, although those testing companies say they have made major efforts to eliminate these biases. Another controversy concerns whether wealthy students who can afford special tutoring seem to unfairly achieve higher scores, whereas poor students without these benefits suffer in comparison. The award of letter grades does not seem to be consistent and fair throughout the nation. In other words, a 4.0 average

Alastair Balderstone/Alamy

Should admission to an ivy league school, such as Harvard University, be based on academic merit only? If so, how should merit be determined?

does not seem to mean the same thing at every high school. If a 4.0 at some high schools might only earn a 3.0 at others, then how should colleges determine what a grade point really means in deciding whom to admit? Test scores and grades are not the only measures of achievement and aptitudes for success. References from teachers and writing samples add to the application materials worth considering, but they do not appear utterly objective and consistent either.

Criteria for admission that are more controversial are characteristics that do not seem to measure academic merit, such as wealth or being the child of a graduate of that college or university. Many schools grant special admissions preference to successful athletes, regardless of grades and test scores. Some schools say they give comparable preference to talented artists, musicians, painters, and novelists. The experiences of veterans, especially of recent wars in Iraq and Afghanistan, are counted toward the totality of criteria in selecting candidates for admission at some schools. In other words, many factors have been acknowledged by colleges and universities in addition to or in place of pure academic merit.

When certain groups by race or gender have been underrepresented at a university, affirmative action advocates have urged that the institution has an interest and even a duty in ensuring increased representation of these groups. How this increased representation should occur is itself controversial. A college might simply make more recruitment efforts while using consistent academic standards, but casting a wider "net" to include more people in the applicant pool, especially more people of diverse races and gender. More aggressive types of policies amount to affirmative action or what some call preferential admissions. But insisting on a one-size-fits-all requirement for grade point average and test scores seems unrealistic and unfair. For example, if wealthy parents in Beverly Hills can afford the very best schools and private tutoring to help raise their children's SAT scores, these children seem to have an unfair advantage over children from impoverished inner-city schools when it comes to gaining admission to the most competitive universities. Colleges might then look at the totality of an applicant's strength. This might include "overcoming unusual challenges," which might be an impoverished childhood or racial segregation, which explain somewhat lower test scores.

Somewhat different issues arise with regard to persons with disabilities. Such individuals, admitted on

> **Under the Americans with Disabilities Act (ADA) of 1990, schools are now required to make reasonable accommodations for students with disabilities.**

the basis of high grades, might find it difficult to succeed in school without some extra assistance. This might take the form of ramps to be able to enter classroom buildings or sign language translators to enable them to comprehend what is being said in a lecture hall. Under the Americans with Disabilities Act (ADA) of 1990, schools are now required to make reasonable accommodations for students with disabilities. But critics of ADA complain that it goes too far in providing assistance that amounts to an unfair advantage for success in the classroom. For example, it might be objected that providing extra time for test completion for students with Attention Deficit Disorder is unfair to other students without this disability.

8-1b Employment

In an employment setting, hiring criteria are important to consider. As with education, we need to ask what characteristics are relevant in hiring decisions and which ones are not. This question in turn leads to wondering what specific skills, training, or education may be required to perform a particular job. For example, in the beginning of the U.S. space program in the 1960s, only men were selected as astronauts, in part because NASA required that all astronauts first be test pilots in the Air Force, which women were not allowed to be. As the space program developed, however, it became clear that test-pilot skills and experience were not essential in performing an astronaut's duties, and that being an experienced scientist or engineer was equally, or even more, necessary for at least some astronauts. The first female astronaut was Sally Ride, who was a shuttle crew member in 1983. She held a Ph.D. in physics from Stanford University and had never been a test pilot.

Another example concerns the need for a group of workers to function well as a team. Here the questions include whether there are situations when "unit cohesion" and whether a person will fit in well are relevant employment requirements. In 1948, when President Harry Truman issued an executive order to desegregate the U.S. military, the argument that white and black soldiers could not maintain unit cohesion was raised by critics of this desegregation initiative. The same argument was raised more recently against allowing openly homosexual soldiers to serve in the military. The "don't ask don't tell" policy in place since 1993 relied on the belief that the presence of openly homosexual soldiers would weaken military cohesion. This policy was abolished in 2011. Today, women are banned from combat operations for similar reasons, although that is increasingly under scrutiny.

Societies have gone through a long process of looking closely at genuinely relevant job requirements to gradually break down old biases against certain groups, and surely more need to be reexamined. In a legal realm, these legal requirements are typically referred to as "bona fide occupational qualifications," but the demands are just as important in an ethical realm. As the examples given show, historically in societies, types of discrimination seem to take root for various reasons. These then come to be questioned when they have an adverse impact on the overall development of a given society. To

look out for its continued welfare, a society might consequently implement measures to counteract these negative effects.

A more controversial form of affirmative action occurs when a certain group has been historically excluded from certain professions and the government orders the use of policies to help give access to these jobs to more members of that excluded group. Affirmative action is not the same thing as "preferential treatment," although critics often allege that they are the same. Positive steps must be taken to recruit and give serious consideration to persons who meet the legitimate qualifications for a job. This does not mean that unqualified persons must be hired or promoted. In some contexts in which there has been an explicit policy of excluding certain races or genders, courts sometimes issue orders to aim for certain "goals" in hiring over a long period of time. Goals are not the same as "quotas," however, although critics again often allege that they are the same. With these hot-button issues, language can become a misleading weapon to turn people against policies they might otherwise support.

The situation of the disabled raises different issues. Under the ADA, employers must make reasonable accommodations for the disabled to be able to carry out the job requirements. Exactly what should count as reasonable accommodations is the subject of continuing debate.

8-1c Housing and Credit

Access to housing and credit also affects a person's ability to pursue his or her dreams and earn a good living. In recent decades, many government laws and programs have aimed at addressing discrimination in these areas—particularly as it has affected significant groups such as women and racial minorities. Only a few decades ago, women were routinely denied credit because it was assumed they would get married and drop out of the workforce, if they were ever employed at all. Now those decisions are made based on the likelihood that a woman can repay her debts, that is, by the same measures used for men. Discrimination continues to affect these groups today, but a call for the application of affirmative action measures has not been made as it has in education and employment.

Discrimination exists in almost every area of life. Some of it is justified, some of it not. The challenge in all these areas is to identify relevant criteria that are fair and based on appropriate decision making.

In CourseMate, watch a video and take the quiz.

Astronauts Memorial Foundation/HO/AP Photos

The Supreme Court decision in *Brown v. Board of Education* in 1954 mandated desegregation in public K–12 education and contributed to the continuing decline of discrimination against African Americans in the United States. The process of reversing laws that kept African Americans from enjoying the same opportunities as white Americans enabled many blacks to flourish. For example, Robert H. Lawrence Jr. officially became an astronaut on June 10, 1967, and was the first African American astronaut.

8-2 PHILOSOPHICAL APPROACHES FOR ANALYZING DISCRIMINATION

In analyzing the ethics of discrimination of all kinds, familiar philosophical theories will be helpful. Debates typically pit the human rights of individuals to be treated fairly against the consequences of practices in hiring or education, for example, on society. This discussion amounts to an analysis of these questions using the Kantian principle of the dignity and autonomy of persons or the utilitarian principle of the greatest happiness for the greatest number.

According to the Kantian approach, every person has a right to be treated with dignity and respect, and their autonomy is to be recognized. So, in hiring, we can argue that we should be treated with respect for our actual abilities and qualifications and not be excluded for irrelevant reasons and rationalizations that have nothing to do with our qualifications. Therefore, if I am rejected for a job solely because I happen to be female, African American, or in need of a wheelchair for mobility, it means that the employer is not respecting the full range of my abilities in considering me for the job. I simply want to be treated fairly, that is, by the same job-related standards applied appropriately to everyone else.

A utilitarian approach might end up with the same conclusions in many cases, but the reasoning would be different. The utilitarian would look at the results for different choices. If we make hiring decisions based on relevant qualifications and not on irrelevant preferences, the good results would be many. The employer would benefit from more effective work from the new employee. Current employees would benefit from work being performed better and more efficiently by new coworkers. Future employees would benefit from knowing that obtaining relevant qualifications will help them get jobs in the future.

In CourseMate, apply what you've learned to the real-life scenario in the simulation.

In CourseMate, practice what you learned by taking the chapter quiz.

8-3 APPLICATIONS TO CONTEMPORARY ISSUES

Affirmative action programs originated in the 1970s and remain highly contentious today. With regard to affirmative action programs in education and employment, both types of reasoning explored in the prior section can be found in philosophical debates, as well as in the reasoning of courts called on to examine these programs. From a Kantian perspective, we might insist that justice and equity to make up for past wrongs justifies preferential hiring now for groups that have been excluded in the past. In other words, past injustice is remedied by being given that job now and restoring our respect for the dignity of that entire group of persons. This argument seems weak because it seeks to redress a grievance affecting individuals in the past by taking action benefitting individuals in the present who were not directly affected by this discrimination, as critics of the program charge. These opponents of affirmative action are citing Kantian principles when they say that the person who wants a job now should not be denied their rights because

> [I]n hiring, we can argue that we should be treated with **respect for our actual abilities and qualifications ...**

The advent of technology has taken away the advantage that great physical strength gives a person in performing certain tasks, such as lifting heavy loads.

Cathy Yeulet/Photos.com

Joseph Schwartz/CORBIS

The Jim Crow laws were state and local laws enacted in the United States between 1876 and 1965. They imposed racial segregation in public facilities in Southern states, using a "separate but equal" status for black Americans.

others discriminated against other persons in that group in the past.

Utilitarian reasoning is also prominent in the affirmative action debates. Supporters argue that the benefits, to society as a whole, of bringing previously excluded groups into certain professions should be paramount. If African Americans were systematically excluded from law schools and medical schools (as they were for much of our history), it would benefit society as a whole to get an infusion of members of those groups into these professions to better serve these minority communities, or so that argument goes. The profession itself also would benefit from an influx of different points of view, experiences, and even familiarity with group-specific conditions or disorders, as could, ultimately, the wider community. Here, good consequences are said to outweigh any individual rights that might seem trampled upon.

But critics of affirmative action also cite utilitarian arguments. They are troubled that insufficiently qualified or unqualified people might be admitted to competitive programs, resulting

> **Enabling the disabled to participate in education and employment has beneficial results for disabled persons and also for society at large ...**

in poor performance in school and later in their careers. They worry that beneficiaries of affirmative action will suffer in the long run by being "branded" as unqualified. They cite the corrosive effects of making decisions based on something other than pure merit.

As mentioned, the legal reasoning of courts considering various discrimination and affirmative action cases typically uses both Kantian appeals to individual human rights and utilitarian arguments. In one of the most famous cases concerning affirmative action, *Regents of the University of California v. Bakke* (1978), Allan Bakke was denied admission to the medical school at the University of California, Davis. He argued that if he had been a member of certain underrepresented racial groups, which were held to different standards for admission tests and grades, he would have met the threshold for admission. The U.S. Supreme Court considered several utilitarian arguments presented by the university, especially the argument that society would benefit from more minority physicians. The Court said that those benefits to society did not override Mr. Bakke's individual rights and ordered that he be admitted. But the Court also said that having diverse classrooms was a worthwhile consequence of affirmative action programs for all students, so it was acceptable for universities to "take race into account," so long as race did not function as an absolute quota or barrier for anyone. Thus, the Court used both what we have called Kantian reasoning and consequentialist reasoning to reach its conclusions. These basic holdings were reaffirmed by the Court in 2003 in the decision for *Grutter v. Bollinger*, although they remain controversial to this day.

In addition to affirmative action, one of the more contentious areas today in discrimination debates concerns the rights of the disabled and the obligations of society to make accommodations for those disabilities in different settings. Here again, it is helpful to use both Kantian and utilitarian reasoning to more carefully examine the viewpoints. The rights of individuals to be treated with dignity and respect seem to dictate that we make such accommodations as ramps for persons needing wheelchairs, assistance for persons with hearing problems, and special computers to enable the blind to work at certain jobs. A utilitarian approach considers different factors. Enabling the disabled to participate in education and employment has beneficial results for disabled persons and also for society at large in making it possible for them to earn a living, support themselves, and avoid the need for public assistance. The consequentialist approach

also looks at the economic cost to society of providing that assistance and balances the results of the different alternatives.

Now that you have studied how various types of reasoning apply to the topics discussed, review Critical Thinking Table 8.1 to follow the process of examining an ethical claim on a related topic.

In CourseMate, listen to the audio summary of the chapter.

Table 8.1 Critical Thinking Steps and Their Application in an Example

{ "If we really believe in equal opportunity for all, then we should no longer consider race or gender in hiring or higher education admissions." }

Critical Thinking Steps	Application
1. Examine and clarify key terms and concepts. • Look words up in a dictionary as a start if necessary. • Unravel or unpack the complexities and nuances of a central term, such as *justice*, *right*, or *good*.	• What do we understand as "equal opportunity"? Does that mean we should all be treated exactly the same, regardless of our differences in intellectual and other abilities? • If we are not to be treated in the same way, can we be treated in a comparable way? Is that a better way of making sense of equal opportunity? • If we no longer consider race or gender, what should we consider when making decisions about employment and education?
2. Work through the meaning of the key terms and concepts to make sure you will use them consistently. • Consider the ways the term can be used by including it in different sentences and contexts to zero in on the particular meaning you are after. • Ask yourself what words are potential synonyms for the concept. Do those capture everything you want to understand about that term?	• Should equal opportunity be measured only in terms of the level playing field when we apply for education or employment? • What should be included in assessing that level playing field? Can we compare all life experiences and schooling? If not, what are the measures of a level playing field? • Should we also measure it in terms of results and outcome to test whether that opportunity was really equal?
3. Build premises and bring any assumptions to light. • Put together short and clear sentences to build each of your premises. • Think through what you may be taking for granted in your reasoning. What assumptions are you making? • Once you have identified assumptions, articulate them in your premise, so that your audience has the same understanding of a term or a concept as you.	The premises of the argument could be constructed as follows: (i) Equal opportunity means that only relevant characteristics of merit should be considered in employment and education. (ii) Race and gender are not relevant characteristics in employment and education. CONCLUSION: Equal opportunity means that race and gender should not be considered in employment or education.

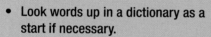
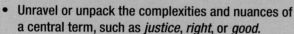

(Continued)

Table 8.1 Continued

Critical Thinking Steps	Application
4. Test/Verify your premises. • Now that you have stated your premises explicitly, do you want to stick with them? • Are you relying on premises drawn from unsubstantiated sources or from questionable authorities? • Are you consistent in your premises? Or are you appealing to different and inconsistent foundations in your reasoning? • Reformulate your premises if they have proven to be faulty.	Each of these premises should be examined. (i) Is it always clear what counts as merit in decisions concerning employment and education? Are we sure we want to eliminate all consideration of good consequences in these decisions, such as giving somebody from a deprived background an extra chance? (ii) Are there situations in which race and gender are relevant in employment and education situations? Is providing a diverse classroom experience relevant to all students and thus sometimes a justification for racial and gender diversity? If we are trying to sell our products to a certain market identified by race or gender, is it appropriate to try to hire people who can communicate effectively with those groups? If you do not accept all of these premises, then you will not accept the conclusion either. But if you do accept all of them, then you would find the conclusion valid and justified.
5. Confirm that the conclusions you draw are logical. Check for reliance on fallacies and correct any premise that you identify as relying on a fallacy.  Joseph Schwartz/CORBIS	This argument is especially vulnerable to criticism as the fallacy of equivocation, especially regarding the words *merit* and *equal*. This fallacy relies on shifting between differing meanings for the same term. Merit might sometimes be used as shorthand for *academic merit*, but in other cases as shorthand for *deserving for some reason*, including military service or athletic talent. *Equal* is sometimes used as *identical* and sometimes used as *comparable*.

Bernard Boxill

Bernard Romaric Boxill is the Pardue Professor of Philosophy at the University of North Carolina at Chapel Hill, where he has taught since 1991. One of several distinguished African American philosophers working today, he has published extensively on issues of race, racism, and social justice. He received his Ph.D. in philosophy from UCLA in 1971, after majoring in mathematics at La Salle College.

Boxill rejects a goal of some that we should be a color-blind society. He has argued that giving special consideration to racial minorities in employment and education can be justified, especially if educating black lawyers and doctors means, for example, that more will be available to serve those communities. He thus relies on a utilitarian approach and rejects a purely egalitarian principle of selection that decisions should be made solely on a color-blind basis of pure merit, however that is understood. His books on this issue include *Race and Racism* (2001) and *Blacks and Social Justice* (1984, 1992), as well as numerous journal articles and chapters in various collections.

Bernard Boxill (1937–)

The University of North Carolina at Chapel Hill

CHAPTER 8 Case Study

Reparations for Groups Held in Slavery

Reparations are typically damages paid to its victims by the losing party in a war, but it can more generally refer to compensation for a wrong done to a person or a group. In 1988, the United States Congress agreed to pay $20,000 each to more than 82,000 Japanese Americans (or their heirs) who were wrongly interned during World War II, a conflict that had ended over four decades earlier.

Several African American leaders in recent years have argued that the United States also should pay reparations to the descendants of slaves freed during the Civil War, which ended in 1865. The National Coalition of Blacks for Reparations in America was established in 1987 to pursue such reparations. These would not necessarily involve cash payments to the descendants of slaves, but rather a wide range of social programs and recognition of the legacy of slavery in the United States, Charles J. Ogletree, the Jesse Climenko Professor of Law at Harvard University, is cochair of the Reparations Coordinating Committee, which is pursuing legal avenues to obtain reparations for African Americans. Professor Ogletree and his organization urge that the U.S. government establish a trust fund that would assist the poorest members of the group descending from slaves to overcome the legacy of slavery and Jim Crow (the racial segregation laws in the states of the old Confederacy after the Civil War).

Reparations also have been sought for violence, as well as destruction of property of African Americans; lawsuits have not been successful because of the statute of limitations, which bars recovery after a certain amount of time. For example, in 1898, sixty African American residents of Wilmington, North Carolina, were murdered by white supremacists and thousands more were driven from the city. In 1921, a race riot in Tulsa, Oklahoma, resulted in the deaths of as many as 300 black residents, and more than 1,000 homes in their community were burned to the ground. Although a 2001 report commissioned by the state legislature concluded that the damage was the fault of white mob violence, assisted by the Tulsa police, no damages were ever paid because of the passage of too much time since the incident.

Some prominent African American intellectuals have opposed reparation payments on the grounds that many governmental programs, such as affirmative action, have already benefitted the descendants of slaves and no further efforts are needed to enable blacks to compete fairly with whites. These critics include John H. McWhorter, a Senior Fellow at the Manhattan Institute, and Glen C. Loury, Professor of Economics at Boston University.

1. Granted that the institution of slavery in the United States before the end of the Civil War was an atrocious violation of human rights, what reparations should be paid now, if any, to descendants of those slaves? How would we identify the persons deserving of those reparations today? Who are the wrongdoers who should pay? Are affirmative action programs and other social action efforts sufficient as compensation?

2. The victims of the Holocaust during World War II, their descendants, and persons forced into slave labor by the Nazis have received substantial reparations from the current government of Germany, as well as corporations that used that slave labor. Is this reparation justified? How is this similar to and different from reparations sought by descendants of African slaves in the United States?

3. Many immigrant groups have suffered blatant discrimination in the history of the United States. Are they deserving of reparations? How should we decide which groups and individual persons are deserving and by what criteria?

For additional case studies, please see the CourseMate for this text.

The Art Archive/Alamy Limited

President Franklin D. Roosevelt's Executive Order 9066, issued February 19, 1942, authorized the relocation and internment of some 110,000 Japanese Americans and Japanese who resided on the west coast of the United States. On January 2, 1945, the exclusion order was rescinded and internees were able to start leaving the camps.

Reading Excerpt: Mary Wollstonecraft, *A Vindication of the Rights of Woman* (1792)

INTRODUCTION

Mary Wollstonecraft's *A Vindication of the Rights of Woman*, published in England in 1792, is recognized as the first major feminist treatise. She wrote and published broadly on moral and political philosophy, not just women's issues. Raised in a chaotic family environment and lacking in formal education, she read widely and traveled extensively as an adult through Scandinavia, Portugal, and France. She urged that with rights for women came responsibilities, and she hoped that women would achieve full citizenship. The excerpt here is from Chapter XIII, the final chapter of her book, on "Concluding Reflections on the Moral Improvement That a Revolution in Female Manners Might Naturally Be Expected to Produce."

Mary Wollstonecraft
(1759–1798)

QUESTIONS FOR REFLECTION

1. What is the role of reason and education in the pursuit of virtue and liberty? How have women been held back by their lack of education? Do Wollstonecraft's observations about education still apply today more than two centuries later?

2. What similarities does Wollstonecraft note between women and oppressed social groups in general? What does she see as the path to their respective improvements in life?

3. What should we expect from women if they are emancipated politically? Do you agree that women cannot be expected to be virtuous if they are restrained politically and not educated? What form of education would you recommend to address this?

READING

... Moralists have unanimously agreed, that unless virtue be nursed by liberty, it will never attain due strength—and what they say of man I extend to mankind, insisting that in all cases morals must be fixed on immutable principles; and, that the being cannot
5 be termed rational or virtuous, who obeys any authority, but that of reason.

> **❝** *[T]he being cannot be termed rational or virtuous, who obeys any authority, but that of reason.* **❞**

To render women truly useful members of society, I argue that they should be led, by having their understandings cultivated on a large scale, to acquire a rational affection for their country, founded
10 on knowledge, because it is obvious that we are little interested about what we do not understand. And to render this general knowledge of due importance, I have endeavored to show that private duties are never properly fulfilled unless the understanding enlarges the heart; and that public virtue is only an aggregate of
15 private. But, the distinctions established in society undermine both, by beating out the solid gold of virtue, till it becomes only the tinsel-covering of vice; for while wealth renders a man more respectable than virtue, wealth will be sought before virtue; and while women's persons are caressed, when a childish simper shows an absence
20 of mind—the mind will lie fallow. Yet, true voluptuousness must proceed from the mind—for what can equal the sensations produced by mutual affection, supported by mutual respect? What are the cold, or feverish caresses of appetite, but sin embracing death, compared with the modest overflowings of a pure heart and exalted
25 imagination? Yes, let me tell the libertine of fancy when he despises understanding in woman—that the mind, which he disregards, gives life to the enthusiastic affection from which rapture, short-lived as it is, alone can flow! And, that, without virtue, a sexual attachment must expire; like a tallow candle in the socket, creating
30 intolerable disgust. To prove this, I need only observe, that men who have wasted a great part of their lives with women, and with whom they have sought for pleasure with eager thirst, entertain the meanest opinion of the sex.—Virtue, true refiner of joy!—if foolish men were to fright thee from earth, in order to give loose to all their
35 appetites without a check—some sensual being of taste would scale the heavens to invite thee back, to give a zest to pleasure!

Mary Wollstonecraft, *A Vindication of the Rights of Women,* 1792, excerpts.

That women at present are by ignorance rendered foolish or vicious, is, I think, not to be disputed; and, that the most salutary effects tending to improve mankind might be expected from a 40 REVOLUTION in female manners, appears, at least, with a face of probability, to rise out of the observation. For as marriage has been termed the parent of those endearing charities which draw man from the brutal herd, the corrupting intercourse that wealth, idleness, and folly, produce between the sexes, is more universally 45 injurious to morality than all the other vices of mankind collectively considered. To adulterous lust the most sacred duties are sacrificed, because before marriage, men, by a promiscuous intimacy with women, learned to consider love as a selfish gratification— learned to separate it not only from esteem but from the affection 50 merely built on habit, which mixes a little humanity with it. Justice and friendship are also set at defiance, and that purity of taste is vitiated which would naturally lead a man to relish an artless display of affection rather than affected airs. But that noble simplicity of affection, which dares to appear unadorned, has few attractions 55 for the libertine, though it be the charm, which by cementing the matrimonial tie, secures to the pledges of a warmer passion the necessary parental attention; for children will never be properly educated till friendship subsists between parents. Virtue flies from a house divided against itself—and a whole legion of devils take 60 up their residence there.

The affection of husbands and wives cannot be pure when they have so few sentiments in common, and when so little confidence is established at home, as must be the case when their pursuits are so different. That intimacy from which tenderness 65 should flow, will not, cannot subsist between the vicious.

Contending, therefore, that the sexual distinction which men have so warmly insisted upon, is arbitrary, I have dwelt on an observation, that several sensible men, with whom I have conversed on the subject, allowed to be well founded; and it is 70 simply this, that the little chastity to be found amongst men, and consequent disregard of modesty, tend to degrade both sexes; and further, that the modesty of women, characterized as such, will often be only the artful veil of wantonness instead of being the natural reflection of purity, till modesty be universally respected. 75

From the tyranny of man, I firmly believe, the greater number of female follies proceed; and the cunning, which I allow makes at present a

In 1792, the year Wollstonecraft's book was published, on December 3, George Washington was reelected President of the United States.

part of their character, I likewise have repeatedly endeavored to 80 prove, is produced by oppression.

Were not dissenters, for instance, a class of people, with strict truth characterized as cunning? And may I not lay some stress on this fact to prove, that when any power but reason curbs the free spirit of man, dissimulation is practiced, and the various shifts of 85 art are naturally called forth? Great attention to decorum, which was carried to a degree of scrupulosity, and all that puerile bustle about trifles and consequential solemnity, which Butler's caricature of a dissenter, brings before the imagination, shaped their persons as well as their minds in the mould of prim littleness. I speak col- 90 lectively, for I know how many ornaments to human nature have been enrolled amongst sectaries; yet, I assert, that the same narrow prejudice for their sect, which women have for their families, prevailed in the dissenting part of the community, however worthy in other respects; and also that the same timid prudence, or head- 95 strong efforts, often disgraced the exertions of both. Oppression thus formed many of the features of their character perfectly to coincide with that of the oppressed half of mankind; for is it not notorious that dissenters were, like women, fond of deliberating together, and asking advice of each other, till by a complication of 100 little contrivances, some little end was brought about? A similar attention to preserve their reputation was conspicuous in the dissenting and female world, and was produced by a similar cause.

Asserting the rights which women in common with men ought to contend for, I have not attempted to extenuate their faults; but to 105 prove them to be the natural consequence of their education and station in society. If so, it is reasonable to suppose that they will change their character, and correct their vices and follies, when they are allowed to be free in a physical, moral, and civil sense.

Let woman share the rights and she will emulate the virtues 110 of man; for she must grow more perfect when emancipated, or justify the authority that chains such a weak being to her duty.—If the latter, it will be expedient to open a fresh trade with Russia for whips; a present which a father should always make to his son-in-law on his wedding day, that a husband may keep his whole family 115 in order by the same means; and without any violation of justice reign, wielding this sceptre, sole master of his house, because he is the only being in it who has reason:—the divine, indefeasible earthly sovereignty breathed into man by the Master of the universe. Allowing this position, women have not any inherent rights 120 to claim, and by the same rule, their duties vanish, for rights and duties are inseparable.

Be just then, O ye men of understanding! and mark not more severely what women do amiss, than the vicious tricks of the horse or the ass for whom ye provide provender—and allow her 125 the privileges of ignorance, to whom ye deny the rights of reason, or ye will be worse than Egyptian task-masters, expecting virtue where nature has not given understanding!

Reading Excerpt: Frederick Douglass, *Reconstruction* (1866)

INTRODUCTION

Born into slavery, Frederick Douglass taught himself to read and suffered the worst indignities of slavery. He escaped from his slave masters at the age of twenty while working at a shipyard in Baltimore and made his way to the North. Douglass was a tireless abolitionist, through speaking, writing, and publishing his own newspaper. He worked for social justice for all, including women's rights, attending the first women's rights convention in 1848 in Seneca Falls. He also became a trusted advisor to many government officials, most importantly, President Abraham Lincoln. This essay was originally published in *The Atlantic Monthly*, December 1866, a year after the end of the Civil War.

Frederick Douglass
(1818–1895)

QUESTIONS FOR REFLECTION

1. Although the North had won the Civil War and the Thirteenth Amendment prohibiting slavery had been ratified by the states in December 1865, before he wrote this essay, Douglass saw a difficult road ahead in ending the practices and customs of slavery. What barriers did he see? Are some of those practices and customs still barriers to full racial equality today?

2. Douglass has great confidence in the power of giving people the right to vote. Is that confidence justified? What problems do you see in trusting that avenue to equality?

3. What other measures would Douglass likely approve in ending the cultural biases resulting from the institution of slavery? Has the nation done enough through reconstruction that it can now be truly color-blind and race-blind?

READING

The assembling of the Second Session of the Thirty-ninth Congress may very properly be made the occasion of a few earnest words on the already much-worn topic of reconstruction.

5   Seldom has any legislative body been the subject of a solicitude more intense, or of aspirations more sincere and ardent. There are the best of reasons for this profound interest. Questions of vast moment, left undecided by the last session of Congress, must be manfully grappled with by this. No political skirmishing will avail. The occasion demands statesmanship.

10   Whether the tremendous war so heroically fought and so victoriously ended shall pass into history a miserable failure, barren of permanent results,—a scandalous and shocking waste of blood and treasure,—a strife for empire, as Earl Russell characterized it, of no value to liberty or civilization,—an attempt to re-establish a

15 Union by force, which must be the merest mockery of a Union,—an effort to bring under Federal authority States into which no loyal man from the North may safely enter, and to bring men into the national councils who deliberate with daggers and vote with revolvers, and who do not even conceal their deadly hate of the

20 country that conquered them; or whether, on the other hand, we shall, as the rightful reward of victory over treason have a solid nation, entirely delivered from all contradictions and social antagonisms, based upon loyalty, liberty, and equality, must be determined one way or the other by the present session of Congress.

25 The last session really did nothing which can be considered final as to these questions.

    The Civil Rights Bill and the Freedmen's Bureau Bill and the proposed constitutional amendments, with the amendment already adopted and recognized as the law of the land, do not

30 reach the difficulty, and cannot, unless the whole structure of the government is changed from a government by States to something like a despotic central government, with power to control even the municipal regulations of States, and to make them conform to its own despotic will. While there remains such an idea as the right

35 of each state to control its own local affairs,—an idea, by the way, more deeply rooted in the minds of men of all sections of the

Frederick Douglass, *Reconstruction,* 1866, excerpts.

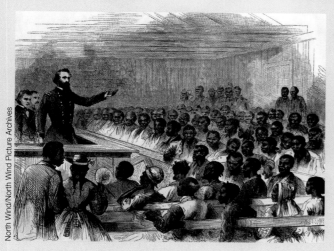

The Civil Rights Act of 1866 granted full citizenship to all persons born on U.S. soil, except Native Americans. The law gave legally emancipated former slaves, who came to be known as freedmen, rights not specifically guaranteed in the Thirteenth Amendment abolishing slavery: rights to own property, enforce contracts, and give evidence in courts. This image shows U.S. Generals Stedman and Fullerton conferring with Freedmen in 1866, following the enactment of the new law.

country than perhaps any one other political idea,—no general assertion of human rights can be of any practical value. To change the character of the government at this point is neither possible
40 nor desirable. All that is necessary to be done is to make the government consistent with itself, and render the rights of the States compatible with the sacred rights of human nature.

> *All that is necessary to be done is to make the government consistent with itself, and render the rights of the States compatible with the sacred rights of human nature.*

The arm of the Federal government is long, but it is far too short to protect the rights of individuals in the interior of distant
45 States. They must have the power to protect themselves, or they will go unprotected, in spite of all the laws the Federal government can put upon the national statute-book.

Slavery, like all other great systems of wrong, founded in the depths of human selfishness, and existing for ages, has not
50 neglected its own conservation. It has steadily exerted an influence upon all around it favorable to its own continuance. And today it is

so strong that it could exist, not only without law, but even against law. Custom, manners, morals, religion, are all on its side every-where in the South; and when you add the ignorance and servility
55 of the ex-slave to the intelligence and accustomed authority of the master, you have the conditions, not out of which slavery will again grow, but under which it is impossible for the Federal government to wholly destroy it, unless the Federal government be armed with despotic power, to blot out State authority, and to station a Federal
60 officer at every cross-road. This, of course, cannot be done, and ought not even if it could. The true way and the easiest way is to make our government entirely consistent with itself, and give to every loyal citizen the elective franchise,—a right and power which will be ever present, and will form a wall of fire for his protection.
65 One of the invaluable compensations of the late Rebellion is the highly instructive disclosure it made of the true source of danger to republican government. Whatever may be tolerated in monarchical and despotic governments, no republic is safe that tolerates a privileged class, or denies to any of its citizens equal
70 rights and equal means to maintain them.

It remains now to be seen whether we have the needed cour-age to have that cause [for rebellion] entirely removed from the Republic. At any rate, to this grand work of national regeneration and entire purification Congress must now address itself, with full
75 purpose that the work shall this time be thoroughly done.

If time was at first needed, Congress has now had time. All the requisite materials from which to form an intelligent judgment are now before it. Whether its members look at the origin, the progress, the termination of the war, or at the mockery of a peace
80 now existing, they will find only one unbroken chain of argument in favor of a radical policy of reconstruction.

The people themselves demand such a reconstruction as shall put an end to the present anarchical state of things in the late rebellious States,—where frightful murders and wholesale
85 massacres are perpetrated in the very presence of Federal sol-diers. This horrible business they require shall cease. They want a reconstruction such as will protect loyal men, black and white, in their persons and property: such a one as will cause Northern industry, Northern capital, and Northern civilization to flow into the
90 South, and make a man from New England as much at home in Carolina as elsewhere in the Republic. No Chinese wall can now be tolerated. The South must be opened to the light of law and liberty, and this session of Congress is relied upon to accomplish this important work.
95 The plain, common-sense way of doing this work is simply to establish in the South one law, one government, one administra-tion of justice, one condition to the exercise of the elective fran-chise, for men of all races and colors alike. This great measure is sought as earnestly by loyal white men as by loyal blacks, and is
100 needed alike by both. Let sound political prescience but take the place of an unreasoning prejudice, and this will be done.

CHAPTER 9

Health Care

" In nothing do men more nearly approach the gods than in giving health to men. "

—Marcus Tullius Cicero, Roman philosopher,
first century, B.C.E.

" The health of the people is no more a subject for legislation than their religion; . . . no man can reasonably require the state to take that care of his body which he will not take himself. "

—Herbert Spencer, "The Proper Sphere
of Government," 1843

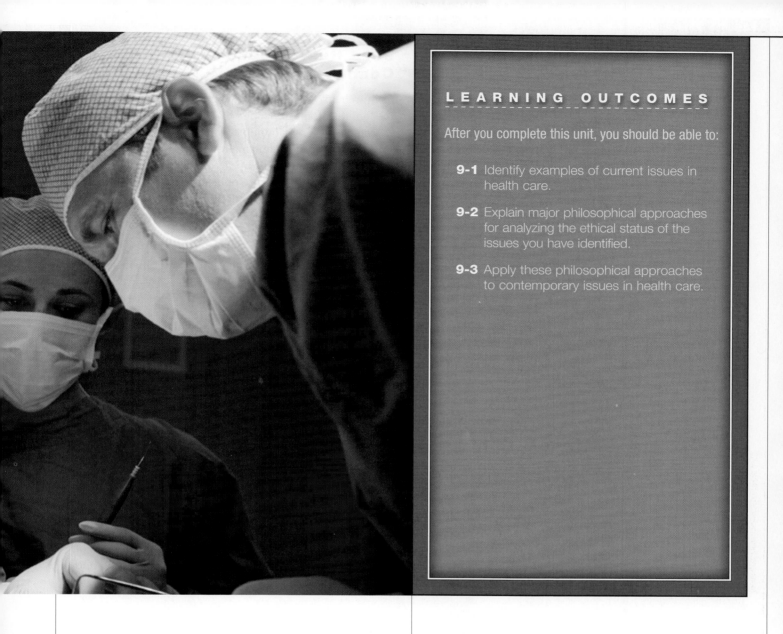

LEARNING OUTCOMES

After you complete this unit, you should be able to:

9-1 Identify examples of current issues in health care.

9-2 Explain major philosophical approaches for analyzing the ethical status of the issues you have identified.

9-3 Apply these philosophical approaches to contemporary issues in health care.

Rapid advances in medical science and technology raise numerous ethical questions for the medical profession and general public alike. Many of the questions we face today were unheard of just a few decades ago, and questions you are likely to face later in your life may not have yet been recognized. For example, the first successful heart transplant occurred in 1967 in South Africa, and the patient lived only eighteen days. The first successful bone marrow transplant occurred in Baltimore, Maryland, in 1972—today such procedures are frequently used to treat leukemia, sickle cell anemia, and other devastating diseases. Many other treatments such as these now seem almost routine. This particular area of human endeavor is in constant flux and new discoveries promise to not only stretch the current limits of our understanding and capacity to heal but also of ethical behavior.

Overview

We have tackled some bioethical issues in previous chapters, including abortion, suicide, assisted suicide, and euthanasia. In this chapter, we will focus on a few additional topics—namely health care as a right or a responsibility, genetic engineering, genetic testing,

What do **you** think?

Health care is a basic human right that should be available to everyone, regardless of ability to pay.

Strongly Disagree						Strongly Agree
1	2	3	4	5	6	7

transplants, and the ethics of medical research, and attempt to map out a philosophical framework useful for these issues and for questions in the future that we cannot now anticipate. Finally, we study the views by a leading U.S. bioethicist, Arthur L. Caplan, and a leading national expert on legal issues in health care, Karen Rothenberg.

9-1 CURRENT ISSUES IN HEALTH CARE

Public debates about health care are found everywhere, on the Internet, television, in newspapers, and everyday conversations. Perhaps because they pertain to such personal matters and involve our very lives and the quality of those lives, health care discussions seem all the more contentious and difficult to tackle. We here focus on just a few examples of current issues that have been grabbing the headlines, even though rapid developments in medical science and technology mean that the most urgent issues of the day will evolve and change in the coming years in ways we cannot yet even imagine. Note that issues in health care cover a broad range of concerns, from whether we have a right to health care at all to ethical issues surrounding medical research and therapeutic techniques themselves, regardless of how those are provided and paid for. In assessing the public debates, it is important to first get clear on precisely what is at issue, which is always the first step in good reasoning.

9-1a Health Care: A Right or a Commodity?

Comprehensive medical care is expensive and far beyond the ability of most people to pay for themselves—far more expensive, for example, than groceries or gasoline. President Harry S. Truman after World War II proposed that the government set up a comprehensive system to help provide some measure of health care for everyone in the United States, but he failed to get Congress to adopt his proposal. Since then, health care has remained the subject of much reflection and debate in the nation, in particular in considering whether health care is a privilege conferred only to those who can afford it or if it is a right, and if the latter, a right for whom; see Feature 9.1 for citations pertinent to this debate. U.S. presidents since Truman have continued to try to address health care needs and the discussion is ongoing today.

Many disciplines, from political science to sociology to economics, study these issues. In philosophy, we are concerned with finding ways to look at the big picture and sift through the ethical issues involved. For example, is health care a basic human right of every person? Is it a right that the government must pay for? In considering human rights, we need to distinguish between rights to do something on our own and rights that are so fundamental that the government must pay for them if you cannot afford them yourself. For example, even if you have the right to own a gun in the United States, we have not adopted the more extreme view that the government is required to buy you a gun, if you cannot afford one yourself. In contrast, if you are arrested and

Feature 9.1: Is Health Care a Right?

Should health care be treated as a right or as a responsibility for each individual? Some international charters have declared that health care is a human right, but not everyone agrees.

*Everyone has the right to a standard of living adequate for the health and well-being of himself and of his family, including food, clothing, housing and **medical care** and necessary social services, and the right to security in the event of unemployment, sickness, disability, widowhood, old age or other lack of livelihood in circumstances beyond his control.*

—United Nations Universal Declaration of Human Rights, Article 25 (1948) (emphasis added)

Health Care: Everyone has the right of access to preventive health care and the right to benefit from medical treatment under the conditions established by national laws and practices. A high level of human health protection shall be ensured in the definition and implementation of all Union policies and activities.

—Charter of Fundamental Rights of the European Union, Article 35 (2000)

During the 2008 Presidential campaign debate on October 7, Barack Obama and John McCain were asked: "Is health care a right or a responsibility?"

"I think it should be a right for every American." Then-Senator Barack Obama

"I think it's a responsibility. . . . it is certainly my responsibility. It is certainly small-business people and others, and they understand that responsibility." Senator John McCain

The U.S. justice system and the fundamental rights it relies on are the subject of many TV shows, such as *The Good Wife*. One such right, that to a fair trial when charged with a crime, is guaranteed under the Sixth Amendment to the U.S. Constitution. A 1963 U.S. Supreme Court decision also ensured that those who do not have the necessary means to hire an attorney for their defense when they face imprisonment are represented in both state and federal courts of law at the government's expense.

face criminal charges, the government must pay for an attorney to represent you and help you obtain a fair trial because the right to a fair trial is such a fundamental right. So, here we can ask: If health care is a right, is it more like the right to own a gun, that is, at your own expense, or the right to an attorney in a criminal proceeding, that is, at the government's expense? If it is a right, where does that right come from? Is it a "natural right" possessed by all persons? Or is it a right only if your government says so in its constitution? If health care is not a right, is it more like a commodity, something you can purchase if you earn enough money to pay for it, like a car or a house?

9-1b Stem Cell Research

One of the more controversial forms of medical research today is research on stem cells. We consider this issue here as one of the most relevant topics today under the health care umbrella—note that Chapter 3 devoted its discussion on this topic on bioethical issues dependent on the concept of a "person." Embryonic stem cells are those from fertilized eggs, typically left over from attempts at in vitro fertilization (IVF). Supporters of

this research hold out the promise that these stem cells could be used to regenerate parts of the human body, whether the brain or paralyzed nerve endings or many other organs or parts of organs that are afflicted by traumatic injury. The controversy here is that some people believe that these fertilized eggs are persons with all the rights of persons, including the right not to be destroyed. In August 2001, President George W. Bush issued a policy that permitted experimentation on existing stem cells, but prohibited use of future stem cells from IVF or other sources. Shortly after taking office in 2009, President Barack Obama issued an Executive Order lifting this research ban and asked the National Institutes of Health to develop guidelines for the ethical use of embryonic stem cells. Today, some states are considering constitutional amendments that would define "person" in such a way that this stem cell research would be banned on the basis that it amounts to the taking of a human life.

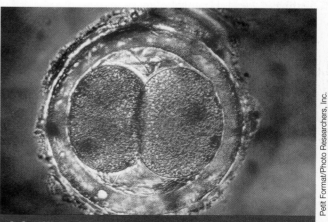

A fertilized human egg in the second stage of development, showing one cell division. In the beginning of its life, a fertilized egg divides and grows into several cells. The cell division continues during the egg's journey through the fallopian tube and the uterus.

9-1c Genetic Engineering

The manipulation of DNA in humans, as well as plant and animal life, raises exciting prospects for medical advances if it can be used to treat or avoid genetically inherited diseases. The cloning of human beings is alive in science fiction, such as the films *The Boys from Brazil* (in which Adolf Hitler clones were mass-produced), *Blade Runner*, or *The Island.* But the possibility that humans might be cloned for purposes of providing substitute limbs and other body parts remains a troubling possibility to many. Science has moved with great speed in the area of genetics. In ethics, we are concerned about the uses made of these technologies, whether they should be regulated (and, if so, how), and what rights and obligations we have as persons to use them wisely. In the 1990s President Bill Clinton signed an order banning research on human cloning of full humans, continued by later presidents. But genetic research other than cloning remains a possibility and the ethical issues it presents are enormous.

9-1d Testing

Testing in medical research raises many ethical questions. For instance, how should we test new and experimental medicines? Even after animal testing, some testing on humans is probably necessary before distribution to a general public. Should those persons used for tests be fully informed of the risks? Should they be paid? If the new drugs are very risky, how should we set the payment? Is it fair to exploit human subjects in desperately poor neighborhoods and countries because we know they are more likely to take the money?

Genetic testing is quite controversial today. Testing a person's genetic makeup can reveal whether a person has a propensity to develop certain diseases. Ongoing research continues producing new tests of this sort to help identify more and more particular predispositions to specific diseases. Such knowledge can be considered positive, if, for example, steps could be taken to lessen the impact of a disease on the person's life in the future with preventative measures, if they exist. But many worry that the results of this genetic testing could be used to make it far more difficult for persons to obtain health insurance or even employment. These persons could be seen as presenting too much of a costly risk because of the potential for developing health issues that the tests would have uncovered.

9-1e Transplants

Another troubling area for ethics is the transplantation of organs. The medical techniques are well developed, but the ethical challenges are still unresolved. For example, the sale of organs is banned in the United States under the National Organ Transplant Act of 1984. But if a poor person wants to sell an organ to a wealthy recipient and is fully informed of the risks, why is this option not legal? Would more organs be available and more lives saved if we lifted this prohibition? Also, currently, when a person dies in the United States, the organs cannot be extracted for transplant until the person or immediate family gives permission. What if we reversed that presumption and said that organs may always be removed for transplant, unless the donor has explicitly said *no* prior to his or her death? Should family members be obligated to donate organs to other family members while they are alive, if they are a good match? This scenario became reality in the complicated case of two sisters, both incarcerated in Mississippi for armed robbery, who were freed from prison in January 2011, on condition that one of the sisters donate a kidney to her sister. If a stranger is a perfect match, should that person be compelled to be an organ donor if no other matches can be found? Although it seems unlikely that such a legal obligation would ever be established, ethical pressures on family members are pervasive and challenging.

In CourseMate, watch a video and take the quiz.

Joel Page/AP Photos

The world's first organ donor was Ronald Herrick, here pictured at his home in Belgrade, Maine. On December 23, 1954, Ron, aged twenty-three, donated a kidney to his twin brother Richard. The kidney recipient went on to live another eight years.

9-2 PHILOSOPHICAL APPROACHES FOR ANALYZING HEALTH CARE ISSUES

Some reasoning frameworks are most helpful in working through these contemporary issues. We can start with the Kantian approach: every person has a right to be treated with dignity and respect, and their autonomy is to be recognized. In applying this Kantian principle, we need to consider all persons affected by these medical issues. The patients, families, medical personnel, and future generations all deserve that same respect and dignity. We also need to consider at what point in the life cycle one is a person deserving of that respect and dignity, whether at conception, when one develops a functioning brain, or at birth.

The utilitarian approach looks at results of actions as they affect everyone, both the person pursuing a certain action and all other persons. This can lead to results that might be troubling. If experimentation on a small group of people results in their deaths, but the knowledge gained is enormously beneficial to a much larger group of people, such testing might be justifiable from the consequentialist perspective, but troubling from the vantage point of human respect and dignity.

As always, our goal must be to think from the vantage of the big picture in our reasoning, so we can adapt to new empirical evidence and developments in science, while consistently holding to our ethical principles.

In CourseMate, apply what you've learned to the real-life scenario in the simulation.

In CourseMate, practice what you learned by taking the chapter quiz.

9-3 APPLICATIONS TO CONTEMPORARY ISSUES

9-3a Health Care

Treating every person with respect and dignity might seem to include providing every person with reasonable health care, whether or not they can personally afford to pay for it. But others might instead argue that subsidies, whether for health care, food, or housing, disrespects persons by implying they are incapable of earning the money needed to purchase those things themselves. Even those who object to providing subsidies as a general principle might agree that children, the severely disabled, or grievously wounded from wars are either unable or limited in their ability to earn the needed funds, so we might need to find a way to make exceptions to provide for them without concluding that we are disrespecting them. The key here is to consider what it means in this application to treat someone with respect and dignity, which itself can be contentious.

From a utilitarian perspective, we need to consider all persons, not just the sick ones. Many diseases are communicable and could spread to an entire community of innocent persons if not treated. Tuberculosis, AIDS, malaria, flu, and many other diseases are highly contagious. So if as a society we decide to provide free care to all persons with those diseases, we would not be benefitting only that person but also all who might contract that disease in an epidemic. But the consequentialist would also consider the economic costs to all persons of providing care. If many cannot afford state-of-the-art care on their own, would it bankrupt the rest of a given community to provide that care with our tax or insurance dollars? It might seem harsh to make these judgments based on money and who can afford to be treated, but economic consequences is one of many legitimate results that must be considered.

> **Many diseases are communicable and could spread to an entire community of innocent persons if not treated.**

9-3b Stem Cell Research

As we have seen in so many other situations, the Kantian right to respect and dignity turns on what we count as a person, and this is especially relevant in embryonic stem cell research. Beyond this threshold question, we must then turn to the dignity we owe to persons with debilitating diseases and injuries who might be saved as a result of this research. Famous persons otherwise opposed to abortion, including Nancy Reagan, wife of the former president, and Senator Orin Hatch, support stem cell research because of the potential for lifesaving cures. Others oppose it, despite this potential, because of their beliefs about the nature of "personhood."

The utilitarian seems to have an easier time sorting through this issue. The fact that the research would benefit a huge number of people might outweigh the harm to a single individual, even if that embryonic stem cell is considered a person. This seems harsh, but pure

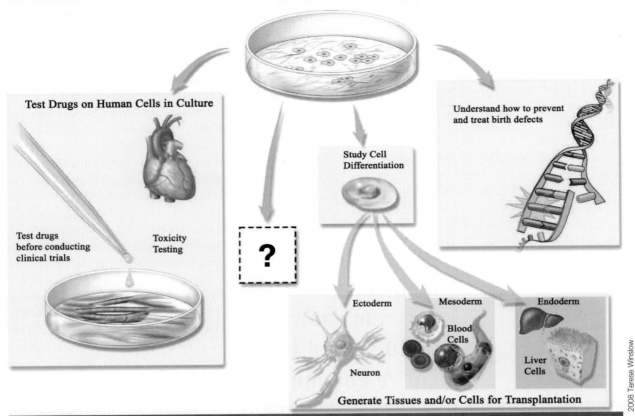

Test Drugs on Human Cells in Culture

Test drugs before conducting clinical trials

Toxicity Testing

?

Study Cell Differentiation

Understand how to prevent and treat birth defects

Ectoderm

Neuron

Mesoderm

Blood Cells

Endoderm

Liver Cells

Generate Tissues and/or Cells for Transplantation

2008 Terese Winslow

This National Institutes of Health illustration shows in what various areas of scientific exploration stem cell research can be applied. To many, none of the possible medical discoveries resulting from this research warrants the use of stem cells.

consequentialism, as we have seen, often leads to challenging conclusions. On the other hand, a utilitarian might respond that using a stem cell in research would devalue the human life it embodies, which would have the negative consequences of coarsening society. In turn, those results would outweigh the benefits to the greater public of any medical advances.

9-3c Genetic Engineering

From a Kantian perspective, we must consider the dignity and worth of all concerned, not just the patients who might benefit from manipulation of DNA or even cloning, but all others affected. Would cloned persons (should scientists be able to produce such entities someday) have the same rights as "uncloned" persons? If they were cloned solely to provide body parts

> Would cloned persons (should scientists be able to produce such entities someday) have the same rights as "uncloned" persons?

for the injured original, whose rights and dignity take priority? Although this scenario seems far-fetched, other techniques we now take for granted, such as organ transplants, were once thought to belong only to the realm of science fiction. The issue, from a Kantian viewpoint, seems to be that a cloned person created solely for selfish reasons is being treated as a means to an end and not as a being whose very existence is valuable in and of itself.

Utilitarians would need to look at results for all in the broader scope of any specific medical research. DNA manipulation might benefit a patient, but could it have unforeseen consequences for others? For example, if wealthy parents can manipulate genes to have the "perfect child," however that is understood, are we harming parents and their children who cannot afford these expensive procedures by shifting societal standards for perfection?

9-3d Testing

Testing experimental drugs on human beings raises basic issues from a Kantian perspective. Those human subjects must be treated with respect and dignity. This should include making sure that they are fully informed of the risks of participating in an experiment, so they can make a meaningful choice of whether or not to participate. Respect would also entail providing medical care should the experiment prove damaging to their health.

Testing of experimental medicines creates consequences for many people, all of which need to be taken into account by the utilitarian. The persons on whom the tests are conducted could be happy that the experimental drugs improved their medical condition. During the early years of the AIDS epidemic, for example, seriously ill patients were eager to volunteer for new, untested medicines in the hopes that they might be beneficial, even if they had not passed the usual safety and efficacy testing required for drugs. Some persons might be happy with the payment they received for participating in the tests, even knowing the risks involved. The potential unhappiness of the test subjects cannot be ignored, however. Taking new, unproven drugs can cause serious harm, even death, to the test subjects, which would result in unhappiness for them and their family and friends.

Also relevant to the utilitarian is the happiness and unhappiness of the patients who would benefit from the proof that a new drug works. They would also benefit from testing that showed that an experimental medicine was harmful, although they might not ever realize this if the drug never made it beyond the testing stage. So, the universe of persons whose happiness and unhappiness would need to be weighed is large and complex for the utilitarian.

Familiar reasoning tools also help us address the issues of genetic testing. The persons being tested should be treated with Kantian respect and dignity, which would include fully informing those persons of the risks and benefits of the tests so they can make appropriate decisions. The results of those tests should also be shared with the patient to respect their humanity and rights. But respectful treatment also would seem to include treating those test results with care to protect the privacy of the patient, so they would not be embarrassed or harmed by others who might have access to their test results. Some might wonder if treating a person with more respect would entail withholding genetic information that

reveals they had a terrible disease with the potential to kill them at an early age. Some might wonder if it would be better for them to live their life to the fullest without their having to worry about that fate. These sticky issues center on how we view and define the autonomy and dignity of the persons involved.

Genetic testing can also be analyzed from the perspective of utilitarianism. Consider all the persons who would be happier knowing the results of the test, especially if that knowledge made it possible to exploit available treatments while there was still time. The persons affected by this knowledge would include not only the patient but also the family and friends of that patient. But negative consequences also need to be weighed in the analysis. These might include restrictions by insurance companies or employers who did not want to insure or hire somebody with a genetic disease potentially expensive to treat. The unhappiness would extend to financially bankrupting the patient and family in obtaining treatment, while the insurance company and prospective employer would be happy to have avoided taking on that expense themselves.

9-3e Transplants

The rapid advances in transplant technology in the last half-century have generated a myriad of new ethical questions. From the vantage point of the patient who needs a transplant, we should ask whether society should do all it can to make transplants possible as a way of treating that patient with Kantian dignity and respect, even if the medical costs are high or even if the patient might not seem the most "deserving" for a transplant. With the continuing shortage of available organs for transplant, wrenching decisions must be made about who should get them first. Should all patients be treated equally, first-come-first-served (assuming all are medically able to accept a transplant)? Would that be the best way to treat all of them with respect and dignity? Or should we come up with a ranking system, say, giving priority to the young, the well-educated, the wealthy, or those without a criminal record?

The organ donors also must be considered. To treat them with dignity and respect, we should make sure that they are fully informed of any risks and obtain their clear consent to the procedure. If things go awry during the procedure, we should ensure that they will receive appropriate medical attention themselves.

> With the continuing shortage of available organs for transplant, wrenching decisions must be made about who should get them first.

The utilitarian would ask us to consider the happiness and unhappiness of all the persons involved in a transplant procedure. Presumably a transplant would bring happiness to the patient benefitting from it, as well as the patient's family and friends. But each case would need to be examined carefully. A very elderly patient might not want the agony of this surgery to prolong his or her life and might just want to die peacefully.

The consequences for the donor would also need to be factored into the utilitarian calculus. Consider a family member who is a good match for donation being pressured by other family members to consent to the transplant and reluctantly agreeing to do it. Their unhappiness, for whatever reason, would be relevant in weighing the overall happiness and unhappiness associated with this procedure.

Now, equipped with the knowledge you acquired about the types of reasoning that can be applied to the topics discussed, review Critical Thinking Table 9.1 to follow the examination of an ethical claim on a related topic.

In CourseMate, listen to the audio summary of the chapter.

Table 9.1 Critical Thinking Steps and Their Application in an Example

{"All stem cell research should be banned because life begins at conception."}

Critical Thinking Steps	Application
1. **Examine and clarify key terms and concepts.** • Look words up in a dictionary as a start if necessary. • Unravel or unpack the complexities and nuances of a central term, such as *justice, or right*, or *good*.	• What is "stem cell research"? • Precisely how do we understand "conception"? Is conception synonymous with any fertilized egg?
2. **Work through the meaning of the key terms and concepts to make sure you will use them consistently.** • Consider the ways the term can be used by including it in different sentences and contexts to zero in on the particular meaning you are after. • Ask yourself what words are potential synonyms for the concept. Do those capture everything you want to understand about that term?	• Is stem cell research shorthand for embryonic stem cell research? Does it also include adult stem cell research? Are the ethical issues the same? • How expansively do we understand "research"? Is this mainly a concern for research that destroys or alters stem cells? • What do we mean by "life"? Is life synonymous with "person"?
3. **Build premises and bring any assumptions to light.** • Put together short and clear sentences to build each of your premises. • Think through what you may be taking for granted in your reasoning. What assumptions are you making? • Once you have identified assumptions, articulate them in your premise, so that your audience has the same understanding of a term or a concept as you.	The premises of the argument could be constructed as follows: (i) Any research that destroys a person's existence should be banned. (ii) A stem cell is a fertilized egg. (iii) A fertilized egg is a person. (iv) Stem cell research destroys the existence of a person. CONCLUSION: All stem cell research should be banned as life begins at conception.

Petit Format/ Photo Researchers, Inc.

2008 Terese Winslow

Critical Thinking Steps	**Application**
4. Test/Verify your premises.	Each of these premises should be examined.

Critical Thinking Steps

4. **Test/Verify your premises.**

   - Now that you have stated your premises explicitly, do you want to stick with them?

   - Are you relying on premises drawn from unsubstantiated sources or from questionable authorities?

   - Are you consistent in your premises? Or are you appealing to different and inconsistent foundations in your reasoning?

   - Reformulate your premises if they have proven to be faulty.

5. **Confirm that the conclusions you draw are logical. Check for reliance on fallacies and correct any premise that you identify as relying on a fallacy.**

negative/Shutterstock.com

Application

Each of these premises should be examined.

(i)   What do we understand as "research"? As "destroying" a person's existence?

(ii) Is this definition empirically sound? Is this how scientists understand the meaning of stem cell? Is this shorthand for embryonic stem cell?

(iii) Does our concept of a person extend to fertilized eggs?

(iv) Does all research destroy the stem cell? Are there observations and measurements that would not destroy it but might be scientifically useful?

If you do not accept all of these premises, then you will not accept the conclusion either. But if you do accept all of them, then you would find the conclusion valid and justified.

This argument is particularly vulnerable to criticism that it relies on the fallacy of equivocation, especially regarding the words *stem cell*, *research*, and *person*, which are being used in slightly different ways throughout the argument, clouding the validity of the conclusion. Stem cell sometimes refers to embryonic stem cell, whose use in research is the most controversial, and adult stem cell, whose use sparks less controversy. Person is a highly contentious term, with some stipulating that one is a person from conception, others from viability outside the womb, and others from the moment of birth.

Frances Kamm

Frances Kamm

Frances Kamm is one of the most distinguished philosophers today working on the issues of health care, bioethics, and human rights. She is the Littauer Professor of Philosophy and Public Policy in the Kennedy School of Government and Professor of Philosophy at Harvard University. She has received numerous fellowships and honors for her influential work.

Her books include *Intricate Ethics: Rights, Responsibilities, and Permissible Harm* (2007), *Morality, Mortality, Vol. 1: Death and Whom to Save from It* (1993); *Morality, Mortality, Vol. 2: Rights, Duties, and Status* (1996); *Creation and Abortion* (1992). Kamm rejects utilitarianism and pursues a Kantian approach to human rights, especially as developed by the late John Rawls, who had also been a philosophy professor at Harvard.

In her 2002 essay, "Health and Equity," for the World Health Organization, she meticulously works through how to prioritize access to health care and the difficult issue of rationing. She uses principles of goodness, fairness, and justice to consider an extensive series of hypothetical situations that illustrate how difficult it is to resolve these issues in an era of limited resources.

Martha Stewart

CHAPTER 9 Case Study

Research on Human Subjects: The Guatemala Experiments

From 1946 to 1948, the U.S. Public Health Service (PHS) conducted research in Guatemala on sexually transmitted diseases (STDs) on 5,500 prison inmates, orphans, school children, soldiers, psychiatric patients, and commercial sex workers. In 2010, information was revealed that 1,300 of these research subjects were intentionally exposed and infected to STDs without their consent. At least 83 of the subjects died. The Presidential Commission for the Study of Bioethical Issues conducted a thorough investigation of this episode, including review of 125,000 pages of original documents, a fact-finding trip to Guatemala, and meetings with that country's own investigative committee.

In September 2011, the commission released its own report, titled *Ethically Impossible STD Research in Guatemala from 1946 to 1948*, which it posted on the commission's website at http://www.bioethics.gov. The commission discovered that the U.S. researchers in Guatemala were given great latitude in their conduct of the experiments and little oversight from the PHS. They also went to great lengths to keep their activities secret. Even though some of the researchers, when they worked in the United States, had previously sought consent on experiments with human subjects, they knowingly skipped this procedure in Guatemala, in a "double standard" that the commission found "shocking." The behavior of the researchers, in the words of the commission report, "shows understanding of, and disregard for, generally accepted moral principles such as respect for human dignity in the course of their work in Guatemala."

According to the historical records, the idea for conducting the research in Guatemala came from a Guatemalan physician who was in the United States for a study program with the government. The United States already had in place an extensive program of medical assistance to Guatemala, and funding for the research was reviewed and approved by a panel at the National Institutes of Health. Agreements were signed with several governmental officials in Guatemala for wide-ranging research on STDs. The U.S. researchers provided extensive assistance with the provision of scarce medicines and other benefits to ensure the continued cooperation of the Guatemalan officials.

The chair of the commission, Amy Gutmann, is President of the University of Pennsylvania and a distinguished political philosopher and ethicist. In her statement accompanying release of the report, she said, "A civilization can be judged by the way it treats its most vulnerable individuals. It is our moral responsibility to care for those who cannot protect themselves and clearly in this dark chapter of our medical history we grievously failed to keep that covenant."

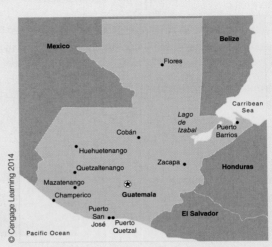

© Cengage Learning 2014

Guatemala is a country located in Central America. It has a population of about 14.7 million inhabitants and is about the size of the state of Tennessee.

1. If the research subjects had been notified of the plans to infect them and they had given their consent, would this research have been ethically justifiable? Would these research subjects genuinely feel free to refuse because they were all dependent on state support in some way as prisoners, orphans, and soldiers? What tests would you insist upon to ensure that they had genuinely and freely consented?

2. Would it be more ethical if, along with consent, the research subjects had been paid a significant amount of money for their participation? If the subjects were desperately impoverished, would the offer of money be coercion or could they still freely give consent to participate?

3. Experiments of this kind might generate significant new knowledge about the nature of these diseases and effective treatments once infected. Would this knowledge benefiting large numbers of people elsewhere be a consequence that would justify the likely harm to the relatively small number of research subjects? In other words, would a philosophical theory of consequentialism justify this type of research? Would an approach emphasizing human autonomy and dignity outweigh any beneficial consequences to this type of research?

4. If you were designing a research study on these diseases, what conditions would you insist upon to make the study ethical?

For additional case studies, please see the CourseMate for this text.

Reading Excerpt: Arthur L. Caplan, *Testimony on Synthetic Biology* (2010)

INTRODUCTION

Synthetic biology is a new area of scientific research that has led to the successful creation of biological elements in the laboratory by relying on artificially created DNA. It promises dramatic advances in the treatments of many diseases, vaccines, medicines, and artificial organs, as well as in other scientific areas such as biofuels. The Presidential Commission for the Study of Bioethical Issues conducted a thorough study of the issues raised by these new technologies, held hearings around the country, and issued a report with recommendations to the president in December 2010.

Arthur L. Caplan was among the experts providing testimony to the commission in its investigations. One of the country's leading bioethicists, he directed the Center for Bioethics at the University of Pennsylvania for many years, and now directs a new medical ethics program at New York University. The author or editor of twenty-nine books and more than 500 papers, he has received numerous awards for his leadership in bioethics research. Following is the testimony he provided in September 2010 at the governmental hearings of the commission on synthetic biology.

Arthur L. Caplan

QUESTIONS FOR REFLECTION

1. Synthetic biological life forms offer great promise but also great risks. How would a consequentialist balance promise and risk to draw conclusions about the direction of this scientific research? Would the restraints recommended by Caplan also restrict in unacceptable ways the benefit of this research to humans?

2. Does the creation of these synthetic biological elements threaten our concept of the dignity and autonomy of persons?

Does that classic philosophical perspective fail to account for these new directions in research?

3. If synthetic biology could lead to the creation of a human being, should that human being have the same rights and responsibilities as a naturally created person?

READING

Philosophy Matters

Thank you for allowing me to share some of my thinking about the religious, philosophical and spiritual significance of synthetic biology with the distinguished members of this commission. I know
5 that the President has asked you to report to him about developments in this rapidly evolving field of biology and I hope that this testimony will prove useful to you in carrying out that assignment.

I think much of the ethical commentary concerning synthetic biology has centered on the benefits that synthetic biology may
10 bring, the potential risks involved in pursuing those benefits to human health and well-being as well as questions about the ownership of the key techniques used by synthetic biologists.

These are very legitimate topics for ethical reflection and policy development. I am going to comment on them myself.
15 However I want to persuade you that there are deeper philosophical concerns that, while perhaps harder to pinpoint, underlie some of the disquiet about the field of synthetic biology. I think this commission should attempt to wrestle with some of these issues in its recommendations to the President. As we have seen with many
20 other breakthroughs in the biomedical sciences ranging from cloning to the reproductive technologies to stem cell research, more is involved in evincing public concerns about new directions in science than worries about safety.

A Short Aside—What Do I Mean by Synthetic
25 Biology?

There is no real consensus definition of synthetic biology. I want [to] offer a comment on how I see the field since the commission may find it useful in their analysis.

Synthetic biology is a sub-part of the field of genetic engineer-
30 ing. Synthetic biology tries to create novel sets of genes or entire genomes by building them de novo from genetic elements or 'bio-blocks,' or by stripping down existing genomes or by combining existing genomes. The aim of much of the work of synthetic biology is to create novel organisms with specific capabilities permitting the creation of useful products and activities.
35 permitting the creation of useful products and activities.

To date, most of the public attention given to synthetic biology has focused on efforts to create novel life-forms. But synthetic biology may also involve the transfer of large segments of genetic information between species to produce novel properties or repairs. For example, it may be possible to utilize the transfer of genomic information from a bacterium to supplement genetic failure in human disease in the eye or gut. This kind of genomic transfer, synthetic prosthetic genomics, is a part or will be a part, I predict, of synthetic biology as well.

Is Synthetic Biology 'Opposed' by Organized Religion?

I became interested in synthetic biology in 1997 when I had the opportunity to give a lecture at the National Academy of Sciences along with J. Craig Venter. Venter's talk quickly persuaded me that there were a number of important ethical issues surrounding the nascent attempt to create a new microbial life-form.

I organized a group at our Center for Bioethics at Penn to discuss this emerging field. I was careful to include many representatives from major religious traditions since I felt uncertain as to what sort of reception synthetic biology might receive from communities of faith. This group had a number of meetings at Penn and ultimately produced a paper in Science—"Ethical Considerations in Synthesizing a Minimal Genome"—which was published in December of 1999.

At the time few members of our group had ever heard of synthetic biology. But, as they began to understand what Venter[,] his collaborators and other groups were undertaking I was surprised to learn that the theologians in the group, drawn from traditions including Catholicism, Conservative and liberal Protestantism, Buddhism and conservative Judaism, had no 'in principle' object to the creation of new life forms. Their concerns were primarily about the impact of synthetic organisms on the environment and with social justice—ensuring equitable access to the benefits that might flow from synthetic biology.

> " *[T]he theologians in the group ... had no 'in principle' object to the creation of new life forms.* "

I think little has changed in the past dozen years with respect to religious attitudes. Among those few theologians around the world who are acquainted with synthetic biology, the creation of novel life forms is not seen as any more threatening to the dignity of humanity then the creation of tangerines, French poodles, or Basmati rice. The notions that humanity holds dominion over the earth and that man is entitled to manipulate nature to serve human needs are especially strong in Judeo-Christian thought.

Where philosophical and theological concerns, and popular concerns according to recent polls, tend to concentrate is around safety worries for the environment posed by novel life-forms.

Can we be sure that whatever is made will stay where its creators want it to? And, can we be sure that those who[se] aims are malevolent will not gain access to the techniques for designing novel life that could do enormous harm?

There is very little about the history of human activities involving animals and plants that provides confidence that we can keep novel life forms in their place. We do not have the national or international oversight and regulation requisite to minimize the risk of the creations of synthetic biology causing harm by showing up uninvited due to accident, inadvertence or negligence. People have been inadvertently introducing new life forms for hundreds of years into places where they create huge problems. Rabbits, kudzu, starlings, Japanese beetles, snakehead fish, rabies, fruit-flies, zebra mussels, and long-horned beetles are but a short sample of living things that have caused havoc for humanity simply by winding up in places we do not want them to be. Sometimes those involved in creating new life forms have accidentally lost track of the animals, insects or plants they were working with as happened

J.K. York/Shutterstock.com

Kudzu is a vine that grows quickly and climbs over trees or shrubs. It spreads easily, covering other plants and smothering them with its leaves. It was introduced into the United States from Japan at the 1876 Centennial Exposition in Philadelphia. It has since continued spreading in the United States.

with the introduction of 'killer bees' into South, Central and North America. In other cases inadequate attention to oversight allowed life forms to escape and wind up in places they were not wanted such as GMO corn's invasion of native strains of Mexican maize.

What standards of control should govern the creation, introduction and release of novel life forms? Should there be specific restrictions on the kind of life forms that can be engineered so as to minimize threats to human, animal and plant health? Should synthetic lifeforms be engineered when possible to naturally expire after a finite period of time? And if these rules are articulated, which agencies will have clear responsibility and authority for enforcing them? And can enforcement be made uniform and coordinated around the globe?

Not only is there a lack of agreed upon regulations and regulators in place to help manage the products of synthetic biology, few provisions have been made to make sure that the techniques involved or the knowledge generated do not fall into the wrong hands. In an age of terrorism and bio-weapons that is not ethically sound public policy.

With the appearance of the nuclear bomb at the end of World War II, great efforts were made by the United States and other nations to keep the knowledge of the creation of these deadly weapons secret. International organizations sought treaties that would control the proliferation of these weapons and even attempt to place the creation of some forms of weapons off limits. National restrictions were placed on who could work on nuclear weapons and what could be published about them. None of this has been done for synthetic biology despite the danger posed by the creation of weaponized microbes, germs and viruses that could decimate our food supply, poison our water, or cause pandemic horror in human populations.

Both environmental control and protections against misuse merit more attention than they have received. International coordination is essential if the public is to feel comfortable that safety is being properly managed. Neither poses an insurmountable obstacle to the advancement of synthetic biology. But, a failure to vigorously attend to both could set the field back just as the promise of synthetic biology is poised to begin to deliver much good.

Let me offer four general principles that I think are essential to securing public confidence in the safety of organisms created by synthetic biology.

First, since national security and public health must have top ethical priority, it is appropriate to implement controls over the publication of scientific details, the selection of locations of laboratories, and who is permitted to train in them.

Second, to ensure the responsible handling of synthetic life, all synthetic organisms should be marked or branded in some way so as to make it easy to distinguish them from natural life-forms. Venter's team inserted several DNA "watermarks" into their recently created novel bacteria, and that precedent ought be routinized.

Third, to ensure the safety of the environment from accidents, every synthetic life form at this point in time ought to have some limit on its lifespan engineered into it.

Fourth, a single agency should have clear-cut, responsibility for approving the release of any entity created by synthetic biology outside the controlled environment of a laboratory.

These ideas may help tamp down some of the practical concerns about making new life forms.

All that said, I still believe that there are philosophical, religious, and metaphysical anxieties about creating life or creating prosthetic repairs using genomic transfers that ought to be acknowledged and addressed. While these do not now dominate popular or religious expressions of concern they may come to do so in the future.

How Might the Emergence of Synthetic Biology Broadly Understood, Bear upon Spiritual Matters and Religious Understanding?

I think there are three ways in which the creation of new life forms and manipulating whole or partial genomes for medical or industrial purposes trigger philosophical anxieties. These are (1) concerns about 'playing god'; (2) the end of the view that life is special or exceptional, and (3) worries about the mixture or placement of large portions of genomes across species.

Playing God

These is plenty of room for arguing about what it would take in terms of biological creation to lay claim to the mantle of the scientist who creates the first novel life form. Some argue that viruses should not count because they are parasitical—needing another creature's genome to reproduce. The prize probably will go to the first team to be able to create a creature capable of replicating under the power of its own novel genetic program. Still, however life is defined, there should be no doubt that someone is going to create a new critter in the not too distant future.

The possibility that humans can create life, either from pre-existing organic parts or from inorganic materials, has been the subject of considerable cultural worry and commentary from Mary Shelley's *Frankenstein* to Gene Roddenberry's creation of the android Data in *Star Trek The Next Generation*. While no one will be making living people from scratch anytime soon, the idea that humans can create even primitive life forms seems to some to violate the prohibition that humans should not play god.

The key admonition about not to playing God I think is not about the divinity but about the notion of 'playing.' Playing brings to mind carefree, lighthearted, even irresponsible activity—not the sort of thing that lends credibility to having confidence in those making new life forms. Cautions about playing god use the notion of play to suggest that scientists are at best cavalier and at worst just screwing around when it comes to making artificial or novel life forms.

That criticism seems unfair. Those involved in the creation of synthetic new life forms do so not as a game but in the hope that they can better understand how life works and, further, perhaps

Fiction is replete with examples of creatures that are man-made, such as the android Data in the show *Star Trek: The Next Generation*. An android is an automaton, or a robot, that looks and behaves like a human being.

CBS /Landov Media

make microbes that can benefit us all. I would maintain that play is not much in evidence in the motivation for or, just as importantly, the funding of synthetic biology.

200 Well then what about the challenge of being godlike in making new life? Some fear that when the creation of life at human hands happens this will knock down a key theological tenet that only God can create life from non-life. Others worry that in creating new forms of life we will create something that we can neither contain nor control.

205 It is heard to credit the view that God would give us the abilities to make new life forms and then argue that to do so crosses a line that God does not want crossed. If one takes a more secular view, the fact that human beings can mimic random processes that allowed life to emerge is not especially threatening to faith in a divinity.

210 What about hubris? Our inability to control what we might make is a problem. It is not clear that we can completely control new life forms. But, surely it is clear that we would be prudent to both create mechanisms for identifying and tracing new life forms and for insuring that they are fragile should they go places they 215 are not wanted. So heeding the warnings against arrogance we should be certain we can control where novel life-forms go but still build in insurance that if they get out they will do no harm anyway.

> ❝ *It is not clear that we can completely control new life forms.* ❞

The Exceptionalism of 'Life'

Just over one hundred years ago, the French philosopher Henri 220 Bergson claimed that life could never be explained simply by mechanistic explanations. Nor could life be artificially created by synthesizing molecules. There was, he argued, an elan vital—a

vital force—that was the ineffable current of life, which distinguished the living from the inorganic. Life transcended the 225 material world and could only exist by means of a special force or power—most likely issuing from the divinity.

Bergson was hardly alone in his view that something mystical and special drives life. Vitalism has come in many forms in Western thought from Galen's talk of the 'vital spirit,' to Swann 230 and Pasteur's positing of 'vital action' in their explanations of how life comes to exist to the 20th century biologist Hans Driesch's positing of the mysterious metaphysical 'entelechy' as requisite for life. While materialistic reductionism dominates biological thinking today, there are no exceptionalists in the foxholes of the 235 NIH institutes, many outside the biological sciences still hold the view that life is a mystery beyond human comprehension and that the mystery of life is linked to the will of God.

All of these deeply entrenched metaphysical views are cast into doubt by the demonstration that life can be created from non-living 240 parts. The achievement of the creation of synthetic life will end the argument that life requires a special force or power to exist. Likely more troubling to many, the achievement suggests that neither microbial nor human life are fueled by a transcendent vital force.

The belief in the special, mysterious nature of life, including 245 the long-standing belief that we ourselves are infused with a special, mysterious force that permits us to live, is called into question when life can be created from non-living elements. Learning to live in a world where life has been shown by science to be the product of material forces subject to human control will likely prove for 250 many a challenge to rival worries about safety.

Mixing and Purity

The last deeper metaphysical and spiritual worry about living things or products created by synthetic biology concerns mixing what is seen as foreign, unnatural or alien into our bodies. If it were pos255 sible to move a large portion of a genome from a bacterium into the human eye to restore a form of vision many would celebrate but some might balk. Making a microbe that can eat cholesterol from our arteries or immunize us against infectious diseases will leave some cold just as there are worries today about vaccines and 260 drugs in some quarters. Still others may be concerned if genomic transfers could be used to alter our natural abilities or capacities.

These are very real if difficult to engage concerns. The future of synthetic biology depends in part on recognizing these worries and finding ways to engage and debate them.

265 ### Conclusion

I know this group understands the importance of coming to grips with concerns over the safety of the creations of synthetic biology. I believe it is equally important to begin the process of coming to terms with deeper metaphysical and spiritual concerns that are stirred by 270 the demonstration that humans can create novel life-forms.

Reading Excerpt: Karen Rothenberg, *Protecting Workers from Genetic Discrimination* (2007)

INTRODUCTION

Rapid advances in science have made possible genetic testing to determine our likelihood of contracting many diseases. Yet this knowledge can be a two-edged sword. It might alert us to a disease we will likely suffer as we get older so we can take precautions to slow its advance. But it might also discourage us if we knew that disease cannot be successfully avoided or treated.

This testimony by Karen Rothenberg was presented to the Sub-committee on Health, Employment, Labor and Pensions, Committee on Education and Labor, in the U.S. House of Representatives, Washington, D.C., on January 30, 2007. At the time, she was Dean, Marjorie Cook Professor of Law, and the founding Director of the Law and Health Care Program at the University of Maryland School of Law. The hearing was held to consider whether there should be a federal law prohibiting discrimination based on genetic testing. The Genetic Information Non-Discrimination Act was signed into law in 2008.

University of Maryland Francis King Carey School of Law

Karen Rothenberg

QUESTIONS FOR REFLECTION

1. If you learned through genetic testing that you were likely to develop a disabling condition later in life, would you feel obligated to inform your siblings and children of your condition, in case they have the same genetic tendency? Would this knowledge alter your quality of life in the future? Would you think it better not to know of this impending condition?

2. If a couple learned through genetic testing that it was likely to produce a child with a severe disease for which there is no effective treatment, would that knowledge support an abortion of that fetus?

3. If a physician knows that his patient has suffered from clinical depression and suicidal tendencies in the past, should that doctor share with the patient the knowledge that genetic test-ing revealed the patient was likely to contract a severe disease later in life for which treatment is ineffective? If the physician does share that information and the patient commits suicide, should the doctor be held ethically responsible?

READING

. . . I am Karen H. Rothenberg, Dean, Marjorie Cook Professor of Law, and the founding Director of the Law & Health Care Program at the University of Maryland School of Law. Over the last decade or so, a primary area of my research has been on the ethical,
5 legal, and social implications of genetic information and I have published numerous articles on genetics and public policy. I also chaired the Committee on Genetic Information and the Workplace (a joint project of the NIH-DOE Working Group and National Action Plan on Breast Cancer) that developed the framework for state and
10 federal legislative proposals. Most recently, I co-authored an article in Science with my colleague Diane Hoffmann of the University of

Maryland School of Law on the use of genetic information in the courtroom.

I would like to begin by putting in context our concerns about
15 genetic discrimination in the workplace. Almost 20 years ago, Congress committed to investing in the Human Genome Project because it shared the vision of a revolution in medicine that would improve the health of all Americans. Their goal was not to provide health insurers and employers new tools to weed out individuals
20 that might someday generate large health care costs. To date, close to three-and-a-half billion dollars has been appropriated to fund the promise of genomic research for the American people.

The return on this investment is substantial and has the potential to transform medicine as we know it. But, unless Congress acts to address the perils associated with unauthorized dissemination of citizen's genetic information, we may never be able to make the transition from the research laboratory into the doctor's office.

Even in the early days of the Human Genome Project, people were concerned about the social risks associated with genetic research and anticipated that strong protections against misuse of genetic information would be established. Yet here we are almost 20 years later, with enormous advances in scientists's ability to sequence and interpret our DNA, and we have yet to achieve a federal law to safeguard genetic information. The tremendous promise of genomics is hamstrung by fear. How extensive is this fear of genetic discrimination, and why does it matter?

- Fear of genetic discrimination is widespread in the American public. A 2006 survey by Cogent Research showed that 72 percent of respondents agreed the government should establish laws and regulations to protect the privacy of genetic information. Eighty-five percent believed that without a specific law on point, employers will discriminate. Sixty-four percent believed that insurance companies will do everything possible to use genetic information to deny health coverage. Recent polls conducted by the Wall Street Journal Online/Harris Interactive Health Care and the Genetics and Public Policy Center showed similar results.

> " *Genetic research holds tremendous promise to unlock new diagnoses and new treatments . . .* "

- Fear of genetic discrimination has a negative impact on biomedical research and potentially, health care decision making. Genetic research holds tremendous promise to unlock new diagnoses and new treatments, and even to assist in the creation of pharmaceutical therapies tailored to an individual's genetic makeup. However, scientific research and development cannot progress without clinical trials, and these trials can move forward only if individuals who could benefit are willing to participate. Fear that information will become available to and be misused by health insurers or employers has chilled participation in many studies of genetic conditions. For example, in a 2003 NIH study of families at risk for heredity nonpolyposis colorectal cancer (HNPCC), the number one concern expressed by participants regarding genetic testing was concern about losing health insurance should the knowledge

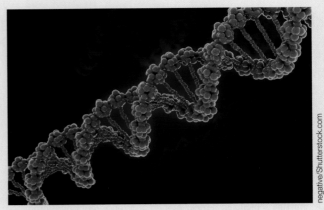

DNA is one of the fundamental constituents of life. It consists of the genetic material that determines the makeup of all living cells.

of their genetic test result be divulged or fall into the "wrong hands." Thirty-nine percent of participants cited this as the most distressing issue relating to genetic testing. Nearly half of family members at 50 percent risk for inheriting a cancer-inducing mutation were not willing to participate in any aspect of the study because of their fear of discrimination.

Where does this fear of genetic discrimination come from; and is it justified?

Perhaps it would be helpful to place these questions in historical context. In the early 1900's, Congress relied on the use of "genetic science" and the "genetic inferiority" of racial, ethnic, and disadvantaged groups to restrict their immigration into this country. State legislatures promoted sterilization laws based on the same rationale and eugenics was the "scientific justification" for killing millions during the Holocaust. During the early 1970's, African Americans who were carriers for the gene mutation associated with sickle cell disease were denied insurance coverage, charged higher rates, and lost their jobs. More recently, the Burlington Northern Santa Fe Railway Company paid up to $2.2 million to settle a 2002 lawsuit brought by employees who were secretly tested for a genetic variation purported to be associated with carpal tunnel syndrome

Nevertheless, because there is currently little evidence of major problems with widespread discrimination, some might argue that there is no need for legislation. It is true that in recent years we have not been able to quantify the incidence of genetic discrimination. Why? First, we do not have widespread utilization of genetic services.

Second, individuals often will not know or understand the underlying basis for an insurance or employment decision. Third, without clear legal remedies, healthy individuals with a genetic predisposition for a medical condition may be averse to risking loss of privacy for themselves and their families by going public with a discrimination claim, a greater risk than if the claim were based on race or sex. Finally, there may in fact be discrimination cases settled or resolved at the trial court levels that are never formally reported.

100   This raises an interesting public policy question: is it prudent to pass preventive federal legislation based on a fear of genetic discrimination? I would argue "yes," if we are to fully benefit from the promise of genetic research.

    Over the last decade, most states have enacted genetic 105 nondiscrimination legislation, although the scope of protection varies widely. Forty-one states have passed laws on discrimination in the individual health insurance market and thirty-four states have passed laws on genetic discrimination in the workplace.

There have also been patchwork approaches at the federal level. 110 For example, President Clinton's Executive Order 13145 protects federal employees from genetic discrimination in the workplace. Federal laws such as HIPPA, the ADA, and Title VII of the Civil Rights Acts may provide some protection, but there remain loopholes and gaps in coverage:

115 •   HIPAA prohibits raising rates for or denying coverage to an individual based on genetic information within the group coverage setting, but HIPPA protections are limited to only the group market. It does not cover individual insurance plans. The Federal Privacy Rule, authorized by HIPAA, protects 120   the use and disclosure of individually identifiable health

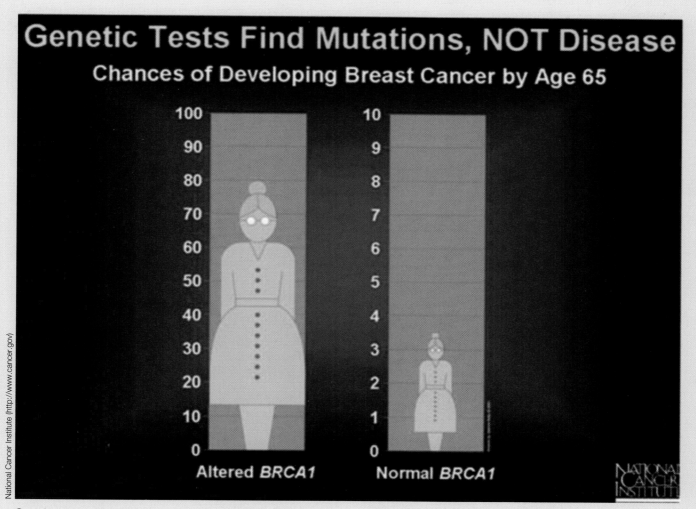

National Cancer Institute (http://www.cancer.gov)

Genetic testing offers what may be the opportunity to learn precious information that could lead to saving someone's life. But some people might not wish to know they have gene mutations and thus increased chances to develop a disease. The Genetic Information Nondiscrimination Act, signed into law in May 2008, prohibits insurance companies and employers from discriminating based on this genetic information, but some worry that it will not be effectively enforced.

information, including genetic information. The Rule does not prohibit the use of genetic information in underwriting. If a company determines that the individual is likely to make future claims, they could be charged higher premiums or denied coverage.

- The ADA was designed to protect those individuals who are living with a disability. The ADA defines disability as 1) a physical or mental impairment that substantially limits one or more of the major life activities of an individual; 2) a record of such impairment; or 3) being regarded as having such an impairment. While the ADA provides protections for people who have current disabling genetic illnesses, it is not at all clear whether the law covers individuals who have a genetic mutation that predisposes them to disease. Although guidance issued by the Equal Employment Opportunity Commission (EEOC) suggested a number of years ago that the ADA could apply in situations where an employer treats or regards an employee as impaired based on their genetic makeup, no court has ruled specifically on this issue. To the contrary, recent court cases have established a general trend of narrowing the ADA's scope stretching the ADA's definition of "impairment" to cover genetic predisposition to disease is inconsistent with the current judicial interpretation of the ADA.

- It is not clear whether Title VII of the 1964 Civil Rights Act would provide protection for those claiming genetic discrimination in most circumstances. Protection under this law is available only where an employer engages in discrimination based on a genetic trait that is substantially related to a particular race or ethnic group.

Thus, there is no uniform protection against the use of, misuse of, and access to genetic information in the workplace. As a matter of public policy, we still need to achieve a comprehensive approach that includes the following:

(1) Employers should be prohibited from using genetic information in hiring, firing, and determination of employee benefits.

(2) Employers should be prohibited from requesting or requiring collection or disclosure of genetic information unless they can show that the disclosure is relevant to the job. This is a very high standard and one that will rarely be met. Written and informed consent should be collected for each request, collection, or disclosure of genetic information.

(3) Employers should be restricted from access to genetic information contained in medical records released as a condition of employment, in claims filed for health care benefits, or any other sources.

(4) Employers should be prohibited from releasing genetic information without prior written authorization of the individual for each and every disclosure.

(5) Employers who violate these provisions should be subject to strong enforcement mechanisms, including a private right of action.

I understand that there might be concern that new federal legislation may place an undue burden on the business community. This is unlikely for two reasons: First, if we are to assume that employers are complying with applicable state laws then a federal law should not represent a significant new burden. Second, employers and those representing the insurance community have long maintained that they are not currently using genetic information to determine eligibility or employment status. If so, a federal prohibition should not burden their business practices. It would simply prevent the misuse of genetic information and be integrated into their legal compliance efforts. I am not aware of any data that demonstrates increased costs to employers for complying with these state laws.

In conclusion, the era of genomic medicine is here, but fear continues to paralyze its future. In the words of Dr. Francis Collins, Director of the NIH Human Genome Research Institute:

> **"** *[T]he era of genomic medicine is here, but fear continues to paralyze its future.* **"**

Unless Americans are convinced that their genetic information will not be used against them, the era of personalized medicine may never come to pass. The result would be a continuation of the current one-size-fits-all medicine, ignoring the abundant scientific evidence that the genetic differences among people help explain why some patients benefit from a therapy and, while some do not, and why some patients suffer severe adverse effects from a medication, while others do not.

It is my hope that passage of comprehensive federal legislation will move us forward to honoring our commitment to improving our understanding of genetics and its positive impact on the health of all Americans. . . .

THINKING IT THROUGH

H ere again is our example—the ethical claim we are investigating:

> **"Cheating in college is acceptable, so long as you don't get caught because everybody does it and good grades are necessary to get a good job after graduation."**

This third step in critical thinking is probably the most important of all because we are seeking to spell out the reasoning premises that lead logically to the conclusion. In addition, some notions or concepts may be implicit, unstated, or not obvious at first. It is important to uncover those implicit ideas or assumptions to bring to light the strength or weakness of the reasoning that leads to the conclusion.

What are the consequences for someone caught cheating in college? In the professional world?

Step III. Build premises and bring any assumptions to light.

- Put together short and clear sentences to build each of your premises.

- Think through what you may be taking for granted in your reasoning. What assumptions are you making?

- Once you have identified assumptions, articulate them in your premises, so that your audience has the same understanding of a term or a concept as you.

---

1. Put together short and clear sentences to build each of your premises.

Premises and Conclusions. In assessing whether we have effectively applied critical thinking to the formulation of our claim, we need to make sure that its premises make sense and lead logically to our conclusion. Premises express the foundational reasons that lead to the conclusion. So we need to draw out from our claim what the premises are. But it is often easiest to identify the conclusion first. In arguments, conclusions are not always found at the end and may be found anywhere.

Connections. It is also sometimes possible to identify a conclusion easily by finding words that connect one part of a sentence to another and indicate a relationship between these sentence segments. For example, a connector word, such as *because*, points to a cause-and-effect relation between the segments before and after it. Usually, what immediately follows *because* is the cause and what precedes it is the effect. In the sentence, "I could not get the job because I missed the interview," missing the interview caused the speaker to fail getting the job. The cause of the failure to get hired was the inability to get to the interview. The effect of the missed meeting was not getting the position sought. Beware that placement alone can be misleading. The effect is expressed in a clause that follows the one introduced by *because* in the statement, "Because I got sick, I could not take the final."

In this case, getting sick caused the speaker to be unable to take the final. The cause of the unfortunate failure to take the final was the sickness. For our claim, what follows *because* seems to justify the statement, "Cheating in college is acceptable."

STRATEGY:
Make sure that you can identify or learn to identify such elements as connector or transition words to help you distinguish premises from conclusions.

The fact that everybody cheats and that good grades are necessary to get a good job seems to lead to the conclusion from the original claim:

"Cheating in college is acceptable, so long as you don't get caught."

ASK YOURSELF: Have I identified the precise conclusion I seek to reach?

From Conclusion to Premises. We next need to ask what premises would logically get us to that conclusion. We will build our premises by "extracting" the general essence from our claim's statements. So let us first identify the statements in our claim that make up

Is graduation from college sufficient to get a good job after one's studies—even with average grades?

the different premises. Let us give them identifiers: s1 for the first statement, s2 for the second, and so on.

s1: Everybody cheats in college.
s2: Good grades are necessary to get a good job after graduation.
s3: One should do one's best not to get caught.

From each of these statements, we can build the following premises (p), with corresponding identifiers:

p1: Cheating in college is something everybody does.
p2: Getting a good job after graduation is the reason for going to college and good grades are necessary to get a good job.
p3: One should not get caught cheating.

2. Think through what you may be taking for granted in your reasoning. What assumptions are you making?

Let us now look at each of the premises and give them identifiers that show their relation to the original statements and premises.

For p1, can we go logically from asserting that cheating in college is something everybody does to stating that cheating in college is acceptable? It seems that we cannot go from the first assertion to the second statement without assuming that:

p1b: When everybody does something, then it (this something) is acceptable.

STRATEGY:
To uncover possible assumptions, for each statement, try to move from particulars to general principles—for example, here, we moved from cheating in college as something everybody does to everybody doing something being acceptable.

For p2, do we need to rely on further specifics to go from this statement to our conclusion? In this case, again, an assumption is made. A condition to getting a good job after graduation is obtaining good grades, but we can assert that cheating in college is acceptable if we assume that securing good grades justifies cheating. So, we are assuming here that:

> **p2b:** Any behavior that results in the good grades necessary to get a good job after graduation is acceptable.

Finally, for p3, let us apply the same process. We can get from the need not to get caught to cheating in college being acceptable if we accept that not getting caught doing something bad means that that action is acceptable. So, here we assume that:

> **p3b:** Doing something as long as one does not get caught doing it is acceptable.

{ ASK YOURSELF: Have I uncovered all possible assumptions included in the premises of my argument? }

3. Once you have identified assumptions, articulate them in your premise, so that your audience has the same understanding of a term or a concept as you.

Let's include these assumptions into our premises.

> **[p1]** Cheating in college is something everybody does and **[p1b]** when everybody does something, then it (this something) is acceptable.
> **[p2]** Getting good grades is necessary to get a good job, and **[p2b]** any behavior that results in the good grades necessary to get a good job after graduation is acceptable.
> **[p3]** One should not get caught cheating and **[p3b]** doing something as long as one does not get caught doing it is acceptable.

Myriam Abdelaziz/Redux

Does knowingly purchasing pirated software amount to cheating?

Let us break these down into simple and short premises:

> **PI:** Cheating in college is something everybody does.
> **PII:** When everybody does something, then it is acceptable.
> **PIII:** Good grades are necessary to get a good job.
> **PIV:** Any behavior that results in the good grades necessary to get a good job after graduation is acceptable.
> **PV:** One should not get caught cheating.
> **PVI:** Doing something as long as one does not get caught doing it is acceptable.
>
> **Therefore:** Cheating in college is acceptable.

At this point, we are not considering whether any of these premises is justifiable or empirically true—that is, whether we can prove any of them to be true. We will be engaging in this activity in our next step in **Thinking It Through 5**.

{ ASK YOURSELF: Have I identified precisely all of the elements needed to get to my conclusion? }

Now, take a moment to go back to your own claim and apply the steps we just took to extract the statements from our claim to build premises, examine each to find any assumptions, and articulate these in your premises.

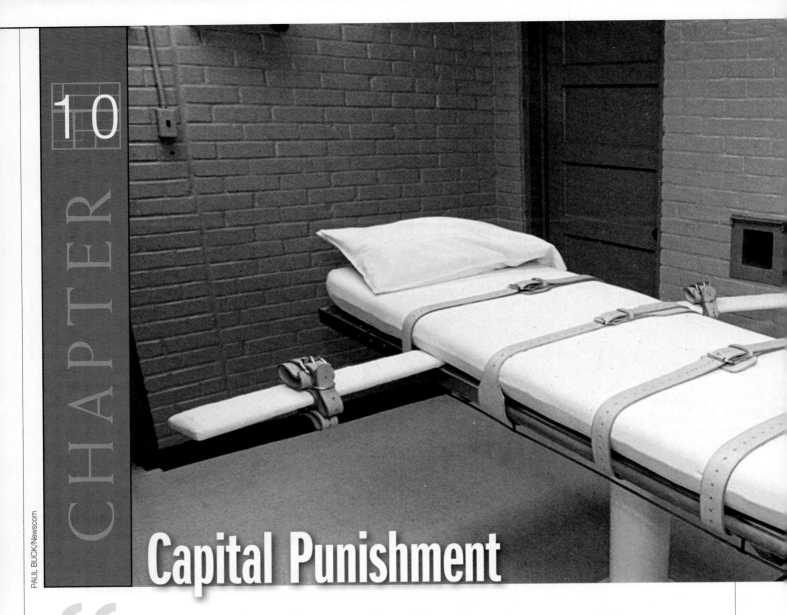

CHAPTER 10

Capital Punishment

"I defend this penalty, when confined to atrocious cases, on the very ground on which it is commonly attacked—on that of humanity to the criminal; as beyond comparison the least cruel mode in which it is possible adequately to deter from the crime."

—John Stuart Mill, Speech to the English Parliament, 1868

"The death penalty, unnecessary to promote the goal of deterrence or to further any legitimate notion of retribution, is an excessive penalty forbidden by the Eighth and Fourteenth Amendments."

—Justice Thurgood Marshall, dissenting opinion, *Gregg v. Georgia*, 428 U.S. 153 (1976)

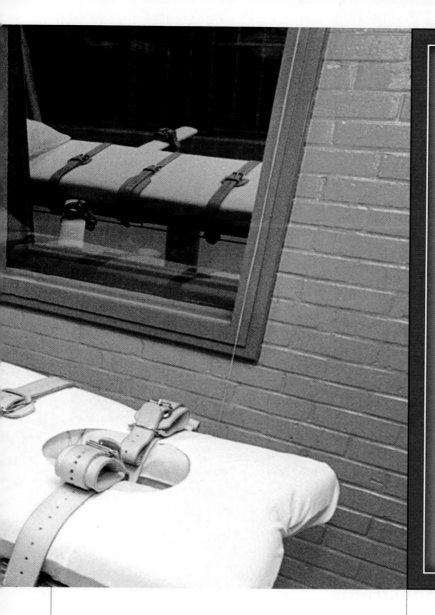

LEARNING OUTCOMES

After you complete this unit, you should be able to:

10-1 Describe the nature of punishment in general.

10-2 Identify and describe theories of punishment.

10-3 Explain how these theories apply to the justification of capital punishment.

10-4 Describe how scientific developments in DNA testing have affected our thinking about capital punishment.

10-5 Identify situations in which we should make exceptions to capital punishment.

10-6 Explain issues of fairness remaining today in the imposition of the death penalty, especially by race, class, and gender.

10-7 Identify and justify crimes, other than murder, that are subject to capital punishment.

10-8 Explain how legal reasoning compares with ethical reasoning regarding capital punishment.

Recent polls show that almost two-thirds of the United States population believe that capital punishment, the "death penalty," is justified. This support has remained steady for the last decade. Almost all of the executions worldwide are carried out in five countries: China, Iran, Pakistan, Saudi Arabia, and the United States. The continued debate over this form of punishment draws on broad philosophical principles for the ethical treatment of others, including the justification of all forms of punishment in general.

Overview

In this chapter, we will review theories of punishment in general and then apply them specifically to capital punishment to see whether the death penalty can be supported with them. We will ask whether new scientific techniques in DNA testing have cast doubt on the appropriateness of capital punishment because once we execute an innocent person, we have no way to correct the mistake. We will consider how evolving standards of public decency have led us to exempt from the threat of capital punishment the mentally and intellectually challenged, as well as young people. Whether any crimes other than murder, such as the rape of a child, should be subject to the death penalty is another challenge. We will see how closely intertwined philosophical reasoning is with legal reasoning in

What do you think?

Capital punishment is justified punishment for premeditated murder when guilt has clearly been proven.

Strongly Disagree						Strongly Agree
1	2	3	4	5	6	7

determining the justifiability, if any, of the death penalty in the twenty-first century. Finally, the topic is discussed in two readings, one by John Stuart Mill, and the other by Justice Thurgood Marshall, supporting arguments that respectively favor and reject the death penalty.

10-1 THE NATURE OF PUNISHMENT

Clarity in the use of key terminology is essential for good reasoning and philosophical analysis. We often step back to look at broader concepts to gain this clarity and then apply them to specific problems. So, before looking at capital punishment, we should first look at punishment in general. In philosophy, ethics, legal studies, and criminal justice, certain common traits of punishment are widely recognized:

- **Unpleasantness:** Punishment might involve incarceration or a monetary fine or restrictions on travel, all of which are undesirable impositions, whether meted out for criminal behavior or in a private setting such as a family home, a dormitory, or another setting where rules have been violated.

- **Violation of established standards, rules, or laws:** Punishment is inflicted when the wrongdoer violates some code for conduct that is understood in that setting. This might be a private set of rules in a family or a public set of laws in a governmental setting.

- **Infliction on a rule or law breaker:** Some process is needed for determining whether the alleged wrongdoer has indeed broken those rules or laws, followed by imposition of the punishment on that wrongdoer.

- **Imposition of the punishment by someone else:** Some system is needed for a judge to determine whether rules or laws have been violated and then impose the appropriate punishment. The judge might be a parent in a family or a judge in a criminal court of an established government.

- **Legitimacy of the authority to punish:** Whatever system we are considering, the person making the determination of a violation and the imposition of punishment needs to be someone recognized in that system as having the authority to do these things.

Article III of the U.S. Constitution established the judicial branch, which is charged with interpreting and applying the law. Under the separation of powers political doctrine, the legislative, executive, and judicial branches of the U.S. government are kept distinct to prevent abuse of power.

In CourseMate, watch a video and take the quiz.

⌐Punishment might involve ... undesirable impositions, whether meted out for criminal behavior or in a private setting such as a family home ...⌐

10-2 THEORIES OF PUNISHMENT

Why do we even need a "theory" of punishment? Is it not enough to just come up with some good reasons to explain why we think it is justified? The challenge arises because the things we use as punishment, whether in a family or in a criminal justice system, are unpleasant things, which, in isolation or on their own, would be wrong for us to do. If you locked somebody in a room against their will for many years, it would be wrong on the face of it (prima facie). So if, as a society, we lock people up in jail cells against their will for many years, we need a good justification for doing this. If you take somebody's money against their will, that, too, would be wrong on the face of it. So if, as a society, we fine people significant amounts of their money, we need a good justification for that, too. And in the most extreme case, if we killed somebody, that would be wrong on the face of it; thus, if we as a government want to execute somebody, we need a good reason for that. Theories of punishment give us the rationale and justification for doing these things which would otherwise be wrong prima facie.

Theories of punishment have evolved in law, philosophy, ethics, and criminal justice studies along the same lines. They typically appeal to historic philosophical views about ethics, even if we do not always name those sources.

10-2a Retribution

This theory centers on the notion of paying people back or giving them what they deserve for something they have done wrong. It is a way of evening the score. **Retribution** can be found in the Old Testament described as an "eye-for-an-eye," and we still hear that rationale today in non-religious discussions of punishment. The great German philosopher Immanuel Kant focused on retribution in his theories of ethics and the law as the justification for punishment and many contemporary philosophers have adopted this Kantian approach. The U.S. Supreme Court Justices, in analyzing cases about forms of punishment, including capital punishment, typically discuss whether the punishment can be justified as retribution. So this approach to justifying punishment is widely recognized and accepted.

One dispute regarding retribution is whether it should literally mean the identical conduct as punishment for that which is being punished, or whether it means only that the punishment should be proportionate to the crime or wrongdoing in question. If it literally means identical conduct, then executing someone for a murder makes sense. But does an eye-for-an-eye make sense for other crimes (see Feature 10.1 Eye-for-an-Eye)? If we convict someone of the crime of arson, should the punishment be that society gets to burn down the felon's house? If we convict someone of battery, should the punishment be that society has the convicted felon beaten up as retribution?

Proportionality is a milder sense of retribution and is summed up in the slogan that "the punishment should fit the crime." If you are convicted of jaywalking on a public street, life in prison without parole seems excessive. If you murder dozens of people, a fine of five dollars does not seem adequate to the seriousness of the crime. Finding proportionality in wrongdoing and punishment seems essential to have a functioning and effective justice system that people respect.

Retribution is sometimes criticized as simply being another term for *revenge*—by society against the wrongdoer. But the vengeful aspect highlighted by some is only one way of understanding the motive for retribution. Ultimately, any form of retribution comes with a real limitation: it makes a judgment in isolation from

Feature 10.1: Eye-for-an-Eye?

Supporters of capital punishment sometimes cite the language of an eye for an eye from the Old Testament of the Judeo-Christian bible as justification for its application. This expression is derived from the Latin phrase *lex talionis* (Latin, *lex* [law] and *talio* [like]) or the law of equivalency. This concept appears in the following Old Testament passage:

And if any mischief follow, then thou shalt give life for life, eye for eye, tooth for tooth, hand for hand, foot for foot, burning for burning, wound for wound, stripe for stripe. Exodus 21: 23–25

(This idea also can be found in two other passages of the Old Testament: Lev. 24:19–20; and Deut. 19:21.) If this supports execution by the state as punishment for the crime of murder, does it also support punishments for other crimes in contemporary society? What would be analogous punishment for arson? For theft? For assault?

Does an eye for an eye literally mean that the punishment should be the same act as the crime? Or does it mean merely that the punishment should be comparable in severity to the crime?

The expression, "an eye for an eye makes the whole world blind," is attributed to India's Mahatma Gandhi, the nonviolent political and spiritual leader.

what might be good for society as a whole. Indeed, we need effective systems of punishment, in which motivation should go beyond revenge and in which more effective justifications with better outcomes for everybody should be sought. The next four theories justify punishment based on the beneficial results produced for society, rather than merely on what criminals deserve through retribution.

10-2b Deterrence

This theory of punishment relies on producing good results from the form of punishment that is threatened or inflicted. It is consistent with the consequentialist or utilitarian views of such philosophers as John Stuart Mill because it looks toward producing results, namely, the greatest happiness (or least unhappiness) for the greatest number of people. **Deterrence** can happen in several ways. If we know what the punishment will be for a certain infraction, most of us will avoid that wrongdoing. If we know that parking in a handicapped spot will result in a one-hundred-dollar fine if we are caught, then we are deterred or discouraged from taking the chance and park elsewhere. This deterrence is even more effective if we have a friend who got caught and had to pay the fine or if we ourselves have previously had to pay one. So deterrence depends on our knowledge of the unpleasant consequences that will follow if we violate a rule or law.

We sometimes see public spectacles in which law officials want the rest of us to see what happens when people break the law. The notorious perp walk of alleged fraudsters on Wall Street should function as a strong deterrent to others thinking of trying to commit such fraud. But in contemporary society, we balk at too much publicity, even if it were an effective deterrent. In previous centuries, public hangings of lawbreakers were commonplace. Today, we do not televise executions, even though some have suggested that this might be a more effective deterrent to law breaking.

> In previous centuries, public hangings of lawbreakers were commonplace.

10-2c Prevention

Another justification of punishment is the **prevention** of further law breaking by the criminals themselves. This theory also relies on producing good consequences for society as a whole. We might accomplish prevention by locking up a criminal for a long time so he or she could not commit additional crimes on the general public. Prevention could also occur in more humanitarian ways, such as providing better education and job skills to young people so they did not feel compelled to commit crimes to "earn" a living.

10-2d Rehabilitation

The **rehabilitation** justification again focuses on results. If we reform or rehabilitate criminals while they are locked up, according to theory, we are benefitting them in making them employable when they are released. We are also improving the safety in society at large by reducing repeat crimes by these people.

10-2e Protection of Society

Yet another results-oriented theory focuses on the **protection of society** from otherwise innocent persons who we suspect might have a strong disposition to commit crimes and thus pose a special danger to others. But we do not simply lock people up because we have a hunch they might commit a crime someday because that would be a violation of basic principles of justice and subject to serious abuse against unpopular groups of persons. This approach to punishment has been problematic in dealing with persons with serious mental illness who we fear might harm others but have not yet committed any wrongdoing.

Frances M. Roberts/Alamy Limited

The "perp walk" has become a common practice by U.S. law enforcement. Parading a suspect under arrest in front of members of the media creates opportunities for photographs and video of the "perpetrator" to be taken.

10-3 FROM THEORY TO JUSTIFICATION

By looking at punishment in general, we are better equipped to look carefully at the theories attempting to justify capital punishment in particular.

10-3a Retribution

The theory of an eye-for-an-eye is often invoked to justify capital punishment. The criminal murdered somebody, so we as a society should get to kill him in return, to even out the score and give him or her what they deserved. This theory remains exceedingly persuasive to many, including philosophers, legal theorists, and the U.S. Supreme Court.

Critics urge that retribution should mean only that the punishment is comparable in severity to the crime, not that they be identical actions. Life in prison without the possibility of parole is a severe punishment. Indeed, Mill thought it was worse than execution and was the centerpiece of his argument in support of capital punishment. Critics also argue that retribution is an uncivilized form of societal revenge, and we should be able to come up with more enlightened solutions that punish appropriately and protect society.

10-3b Deterrence

The threat of the death penalty is assumed to be a strong deterrence to committing murder, at least according to death penalty supporters. But even the most ardent supporters, including justices on the U.S. Supreme Court, acknowledge candidly that solid empirical evidence to prove that the threat of the death penalty as a deterrent does not exist. More tellingly, it is difficult to imagine how one would set up such a study because of the many variables involved. Should we compare murder rates in a state such as California with the death penalty to the murder rate in a state such as New Hampshire that does not have the death penalty? Should we compare the murder rate in a state that ended its death penalty and then brought it back, such as New York? Consider all the other variables in any such study—rates of gun ownership, violence on television, demographics, gang eradication programs, quality of education, and the numerous other factors that might contribute to fluctuations in the murder rate. It does not seem possible to prove convincingly either that the death penalty is a deterrent or that it is not.

Supporters of the death penalty also acknowledge that certain groups of murderers are not deterred by the threat of death. The news is too often filled with reports of murder-suicides in which families or couples are murdered and the murderer then commits suicide. The threat of death is no deterrent in those all-too-common tragic situations.

The deterrent effect of the death penalty remains intellectually persuasive in this debate, however, and it is commonly discussed in Supreme Court decisions as relevant.

10-3c Prevention

One goal of the death penalty is to ensure that the convicted murderer will never be able to murder anyone else. Even with life without parole, supporters argue that convicted murderers remain a threat to other prisoners and to prison guards. Critics of the death penalty respond that more effective means of securing prisons should be the appropriate response of a civilized society.

10-3d Rehabilitation

Rehabilitation does not seem to make sense for a convicted murderer who will never again walk the streets in freedom. Yet the claim of rehabilitation has arisen in recent years because prisoners sentenced to death claim they have been rehabilitated and can accomplish good within prison, if their sentence is reduced to life without parole. Critics of the death penalty might find

REUTERS/Landov

Karla Faye Tucker, convicted of murder in Texas in 1984, was put to death in 1998. Her case gained attention because she was the first woman to be executed in the United States since 1984, and she claimed to have converted to Christianity while in prison.

this an attractive argument, but it has not succeeded in sparing the lives of such notorious murderers as Karla Fay Tucker in Texas or Stanley "Tookie" Williams in California, who were both executed despite claims of rehabilitation.

10-4 DNA TESTING'S IMPACT

The dramatic developments in DNA testing in recent years have led many to have second thoughts about capital punishment. These scientific techniques can determine definitively whether someone accused of a crime actually committed it. The ability to make this determination depends on finding sufficient samples for DNA testing, but the continuing improvements in testing enable forensic scientists to accomplish this with very small samples.

For individuals now on trial for a murder, DNA testing could prove conclusively that they were guilty or innocent and would be very relevant at a trial (see Feature 10.2). But we are now in a transitional period where many sitting on death row did not have this advantage at their own trials and now want to go back and have the evidence tested to prove their own innocence. If the evidence has been stored properly and is still available, this testing is possible. Groups, such as Project Innocence, have proven that 265 people were wrongly convicted,

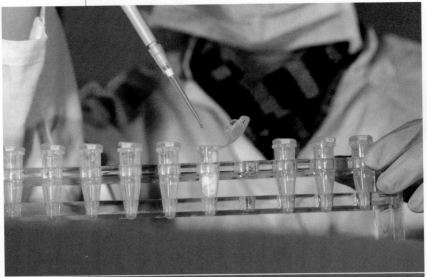

DNA typing, since it was introduced in the mid-1980s, has revolutionized forensic science and the ability of law enforcement to match perpetrators with crime scenes.

imagebroker.net/SuperStock

For individuals now on trial for a murder, DNA testing could prove conclusively that they were guilty or innocent ...

including 13 who were on death row. These people are not getting off on a "technicality" and getting a new trial: their actual innocence has been proven through that DNA testing.

These astonishing results have given pause to many who otherwise supported the death penalty. If this many people have already been proven innocent, long after their convictions, how many other innocent people might be sitting on death row? How many people have been executed wrongly when they were in fact innocent? The death penalty is unique in its irrevocability. If someone is wrongly imprisoned, society can give them their

Feature 10.2: DNA Testing

Several types of DNA testing have been developed in recent decades that can help identify both criminals and victims with certainty as a result of the uniqueness of our DNA.

According to the Human Genome Project of the U.S. government, all fifty states require convicted sex offenders to submit DNA, and convicted felons are required to submit DNA in forty-four states. DNA records have enabled law enforcement to solve many "cold cases." Ethical concerns include the

possible violation of privacy rights when government agencies have such extensive information about DNA profiles on file.

The federal Innocence Protection Act, enacted in 2004, gives all federal inmates the right to petition a federal court for DNA testing to prove they are innocent. The Act also encourages states to make DNA testing available after conviction.

Sources: Genomic Science Program, U.S. Department of Energy; The Innocence Project.

freedom first, and then monetary compensation for those lost years. But that is not an option when someone has been wrongly executed.

10-5 JUVENILES AND THE MENTALLY IMPAIRED

Even among supporters of the death penalty, certain situations have been recognized when capital punishment is not appropriate, including in the case of murder with clear evidence proving "guilt beyond a reasonable doubt."

In 2002, the U.S. Supreme Court held in *Atkins v. Virginia* that it was an unconstitutional violation of the protection against cruel and unusual punishment to execute someone with mental retardation. The Court focused on the two major justifications for punishment, retribution and deterrence, and concluded that they do not make sense for persons unable to understand the laws or the threat of punishment. This reasoning coincides with the approach philosophers take in asking when we should hold someone responsible for their actions. Critics of this approach, however, worry that the accused might succeed in faking retardation to escape punishment, and the Court did not set out any guidelines for how to define retardation sufficient to come under this protection.

> ⌈**[R]etribution and deterrence ... do not make sense for persons unable to understand the laws...**⌋

Similar reasoning was used in 2005 when the U.S. Supreme Court in *Roper v. Simmons* held that a juvenile offender cannot be executed. Young people cannot understand fully the threat of punishment or take full responsibility for their actions, so neither retribution nor deterrence justifies execution. Critics of this conclusion worry that organized gangs encourage juveniles to commit murders for them, knowing the juveniles will not be executed if caught and convicted.

Mental illness has long raised special issues in the criminal justice system. Dating back to the mid-nineteenth century in England, legal struggles have long centered on finding a way to articulate when someone with a mental disease or defect should be excused from their actions. The key seems to be whether the person knew the difference between right and wrong and knew that what they were doing was wrong. If they did not, then the rationale of retribution or deterrence makes little sense in justifying any punishment, including the

death penalty. Yet protection of society from persons who might cause further harm remains a legitimate concern, which has led to justifying locking people up in hospitals for the criminally insane.

10-6 CAPITAL PUNISHMENT AND FAIRNESS

Especially since the 1976 reforms required in *Gregg v. Georgia*, many who have been convicted of murder have not been subject to the death penalty. The states with the death penalty have imposed stringent requirements for when the death penalty could be considered. These include first-degree murder or aggravated murder or murders of multiple persons. That also means that many convicted murderers are not even considered for the death penalty.

Despite these reforms, troubling questions remain about the fairness of the justice system. Although everyone has a right to an attorney, they do not have a right to the best or most expensive attorney, and poor quality representation, even of alleged murderers, has been well documented. Everyone has a right to a fair trial, but is that what every accused is receiving? The gross disparities in our justice system led the U.S. Supreme Court to strike down the death penalty temporarily in 1972 in *Furman v. Georgia* until some of the most egregious practices were curtailed. The death penalty was reinstated four years later in *Gregg v. Georgia* when states agreed to automatic appeals, separation of the trial from the penalty phase, and abolishment of mandatory death sentences. Even with these improvements in the justice system, many remain concerned about the great disparities in the imposition of the death penalty by race, class, and gender.

In the case of *McClesky v. Kemp*, in which a black man was sentenced to death for the killing of a white policeman, the defendant's lawyers produced extensive data showing that convicted killers of white victims were far more likely to receive the death penalty than killers of black victims—the statistics in Figure 10.1 show specific differences in the capital punishment application rate by race in the recent past. Even so, the U.S. Supreme Court upheld the constitutionality of the death penalty in a 5–4 decision.

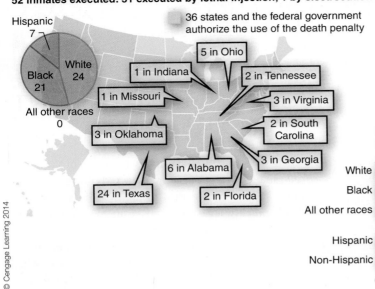

52 inmates executed: 51 executed by lethal injection; 1 by electrocution

36 states and the federal government authorize the use of the death penalty

Hispanic 7

Black 21

White 24

All other races 0

5 in Ohio

1 in Indiana

2 in Tennessee

1 in Missouri

3 in Virginia

2 in South Carolina

3 in Oklahoma

3 in Georgia

6 in Alabama

24 in Texas

2 in Florida

© Cengage Learning 2014

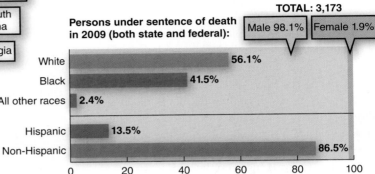

Figure 10.1 Capital punishment by race in the United States in 2009

Source: Bureau of Justice Statistics, U.S. Department of Justice

Persons under sentence of death in 2009 (both state and federal):

TOTAL: 3,173

Male 98.1%   Female 1.9%

White 56.1%
Black 41.5%
All other races 2.4%
Hispanic 13.5%
Non-Hispanic 86.5%

10-7 CAPITAL PUNISHMENT FOR OTHER CRIMES

Although most popular discussion of the death penalty focuses on punishment for the crime of murder, laws exist in the United States today for other crimes subject to capital punishment. At the level of the federal government, although most offenses involve murder, espionage and treason remain subject to the death penalty. The most recent executions for espionage were Julius and Ethel Rosenberg, who were executed by electric chair in 1953 for passing nuclear secrets to the Soviet Union. The death penalty is also still available for treason. According to the Navy Historical Center, U.S. Navy, Herbert Hans Haupt was executed for treason during World War II. Born in Germany, he had become a naturalized U.S. citizen in 1930 but returned to Germany to assist in their war effort. He was convicted as part of a group that attempted to sabotage the U.S. war effort after landing on a beach in Florida. In the states—as opposed to the federal level—most crimes subject to the death penalty involve murder. Treason is subject to the death penalty in Louisiana.

The challenging question today is the rationale for this punishment. Traditionally, those striking at the very heart of the government's existence, through

In the states ... most crimes subject to the death penalty involve murder.

espionage or treason, did not deserve to continue existence in that society. Given the danger of these crimes to society, both retribution and deterrence seem also to provide support, if there is support at all, for the death penalty.

Of more immediate concern is capital punishment for rape. In 1977, the U.S. Supreme Court, in *Coker v. Georgia*, held that this punishment was excessive and thus unconstitutional, while acknowledging the horrors of the crime of rape of an adult. It was not until 2008 that the Court decided that capital punishment for the rape of a child was also excessive, in the case of *Kennedy v. Louisiana*. Of course, capital punishment remains as an option for rape-murder crimes, but not for rape alone, as horrible as that crime might be. Here, the court was appealing to proportionality of punishment to crime, a mild version of retribution theory.

Now that you have studied how various types of reasoning apply to the topics discussed, review Critical Thinking Table 10.1 to follow the process of examining an ethical claim on a related topic.

In CourseMate, apply what you've learned to the real-life scenario in the simulation.

In CourseMate, practice what you learned by taking the chapter quiz.

Table 10.1 Critical Thinking Steps and Their Application in an Example

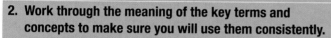

{ "An 'eye-for-an-eye' means that anybody who commits a murder deserves to be executed." }

Critical Thinking Steps	Application
1. **Examine and clarify key terms and concepts.** PAUL BUCK/ Newscom • Look words up in a dictionary as a start if necessary. • Unravel or unpack the complexities and nuances of a central term, such as *justice*, *right*, or *good*.	• What does "eye-for-an-eye" really mean? • Does "murder" include all killing or only certain kinds of killing? • Does "execute" include any form of killing by the state?
2. **Work through the meaning of the key terms and concepts to make sure you will use them consistently.** • Consider the ways the term can be used by including it in different sentences and contexts to zero in on the particular meaning you are after. • Ask yourself what words are potential synonyms for the concept. Do those capture everything you want to understand about that term?	• Do we really accept eye-for-an-eye in all situations? Do we literally mean an identical response to the crime or merely something of comparable severity? If someone is convicted of arson in burning down a house, do we literally think the appropriate punishment is burning down the criminal's house? • Are we sure we want our conclusions to apply to everybody, including children, the mentally challenged, and the mentally ill? • Murder comes in many varieties and degrees; we also seem to treat the murders of some persons more severely, such as police officers or witnesses in a trial. Should they all be treated the same with regard to punishments? • Are some forms of execution off limits today or do we want to accept any form of execution in our conclusion? Would boiling in oil or dismembering somebody on the medieval rack be okay?
3. **Build premises and bring any assumptions to light.** 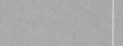 REUTERS/Landov • Put together short and clear sentences to build each of your premises. • Think through what you may be taking for granted in your reasoning. What assumptions are you making? • Once you have identified assumptions, articulate them in your premise, so that your audience has the same understanding of a term or a concept as you.	The premises of the argument could be constructed as follows, using these clarifications of terminology: • An *eye-for-an-eye* means that the appropriate punishment is the same act as the crime itself. • *Execution* is the same act as the crime of murder. CONCLUSION: An eye-for-an-eye means that execution is the appropriate punishment for murder.
4. **Test/Verify your premises.** • Now that you have stated your premises explicitly, do you want to stick with them? • Are you relying on premises drawn from unsubstantiated sources or from questionable authorities?	Each of these premises should be examined. • Although we typically rely on eye-for-an-eye with regard to murders and execution, we are less comfortable applying this principle to all possible crimes.

(Continued)

Table 10.1 Continued

Critical Thinking Steps	Application
• Are you consistent in your premises? Or are you appealing to different and inconsistent foundations in your reasoning? • Reformulate your premises if they have proven to be faulty.	• The physical act of termination of a life seems to be the same act, but the intentions and the persons carrying out the act differ. The murder is committed by a criminal, while the execution is carried out by the state. Is this a difference we should be concerned about? If you do not accept all of these premises, then you will not accept the conclusion either. But if you do accept all of them, then you would find the conclusion valid and justified.
5. Confirm that the conclusions you draw are logical. Check for reliance on fallacies and correct any premise that you identify as relying on a fallacy. HO/U.S. Marshals Service/Reuters/Landov	The fallacy of sweeping generalization seems to be at play here in the key terminology. Although the terms seem persuasive if we are only talking about vicious murders, the claims are less obvious when stated in general terms for other crimes.

Timeline 10.1 Landmark legal cases of the U.S. Supreme Court on Capital Punishment

1972 *Furman v. Georgia,* 408 U.S. 238: Death penalty constitutes cruel and unusual punishment in violation of eighth amendment due to grossly unfair implementation by race and class.

1976 *Gregg v. Georgia,* 428 U.S. 153: Death penalty constitutional if procedural safeguards are implemented, e.g., automatic appeal, separation of guilt, and penalty phases.

1977 *Coker v. Georgia,* 433 U.S. 584: Death penalty for rape of an adult unconstitutional as excessive.

1987 *McClesky v. Kemp,* 481 U.S. 279: Statistical evidence of racially disparate imposition of death penalty does not violate Equal Protection Clause of the Constitution.

10-8 LEGAL AND ETHICAL REASONING COMPARISON

In many areas of ethical reasoning, there is clear overlap with legal reasoning in our judicial system. This is particularly obvious in the area of capital punishment, which remains a major issue both in ethics and in the law. Of special note, as we have pointed out here, is the similarity of reasoning in these two domains. Deterrence and retribution are central in both philosophical and legal reasoning. Many court opinions read almost like philosophical treatises in their approach.

The main difference is that legal reasoning makes an ultimate appeal to the U.S. Constitution, in particular, the Eighth Amendment protecting against

> **[L]egal reasoning makes an ultimate appeal to the U.S. Constitution, in particular, the Eighth Amendment protecting against "cruel and unusual punishment."**

"cruel and unusual punishment." Although philosophers do not explicitly appeal to that amendment in their analyses, they do use reasoning that is consistent with the spirit of that amendment in their appeals to justice and fairness in the administration of our system of laws and ethics.

Another major difference is that in legal reasoning, the precedent of previous decisions is weighed heavily, whereas philosophical reasoning is not bound by such authority. Our legal system, based on the common law of England as well as the written constitution of the United States, places great weight on stare decisis (stay the course). People need to know what the law is if they are expected to follow it. That law includes not only the Constitution and the written statutes passed into law by Congress, but also the judge-made law and precedent of

1993 *Herrera v. Collins,* 506 U.S. 390: Proof of actual innocence does not guarantee additional appeals.

2005 *Roper v. Simmons,* 543 U.S. 551: Execution of juvenile offenders younger than eighteen is excessive and violates the Constitution.

2008 *Kennedy v. Louisiana,* 554 U.S. 407: Death penalty for rape of a child unconstitutional as excessive.

2002 *Atkins v. Virginia,* 536 U.S. 304: Execution of the mentally retarded is excessive and violates the Constitution.

Gyuszkofoto/Shutterstock

our legal system. Although judges do from time to time modify or even overturn precedents, they tend to avoid this except in the most extreme situations in which justice seems to demand nothing less. Philosophers are interested in the wisdom of Kant and Plato and great thinkers who came before, but they do not accord them the status of authorities, as the legal system does with precedents.

In CourseMate, listen to the audio summary of the chapter.

Hugo Adam Bedau

Hugo Bedau was probably the most prominent American philosopher opposing the death penalty in the twentieth century. Educated at the University of Redlands, Boston University, and Harvard University, he taught for most of his career at Tufts University in Massachusetts, from 1966 until he retired in 1999 as the Austin B. Fletcher Professor of Philosophy Emeritus. In 1994, he was named the Romanell-Phi Beta Kappa Professor of Philosophy for the 1994–1995 academic year. He previously taught at Reed College, Princeton University, and Dartmouth College.

His first book, *The Death Penalty in America* (1964), was not only a pioneering work on capital punishment but also one of the earliest examples of applied ethics, demonstrating the insights that professional philosophers can bring to bear on important public policy issues. That book went through several editions, becoming *The Death Penalty in America: Current Controversies* in 1997. With Michael L. Radelet and Constance E. Putnam, Bedau published another ground-breaking book in 1992, *In Spite of Innocence: Erroneous Convictions in Capital Cases*. He wrote more than 150 articles on justice and civil rights, and on legal and political philosophy; he also edited numerous books. Among his major works on capital punishment are three collections of his own essays: *The Courts, The Constitution, and Capital Punishment* (1977), *Death is Different* (1987) and *Killing as Punishment* (2004). In addition to his

Hugo Adam Bedau (1926–2012)

extensive academic work on capital punishment, he was active in political efforts to abolish the death penalty. He was a founding member of the National Coalition to Abolish the Death Penalty, a long-time member of the American Civil Liberties Union, and a member of the speakers's bureau for Amnesty International USA.

For much of his career, Bedau engaged in print dialogue with a sociologist well known for his support of the death penalty, Ernest van den Haag. Bedau argued that there is no conclusive evidence that the death penalty deters crime or even that it deters convicted murderers from murdering again. He also expressed alarm at the unfair applications of the death penalty to those disadvantaged by race, gender, and economic resources. Van den Haag, in his extensive writings on the death penalty, agreed that we do not have solid statistical evidence that the death penalty deters potential murderers, but believed that capital punishment was justified as a psychological deterrent anyway. He also argued that the death penalty can be justified through a utilitarian analysis of costs and benefits to society overall. He and Bedau were also frequent adversaries in oral debates.

CHAPTER Case Study

Capital Punishment

Jared Loughner is alleged to have shot nineteen people, including Congresswoman Gabrielle Giffords, on January 8, 2011, in the parking lot of a shopping center in Tucson, Arizona. Six of the nineteen were killed. Federal law prohibits the murder of federal officials, so he will be tried first for the murders of U.S. District Judge John Roll and congressional aide Gabe Zimmerman. Under federal law, the death penalty is available for these murders, if he is convicted. After the federal case is tried, he can also be tried

A photo showing the aftermath of the January 8, 2011 shooting in Tucson, Arizona, that claimed the lives of six people and injured thirteen.

2. If we conclude that those who truly do not know the difference between right and wrong should not be executed, what would be a justifiable response by society to those persons, whether ethically or legally? Should they be punished in some other way? Are we justified in locking them in prison solely to protect society even if they do not understand deterrence or retribution?

3. Check the progress of the Loughner trials on the Internet from reliable sources. What arguments are the defense attorneys making on his behalf? How are the prosecutors responding? What issues are being raised concerning his mental condition? Do you consider them justifiable excuses for his behavior? What punishment or other response seems justifiable to you?

For additional case studies, please see the CourseMate for this text.

under Arizona state law for the murders of the other four victims, for which the death penalty is also available.

Loughner entered a "not guilty" plea for the federal charges. Numerous press reports and commentators have wondered whether Loughner is mentally ill and thus might escape punishment through the so-called "insanity defense." Although this defense is generally available in some form in all states and at the federal level, it is not easily used. The Unabomber Ted Kaczynski was found sane for his trial and conviction, even though he was a diagnosed paranoid schizophrenic. Andrea Yates, convicted in Texas of drowning her five children, also was found sane and convicted, although she too had been a diagnosed paranoid schizophrenic.

Mental illness alone does not meet the requirement of the insanity defense. First recognized in England in the mid-nineteenth century, the defense has been stated in many forms in this country. The most essential element is that the wrongdoer does not know the difference between right and wrong and is unable to make those choices in how to behave properly.

1. Should we treat insane people differently in meting out justice, whether in our ethical judgments or in our legal system? Does the justification of retribution make sense for those who are genuinely insane? Does capital punishment or any other form of punishment have any deterrent effect for those who are insane? What other justification might we have to execute the insane? What tests would you propose for making the decision on whether and, if so, when to execute the insane?

Jared Loughner, the man accused of gunning down nineteen people in 2011.

Reading Excerpt: John Stuart Mill, "In Support of Capital Punishment" (1868)

INTRODUCTION

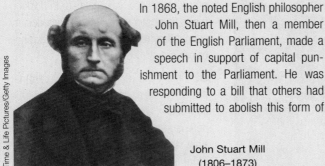

Time & Life Pictures/Getty Images

John Stuart Mill
(1806–1873)

In 1868, the noted English philosopher John Stuart Mill, then a member of the English Parliament, made a speech in support of capital punishment to the Parliament. He was responding to a bill that others had submitted to abolish this form of punishment. He argues that the most effective deterrent to crime is the death penalty, which is more humane than life in prison. His approach to the issues appeals to his utilitarianism, considering which alternative will produce the greatest happiness (or least unhappiness) for the greatest number. He does not appeal to retribution as a justification because this would be contrary to his utilitarian approach, which focuses only on consequences.

QUESTIONS FOR REFLECTION

1. Has Mill effectively argued that capital punishment is the most humane punishment, compared with life imprisonment? Does his argument depend on empirical facts about the prison system in England which might not apply today?

2. What language in his speech directly appeals to his utilitarian principles?

3. What reasoning does Mill use to conclude that the threat of death is an effective deterrent?

4. Does Mill effectively respond to critics that innocent people might be executed, with no recourse available to society?

READING

. . . aggravated murder is now practically the only crime which is punished with death by any of our lawful tribunals; and we are even now deliberating whether the extreme penalty should be retained in that solitary case. This vast gain, not only to humanity,
5 but to the ends of penal justice, we owe to the philanthropists; and if they are mistaken, as I cannot but think they are, in the present instance, it is only in not perceiving the right time and place for stopping in a career hitherto so eminently beneficial.

Sir, there is a point at which, I conceive, that career ought to
10 stop. When there has been brought home to any one, by conclusive evidence, the greatest crime known to the law; and when the attendant circumstances suggest no palliation of the guilt, no hope that the culprit may even yet not be unworthy to live among mankind, nothing to make it probable that the crime was an
15 exception to his general character rather than a consequence of it, then I confess it appears to me that to deprive the criminal of the life of which he has proved himself to be unworthy—solemnly to blot him out from the fellowship of mankind and from the catalogue of the living—is the most appropriate as it is certainly the
20 most impressive, mode in which society can attach to so great a crime the penal consequences which for the security of life it is indispensable to annex to it.

I defend this penalty, when confined to atrocious cases, on the very ground on which it is commonly attacked—on that of human-
25 ity to the criminal; as beyond comparison the least cruel mode in which it is possible adequately to deter from the crime. If, in our horror of inflicting death, we endeavor to devise some punishment for the living criminal which shall act on the human mind with a deterrent force at all comparable to that of death, we are driven
30 to inflictions less severe indeed in appearance, and therefore less efficacious, but far more cruel in reality. Few, I think, would venture to propose, as a punishment for aggravated murder, less than imprisonment with hard labor for life; that is the fate to which a murderer would be consigned by the mercy which shrinks from
35 putting him to death.

What Punishment Is Merciful?

But has it been sufficiently considered what sort of a mercy this is, and what kind of life it leaves to him? If, indeed, the punishment is not really inflicted—if it becomes the sham which a few years
40 ago such punishments were rapidly becoming—then, indeed, its adoption would be almost tantamount to giving up the attempt to repress murder altogether. But if it really is what it professes to be, and if it is realized in all its rigor by the popular imagination,

as it very probably would not be, but as it must be if it is to be
45 efficacious, it will be so shocking that when the memory of the
crime is no longer fresh, there will be almost insuperable difficulty
in executing it.

What comparison can there really be, in point of severity,
between consigning a man to the short pang of a rapid death, and
50 immuring him in a living tomb, there to linger out what may be a
long life in the hardest and most monotonous toil, without any of
its alleviations or rewards—barred from all pleasant sights and
sounds, and cut off from all earthly hope, except a slight mitigation
of bodily restraint, or a small improvement of diet? Yet even such a
55 lot as this, because there is no one moment at which the suffering
is of terrifying intensity, and, above all, because it does not contain
the element, so imposing to the imagination, of the unknown, is
universally reputed a milder punishment than death—stands in
all codes as a mitigation of the capital penalty, and is thankfully
60 accepted as such. For it is characteristic of all punishments which
depend on duration for their efficacy—all, therefore, which are
not corporal or pecuniary—that they are more rigorous than they
seem; while it is, on the contrary, one of the strongest recommendations a punishment can have, that it should seem more rigorous
65 than it is; for its practical power depends far less on what it is than
on what it seems.

> " *What comparison can*
> *there really be, in point*
> *of severity, between*
> *consigning a man to the*
> *short pang of a rapid death,*
> *and immuring him in a*
> *living tomb ... [?]* "

There is not, I should think, any human infliction which
makes an impression on the imagination so entirely out of
proportion to its real severity as the punishment of death. The
70 punishment must be mild indeed which does not add more to
the sum of human misery than is necessarily or directly added
by the execution of a criminal. As my hon. Friend the Member
for Northampton (Mr. Gilpin) has himself remarked, the most that
human laws can do to anyone in the matter of death is to hasten
75 it; the man would have died at any rate; not so very much later,
and on the average, I fear, with a considerably greater amount
of bodily suffering. Society is asked, then, to denude itself of an
instrument of punishment which, in the grave cases to which

Newgate Prison in London, estimated to date back to the
twelfth century, was rebuilt several times. Located close to the
Old Bailey and Saint Paul's Cathedral, it became the site where
executions took place in London, until 1868 when these public
hangings came to an end.

alone it is suitable, effects its purposes at a less cost of human
80 suffering than any other; which, while it inspires more terror, is
less cruel in actual fact than any punishment that we should
think of substituting for it.

My hon. Friend says that it does not inspire terror, and that
experience proves it to be a failure. But the influence of a punish-
85 ment is not to be estimated by its effect on hardened criminals.
Those whose habitual way of life keeps them, so to speak, at all
times within sight of the gallows, do grow to care less about it;
as, to compare good things with bad, an old soldier is not much
affected by the chance of dying in battle. I can afford to admit all
90 that is often said about the indifference of professional criminals
to the gallows. Though of that indifference one-third is probably bravado and another third confidence that they shall have
the luck to escape, it is quite probable that the remaining third
is real. But the efficacy of a punishment which acts principally
95 through the imagination, is chiefly to be measured by the impression it makes on those who are still innocent; by the horror with
which it surrounds the first promptings of guilt; the restraining
influence it exercises over the beginning of the thought which, if
indulged, would become a temptation; the check which it exerts
100 over the graded declension towards the state—never suddenly
attained—in which crime no longer revolts, and punishment no
longer terrifies.

Death as a Deterrent
As for what is called the failure of death punishment, who is able
105 to judge of that? We partly know who those are whom it has not
deterred; but who is there who knows whom it has deterred, or
how many human beings it has saved who would have lived to be

Bettmann/Corbis

murderers if that awful association had not been thrown round the idea of murder from their earliest infancy? Let us not forget that the most imposing fact loses its power over the imagination if it is made too cheap. When a punishment fit only for the most atrocious crimes is lavished on small offences until human feeling recoils from it, then, indeed, it ceases to intimidate, because it ceases to be believed in.

The failure of capital punishment in cases of theft is easily accounted for; the thief did not believe that it would be inflicted. He had learnt by experience that jurors would perjure themselves rather than find him guilty; that Judges would seize any excuse for not sentencing him to death, or for recommending him to mercy; and that if neither jurors nor Judges were merciful, there were still hopes from an authority above both. When things had come to this pass it was high time to give up the vain attempt.

When it is impossible to inflict a punishment, or when its infliction becomes a public scandal, the idle threat cannot too soon disappear from the statute book. And in the case of the host of offences which were formerly capital, I heartily rejoice that it did become impracticable to execute the law. If the same state of public feeling comes to exist in the case of murder; if the time comes when jurors refuse to find a murderer guilty; when Judges will not sentence him to death, or will recommend him to mercy; or when, if juries and Judges do not flinch from their duty, Home Secretaries, under pressure of deputations and memorials, shrink from theirs, and the threat becomes, as it became in the other cases, a mere *brutum fulmen* [A display of force]; then, indeed, it may become necessary to do in this case what has been done in those—to abrogate the penalty.

That time may come—my hon. Friend thinks that it has nearly come. I hardly know whether he lamented it or boasted of it; but he and his Friends are entitled to the boast; for if it comes it will be their doing, and they will have gained what I cannot but call a fatal victory, for they will have achieved it by bringing about, if they will forgive me for saying so, an enervation, an effeminacy, in the general mind of the country. For what else than effeminacy is it to be so much more shocked by taking a man's life than by depriving him of all that makes life desirable or valuable? Is death, then, the greatest of all earthly ills? *Usque adeone mori miserum est*? [Is it so hard a thing to die?] Is it, indeed, so dreadful a thing to die? Has it not been from of old one chief part of a manly education to make us despise death—teaching us to account it, if an evil at all, by no means high in the list of evils; at all events, as an inevitable one, and to hold, as it were, our lives in our hands, ready to be given or risked at any moment, for a sufficiently worthy object?

I am sure that my hon. Friends know all this as well, and have as much of all these feelings as any of the rest of us; possibly more. But I cannot think that this is likely to be the effect of their teaching on the general mind. I cannot think that the cultivating of a peculiar sensitiveness of conscience on this one point, over and above what results from the general cultivation of the moral sentiments, is permanently consistent with assigning in our own minds to the fact of death no more than the degree of relative importance which belongs to it among the other incidents of our humanity.

The Horror of Death

The men of old cared too little about death, and gave their own lives or took those of others with equal recklessness. Our danger is of the opposite kind, lest we should be so much shocked by death, in general and in the abstract, as to care too much about it in individual cases, both those of other people and our own, which call for its being risked. And I am not putting things at the worst, for it is proved by the experience of other countries that horror of the executioner by no means necessarily implies horror of the assassin. The stronghold, as we all know, of hired assassination in the 18th century was Italy; yet it is said that in some of the Italian populations the infliction of death by sentence of law was in the highest degree offensive and revolting to popular feeling.

Much has been said of the sanctity of human life, and the absurdity of supposing that we can teach respect for life by ourselves destroying it. But I am surprised at the employment of this argument, for it is one which might be brought against any punishment whatever. It is not human life only, not human life as such, that ought to be sacred to us, but human feelings. The human capacity of suffering is what we should cause to be respected, not the mere capacity of existing.

And we may imagine somebody asking how we can teach people not to inflict suffering by ourselves inflicting it? But to this I should answer—all of us would answer—that to deter by suffering from inflicting suffering is not only possible, but the very purpose of penal justice. Does fining a criminal show want of respect for property, or imprisoning him, for personal freedom? Just as unreasonable is it to think that to take the life of a man who has taken that of another is to show want of regard for human life. We show, on the contrary, most emphatically our regard for it, by the adoption of a rule that he who violates that right in another forfeits it for himself, and that while no other crime that he can commit deprives him of his right to live, this shall.

Executing the Innocent

There is one argument against capital punishment, even in extreme cases, which I cannot deny to have weight—on which my hon. Friend justly laid great stress, and which never can be entirely got rid of. It is this—that if by an error of justice an innocent person is put to death, the mistake can never be corrected; all compensation, all reparation for the wrong is impossible. This would be indeed a serious objection if these miserable mistakes—among the most tragical occurrences in the whole round of human affairs—could not be made extremely rare.

The argument is invincible where the mode of criminal procedure is dangerous to the innocent, or where the Courts of Justice are not trusted. And this probably is the reason why the objection to an irreparable punishment began (as I believe it did) earlier, and is more intense and more widely diffused, in some parts of the Continent of Europe than it is here. There are on the Continent great and enlightened countries, in which the criminal procedure is not so favorable to innocence, does not afford the same security against erroneous conviction, as it does among us; countries where the Courts of Justice seem to think they fail in their duty unless they find somebody guilty; and in their really laudable desire to hunt guilt from its hiding places, expose themselves to a serious danger of condemning the innocent.

If our own procedure and Courts of Justice afforded ground for similar apprehension, I should be the first to join in withdrawing the power of inflicting irreparable punishment from such tribunals. But we all know that the defects of our procedure are the very opposite. Our rules of evidence are even too favorable to the prisoner; and juries and Judges carry out the maxim, "It is better that ten guilty should escape than that one innocent person should suffer," not only to the letter, but beyond the letter. Judges are most anxious to point out, and juries to allow for, the barest possibility of the prisoner's innocence. No human judgment is infallible; such sad cases as my hon. Friend cited will sometimes occur; but in so grave a case as that of murder, the accused, in our system, has always the benefit of the merest shadow of a doubt.

Irreversible Error

And this suggests another consideration very germane to the question. The very fact that death punishment is more shocking than any other to the imagination, necessarily renders the Courts of Justice more scrupulous in requiring the fullest evidence of guilt. Even that which is the greatest objection to capital punishment, the impossibility of correcting an error once committed, must make, and does make, juries and Judges more careful in forming their opinion, and more jealous in their scrutiny of the evidence. If the substitution of penal servitude for death in cases of murder should cause any declaration in this conscientious scrupulosity, there would be a great evil to set against the real, but I hope rare, advantage of being able to make reparation to a condemned person who was afterwards discovered to be innocent.

In order that the possibility of correction may be kept open wherever the chance of this sad contingency is more than infinitesimal, it is quite right that the Judge should recommend to the Crown a commutation of the sentence, not solely when the proof of guilt is open to the smallest suspicion, but whenever there remains anything unexplained and mysterious in the case, raising a desire for more light, or making it likely that further information may at some future time be obtained. I would also suggest that whenever the sentence is commuted the grounds of the commutation should, in some authentic form, be made known to the public.

Thus much I willingly concede to my hon. Friend; but on the question of total abolition I am inclined to hope that the feeling of the country is not with him, and that the limitation of death punishment to the cases referred to in the Bill of last year will be generally considered sufficient. The mania which existed a short time ago for paring down all our punishments seems to have reached its limits, and not before it was time. We were in danger of being left without any effectual punishment, except for small of offences.

Alternative Punishments

What was formerly our chief secondary punishment—transportation [deportation to Australia and the Colonies]—before it was abolished, had become almost a reward. Penal servitude, the substitute for it, was becoming, to the classes who were principally subject to it, almost nominal, so comfortable did we make our prisons, and so easy had it become to get quickly out of them. Flogging—a most objectionable punishment in ordinary cases, but a particularly appropriate one for crimes of brutality, especially crimes against women—we would not hear of, except, to be sure, in the case of garotters, for whose peculiar benefit we reestablished it in a hurry, immediately after a Member of Parliament had been garrotted. With this exception, offences, even of an atrocious kind, against the person, as my hon. and learned Friend the Member for Oxford (Mr. Neate) well remarked, not only were, but still are, visited with penalties so ludicrously inadequate, as to be almost an encouragement to the crime.

> **"** *Penal servitude, … was becoming, to the classes who were principally subject to it, almost nominal, so comfortable did we make our prisons, …* **"**

I think, Sir, that in the case of most offences, except those against property, there is more need of strengthening our punishments than of weakening them; and that severer sentences, with an apportionment of them to the different kinds of offences which shall approve itself better than at present to the moral sentiments of the community, are the kind of reform of which our penal system now stands in need. I shall therefore vote against the Amendment.

Reading Excerpt: Justice Thurgood Marshall, *Gregg v. Georgia*, 428 U.S. 153, dissenting opinion (1976)

INTRODUCTION

Thurgood Marshall is remembered as one of the most important leaders of the civil rights movement of the twentieth century. He was rejected by University of Maryland Law School in 1930, solely because he was not white, even though he had been graduated with honors from Lincoln University. He was graduated first in his class from Howard University Law School in 1933. For the next three decades, he practiced civil rights law, most of that time as chief of the NAACP Legal Defense and Educational Fund. In that capacity, he argued successfully before the U.S. Supreme Court in many landmark legal decisions supporting nondiscrimination. The most important of these was *Brown v. Board of Education*, which in 1954 desegregated the nation's public schools and struck down the odious doctrine of "separate but equal."

In 1961, he was nominated by President John F. Kennedy to the U.S. Court of Appeals and in 1967 he was nominated by President Lyndon Johnson to the U.S. Supreme Court. Marshall was the first African American on the Supreme Court, where he served until 1991. In his own opinions, he always used the term *Negro* because he considered it a term of respect analogous to *Caucasian*, and he shunned the terms *Afro-American* and *African American*.

In 1972, in *Furman v. Georgia*, the U.S. Supreme Court struck down the death penalty as an unconstitutional violation of the Eighth amendment protection against cruel and unusual punishment. However, the court did not conclude that it would be unconstitutional under all conceivable circumstances. Rather, the majority said that the implementation of death penalty statutes in the states was so grossly biased by race and class that it could not continue under those statutes.

Thirty-five states revised their laws to add additional safeguards, such as requiring that

Justice Thurgood Marshall (1908–1993)

the penalty decision be separated from the determination of guilt and that all death penalty sentences were subject to automatic appeal to a higher court for review. When the Court considered the constitutionality of these new statutes, it upheld them in the 1976 decision, *Gregg v. Georgia*. Justice Marshall, however, continued to object to the death penalty, as he explains in this dissenting opinion.

QUESTIONS FOR REFLECTION

1. For most of his opinion, Justice Marshall considers whether the death penalty is needed for the deterrence of the crime of murder and as retribution for that crime. These are the two major lines of argument in the philosophical consideration of the death penalty. How does he conclude that neither supports the continuation of the death penalty?

2. How does Justice Marshall use appeals to utilitarianism in his analysis?

3. Because he concludes that neither deterrence nor retribution can be met only with the death penalty, Justice Marshall then reasons that it is an "excessive" punishment under the Eighth amendment. In what other ways could society's legitimate goals for deterrence or retribution be met, consistently with his concerns?

4. How could you set up a valid study to prove (or disprove) that the threat of the death penalty deters murder? What are the difficulties in setting up such a study?

READING

In *Furman v. Georgia*, I set forth at some length my views on the basic issue presented to the Court in these cases. The death penalty, I concluded, is a cruel and unusual punishment prohibited by the Eighth and Fourteenth Amendments. That continues to be 5 my view.

I have no intention of retracing the "long and tedious journey" ..., that led to my conclusion in *Furman*. My sole purposes here are to consider the suggestion that my conclusion in *Furman* has been undercut by developments since then, and briefly to evalu- 10 ate the basis for my Brethren's holding that the extinction of life is a permissible form of punishment under the Cruel and Unusual Punishments Clause.

In *Furman*, I concluded that the death penalty is constitutionally invalid for two reasons. First, the death penalty is excessive. ... And second, the American people, fully informed as to the purposes of the death penalty and its liabilities, would, in my view, reject it as morally unacceptable....

Since the decision in *Furman*, the legislatures of 35 States have enacted new statutes authorizing the imposition of the death sentence for certain crimes, and Congress has enacted a law providing the death penalty for air piracy resulting in death.... I would be less than candid if I did not acknowledge that these developments have a significant bearing on a realistic assessment of the moral acceptability of the death penalty to the American people. But if the constitutionality of the death penalty turns, as I have urged, on the opinion of an informed citizenry, then even the enactment of new death statutes cannot be viewed as conclusive. In *Furman*, I observed that the American people are largely unaware of the information critical to a judgment on the morality of the death penalty, and concluded that, if they were better informed, they would consider it shocking, unjust, and unacceptable.... A recent study, conducted after the enactment of the post-*Furman* statutes, has confirmed that the American people know little about the death penalty, and that the opinions of an informed public would differ significantly from those of a public unaware of the consequences and effects of the death penalty.

Even assuming, however, that the post-*Furman* enactment of statutes authorizing the death penalty renders the prediction of the views of an informed citizenry an uncertain basis for a constitutional decision, the enactment of those statutes has no

> *A recent study ... has confirmed that the American people know little about the death penalty ...*

bearing whatsoever on the conclusion that the death penalty is unconstitutional because it is excessive. An excessive penalty is invalid under the Cruel and Unusual Punishments Clause "even though popular sentiment may favor" it.... The inquiry here, then, is simply whether the death penalty is necessary to accomplish the legitimate legislative purposes in punishment, or whether a less severe penalty—life imprisonment—would do as well....

The two purposes that sustain the death penalty as nonexcessive in the Court's view are general deterrence and retribution. In *Furman*, I canvassed the relevant data on the deterrent effect of capital punishment.... The state of knowledge at that point, after literally centuries of debate, was summarized as follows by a United Nations Committee:

It is generally agreed between the retentionists and abolitionists, whatever their opinions about the validity of comparative studies of deterrence, that the data which now exist show no correlation between the existence of capital punishment and lower rates of capital crime. The

Air piracy, also known as aircraft hijacking or skyjacking, had become a significant and worldwide problem by the early 1960s. The number of these incidents averaged a little more than one per year, then grew to about five per year between 1958 and 1967. But between 1968 and 1977, the annual average of skyjackings came to a staggering forty-one.

60 available evidence, I concluded in *Furman*, was convincing that "capital punishment is not necessary as a deterrent to crime in our society." ...

The Solicitor General, in his *amicus* brief in these cases, relies heavily on a study by Isaac Ehrlich, reported a year after *Furman*,
65 to support the contention that the death penalty does deter murder. Since the Ehrlich study was not available at the time of *Furman*, and since it is the first scientific study to suggest that the death penalty may have a deterrent effect, I will briefly consider its import.

The Ehrlich study focused on the relationship in the Nation
70 as a whole between the homicide rate and "execution risk"—the fraction of persons convicted of murder who were actually executed. Comparing the differences in homicide rate and execution risk for the years 1933 to 1969, Ehrlich found that increases in execution risk were associated with increases in the homicide rate.
75 But when he employed the statistical technique of multiple regression analysis to control for the influence of other variables posited to have an impact on the homicide rate, Ehrlich found a negative correlation between changes in the homicide rate and changes in execution risk. His tentative conclusion was that, for the period
80 from 1933 to 1967, each additional execution in the United States might have saved eight lives.

The methods and conclusions of the Ehrlich study have been severely criticized on a number of grounds. It has been suggested, for example, that the study is defective because it compares
85 execution and homicide rates on a nationwide, rather than a state-by-state, basis. The aggregation of data from all States—including those that have abolished the death penalty—obscures the relationship between murder and execution rates. Under Ehrlich's methodology, a decrease in the execution risk in one State combined
90 with an increase in the murder rate in another State would, all other things being equal, suggest a deterrent effect that quite obviously would not exist. Indeed, a deterrent effect would be suggested if, once again all other things being equal, one State abolished the death penalty and experienced no change in the murder rate, while
95 another State experienced an increase in the murder rate.

The most compelling criticism of the Ehrlich study is that its conclusions are extremely sensitive to the choice of the time period included in the regression analysis. Analysis of Ehrlich's data reveals that all empirical support for the deterrent effect of
100 capital punishment disappears when the five most recent years are removed from his time series—that is to say, whether a decrease in the execution risk corresponds to an increase or a decrease in the murder rate depends on the ending point of the sample period. This finding has cast severe doubts on the reliabil-
105 ity of Ehrlich's tentative conclusions. Indeed, a recent regression study, based on Ehrlich's theoretical model but using cross-section state data for the years 1950 and 1960, found no support for the conclusion that executions act as a deterrent.

> *" [A] deterrent effect would be suggested if, ... all other things being equal, one State abolished the death penalty and experienced no change in the murder rate, while another State experienced an increase in the murder rate. "*

The Ehrlich study, in short, is of little, if any, assistance in
110 assessing the deterrent impact of the death penalty.... The evidence I reviewed in *Furman* remains convincing, in my view, that "capital punishment is not necessary as a deterrent to crime in our society." ... The justification for the death penalty must be found elsewhere.
115 The other principal purpose said to be served by the death penalty is retribution. The notion that retribution can serve as a moral justification for the sanction of death finds credence in the opinion of my Brothers Stewart, Powell, and Stevent, and that of my Brother White.... It is this notion that I find to be the most
120 disturbing aspect of today's unfortunate decisions.

The concept of retribution is a multifaceted one, and any discussion of its role in the criminal law must be undertaken with caution. On one level, it can be said that the notion of retribution or reprobation is the basis of our insistence that only those who
125 have broken the law be punished, and, in this sense, the notion is quite obviously central to a just system of criminal sanctions. But our recognition that retribution plays a crucial role in determining who may be punished by no means requires approval of retribution as a general justification for punishment. It is the question whether
130 retribution can provide a moral justification for punishment—in particular, capital punishment—that we must consider.

My Brothers Stewart, Powell, and Stevens offer the following explanation of the retributive justification for capital punishment:

"The instinct for retribution is part of the nature of man,
135 and channeling that instinct in the administration of criminal justice serves an important purpose in promoting the stability of a society governed by law. When people begin to believe that organized society is unwilling or unable

to impose upon criminal offenders the punishment they
"deserve," then there are sown the seeds of anarchy—of
self-help, vigilante justice, and lynch law."...

[t]here is no evidence whatever that utilization of imprisonment, rather than death, encourages private blood feuds and other disorders.

It simply defies belief to suggest that the death penalty is necessary to prevent the American people from taking the law into their own hands.

In a related vein, it may be suggested that the expression of moral outrage through the imposition of the death penalty serves to reinforce basic moral values—that it marks some crimes as particularly offensive, and therefore to be avoided. The argument is akin to a deterrence argument, but differs in that it contemplates the individual's shrinking from antisocial conduct not because he fears punishment, but because he has been told in the strongest possible way that the conduct is wrong. This contention, like the previous one, provides no support for the death penalty. It is inconceivable that any individual concerned about conforming his conduct to what society says is "right" would fail to realize that murder is "wrong" if the penalty were simply life imprisonment.

The foregoing contentions—that society's expression of moral outrage through the imposition of the death penalty preempts the citizenry from taking the law into its own hands and reinforces moral values—are not retributive in the purest sense. They are essentially utilitarian, in that they portray the death penalty as valuable because of its beneficial results. These justifications for the death penalty are inadequate because the penalty is, quite clearly I think, not necessary to the accomplishment of those results.

There remains for consideration, however, what might be termed the purely retributive justification for the death penalty—that the death penalty is appropriate not because of its beneficial effect on society, but because the taking of the murderer's life is itself morally good. Some of the language of the opinion of my Brothers Stewart, Powell, and Stevens...appears positively to embrace this notion of retribution for its own sake as a justification for capital punishment. They state:

[T]he decision that capital punishment may be the appropriate sanction in extreme cases is an expression of the community's belief that certain crimes are themselves so grievous an affront to humanity that the only adequate response may be the penalty of death.

...They then quote with approval from Lord Justice Denning's remarks before the British Royal Commission on Capital Punishment:

"The truth is that some crimes are so outrageous that society insists on adequate punishment because the wrongdoer deserves it, irrespective of whether it is a deterrent or not."...

Of course, it may be that these statements are intended as no more than observations as to the popular demands that it is thought must be responded to in order to prevent anarchy. But the implication of the statements appears to me to be quite different—namely, that society's judgment that the murderer "deserves" death must be respected not simply because the preservation of order requires it, but because it is appropriate that society make the judgment and carry it out. It is this latter notion, in particular, that I consider to be fundamentally at odds with the Eighth Amendment.... The mere fact that the community demands the murderer's life in return for the evil he has done cannot sustain the death penalty, for as Justices Stewart, Powell, and Stevens remind us, "the Eighth Amendment demands more than that a challenged punishment be acceptable to contemporary society."... To be sustained under the Eighth Amendment, the death penalty must "compor[t] with the basic concept of human dignity at the core of the Amendment," ...; the objective in imposing it must be "[consistent] with our respect for the dignity of [other] men."... Under these standards, the taking of life "because the wrongdoer deserves it" surely must fall, for such a punishment has as its very basis the total denial of the wrongdoer's dignity and worth.

The death penalty, unnecessary to promote the goal of deterrence or to further any legitimate notion of retribution, is an excessive penalty forbidden by the Eighth and Fourteenth Amendments. I respectfully dissent from the Court's judgment upholding the sentences of death imposed upon the petitioners in these cases.

> " [T]he taking of life "because the wrongdoer deserves it" surely must fall, for such a punishment has as its very basis the total denial of the wrongdoer's dignity and worth. "

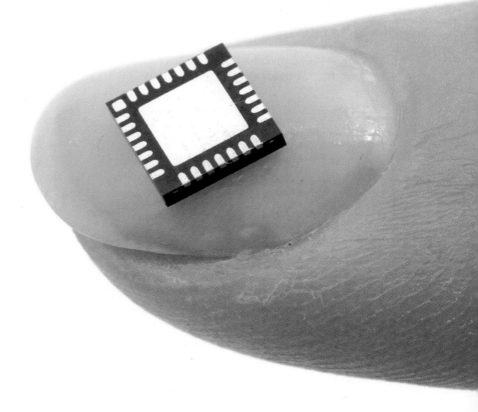

CHAPTER 11

Computer Ethics

"It has become appallingly obvious that our technology has exceeded our humanity."

—Albert Einstein, physicist

"Civilization advances by extending the number of important operations which we can perform without thinking of them."

—Alfred North Whitehead, philosopher

LEARNING OUTCOMES

After you complete this unit, you should be able to:

11-1 Identify major ethical issues presented today by computers and information technology.

11-2 Explain major philosophical approaches for analyzing the ethical status of the issues you have identified.

11-3 Apply those philosophical approaches to contemporary issues of computers and information technology.

It is impossible to imagine daily life nowadays without computers, even though personal computers only date back a few decades. Whether you use a laptop, an iPad, a smartphone, or a desktop, imagine life without your computer and access to the Internet. How would you communicate with friends and family without e-mail and Facebook? How would you research term papers for your classes without Google? How would you purchase many of the items you need for your life without online ordering, eBay, Amazon.com, or Groupon?

Yet, just as computers have changed our daily lives in so many profound ways, they have also presented us with a vast range of ethical problems along the way. Computers actually date back to long before most of us had dreamed we might have our own someday. The Internet traces back to 1969, when the U.S. Defense Department developed what was then called ARPAnet to link defense installations and universities in a way that made it immune to physical attack. The Internet does not use a single computer at one physical location to receive digital content from senders and send it out to recipients; rather, each server location can move content. Even if several of those servers are destroyed through physical attack or incapacity, thousands, and today far more, remain available for routing content.

What do **you** think?

I have a right to complete privacy in all of my Internet activity, whether e-mail or Facebook or any other form of communication.

Strongly Disagree						Strongly Agree
1	2	3	4	5	6	7

E-mail programs date back to 1971. And technology in its many forms goes back to the beginning of civilization. *Technology* does not refer only to computers but also to any invention that provides a tool or system or mechanism to solve a problem, whether the Gutenberg printing press, the wheel, or a quill for writing. In investigating computer ethics, it will be helpful to remember that the ethical problems presented by today's technology can be understood by reflecting on older ones.

Overview

In this chapter, we identify a range of ethical issues presented by computers—although we cannot recognize every one now or in the future. As before, we use philosophical reasoning tools and call on theoretical support to see how we might work through those ethical challenges. Our case study looks at the problem of cyberstalking, and sharing software with friends is considered in a critical thinking exercise. Our readings address the contemporary phenomenon of Google and the much older fear that machines might someday run the world.

11-1 MAJOR ETHICAL ISSUES

We cannot identify every single ethical issue presented by computers today, let alone issues that might arise in the future because this technology continues to evolve in ways unimaginable now, and as Timeline 11.1 shows, the pace of progress in this area seems to increase with ever-greater rapidity. Rather, we want to identify some of the most obvious and pressing issues we face and look at ways to address them. This should help prepare you to identify and carefully consider new issues arising later in life.

11-1a Privacy

Privacy is not a new concern, yet computer technology seems to make it especially urgent. We have always been at the mercy of nosy neighbors able to eavesdrop on confidential conversations or rummage through our garbage to learn information we want to keep secret. But computers open up new vistas for snooping. Has anybody not googled the names of neighbors or former boyfriends and girlfriends to see what they are doing nowadays? This is legal and may be ethical. But massive databases compiled by credit bureaus, government agencies, educational institutions, and employers are proving tempting targets for hackers who illegally grab massive amounts of confidential data. They might use it for identity theft or sell it to tabloid newspapers or use it to blackmail you. A large amount of confidential information is available about us: academic records at one's college or university, health records at one's health provider, or one's credit history at

Timeline 11.1 Computers in our world

- **1910–1913** Bertrand Russell and Alfred North Whitehead publish *Principia Mathematica,* which developed mathematical logic and set the groundwork for the binary language used by computers.

- **1939** Hewlett-Packard, the earliest computer company, founded.

- **1942** Atanasoff-Berry Computer (ABC), thought to be the earliest digital computer in the U.S., completed at Iowa State College.

- **1950** Alan Turing publishes "Computing Machinery and Intelligence," influencing developments in computer science and artificial intelligence, by charting the relationship between the output of computers and the human brain.

- **1952** IBM 701 mainframe computer introduced.

- **1939** Bell Laboratories introduces Complex Number Calculator, an early prototype of modern computers.

- **1950** Earliest work on computer ethics, by Norbert Wiener at MIT, in *The Human Use of Human Beings.*

- **1936** Alan Turing proposes the Turing Test (or Turing Machine).

Norbert Wiener

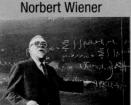

Bettmann/Corbis

the national credit reporting companies. How much privacy should one expect to have concerning our confidential information that is available online? What ethical obligations do we have to each other to protect what we know is confidential?

Should we alert friends if we see what appears to be confidential information on a public website? Should we refrain from sharing information that we believe should be confidential? How much cyberspace privacy should we expect in the workplace? Our educational institutions? Our government? Privacy was an issue before computers and the Internet, but it has taken on more importance as these new techniques allow faster acquisition and sharing of information.

11-1b Harassment

We recognize as unethical the intimidating or aggressive conduct of a person who physically stalks, harasses, or makes death threats. Should such behaviors be considered just as wrong in an online environment? Is cyberstalking as bad as in-person stalking? Are death threats posted on a Facebook page as wrong as those uttered in person? Does the Internet and the distance of

> **A large amount of confidential information is available about us ...**

cybercommunication change the way we should treat these unwelcome advances?

11-1c Free Speech

We are protective of our right to free speech in person, in the physical world, although it is not absolute. Should that right extend to our activities in cyberspace? If it is unethical to defame someone in person or in a written book, is it just as wrong on the Internet? Or should we feel freer to say whatever we want online? If our postings are anonymous, should we have more or less freedom to say what we want, even if it ruins someone's reputation, is upsetting to that person, or is a flat-out lie?

11-1d The Technological "Divide"

The sharp divide between the haves and the have-nots with regard to access to computers and the Internet raises ethical questions. From your own experience, you know how dependent you are on this technology. Much of our educational and employment opportunities now depend on computer literacy. This reality means that those without access to computers or not in a position

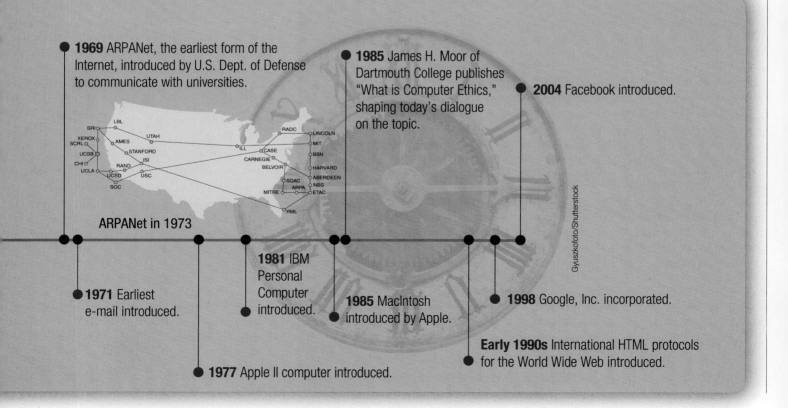

1969 ARPANet, the earliest form of the Internet, introduced by U.S. Dept. of Defense to communicate with universities.

ARPANet in 1973

1971 Earliest e-mail introduced.

1977 Apple II computer introduced.

1981 IBM Personal Computer introduced.

1985 MacIntosh introduced by Apple.

1985 James H. Moor of Dartmouth College publishes "What is Computer Ethics," shaping today's dialogue on the topic.

Early 1990s International HTML protocols for the World Wide Web introduced.

1998 Google, Inc. incorporated.

2004 Facebook introduced.

Gyuszkofoto/Shutterstock

to gain the necessary computer skills are at a disadvantage in securing jobs that depend on technology. Does society have an ethical obligation to find ways to make that technology available to everyone, even if it means diverting tax money or charitable contributions from other worthy causes? This might mean providing good access at public libraries that are reasonably available to everyone. But access at a central library will not help the child in a remote area where libraries have been closed for fiscal reasons. Because of overcrowding, some libraries do not allow the homeless and other socially undesirable people to access their services. It might mean using tax dollars to install high-speed Internet cables to isolated rural areas that otherwise would not have access and finding ways to provide low-cost access to individuals.

11-1e Intellectual Property

As with the other issues broached, intellectual property is not a new ethical challenge, but it has escalated rapidly in importance with the availability of computers and the Internet. If you properly bought software, is it ethical to let your friends borrow it and make copies without paying? Is it ethical to download movies or music from sites that you know obtained it without paying themselves?

In CourseMate, watch a video and take the quiz.

The Business Software Alliance provides a definition of software piracy on its website. It stipulates, "When you purchase software, you are actually purchasing a license to use it, not the actual software." The BSA funds research on the rates of software piracy. It decries the particularly high rates in developing countries.

11-2 APPLYING PHILOSOPHICAL APPROACHES

Using the now-familiar approach of Kant, we can ask whether our actions lead to treating other persons with dignity and respect and to recognizing their autonomy. A special complication with the issues concerning computers and the Internet is the incredible speed with which our actions affect a vast number of persons. In addition, in the case of many ethical challenges we come to face, persons we have not met or might never meet physically need to be taken into account. But with the Internet, we open the possibility that millions or even billions of other Internet users might be affected by a single action we take. We should follow those rules that we would want to be universalized, that is, that everyone should follow; but now the impact of our actions could concern billions of people we will never meet or know. The reasoning principles are the same, but the magnitude of that reasoning increases dramatically.

Utilitarians look at the results of actions as they impact everyone. We should be concerned not only with persons we know among our own family and friends, but also the possibility that our actions might affect millions of people around the world on the Internet. We have no way of knowing how many people might be affected by many of our online actions, making this reasoning technique even more challenging than usual.

Virtue ethics gives us a different vantage point. It is not difficult to carry out many activities on computers and the Internet anonymously. Yet, according to this view, we will know what we have done and what it says about us as a person. Even if we do not know the actual consequences on persons around the world, we can assess whether our actions are ethical or not by evaluating how virtuous our own conduct is because we seek to become a better person and must habitually follow virtuous conduct to achieve this goal.

In CourseMate, apply what you've learned to the real-life scenario in this simulation.

In CourseMate, practice what you learned by taking the chapter quiz.

HOW HWEE YOUNG/EPA/Newscom

Myriam Abdelaziz/Redux

The availability of the Internet and especially the pervasiveness of social media are credited by many for the rise of what is known as the Arab Spring. The Internet offered not only a fast and easy way for protestors to spread the word and recruit more participants, but also millions of potential witnesses.

11-3 APPLICATIONS TO CONTEMPORARY ISSUES

11-3a Privacy

Invading the privacy of another person would seem to be a serious violation of that person's dignity and autonomy, a basic principle in the Kantian approach to ethical reasoning. Pre-Internet, the "zone" or boundaries of our privacy might have extended only to our physical person, the postal service, the newspapers, and television. Our bodies cannot be searched without our consent. Unauthorized opening of our mail is a crime. We can restrict publication of some private information in newspapers or from being broadcast on radios or television. Now that zone could extend globally to include online information of all kinds. We might disagree on the exact sphere of our zone of privacy, but the existence of some such zone seems to be important to almost all people. We can also ask whether we would want all people to respect the privacy of others and

> **Pre-Internet, the "zone" or boundaries of our privacy might have extended only to our physical person, the postal service, the newspapers, and television.**

conclude that, yes, we would want to universalize that rule and thus should follow it ourselves. If we should follow those principles in everyday life, then surely we should also follow them when we use computers and access the Internet, where the possibilities for the invasion of privacy are so much greater.

From the viewpoint of the utilitarians, any invasion of privacy obviously has negative consequences, not only for a few specific individuals that we may target but also for their friends and family members. We must balance these negative consequences against whatever benefit we might get from invading that privacy.

A virtuous person would habitually behave ethically, even if no one else knew about it or might be hurt by acting otherwise. So respecting another's privacy rights might arguably be included in a virtuous person's code of ethics.

Certain rules are put into place to protect many possible types of invasion of privacy in our workplace or educational institution. If you work in a hospital, you are likely bound to keep patient medical records confidential. If you work at an educational institution, you are restricted by rules on what you can say about students and other employees. You might also be subject to legal restrictions, such as the federal privacy laws in certain types of medical and educational institutions. Schools and universities are prohibited under these laws from releasing information about individual students (such as their grades or disciplinary records) without their permission. Medical providers are prohibited from releasing information about the medical histories of their patients. But quite independently of these rules and laws, ethical constraints still apply and indeed might be more sweeping.

11-3b Harassment

Cyberstalking in any form would seem to be a clear violation of another person's dignity. And surely, a proscription against this type of activity is a rule we would want to universalize. Harassment seems an awful thing to do, whether in person or on the Internet.

Legitimate disagreements can exist concerning precisely what counts as "harassment" or "cyberstalking." If flooding someone's e-mail account with unwanted e-mail is harassment, just how many messages count here? If your e-mail program lets you block unwanted senders, you might not even know about the harassment, at least after the first message. What specific form must threats take to be legitimately considered the kind of threat that puts someone in fear of his or her life? Without the benefit of in-person body language to tell us when something is said in jest or sarcastically, do we need different rules for the use of language online?

From a utilitarian viewpoint, you might receive some gratification or enjoy exacting revenge by harassing a person, but does that outweigh the harm to that person? If your repeated harassment on a LISTSERV gets you booted from the list, you might yourself suffer some negative consequences that offset whatever gratification you were getting from the harassment.

A virtuous person would want to habitually behave in a certain ethical way, whether or not anyone knew. Even with so many clever techniques on the Internet for hiding your identity, you might still get caught some day and have to pay the piper, which is a matter of concern to a utilitarian! But a virtuous person would not behave differently, even if his or her identity were secret.

As with privacy, rules in the workplace or at an educational institution might also apply for harassment. In severe cases, persons found to harass someone else might also find themselves subject to state and federal laws prohibiting such cyberstalking.

11-3c Free Speech

Although the constitutions of many countries and the United Nations declarations claim protection for free speech, it is not a universally protected right. In the United States, the First Amendment protection only pertains to restrictions by the government, not by private parties. In other words, the First Amendment prohibits censorship by the government, but it does not prohibit suppression of speech by a private party. If the U.S. Congress prohibited distribution of a book, that would be a violation of the First Amendment. A commercial publisher refusing to publish a book might be considered suppression of the book writer's speech, but that

suppression is not prohibited by the First Amendment. So the ethical arena for free speech is much broader than any laws or declarations that might address the issue.

In thinking about the ethical dimensions of free speech, two angles should be considered, both your rights as a speaker and your obligations with regard to other speakers. As a speaker, are there exceptions to your right to free speech, such as speech that is defamatory, namely, that harms the reputation of another person by spreading lies? Do you think your free speech rights should include distributing obscene materials to anyone, especially children? Do you have a right to disseminate sensitive government secrets that might put the lives of other persons in danger, especially soldiers in a hostile territory? With regard to other speakers, is it ethical to try to shout people down so they cannot be heard? What about repeatedly removing material from Wikipedia to suppress someone else's speech? Is this any different from shouting them down in a public place so they cannot be heard?

If you apply Kantian principles here, your own right of free speech is justified by the fact that to be treated with dignity and respect means being able to voice your opinions. Also, in letting others speak, you are respecting their rights. If you want the freedom to express your own controversial views on politics or religion, then you need to respect the rights of others to express controversial views, no matter how distasteful they might be to you. If you want the freedom to paint a picture that is in questionable taste to others, then you must also respect the rights of

A former U.S. Army intelligence officer, Bradley Manning is accused of leaking sensitive government material to the website WikiLeaks. He has been charged with twenty-two crimes, including "aiding the enemy."

others to create art that you might find in questionable taste. You could recognize some exceptions to these rights (e.g., distributing obscenity to children) by noting that this would violate the dignity of the persons pictured in the obscene material as well as the dignity of the children.

Utilitarians would consider the good and bad results from your actions. The consequences to be balanced in this case are those that affect the protection of everyone's right to free speech with those that generate unpleasantness for some. What is more important: The right of free speech for everyone or the right not to be subjected to the unpleasant or hurtful speech of others? Allowing you to speak, even if your speech is unpleasant, is supported by the importance of protecting that right of free speech for everybody. Permitting others to speak, even if you virulently disagree with their opinions, also protects that right for everyone.

Even with the possibilities for anonymous speech on the Internet, a virtuous person would habitually respect free speech rights for themselves and others.

11-3d Technological "Divide"

Providing educational opportunities of all kinds, whether in the form of public education or public libraries, raises ethical questions. Our reasoning about providing access to computers and the Internet can be seen as one instance of

> [In the United States, ... the **First Amendment prohibits censorship by the government, but it** does **not prohibit** suppression of speech **by a private party.**]

these broader questions. Legitimate debates certainly exist about the extent to which we as a society should provide these educational opportunities, as they exist specifically for computers. But the broader question of access can be tackled regardless of these specific details. Access can be provided through public libraries, through subsidized access in rural areas, or in other ways outside of the traditional public school environment; see Figure 11.1 for recent data on Internet use in the United States.

From a Kantian viewpoint, we can argue that, if we deny people the access they need to compete fairly in education and employment, we are not treating them with dignity and respect. If we found ourselves in a situation in which we do not have access to critical tools or information, we would want that dignity.

From a utilitarian standpoint, if a substantial part of the population has no access to technology, the consequences are not limited to that part of the population. The larger society also loses access to potential labor that is properly qualified to handle today's jobs, which narrows the labor pool. The community is also hurt by facing a situation and its outcomes, where a population is unable to support itself: unemployed individuals become unable to meet their financial obligations. For example, rents or mortgages left unpaid affect other community

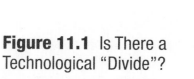

Figure 11.1 Is There a Technological "Divide"?

The U.S. Census Bureau has gathered data on Internet use since 1997. The most recent report (October 2009) shows the households that had no Internet use in the home.

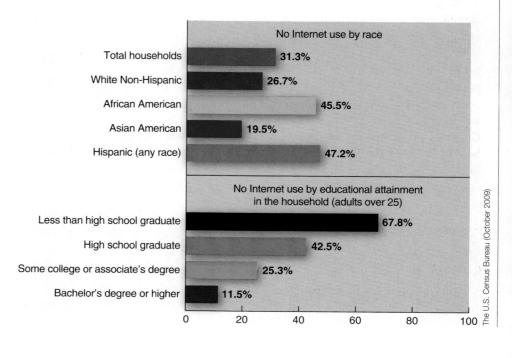

No Internet use by race

Total households	31.3%
White Non-Hispanic	26.7%
African American	45.5%
Asian American	19.5%
Hispanic (any race)	47.2%

No Internet use by educational attainment in the household (adults over 25)

Less than high school graduate	67.8%
High school graduate	42.5%
Some college or associate's degree	25.3%
Bachelor's degree or higher	11.5%

0   20   40   60   80   100

The U.S. Census Bureau (October 2009)

members, in this case, landlords or mortgage holders. Society may find it has an interest in keeping individuals from sinking into destitution, to avoid an increase in crime, for example. To that effect, society may fund public support options, such as housing assistance or food stamps, which means a need for financial input from those in society who have beyond sufficient resources.

Virtuous persons would ask what would count as ethical conduct, independently of these issues. Would virtuous persons do all they could to ensure access to computers to all, perhaps by voting for tax increases or making charitable contributions, whether or not others knew about their efforts? Would a virtuous person volunteer at local community centers to teach computer skills to those who had not had access? Would a virtuous person donate working computers to schools and community centers that were lacking, rather than selling them for personal profit?

> [C]onsider what your views might be **if you had created something new and important and wanted to benefit financially from your innovation ...**

piece of art, an invention, or something else of unique value. And allowing or encouraging anyone to steal anything would not seem to be the sort of rule you would want to universalize.

Utilitarianism seems to provide a rationalization for some who think that just making one more copy will not make any real difference in the profits of a big movie producer or recording studio. You might think that the financial savings for the thief are more important than the financial loss to big business. And although this might sound persuasive to many today, consider how you would feel about these consequences if you were the artist or filmmaker, and others reasoned this way. If it is easy to steal your work, you are probably not just losing one sale, but a great many because your work is distributed by a thief to his or her friends. Changing point of view, as you can see in this case, affects the balancing of consequences.

11-3e Intellectual Property

Technology has long made it possible to copy without permission products that can be reproduced. Photocopying machines, cameras, and dual-tape recorders are among the tools that facilitated copying. Computers and the Internet have simply magnified the possibilities for copying material without permission. Trading files for music or downloading pirated movies might all violate intellectual property principles and can often be done quickly and even secretly. Policies in our workplace or university might restrict this theft, as do federal copyright laws. But ethical perspectives are important to consider independently of these restrictions.

Although many seem to believe that intellectual property should be completely free and unrestricted, consider what your views might be if you had created something new and important and wanted to benefit financially from your innovation, or at least to recover your investment expenses. Perhaps you wrote a popular song or designed a unique artwork that many wanted to buy or made your first film and thought it had potential for broad distribution. From this vantage point, you might feel that you deserve the reward of payments by those who use the product of your work.

Stealing someone else's intellectual property would seem to violate their autonomy as persons who had a good idea and the potential to benefit from that idea, whether a

Photocopiers now can also print, scan, and fax. This type of technology has given people the ability to reproduce anything and disseminate it easily and at great speed. In addition, the hard drives on most of these machines retain all material ever scanned, making them particularly valuable to identity and other thieves.

Virtuous persons do not steal as a matter of habit. Rationalizing that engaging in the activities described does not really amount to stealing requires intellectual contortion that would not be consistent with virtuous conduct.

Now that you have studied how various types of reasoning apply to the topics discussed, review Critical Thinking Table 11.1 to follow the process of examining an ethical claim on a related topic.

In CourseMate, listen to the audio summary of the chapter.

Table 11.1 Critical Thinking Steps and Their Application in an Example

{"I paid for my software, so I should be allowed to give copies to my friends for free."}

Critical Thinking Steps	Application
1. Examine and clarify key terms and concepts. • Look words up in a dictionary as a start if necessary. • Unravel or unpack the complexities and nuances of a central term, such as *justice*, *right*, or *good*. *HOW HWEE YOUNG/ EPA/Newscom*	• What does "allow" mean? Is this permission from the government? The software inventor? The person who sold the software? Ethical rightness? • What do we mean by "friends," only your few very best friends or anyone you "met" on the Internet?
2. Work through the meaning of the key terms and concepts to make sure you will use them consistently. • Consider the ways the term can be used by including it in different sentences and contexts to zero in on the particular meaning you are after. • Ask yourself what words are potential synonyms for the concept. Do those capture everything you want to understand about that term?	• Even when we have "paid" for something, what exactly have we bought? Only the physical thing? Or the right to make copies? Or the right to sell what we bought? Or the right to make copies and sell them? • Who or what should be giving permission that allows this? The government? The software manufacturer? The software vendor? With what justification should any or all of these groups have this authority to allow this? • Are we really giving things away for "free" or are we expecting some favor in return from our friends?
3. Build premises and bring any assumptions to light. • Put together short and clear sentences to build each of your premises. • Think through what you may be taking for granted in your reasoning. What assumptions are you making? • Once you have identified assumptions, articulate them in your premise, so that your audience has the same understanding of a term or a concept as you. *Patrick Semansky/ AP Photos*	The premises of the argument could be constructed as follows: (i) Whenever I have paid for something, I should have complete freedom to copy it and give it away to anyone I choose. (ii) I paid for my software. CONCLUSION: I should be permitted to copy my software and give it to anyone I choose, including my friends.
4. Test/Verify your premises. • Now that you have stated your premises explicitly, do you want to stick with them? • Are you relying on premises drawn from unsubstantiated sources or from questionable authorities?	Both of these premises should be examined. (i) I have bought a lot of things, but did I only buy that one physical object or did I actually buy the rights to make copies? When I bought a distinctive pair of athletic shoes, did I also buy the right to reproduce copies? As an inventor, if I sold one of my inventions to somebody else, would I assume I was selling the right to make copies of my invention?

(Continued)

Table 11.1 Continued

Critical Thinking Steps	Application
• Are you consistent in your premises? Or are you appealing to different and inconsistent foundations in your reasoning? • Reformulate your premises if they have proven to be faulty.	(ii) What exactly did I buy when I bought that software? Did I buy just one download or one physical disk? Did I buy more than that? If you do not accept all of these premises, then you will not accept the conclusion either. But if you do accept all of them, then you would find the conclusion valid and justified.
5. Confirm that the conclusions you draw are logical. Check for reliance on fallacies and correct any premise that you identify as relying on a fallacy. Reha Mark/ iStockphoto.com	• This argument is especially vulnerable to criticism as the fallacy of equivocation, especially regarding the words *buy* and *friend*. In this type of fallacy, key terms are used in different ways in the argument, clouding the validity of the final conclusion. For example, *to buy*, might be construed to mean to purchase a physical product, when the seller might mean that the product in question is a mere license for limited use. *Friends* might mean a small number of people with whom one shares a close relationship, a large number of acquaintances, or even a considerable number of online strangers only connected virtually to oneself.

Alan Turing

Although he did not consider himself a philosopher, Alan Turing's work on computers and intelligence has been enormously influential on philosophical inquiries into computing possibilities and artificial intelligence. A British mathematician, he built on the work on mathematical logic of such distinguished philosophers as Bertrand Russell. After working on top-secret projects to decode the German Enigma machine during World War II, he focused on trying to develop a computer, which he believed could rival the human brain.

Turing's most famous work was a paper published in 1950 that was titled "Computing Machinery and Intelligence." He proposed that if questions were submitted to both humans and suitably advanced computers, we could not tell the difference in the answers. He called this proposition the "Turing Test" or "Turing Machine." He never actually built such a machine but was hypothesizing that the human brain was really nothing but a remarkably sophisticated computer.

This claim has triggered an enormous amount of debate among philosophers, as well as computer scientists. One of Turing's harshest critics was John Searle, a professor of philosophy at University of California, Berkeley, who proposed what he called the Chinese Room. Searle argues that a person could manipulate Chinese symbols and rules and seem to pass the Turing Test, without actually understanding the Chinese language, just as a computer could crank out the right answers. This, Searle claims, shows that there is more to the human brain than merely producing the "right answer" for the Turing Test. We have a good sense of the difference between merely producing the right answer and really understanding something.

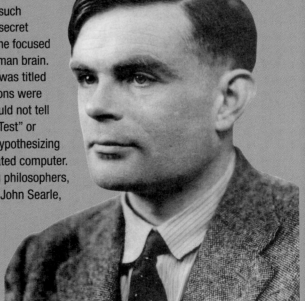

Alan Turing (1912–1954)

Pictorial Press Ltd/Alamy

Turing died mysteriously of cyanide poisoning in 1954 at his home, in what appeared to be a suicide. He had been arrested two years previously for a homosexual affair, and his work on the top-secret Enigma project made him a likely target for assassination or blackmail, according to some credible sources who knew him.

CHAPTER 11 Case Study

Cyberstalking

Two college students at the University of Michigan, Jake Baker and Arthur Gonda, enjoyed trading e-mail about their sexual interest in violence against women and girls. Baker also liked to write fictional stories about the torture, rape, and murder of a young woman with the same name as one of his classmates and posted them on a Usenet news group popular in the mid-90s.

After the young woman saw the story on the Usenet group, she felt fearful and intimidated and sought psychological counseling. Baker was arrested for violating a federal statute that prohibited communications with threats to kidnap or injure another person. Both Baker and Gonda were indicted by a grand jury for violating this statute. We have a good sense of what it means to stalk or threaten someone in person, through repeated, physical behavior and taunts. One challenge here was how to extend that sense to online communication.

When a panel of judges was asked to dismiss the charges, they considered whether a reasonable person would consider the Usenet postings a serious threat or merely a friendly exchange among two guys sharing sexual fantasies. Note that their communication went beyond private e-mail exchanges to posting on the Usenet site where others could see them. The judges ultimately dismissed the charges on the grounds that no reasonable person would take these Internet postings seriously.

1. Would you consider this behavior to be a serious threat to the young woman whose name was used in these postings? What things would you consider as most relevant in deciding when Internet communication could be serious threats? Would calling your fantasies a fictional story that coincidentally uses the name of a classmate relieve you of responsibility?

2. Regardless of the legalities of the behavior of Baker and Gonda on the Internet, do you consider their communication ethical? What standards are you using in reaching your conclusion? If a fictional story using your name were posted on Facebook or sent to a widely read LISTSERV, would you feel you had been treated unethically? Would you feel threatened?

3. Although the charges were ultimately dismissed, the dissenting judges insisted that the details of the fantasy were sufficiently threatening to reasonable people that Baker and Gonda should be tried for this crime. Which side would you take in this dispute? Explain your reasons and justifications.

For additional case studies, please see the CourseMate for this text.

Corbis/Jupiter Images

A grand jury consists of a group of people who are selected and sworn in by a court. Members of a grand jury do not decide the guilt or innocence of a person. They listen to evidence and decide if someone should be charged with a crime.

Reading Excerpt: Gregory Crane, "Reading in the Age of Google" (2005)

INTRODUCTION

Gregory Crane is Professor of Classics at Tufts University in Medford, Massachusetts, where he has taught since 1992. A specialist in computer applications in research and education, he is also an adjunct professor of Computer Science at Tufts. He serves as the editor-in-chief of the Perseus Digital Library, which he created in 1985 and has received almost a million dollars from the National Endowment for the Humanities (NEH), a federal agency. This essay appeared in the NEH publication, *Humanities*, September/October 2005, Vol. 26, No. 5.

Gregory Crane, Professor of Classics at Tufts University, Medford, Massachusetts.

Courtesy of the Perseus Digital Library

QUESTIONS FOR REFLECTION

1. Do you agree with the statement attributed to Socrates that writing says only one thing and that meaning never changes through time? Can you think of counterexamples to that claim? What influences seem to change the meaning of terms?

2. Crane describes enormous online resources connected to the classic texts he works with. Do students with access to such material have an unfair advantage over students who do not?

Do we as a society have an ethical obligation to insist that all students be given access to these online materials so they can fairly compete in school?

3. What do you consider the most important advantages of a community-created resource such as Wikipedia? What are the disadvantages of relying on such a source for knowledge?

READING

Modern information technology began when humans started storing language in physical media—scrolls, stone tablets, steles—that existed separately from their brains. By Plato's time in the fourth century BCE, writing was already thousands of years old
5 and subject to some philosophical criticism.

Tellingly, in the *Phaedrus*, Plato has Socrates commenting that written words are like statues that may imitate life but have no life of their own. He stresses the inert quality of written language: "Writing says one single thing—whatever it may be—the very
10 same thing forever."

We may ask the written word what it means, but it cannot answer or even hear our questions. For at least four thousand years we have been writing ever more numerous books and assembling these in ever more sophisticated libraries. But in the end, like
15 Akkadian-speaking schoolchildren struggling to learn Sumerian, we could only turn to other humans and the reading aids they created, if we could not understand the written words before us.

> " *For at least four thousand years we have been writing ever more numerous books …* "

Twenty years ago, Marvin Minsky, a proponent of artificial intelligence, responded to this ancient challenge and imagined a
20 time when people could not imagine a library in which the books did not talk to each other.

The grand vision of artificial intelligence remains elusive, but simpler approaches have already allowed books to converse with one another and to adapt themselves to the needs of individual
25 human readers. Millions of people have experienced early versions of this idea through e-commerce.

NEH Publication,Humanities September/October 2005 Vol.26 No.5.

When I query Google for "Plato *Phaedrus*," for instance, I not only receive links to a number of online translations of the dialogue but two sponsored links, one to a used-book service, another to a company that sells term papers. A slight variation on this query ("Plato's *Phaedrus*") elicits a link to Google Print and a digitized copy of a translation published by Purdue University Press. As more works are digitized and become available online, the ability of these documents to interact and learn from each other will grow as well.

Amazon.com has already digitized one hundred thousand books, and the Google Print Library Project has set out to digitize the contents of five major libraries, including Harvard's, which contains more than ten million books in five hundred languages.

Google, Amazon, and other companies mine data, analyzing our queries and making inferences about our goals, using as much information as they have to help us spend money.

Many of these same techniques can, however, help us learn. In the Perseus Digital Library, we already have the beginnings of new reading environments that help us understand complex documents in a variety of languages.

For people studying Plato, for example, the Perseus Digital Library can assemble a range of materials relevant to the *Phaedrus*, including a Greek text, English translation, and a list of documents that comment on the opening section of the dialogue. The reader can customize the display by explicitly asking for original source text in Greek, choosing a translation font, and making other decisions about what should be displayed. The reader can ask a question about a particular Greek word, and the system can personalize its response: it recognizes that the reader is looking at a dialogue of Plato and highlights all citations to Plato in the online lexicon entry.

These electronic actions are simple in nature but profound in their implications. Many different books are, in effect, having a conversation among themselves and deciding how best to serve the human reader. The library asks its collection what it knows about a particular work, and then assembles what is, in fact, a virtual book, combining materials derived from multiple print sources into a single integrated display. The Greek edition of the *Phaedrus* recognizes not only that it is being read but also what word in what section the reader is asking about. It can also tell the lexicon that it is being read. The lexicon then adapts itself to the reader, shifting its appearance to suit the needs of individual readers better.

Customization and personalization support changes that we ask for specifically and adaptations that a system makes automatically. Customization can build on extensive information as we have found with language students. For example, a student studying a particular Roman text can tell the Perseus Digital Library which chapters in which edition of *Wheelock's Latin* she

> *Many different books are ... having a conversation among themselves and deciding how best to serve the human reader.*

has studied. The text queries the textbook as to what vocabulary it includes in those chapters and then reports to the reader which words in a new passage of text she has and has not encountered before. Over time, a learning profile evolves, allowing a person to track what has been learned and to develop better ways to work with new documents.

Personalization begins with systems trying to anticipate the readers' needs. At the Perseus Digital Library, machine learning and data mining also have been put to use to discover what questions people have previously asked when they encounter a text. By studying the queries people have made regarding a widely read passage by Ovid, we discovered that readers generally followed a small number of patterns. Once a reader asked about three or four words in a passage, we could predict most of the words about which they would ask next.

Such personalization points to a world where readers using the same materials can identify the parts that are most interesting or most challenging to them. The historian may find pointers to discussions of treaties and international law, while a linguist may get information about the meaning of the subjunctive in a particular passage.

The implications extend beyond the reading of academic texts. As I wrote this, my eighteen-year-old son was familiarizing himself with a new cell phone that includes color screen and keyboard and provides Web access while my fourteen-year-old son was studying three-dimensional graphics.

We are educating a generation that assumes it can ask questions about almost any topic and examine evidence in almost any medium. This generation also has high expectations regarding the availability of materials online and easy means of discovering their content. In response, our libraries are shedding their physical constraints in an effort to meet the expanding needs of a larger and more technologically savvy audience.

We are currently in the incunabulum stage of a long-term shift to electronic publication. Just as early books looked like manuscripts, electronic publications imitate many aspects of printed works. Electronic publications have a few obvious extensions such as linked citations and additional images that would not fit in the print version. But the electronic pages still feel familiar just as

Science and Society/SuperStock

An incunabulum is a rare movable-type edition printed in the last part of the fifteenth century. Gutenberg invented the movable type printing press in 1436. This picture shows an early eighteenth century printing press.

115 the U.S. Navy's first steamship did after it was retrofitted with a complete set of masts and sails.

Habits and preexisting structures constrain the direction of new technology. Even so, there are elements that are already beginning to drive humanities publishing beyond the familiar
120 framework. Larger and broader audiences, documents that learn, the reuse of material for multiple purposes, and decentralized production will all play some role in the making of dictionaries, encyclopedias, translations, commentaries, and other tools that structure information in the humanities.

125 A networked world challenges humanists to reimagine their potential audience. No longer trapped in a tiny network of exclusive academic libraries, ideas can circulate more quickly across the globe.

> **" *No longer trapped in a tiny network of exclusive academic libraries, ideas can circulate more quickly across the globe.* "**

Broadening the audience through electronic publishing raises
130 many questions. Which institutions should sustain this information? Are the humanities well served with a subscription model, where academic work is mainly available in scholarly journals?

Might this model exclude those without access to a university library? If the humanities community chooses to pursue open publication and engage with a broader subset of our fellow citizens, will scholars express themselves in the same way? To what extent will scholars' choices of topics evolve in response to different audiences?

In a print world, publications drift out of date the moment that their authors finish writing. In an electronic world, however, documents can perform more intelligent functions. Rather than creating static content, authors can now prepare data that will drive automated systems, which can then in turn scan much larger bodies of material in order to update information.

The production of traditional reference works may be better suited to such an automated electronic model. A lexicographer, for example, may collect hundreds of instances of a word's use and the different meanings associated with it, but will only have space for a few examples in the print lexicon. This larger set of examples could instead be used with a word-sense disambiguation system.

The word-sense disambiguation system can not only support the lexicographer at work but can be applied to much larger projects. The dictionary entry becomes part of a system to which subsequent editors can add and that can continue organizing data long after the initial project is complete. The same techniques can be used to generate biographies, event descriptions, and other summaries.

The making of all these works will partly depend on granularity: the extent to which reference works can be broken down into smaller chunks and put together for purposes other than the one originally intended.

Humanists tend to write articles and monographs, linear publications roughly fifteen to thirty pages or one hundred and fifty to three hundred pages. Digital environments support and may strongly favor publications that are much larger and smaller than these. Emerging technologies for summarization, question answering, information retrieval, text mining, and visualization now can provide more immediate support for researchers pondering nineteenth-century reviews of Melville, the general reader of *Moby-Dick* imagining Melville's *Pequod*, and the visitor to New Bedford visualizing Ishmael's town. But such services work better when they are able to recombine smaller units of information from a variety of sources. While the article and monograph forms are best suited to some scholarly arguments, successful electronic publications require a shift to more small-scale contributions that can be recombined in novel ways. Ideally, articles and monographs should be structured to make them easier to analyze automatically.

Historically, large research projects have depended upon contributions from a wide range of collaborators, often from non-traditional backgrounds.

Among the more famous was the creation of the *Oxford English Dictionary*, which took seventy years to complete. Thousands of people helped Professor James Murray, including William Chester Minor, an inmate at an asylum for the criminally insane.

The electronic world lends itself to decentralized production with many collaborators. The most important development for the humanities this century may prove to be Wikipedia and the rise of community-driven projects. Wikipedia is an extreme case whose success has so far shocked skeptical scholars. Anyone can contribute to Wikipedia and classic Wikipedia articles do not have single authors. Rather, Wikipedia seems to demonstrate that if a general consensus exists about what a document should look like, and the consenting community can contribute, documents will develop into useful tools of research.

The Wikipedia articles where open production has not worked have generally been on controversial topics such as Israel or the biographies of Kerry and Bush in the 2004 election. While this model of production clearly abandons the distinctive single author's voice, it may better capture the goals of reference works than more professional, centralized efforts.

Wikipedia is immensely interesting for another reason: the relationships between the pieces of data. The 533,000 articles available in May 2005 contained twenty million links to other Wikipedia articles. Of these, fifteen million were disambiguating links, meaning they connected ambiguous terms such as "Springfield" to their referents "Springfield, MA" or "Springfield, IL." A survey of two hundred, randomly selected links revealed only two inaccuracies.

These links demonstrate that communities are willing and able to produce immense amounts of very precise data. Such user input can improve the results of automated processes and can serve as a foundation for authors creating their own reference articles.

As staggering as some changes have been over the past twenty-five years, it is difficult to predict what we will be reading in fifteen, ten, or even five years' time. Subsequent developments may be even more dramatic as old ways of doing things dissolve and a new generation, immersed in electronic information from childhood, takes its place.

The goals we pursue—the hunger for ideas, the desire to understand more, the delight in reasoned, evidence-based debate—will continue to find new modes of expression. Reading has been in flux since writing began to emerge four thousand years ago. The increasing mechanization of print facilitated a shift from intensive reading, where readers repeatedly studied a few texts such as the Bible, Vergil's *Aeneid*, or Shakespeare's plays to extensive reading where readers moved through one novel after another. This shift had many effects, not least of which was laying the foundation for modern democratic society. The restless, question-driven, active reading in the age of Google may lead to a shift that is just as dramatic.

Reading Excerpt: Samuel Butler, *Erewhon*, "The Book of the Machines" (1872)

INTRODUCTION

Samuel Butler was a writer and novelist in nineteenth-century England, greatly influenced by the Industrial Revolution, as well as Charles Darwin's *Origin of Species* (1859). *Erewhon*, published in 1872, is Butler's novel about a Utopian state in which technology is banned because the inhabitants feared that a species of machines would develop and someday dominate the earth. The excerpts here consider these inhabitants' understanding of machines and technology and why they found these advancements so fearsome.

Samuel Butler
(1835–1902)

QUESTIONS FOR REFLECTION

1. Butler worried that some technology, already developed when he wrote this book over 140 years ago, had caused grievous harm to the human race. What more recent technological developments have caused harm to us in our own times? Would we be better off today if that technology had been suppressed long ago?

2. Computers are a leading example of some of the technological changes that took place in the twentieth century. Has the development of this technology helped or hurt the human race, and in what ways?

3. Should we worry that computers might someday become a master race ruling over humans, as the fictional citizens of Erewhon did about the machines they feared in their day? Why or why not?

READING

The writer commences: —"There was a time, when the earth was to all appearance utterly destitute both of animal and vegetable life, and when according to the opinion of our best philosophers it was simply a hot round ball with a crust gradually cooling. Now if a human
5 being had existed while the earth was in this state and had been allowed to see it as though it were some other world with which he had no concern, and if at the same time he were entirely ignorant of all physical science, would he not have pronounced it impossible that creatures possessed of anything like consciousness should be
10 evolved from the seeming cinder which he was beholding? Would he not have denied that it contained any potentiality of consciousness? Yet in the course of time consciousness came. Is it not possible then that there may be even yet new channels dug out for consciousness, though we can detect no signs of them at present?
15 "Again. Consciousness, in anything like the present acceptation of the term, having been once a new thing—a thing, as far as we can see, subsequent even to an individual centre of action and

> ❝ *There was a time, when the earth was to all appearance utterly destitute both of animal and vegetable life* … ❞

to a reproductive system (which we see existing in plants without apparent consciousness) —why may not there arise some new
20 phase of mind which shall be as different from all present known phases, as the mind of animals is from that of vegetables?

"It would be absurd to attempt to define such a mental state (or whatever it may be called), inasmuch as it must be something so foreign to man that his experience can give him

---

Samuel Butler, *Erewhon*, "The Book of the Machines," 1872.

25 no help towards conceiving its nature; but surely when we reflect upon the manifold phases of life and consciousness which have been evolved already, it would be rash to say that no others can be developed, and that animal life is the end of all things. There was a time when fire was the end of all things: another when rocks
30 and water were so."

The writer, after enlarging on the above for several pages, proceeded to inquire whether traces of the approach of such a new phase of life could be perceived at present; whether we could see any tenements preparing which might in a remote futurity be
35 adapted for it; whether, in fact, the primordial cell of such a kind of life could be now detected upon earth. In the course of his work he answered this question in the affirmative and pointed to the higher machines.

"There is no security"—to quote his own words—"against
40 the ultimate development of mechanical consciousness, in the fact of machines possessing little consciousness now. A mollusc has not much consciousness. Reflect upon the extraordinary advance which machines have made during the last few hundred years, and note how slowly the animal and vegetable kingdoms are
45 advancing. The more highly organized machines are creatures not so much of yesterday, as of the last five minutes, so to speak, in comparison with past time. Assume for the sake of argument that conscious beings have existed for some twenty million years: see what strides machines have made in the last thousand! May not
50 the world last twenty million years longer? If so, what will they not in the end become? Is it not safer to nip the mischief in the bud and to forbid them further progress?"

"But who can say that the vapor engine has not a kind of consciousness? Where does consciousness begin, and where
55 end? Who can draw the line? Who can draw any line? Is not everything interwoven with everything? Is not machinery linked with animal life in an infinite variety of ways? ... A 'machine' is only a 'device.' ..."

"Do not let me be misunderstood as living in fear of any
60 actually existing machine; there is probably no known machine which is more than a prototype of future mechanical life.... what I fear is the extraordinary rapidity with which they are becoming something very different to what they are at present. No class of beings have in any time past made so rapid a movement forward.
65 Should not that movement be jealously watched, and checked while we can still check it? And is it not necessary for this end to destroy the more advanced of the machines which are in use at present, though it is admitted that they are in themselves harmless? ... "

70 "It can be answered that even though machines should hear never so well and speak never so wisely, they will still always do the one or the other for our advantage, not their own; that man will be the ruling spirit and the machine the servant; that as soon as a machine fails to discharge the service which man expects
75 from it, it is doomed to extinction; that the machines stand to man simply in the relation of lower animals, the vapor-engine itself being only a more economical kind of horse; so that instead of being likely to be developed into a higher kind of life than man's, they owe their very existence and progress to their power of
80 ministering to human wants, and must therefore both now and ever be man's inferiors."

"This is all very well. But the servant glides by imperceptible approaches into the master; and we have come to such a pass that, even now, man must suffer terribly on ceasing to benefit the
85 machines. If all machines were to be annihilated at one moment, so that not a knife nor lever nor rag of clothing nor anything whatsoever were left to man but his bare body alone that he was born with, and if all knowledge of mechanical laws were taken from him so that he could make no more machines, and all machine-
90 made food destroyed so that the race of man should be left as it were naked upon a desert island, we should become extinct in six weeks. A few miserable individuals might linger, but even these in a year or two would become worse than monkeys. Man's very soul is due to the machines; it is a machine-made thing: he
95 thinks as he thinks, and feels as he feels, through the work that machines have wrought upon him, and their existence is quite as much a *sine qua non* for his, as his for theirs. This fact precludes us from proposing the complete annihilation of machinery, but surely it indicates that we should destroy as many of them as we
100 can possibly dispense with, lest they should tyrannize over us even more completely."

"True, from a low materialistic point of view, it would seem that those thrive best who use machinery wherever its use is possible with profit; but this is the art of the machines—they serve that they
105 may rule. They bear no malice towards man for destroying a whole race of them provided he creates a better instead; on the contrary, they reward him liberally for having hastened their development. It is for neglecting them that he incurs their wrath, or for using inferior machines, or for not making sufficient exertions to invent new ones,
110 or for destroying them without replacing them; yet these are the very things we ought to do, and do quickly; for though our rebellion against their infant power will cause infinite suffering, what will not things come to, if that rebellion is delayed? ..."

"It is said by some with whom I have conversed upon this
115 subject, that the machines can never be developed into animate or *quasi*-animate existences, inasmuch as they have no reproductive system, nor seem ever likely to possess one. If this be taken to mean that they cannot marry, and that we are never likely to see a fertile union between two vapor-engines with the young ones
120 playing about the door of the shed, however greatly we might desire to do so, I will readily grant it. But the objection is not a very profound one. No one expects that all the features of the now

existing organizations will be absolutely repeated in an entirely new class of life. The reproductive system of animals differs widely from that of plants, but both are reproductive systems. Has nature exhausted her phases of this power?"

"Surely if a machine is able to reproduce another machine systematically, we may say that it has a reproductive system. What is a reproductive system, if it be not a system for reproduction? And how few of the machines are there which have not been produced systematically by other machines? But it is man that makes them do so...."

"But the machines which reproduce machinery do not reproduce machines after their own kind. A thimble may be made by machinery, but it was not made by, neither will it ever make, a thimble. Here, again, if we turn to nature we shall find abundance of analogies which will teach us that a reproductive system may be in full force without the thing produced being of the same kind as that which produced it. Very few creatures reproduce after their own kind; they reproduce something which has the potentiality of becoming that which their parents were...."

"It is possible that the system when developed may be in many cases a vicarious thing. Certain classes of machines may be alone fertile, while the rest discharge other functions in the mechanical system, just as the great majority of ants and bees have nothing to do with the continuation of their species, but get food and store it, without thought of breeding. One cannot expect the parallel to be complete or nearly so; certainly not now, and probably never; but is there not enough analogy existing at the present moment, to make us feel seriously uneasy about the future, and to render it our duty to check the evil while we can still do so? Machines can within certain limits beget machines of any class, no matter how different to themselves. Every class of machines will probably have its special mechanical breeders, and all the higher ones will owe their existence to a large number of parents and not to two only."

"We are misled by considering any complicated machine as a single thing; in truth it is a city or society, each member of which was bred truly after its kind. We see a machine as a whole, we call it by a name and individualize it; we look at our own limbs, and know that the combination forms an individual which springs from a single centre of reproductive action; we therefore assume that there can be no reproductive action which does not arise from a single centre; but this assumption is unscientific, and the bare fact that no vapor-engine was ever made entirely by another, or two others, of its own kind, is not sufficient to warrant us in saying that vapor-engines have no reproductive system. The truth is that each part of every vapor-engine is bred by its own special breeders, whose function it is to breed that part, and that only, while the combination of the parts into a whole forms another department of the mechanical reproductive

> **[T]he bare fact that no vapor-engine was ever made entirely by another, ... of its own kind, is not sufficient to warrant us in saying that vapor-engines have no reproductive system.**

system, which is at present exceedingly complex and difficult to see in its entirety."

"Complex now, but how much simpler and more intelligibly organized may it not become in another hundred thousand years? or in twenty thousand? For man at present believes that his interest lies in that direction; he spends an incalculable amount of labor and time and thought in making machines breed always better and better; he has already succeeded in effecting much that at one time appeared impossible, and there seem no limits to the results of accumulated improvements if they are allowed to descend with modification from generation to generation. It must always be remembered that man's body is what it is through having been molded into its present shape by the chances and changes of many millions of years, but that his organization never advanced with anything like the rapidity with which that of the machines is advancing. This is the most alarming feature in the case, and I must be pardoned for insisting on it so frequently."

"... the future depends upon the present, and the present (whose existence is only one of those minor compromises of which human life is full—for it lives only on sufferance of the past and future) depends upon the past, and the past is unalterable. The only reason why we cannot see the future as plainly as the past, is because we know too little of the actual past and actual present; these things are too great for us, otherwise the future, in its minutest details, would lie spread out before our eyes, and we should lose our sense of time present by reason of the clearness with which we should see the past and future; perhaps we should not be even able to distinguish time at all; but that is foreign. What we do know is, that the more the past and present are known, the more the future can be predicted; and that no one dreams of doubting the fixity of the future in cases where he is fully cognisant of both past and present, and has had experience of the consequences that followed from such a past and such a present

In Butler's novel, citizens of Erewhon imagine that machines will be able to reproduce. Some machines, they speculate, will not be able to do so, just like worker or soldier ants. Other machines will be part of a class of "breeders." In the photo above, a soldier ant towers over a smaller worker ant.

on previous occasions. He perfectly well knows what will happen, and will stake his whole fortune thereon.

"And this is a great blessing; for it is the foundation on which morality and science are built. The assurance that the future is no
210 arbitrary and changeable thing, but that like futures will invariably follow like presents, is the groundwork on which we lay all our plans—the faith on which we do every conscious action of our lives. If this were not so we should be without a guide; we should have no confidence in acting, and hence we should never act, for
215 there would be no knowing that the results which will follow now will be the same as those which followed before."

"… the difference between the life of a man and that of a machine is one rather of degree than of kind, though differences in kind are not wanting. An animal has more provision for emer-
220 gency than a machine. The machine is less versatile; its range of action is narrow; its strength and accuracy in its own sphere are superhuman, but it shows badly in a dilemma; sometimes when its normal action is disturbed, it will lose its head, and go from bad to worse like a lunatic in a raging frenzy: but here, again, we are met
225 by the same consideration as before, namely, that the machines are still in their infancy; they are mere skeletons without muscles and flesh…."

"Herein lies our danger. For many seem inclined to acquiesce in so dishonorable a future. They say that although man should
230 become to the machines what the horse and dog are to us, yet that he will continue to exist, and will probably be better off in a state of domestication under the beneficent rule of the machines than in his present wild condition. We treat our domestic animals with much kindness. We give them whatever we believe to be the
235 best for them; and there can be no doubt that our use of meat

has increased their happiness rather than detracted from it. In like manner there is reason to hope that the machines will use us kindly, for their existence will be in a great measure dependent upon ours; they will rule us with a rod of iron, but they will not eat us; they will not only require our services in the reproduction and education of their young, but also in waiting upon them as servants; in gathering food for them, and feeding them; in restoring them to health when they are sick; and in either burying their dead or working up their deceased members into new forms of mechanical existence."

"The very nature of the motive power which works the advancement of the machines precludes the possibility of man's life being rendered miserable as well as enslaved. Slaves are tolerably happy if they have good masters, and the revolution will not occur in our time, nor hardly in ten thousand years, or ten times that. Is it wise to be uneasy about a contingency which is so remote? Man is not a sentimental animal where his material interests are concerned, and though here and there some ardent soul may look upon himself and curse his fate that he was not born a vapor-engine, yet the mass of mankind will acquiesce in any arrangement which gives them better food and clothing at a cheaper rate, and will refrain from yielding to unreasonable jealousy merely because there are other destinies more glorious than their own."

"The power of custom is enormous, and so gradual will be the change, that man's sense of what is due to himself will be at no time rudely shocked; our bondage will steal upon us noiselessly and by imperceptible approaches; nor will there ever be such a clashing of desires between man and the machines as will lead to an encounter between them. Among themselves the machines will war eternally, but they will still require man as the being through whose agency the struggle will be principally conducted. In point of fact there is no occasion for anxiety about the future happiness of man so long as he continues to be in any way profitable to the machines; he may become the inferior race, but he will be infinitely better off than he is now. Is it not then both absurd and unreasonable to be envious of our benefactors? And should we not be guilty of consummate folly if we were to reject advantages which we cannot obtain otherwise, merely because they involve a greater gain to others than to ourselves?"

"With those who can argue in this way I have nothing in common. I shrink with as much horror from believing that my race can ever be superseded or surpassed, as I should do from believing that even at the remotest period my ancestors were other than human beings. Could I believe that ten hundred thousand years ago a single one of my ancestors was another kind of being to myself, I should lose all self-respect, and take no further pleasure or interest in life. I have the same feeling with regard to my descendants, and believe it to be one that will be felt so generally that the country will resolve upon putting an immediate stop to all further mechanical progress, and upon destroying all improvements that have been made for the last three hundred years. I would not urge more than this. We may trust ourselves to deal with those that remain, and though I should prefer to have seen the destruction include another two hundred years, I am aware of the necessity for compromising, and would so far sacrifice my own individual convictions as to be content with three hundred. Less than this will be insufficient...."

THINKING IT THROUGH 5

H ere again is our example—the ethical claim we are investigating:

> "Cheating in college is acceptable, so long as you don't get caught because everybody does it and good grades are necessary to get a good job after graduation."

Step IV. Test/Verify your premises.

- Now that you have stated your premises explicitly, do you want to stick with them?

- Are you relying on premises drawn from unsubstantiated sources or from questionable authorities?

- Are you consistent in your premises? Or are you appealing to different and inconsistent foundations in your reasoning?

- Reformulate your premises if they have proven to be faulty.

1. Now that you have stated your premises explicitly, do you want to stick with them?

Review and Reexamine. We need to take another look at the premises we spelled out in the previous step. Are they precise and accurate? Are they clear? Have we been consistent with the intent of the original claim under examination? We should try to use not only the same words but also the intent they convey.

We should also be careful not to reorder or paraphrase the language in a way that subtly changes that meaning. Let us reexamine our premises, in particular looking to make sure we minimize repetitions and maximize straightforward connections between them.

> PI: Cheating in college is something everybody does.
> PII: When everybody does something, then it is acceptable.
> PIII: Good grades are necessary to get a good job.
> PIV: Any behavior that results in the good grades necessary to get a good job after graduation is acceptable.
> PV: One should not get caught cheating.
> PVI: Doing something as long as one does not get caught doing it is acceptable.

Go Back to the Beginning. Let's start from our conclusion again: "Cheating in college is acceptable." Then, let us work through the premises again to formulate each as a reason given to support the statement that cheating in college is acceptable: Cheating in college is acceptable because . . .

STRATEGY:
If a statement or concept is confusing, go back to the dictionary or the thesaurus to remind yourself of its correct core meaning.

The first two premises:

> PI: Cheating in college is something everybody does.
> PII: When everybody does something, then it is acceptable.

we can reword as:

> P1: Everybody does it, and, if everybody does something, it is acceptable.

The next premises, PIII and IV, become:

> P2: Getting a good job after graduation demands getting good grades; and getting good grades justifies any behavior that will secure these grades.

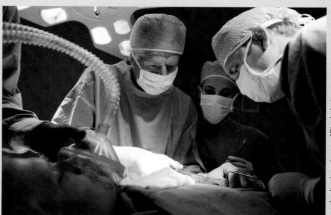

Would "so long as they don't get caught doing something wrong" be an acceptable condition for the work surgeons do in an operating room?

PV and VI become:

P3: Any behavior is acceptable in pursuing one's goals as long as one doesn't get caught.

Our premises seem to meet the test: they connect logically to one another and seem to progress toward the conclusion straightforwardly. We will stick with them.

{ **ASK YOURSELF: Are these premises precisely stated based on the information available?** }

2. Are you relying on premises drawn from unsubstantiated sources or from questionable authorities?

Seek Proof Wherever Possible. To answer this question, let us use one of our premises:

Any behavior is acceptable in pursuing one's goals so long as one doesn't get caught.

How could we prove such a claim? This is not a mere factual or empirical claim that we might test by looking at reliable data. Rather, the word *acceptable* is a value judgment, which is not a matter of simple factual observation. The tip-off is the word *accept-able*, which connotes a value judgment. So, instead, we need to turn to approaches, such as the major ones we reviewed in this book, for justifying value claims.

{ **STRATEGY:**
If you cannot recognize a "value judgment" readily, you should be able to identify it by default: if a claim cannot be resolved by testing or relying on data or quantifiable observation, then it is value-based. }

Use the Time-Tested Theories and Approaches. This statement amounts to the claim that majority or, actually, unanimous, action is right. A utilitarian or a Kantian would not support such a claim. The utilitarian uses the test of the principle of utility, namely, which action would result in the greatest happiness for the greatest number. This notion differs

sharply from the simple contention that majority opinion is all we need to know for establishing ethical rules. The Kantian would use the test of the categorical imperative to determine rightness, not a survey to determine factually what everybody is doing. So we will not find support for our premise using that approach.

Disprove Claims as Needed. A good way to challenge a universal claim is to come up with counterexamples that are clearly true. These counterexamples undercut the claimed universality of the principle being examined. Here, for example, we can counter that even if 100 percent of the prison guards at the Nazi camps participated in the extermination of Jews that would not make it acceptable. Even if 100 percent of the Caucasian political leaders of South Africa supported apartheid (the legally mandated separation of the races) that does not make it acceptable. Even if 100 percent of the plantation owners in the Southern states of the Confederacy owned slaves that does not make it acceptable.

These counterexamples undercut our universal claim in that last premise. If only one premise of our argument fails, then we do not logically reach the conclusion we sought: that cheating in college is acceptable.

{ **ASK YOURSELF: Can each premise be supported or proved through reasoning or reliable factual evidence?** }

3. Are you consistent in your premises? Or are you appealing to different and inconsistent foundations in your reasoning?

In reexamining our language, we have found it to be consistent. We would be inconsistent if, at some point in our deliberations, we accepted the notion that not everybody, but most students, cheat in college, for example.

{ **ASK YOURSELF: Is there anything in the statement of the premises that doesn't seem to "belong"?** }

Slaves working a sugar field, c.1860 (coloured engraving), American School, (19th century)/Private Collection/ Peter Newark American Pictures/The Bridgeman Art Library

Throughout much of history, many reasons were given to justify slavery. How did those who owned slaves and supported the institution of slavery explain or rationalize the ethical dimensions of this practice?

4. Reformulate your premises if they have proven to be faulty.

In our example, the premise that we examined previously fails, and thus so does our sought-after conclusion. You probably suspected that there was something questionable about the ethical claim from the very beginning but were not sure how to explain why it could not be supported. It should now be clear. That premise tried to start from an empirical claim that "everybody does something" and end with a value claim that it was acceptable. But our examination of counterexamples showed us that could not be true. Because that premise was essential to logically get to the conclusion, the argument, and in turn, the conclusion fails. If we were seeking to show a conclusion that we had a hunch was valid, we could revise the troublesome premise to get there. But in this case, it was pretty clear up front that there was something problematic about the original statement.

{ **ASK YOURSELF:** Will reformulation cure the problems with the argument or is the conclusion false? }

Now, revisit your own claim and go through the process described in this module. If some areas seem unclear to you, take note of what they are so that you can try and tease out a strategy to clarify them. You can also use your notes to address these questions later, after you have had a chance to take distance from the work done in this step.

Cathy Yeulet/Photos.com

What reasoning was used to counter the traditional opposition to women entering certain professions or handling certain tasks?

Animals and the Environment

"A thing is right when it tends to preserve the integrity, stability, and beauty of the biotic community. It is wrong when it tends otherwise."

—Aldo Leopold,
A Sand County Almanac (1949)

"[O]nly a small number of companies in each industry are actively integrating social and environmental factors into business decisions."

—United Nations Environment
Program (2002)

LEARNING OUTCOMES

After you complete this unit, you should be able to:

12-1 Identify major ethical issues central to animal rights and environmental ethics.

12-2 Explain major philosophical approaches for analyzing the ethical status of the issues you have identified.

12-3 Apply those philosophical approaches to contemporary issues of animal rights and environmental ethics.

In recent decades, much debate has centered on whether nonhuman animals should be treated humanely and whether we should protect our environment to preserve our quality of life. But as the cliché goes, the devil is in the details. Especially in challenging economic times, how far we should go in pursuing these goals is vigorously questioned.

For a good half-century now, we have become much more sensitive to the treatment of nonhuman animals than our predecessors had been. Philosophers of the past were especially big offenders. Medieval philosopher Augustine argued that animals were irrational and for that reason given to us by God to kill or use for our own purposes. French philosopher René Descartes wrote in the seventeenth century that nonhuman animals are incapable of feeling any sensation and were nothing but biological robots. A century later, Immanuel Kant argued that animals are not self-conscious and are only a means to help achieve our human ends.

However, he did urge that we treat animals kindly, but only because he was concerned that engaging in animal cruelty would have us cultivate bad habits that would make it easier for us to inflict pain on humans.

But we have come a long way in recognizing our obligations to nonhuman animals and to the environment, even if we do not all agree that they have "rights" in the sense that persons have rights. Often these developments in philosophy

What do **you** think?

My economic well-being now is more important than the environment we leave to future generations.

Strongly Disagree						Strongly Agree
1	2	3	4	5	6	7

were motivated by the activism of individuals and groups devoted to improving our awareness of these issues and philosophers sought to apply philosophical inquiry to explain these developments in the context of applied ethics. Some philosophers, as individual activists, have been keenly engaged for decades now in proposing approaches for addressing the ethics of how we treat animals and the environment.

Overview

In this chapter, we will look at the wide range of issues presented by animal and environmental ethics. We will see how philosophical reasoning tools can help us sort through the myriad of challenges. The case study looks at a recent environmental catastrophe, the Gulf Oil Spill. Readings provide an insight into the developments that led to the recent birth of the U.S. Environmental Protection Agency and into the thinking of a classic English utilitarian, Jeremy Bentham, who pioneered an approach for analyzing animal rights that is popular today.

Fracking, or hydraulic fracturing, has become controversial. Supporters of the technique tout the great potential for increase in the domestic production of energy sources such as natural gas and the resulting freedom from dependence on foreign oil. Opponents of fracking cite a number of problems attributed to the technique: local groundwater contamination with hydraulic fracturing chemicals, the potential migration of gases and chemicals to the surface, and the potential mishandling of wastes generated by the technique, among others.

AP Photo/Ralph Wilson

12-1 MAJOR ETHICAL ISSUES

In previous chapters, we have focused on how we treat each other, as human beings, with regard to different issues. In this one, we turn to issues presented by how we treat nonhumans, both nonhuman animals and the other elements of our environment, from plants and rocks to air, water, and the sky. Though the object of our treatment is distinct from the usual one, we can still focus on our relationship to those entities and what moral obligations, if any, we have to them, as well as what rights, if any, they have against us. Although we cannot hope to compile a complete list of all possible issues in this arena, we can identify some of the most current pressing ones. Our analysis

> [W]e need to **ask whether animals** in fact *have* rights, in the way that persons do.

should prepare us with the reasoning tools for tackling issues that might arise in the future and that we do not anticipate presently.

12-1a Animal Ethics

A wide range of issues is apparent when we consider animal rights. First, we need to ask whether animals in fact *have* rights, in the way that persons do. If they have some rights, specifically what rights they have must be considered. Do they have a right not to be tortured or used for scientific experimentation or killed for food? If they do have rights, we need to consider where those rights come from and whether they should be identical to the rights we recognize for persons. If they do not have rights, we still need to consider whether we, as persons, still have some moral obligation to them, and, if so, on what basis. We also need to distinguish "higher" animals, such as

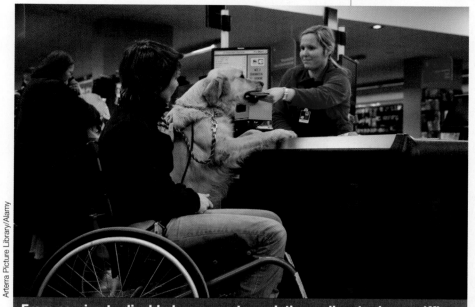

From service to disabled persons, to assisting police, to drug-sniffing, to seizure alert and disease-sniffing, dogs serve human beings in the most diverse capacities.

12-1b Environmental Issues

The most pressing issues regarding the environment cover an enormous range, from the quality of our air and water and the preservation of old-growth forests to acid rain, the disposal of trash, climate change, and the extinction of animal and plant species. But we cannot assess these in isolation. We are continually faced with choices about how much to change our behavior to affect these environmental factors. Particularly in an era of severe economic stress and an explosion of the population globally, we find ourselves balancing goals that might seem incompatible.

dogs, parakeets, or chimpanzees, with an obvious ability to feel pain or to grasp some rudimentary language from, say, insects, viruses, bacteria, amoeba, and sewer rats, and consider whether they should all have identical moral standing or whether we might establish a hierarchy of lower and higher animals, with varying ethical standing.

For example, some argue that strict limits on water quality cost industry money, and in turn, reduce employment opportunities. But others point out that new antipollution requirements have created new industries to address those challenges, and in turn, created employment opportunities. Another balancing question is how much we are willing to pay to improve human health and life expectancy. Should we insist that more be spent to reduce pollution, in hopes that we will save money on health care and quality of life?

Many of these issues require good factual information from scientists. But that data alone cannot make our ethical choices for us. We still need to turn to philosophical tools to sort out how to make these choices, once we have empirical data on our options.

In CourseMate, watch a video and take the quiz.

A Spanish ibex. A subspecies of the Spanish ibex, the Pyrenean ibex, is now extinct. The last natural Pyrenean ibex, a female named Celia, was found dead on January 6, 2000.

12-2 APPLYING PHILOSOPHICAL APPROACHES

Utilitarianism seems to present a promising vehicle for analyzing these ethical choices. But, although it might be clear how to analyze consequences for persons, it is much more debatable whether, and how, to calculate the consequences for nonhuman animals. Utilitarianism seeks to maximize pleasure and minimize pain, so we need first to acknowledge that animals can experience pleasure and pain, even if not in the same way that persons do. Jeremy Bentham, one of the earliest utilitarians, insisted that animals do feel sensation and thus must be included in our calculus. In contemporary times, philosopher Peter Singer has taken up this approach to insist that nonhuman animals must be considered in our utilitarian analysis. Singer and others use this approach to argue for improved treatment of animals in farming, scientific research, and also to argue for a moral obligation on the part of human beings to espouse a vegetarian diet.

With regard to ethical issues in the environment, utilitarianism seems to focus mainly on the consequences of different environmental choices because these outcomes affect human beings. The consequences one might consider may include quality of life now, economic choices, and consequences for future generations.

Kantianism has been proposed by some contemporary philosophers, most notably Tom Regan, to argue in favor of animal rights. All animals, not just humans, should be accorded Kantian dignity and respect. This leads Regan to more extreme conclusions than those reached by the utilitarians. For example, he urges an end to hunting, farming of animals, and scientific experimentation, as well as to eating animal meat. But do we really think nonhuman animals should have the same Kantian status as persons? And although Kantianism is at least worth exploring for animal ethics issues, it does not seem to make sense when analyzing environmental elements such as trees and rivers. For example, is it possible to conceive of rocks and

lakes as worthy of dignity and respect? It does make sense, however, if we think in terms of how our actions impact other people and future generations. If we leave behind a planet that is polluted with toxic substances, nuclear waste, and dramatic climate change, are we respecting the generations in the future that will have to live in such a world?

In debates on environmental ethics, a key distinction has been developed between biocentrism and anthropocentrism. Biocentrism, sometimes called *holism* in this context, argues that we should put the health of the overall ecological system ahead of the health and well-being of human beings. This approach was developed by a famed environmentalist named Aldo Leopold in his book *A Sand County Almanac* (1949). Leopold and his followers focused on what they called the "biotic community," which includes human beings but puts the interests of humans as just part of that community. In contrast, anthropocentrism says that the interests of human beings always come first over the environment considered as a whole. Attention to the environment remains important, but only if it promotes the well-being of human beings.

In CourseMate, apply what you've learned to the real-life scenario in the simulation.

In CourseMate, practice what you learned by taking the chapter quiz.

Elephants are social animals, living in groups and raising their young together. Observation and research have revealed that these animals show concern for each other and take care of weak or injured members of their families.

Villiers Steyn/Shutterstock.com

12-3 APPLICATIONS TO CONTEMPORARY ISSUES

12-3a Animal Ethics

As noted, utilitarianism is a promising approach, developed by Bentham and later by Singer, for providing a rationale for treating animals ethically. To consider our utilitarian balancing and make decisions, we must start with the recognition that animals feel pleasure and pain of some sort.

Utilitarianism might help our analysis of the difficult issue of medical research on new medicines and technologies. Imagine we have a choice between a method that minimizes pain to the animals subjected to medical research and one that does not. The utilitarian calculus rather easily would tell us that the right thing to do is apply the one that minimizes pain. But imagine that our choice is between conducting experiments on animals that might result in some suffering and not testing the experimental drugs at all on animals. Is the minimal pain to the animals outweighed by the risk to humans of taking a drug that has not been tested? That analysis is considerably more difficult, although utilitarianism does give us a mechanism for pursuing it. A utilitarian view would mean considering the physical pain to the animals used for that research against the positive outcomes for the health and well-being of humans measured, including longevity and freedom from pain.

The Kantian approach proposed by Regan, attributing Kantian dignity and autonomy to all animals, seems to provide a way to insist on maximum deference to the rights of nonhuman animals. But it is a difficult approach. It seems to insist that all animals, even higher animals, have the *same* dignity as persons. If you have a choice when entering a burning building, of saving either a human infant or a kitten, does this approach tell you how to make that decision? Does your "gut" tell you that you must first save the human infant? But having attributed identical Kantian dignity to the infant and the kitten, how can you explain that choice? To help answer this question, we could construct a hierarchy of Kantian dignity, in which persons have a higher status than nonhuman animals.

> [W]e could construct a hierarchy of Kantian dignity, in which persons have a higher status than nonhuman animals.

But then we must identify some basis for constructing such a hierarchy. Some animals seem to have better communication skills than infants or severely disabled persons, so the particular criterion of communication skills would not be an appropriate standard to rely on to create our hierarchy. Some higher animals seem to feel sensation as much as some humans, so that would not provide a good basis for such a hierarchy either. Such difficulties with this approach seem to have led many contemporary philosophers to work with the utilitarian alternative to support animal rights.

12-3b Environmental Ethics

Utilitarian analysis is a promising, albeit complicated, tool for analyzing environmental choices. We need to take into account the consequences for all persons now, in the present time, as well as those of future generations. Those consequences would need to include human health and longevity, quality of life and other intangibles, and also economic well-being. And if we recognize that pleasure and pain are felt by nonhuman animals, consequences that result from the pleasure or pain experienced by these animals need to be factored in.

Nuclear power is a good example of how complex the balancing of these calculations can be. Nuclear plants can provide cheap electricity in the present, which yields a positive economic benefit for persons and helps create more jobs. The negative consequences in the immediate future were tragically illustrated by the tsunami that struck Japan and the nuclear contamination in much of the region that was affected. But even without such a catastrophic occurrence, leaving radioactive waste behind that might contaminate huge portions of the planet for thousands of generations to come needs to be included in our analysis.

A Kantian approach encounters similar difficulties. Leaving aside Regan's claims that all animals deserve Kantian dignity, even applying our analysis to persons only is quite complicated. If we are deciding where to build a toxic waste dump, will locating it near a poverty-stricken neighborhood treat those residents with the respect and dignity we would demand for ourselves? If we leave behind ravaged old-growth forests, are we treating future generations with respect and dignity?

On March 11, 2011, a tsunami hit the northeastern coast of Japan. In Okumamachi, the Fukushima Dai-ichi nuclear power plant was struck by giant waves. Several reactors experienced full meltdowns and hydrogen explosions occurred in a couple of the units. Reactor building No. 1 is seen in this photo taken almost a year after the disaster. The incident showed the vulnerability of nuclear facilities in the face of natural disasters.

Mark Eite/Aflo Co. Ltd./Alamy

As we have seen repeatedly, philosophical reasoning does not provide us with any easy answers. But it does provide us with reasoning frameworks for working through issues that will always be difficult and will help us make choices in our everyday life that we can be comfortable making.

Now that you have studied how various types of reasoning apply to the topics discussed, review Critical Thinking Table 12.1 to follow the process of examining an ethical claim on a related topic

In CourseMate, listen to the audio summary of the chapter.

Peter Singer

Peter Singer (1946–)

Najah Feanny/Corbis

Australian-born Peter Singer is the Ira W. DeCamp Professor of Human Values, Princeton University; he also teaches part-time at for Applied Philosophy and Public Ethics. He is best known for rights, especially his 1975 book, *Animal Liberation: A New Ethics for* has published widely on a range of other topics in applied ethics, *Should the Baby Live? The Problem of Handicapped Infants Save: Acting Now to End World Poverty* (2009).

Bioethics at the University Center for the University of Melbourne Centre his pioneering work on animal *our Treatment of Animals.* He also including *Test-Tube Babies* (1982), (1985), and *The Life You Can*

His approach to animal rights is utilitarianism. He has argued that because nonhuman animals can feel pain and pleasure, they, too, should be included in our calculus of right and wrong action. He argued that the animal rights movement is analogous to the drive for rights by race and gender. Privileging *Homo sapiens*, he claimed, amounted to "speciesism," an attitude similar to other forms of bigotry, such as racism and sexism.

Through much of his career, Singer engaged in dialogue with Tom Regan, another prominent philosopher of animal rights. Regan rejects utilitarianism and insists that nonhuman animals should receive the same Kantian dignity we accord to human persons. Regan's approach demanded that all animal farming and hunting end, along with all medical research using animals. Singer's position did not conclude with these more extreme positions, although both Singer and Regan agreed on the ethical necessity of vegetarianism.

Table 12.1 Critical Thinking Steps and Their Application in an Example: "Equal Rights for Animals"

{ "All animals should have the same rights as humans." }

Critical Thinking Steps	Application
1. Examine and clarify key terms and concepts. 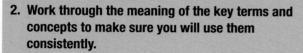 • Look words up in a dictionary as a start if necessary. • Unravel or unpack the complexities and nuances of a central term, such as *justice*, *right*, or *good*.	• What "rights" are of concern here? Rights to do what? • What do we mean by "same"? Does this mean "identical"? • By "animals" do we include all animals? Do we really want to include **all** animals? Do we just mean warm-blooded animals? Or do we also want to include, say, cockroaches and sewer rats?
2. Work through the meaning of the key terms and concepts to make sure you will use them consistently. • Consider the ways the term can be used by including it in different sentences and contexts to zero in on the particular meaning you are after. • Ask yourself what words are potential synonyms for the concept. Do those capture everything you want to understand about that term?	• Where do these rights come from? Does it matter if they are from a constitution or the United Nations Charter? Or as "natural rights" all are born with? How does that make a difference in this dispute? • Are we speaking about rights of humans worldwide or only in certain industrialized first-world countries? • Does same mean "identical" in the sense of "identical twins"? Does it only mean "comparable" or "similar"? • Even if we agree that higher animals have a right to be free from pain do we really want to extend this to such animals as, say, cockroaches and sewer rats? If not, is there a plausible way to draw that distinction?
3. Build premises and bring any assumptions to light. • Put together short and clear sentences to build each of your premises. • Think through what you may be taking for granted in your reasoning. What assumptions are you making? • Once you have identified assumptions, articulate them in your premise, so that your audience has the same understanding of a term or a concept as you.	The premises of the argument could be constructed as follows: (i) Any entity with the same moral status as humans should have the same rights as humans. (ii) All animals have the same moral status as humans. CONCLUSION: All animals should have the same rights as humans.
4. Test/Verify your premises. • Now that you have stated your premises explicitly, do you want to stick with them? • Are you relying on premises drawn from unsubstantiated sources or from questionable authorities? • Are you consistent in your premises? Or are you appealing to different and inconsistent foundations in your reasoning? • Reformulate your premises if they have proven to be faulty.	Both of these premises should be examined. (i) What do we mean by "moral status"? Where do humans get their rights? (ii) On what basis do we conclude that all animals have the same status as humans? Do we really want to insist that cockroaches and sewer rats have the same moral status and rights as humans? If you do not accept all of these premises, then you will not accept the conclusion either. But if you do accept all of them, then you would find the conclusion valid and justified.

(Continued)

Table 12.1 Continued

Critical Thinking Steps	Application
5. Confirm that the conclusions you draw are logical. Check for reliance on fallacies and correct any premise that you identify as relying on a fallacy.	This argument is especially vulnerable to criticism as the fallacy of equivocation, especially regarding the words *rights* and *moral status*. It also seems to be circular in stipulating what amounts to the conclusion sought to be proved.

Villers Steyn/Shutterstock.com

CHAPTER 12 Case Study

Gulf Oil Spill: Jobs, the Environment, and Animals

On April 20, 2010, a Deepwater Horizon oil wellhead blew out in the Gulf of Mexico, about forty miles from the coast of Louisiana. British Petroleum (BP) initially claimed it would have "minimal impact," but it quickly turned into the largest offshore oil spill in U.S. history. Eleven workers were killed by the explosion, and more than 200 million gallons of toxic crude oil were spewed into the Gulf. Some three months after the explosion on the BP rig, the leak was finally stopped on July 15 with a temporary cap over the wellhead. Permanent closure of the well was achieved on September 19. The spill was more than five times larger than the previous record-setter, the spill of the Exxon-Valdez oil tanker in Alaska in 1989. Fishing and tourism businesses that depended on the Gulf were severely affected. Although environmental groups and BP might never agree on the extent of this impact, BP announced that it was cleaning 635 miles of shoreline. The estimates of long-term environmental damage vary, but real damage was inflicted in the immediate aftermath of the disaster, as scenes of devastation showing oil-slicked fish, birds, wetlands, and dying oyster beds made evident.

Many local workers lost their jobs because of the oil spill. A number of them were hired as temporary workers to help clean up the mess, so they had some income. In a settlement with the U.S. government BP agreed to finance a compensation fund of up to $20 billion for business owners and residents who had suffered financial harm. President Barack Obama declared a moratorium on drilling until permits could be reviewed for environmental safety to avoid future disasters. The moratorium was lifted in October 2010, but six months later only three permits to resume drilling had been approved. Many complained that these delays prevented people from resuming their jobs as oil rig workers, especially during a difficult economy. But environmentalists complained that permits had not adequately addressed the environmental concerns, again putting the region at risk for another destructive oil spill.

1. As a utilitarian, how would you calculate the many consequences to the persons involved in trying to decide what to do in the future regarding oil drilling in the Gulf of Mexico? Consider the workers on the oil rig, the owners and managers of BP, the fishermen and business owners on the Gulf, the families of all those people, and others affected by your eventual decision.

2. If you share the view of some utilitarians that all animal life must be included in your calculations of consequences because they feel pleasure and pain, does this change your analysis?

3. How should we calculate the environmental damage for future generations of such oil spills? Is economic harm the only consequence of relevance?

For additional case studies, please see the CourseMate for this text.

Reading Excerpt: U.S. Environmental Protection Agency, "The Birth of EPA" (1985)

INTRODUCTION

The U.S. Environmental Protection Agency (EPA) was founded in 1970 with strongly bipartisan support by Republican President Richard Nixon. It can claim credit for many dramatic improvements in the quality of the nation's air and water and many other environmental elements. However, it continues to be the target of critics who insist that environmental protection is crushing to businesses and costing jobs. Balancing the rights of the general public to a clean environment and jobs with the rights of businesses and other entities that contribute to environmental pollution is a perennial problem. These excerpts from an essay published by EPA staff on the fifteenth anniversary of the agency highlight the events that led to the creation of a national environmental movement and the early problems in pursuing that mandate.

Kurt Strazdins/MCT/Landov

The EPA's mandate is to protect human health and the environment—that is, among other things, land, air, and water.

QUESTIONS FOR REFLECTION

1. All of the language establishing EPA, cited in this article, speaks of the impact of the environment on humans, not animals. Is this justifiable ethically? Should nonhuman animals be included in the mandate of environmental agencies? If so, how would you change the reasoning calculus from what it was in the original mandate?

2. This essay includes details on an early episode of balancing jobs and air quality at Union Carbide's plant in Marietta, Georgia. That year, 1971, the unemployment rate nationally was 5.6 percent. Would a different resolution be desirable if the unemployment rate had been 9 percent, as it was in 2011? How would a utilitarian analyze the impacts of these competing goals of jobs and air quality?

3. The costs associated with environmental protection are often justified by the presumed resulting improvements in human health, longevity, and the quality of life. How could these improvements be quantified for the purpose of using utilitarian analysis? Should agencies like EPA adopt a Kantian approach to justify their actions? What would such an analysis look like?

READING

The official birthday of EPA is December 2, 1970. Like any other birth, EPA's needed progenitors, and a family tree stretching back for years. Surely no factor was more pivotal in the birth of EPA than decades of rampant and highly visible pollution. But pollution

5 alone does not an agency make. Ideas are needed—better yet a whole world view—and many environmental ideas first crystallized in 1962.

That year saw the publication of Rachel Carson's *Silent Spring*, first in serial form in the *New Yorker* and then as a

10 Houghton Mifflin best seller. This exhaustively researched, carefully reasoned, and beautifully written attack on the indiscriminate use of pesticides was not exactly light reading. Yet it attracted immediate attention and wound up causing a revolution in public opinion.

15 An inveterate bird-watcher, Carson derived her missionary zeal from her fear that fewer species of birds would be singing each spring unless pesticide poisoning was curtailed. The readers of her book, however, were less alarmed by the prospect of a "*Silent Spring*" than they were about people dying from any num-

20 ber of hidden poisons lurking in what had previously seemed a benign environment. It was not hard to wax hysterical after reading in Carson's book that "the common salad bowl may easily present a combination of organic phosphate insecticides" that could "interact" with lethal consequences to the unsuspecting salad muncher.

U.S. Environmental Protection Agency, "The Birth of EPA," 1985, excerpts.

<blockquote>
Overpopulation and industrialization had left mankind trapped in a deteriorating environment.
</blockquote>

25   *Silent Spring* played in the history of environmentalism roughly the same role that *Uncle Tom's Cabin* played in the abolitionist movement. In fact, EPA today may be said without exaggeration to be the extended shadow of Rachel Carson. The influence of her book has brought together over 14,000 scientists, lawyers, managers,

ZUMA Press/Newscom

Rachel Carson, born in 1907 in Pennsylvania, grew up on a small family farm. Her early writings were devoted to sharing her wonder about the natural world. But, after World War II, noticing the increasingly extensive use of synthetic pesticide, she turned her attention and research toward studying their effects on nature. She labored to show how human beings, too, were susceptible to the damage wreaked by such poisonous substances as pesticides.

30   and other employees across the country to fight the good fight for "environmental protection."

Skeptics then and now have accused Carson of shallow science, but her literary genius carried all before it. Followers flocked to Carson's cause—rendered all the more sacred by her premature 35   death in 1964. Suddenly, everywhere people looked, they saw evidence of nature's spoilation. Concern over air and water pollution spread in widening eddies from the often-forgotten core of the movement: a highly detailed and intellectually challenging book about commercial pesticides.

40   The disillusioning effect of the Vietnam war enhanced the popularity of *Silent Spring.* When people heard of the defoilation tactics used in the jungles of Indochina, they became more receptive to the "environmental" ideas advanced by Carson and her countless imitators. The cognoscenti even began using a more arcane term— 45   "ecology"—in reference to a science of the environment, then still in its infancy.

The period 1962 to 1970 witnessed a slow erosion in the popularity of the word "conservation," as man himself replaced trees and wildlife as the endangered species, bar none. Overpopulation 50   and industrialization had left mankind trapped in a deteriorating environment. The damage was not just esthetically displeasing but threatening to the very survival of man. Environmentalism gained strength as a movement dedicated to ending—and if possible— reversing this decline in the human environment....

55   ... The Nixon Administration, although preoccupied with an unpopular war and a recession-ridden economy, took some stop-gap action on the environmental front in 1969. In May, President Nixon had set up a Cabinet-level Environmental Quality Council as well as a Citizens' Advisory Committee on Environmental Quality. 60   His critics charged that these were largely ceremonial bodies, with almost no real power.

Stung by these charges, President Nixon appointed a White House committee in December 1969 to consider whether there should be a separate environmental agency.... It was at just this time 65   that Congress sent to the President a remarkable bill known as the

<blockquote>
Environmental Impact Statements ... were now required of all federal agencies planning projects with major environmental ramifications.
</blockquote>

National Environmental Policy Act (NEPA).... A tone of high-minded idealism pervades this statute. NEPA's stated purposes were:

- "To declare a national policy which will encourage productive and enjoyable harmony between man and his environment."

70 - "To promote efforts which will prevent or eliminate damage to the environment and biosphere and stimulate the health and welfare of man."

- "To enrich our understanding of the ecological systems and natural resources important to the Nation."

75 To further these ends, NEPA called for the formation of a Council on Environmental Quality (CEQ) to give the President expert advice on environmental matters. The CEQ was also charged with reviewing Environmental Impact Statements, which were now required of all federal agencies planning projects with major envi-
80 ronmental ramifications.

In an era of bitter ideological disputes, public opinion was virtually unanimous on the need for the national environmental policy NEPA would generate. Turning his reluctant consent into a show of visionary statesmanship, President Nixon chose to
85 sign NEPA on New Year's Day, 1970—thus making the signing his "first official act of the decade." He named future EPA Administrator Russell E. Train to be the first CEQ Chairman.

NEPA's New Year's Day signing did prove to have more than symbolic significance. Enactment of this law set the stage for
90 a year of intense activity on the environmental front. Senator Gaylord Nelson recalls that right after the passage of NEPA, "the issue of the environment exploded on the country like Mount St. Helens." The authors of the first CEQ Annual Report on Environmental Quality had the same sense of an unprec-
95 edented watershed. In August 1970, they wrote: "Historians may one day call 1970 the year of the environment—a turning point, a year when the quality of life [became] more than a phrase ... "

It was in this atmosphere of intense concern for environ-
100 mental issues that President Nixon delivered his 1970 State

> ❝ [T]he first Earth Day celebration brought 20 million Americans out into the spring sunshine for peaceful demonstrations in favor of environmental reform.... ❞

of the Union Address. Speaking to both houses of Congress on January 22, the President proposed making "the 1970s a historic period when, by conscious choice, [we] transform our land into what we want it to become." He continued this activist
105 theme on February 10, when he announced a 37-point environmental action program. The program gave special emphasis to strengthening federal programs for dealing with water and air pollution.

Two months later, on April 22, the first Earth Day celebration
110 brought 20 million Americans out into the spring sunshine for peaceful demonstrations in favor of environmental reform.... The first Earth Day lives in popular memory to this day as a joyous and life-affirming moment in American history. The theatrical flair of some of the demonstrators had a great deal
115 to do with its success. Oil-coated ducks were dumped on the doorstep of the Department of the Interior ... A student disguised as the Grim Reaper stalked a General Electric Company stockholders' meeting ... Demonstrators dragged a net filled with dead fish down Fifth Avenue, and shouted to passers-by,
120 "This could be you!"

The phenomenal success of Earth Day gave greater priority than ever to environmental issues.... President Nixon called for "a strong, independent agency." The mission of this "Environmental Protection Agency" would be to:

125 - Establish and enforce environmental protection standards.

- Conduct environmental research.

- Provide assistance to others combating environmental pollution.

- Assist the CEQ in developing and recommending to the President new policies for environmental protection.
130

The components of the new agency were pieced together from various programs at other departments. From the Department of Health, Education and Welfare (HEW) came several functions: those of the National Air Pollution Control Administration, the
135 bureaus of Water Hygiene and Solid Waste Management, and some functions of the Bureau of Radiological Health. The Food and Drug Administration of HEW gave up to EPA its control over tolerance levels for pesticides.

The Department of the Interior contributed the functions of
140 the Federal Water Quality Administration and portions of its pesticide research responsibilities. EPA gained functions respecting pesticide registration from the Department of Agriculture. From the Atomic Energy Commission and the Federal Radiation Council, the new agency gained responsibility for radiation criteria and
145 standards....

One of EPA's goals was to give real bite to the federal enforcement bark. But this would clearly be impossible unless EPA's first

Administrator was able to fuse the air and water programs as well as those for pesticides and radiation into one effective working entity.... But President Nixon made the task facing EPA's first Administrator even greater by insisting upon the importance of viewing "the environment as a whole." The President's charge to the first EPA Administrator was to treat "air pollution, water pollution and solid wastes as different forms of a single problem." The main purpose of the reorganization that gave birth to EPA was to introduce a "broad systems approach [that] … would give unique direction to our war on pollution."

This daunting assignment went to a 38-year-old Assistant Attorney General named William D. Ruckelshaus. ... On December 1, at his Senate confirmation, Ruckelshaus received a magnanimous blessing from the Democratic Party's leading environmental activist, Senator Edmund Muskie (D-Maine): "I hope that you pre-empt the title that has been tossed about loosely in recent years. I hope that you become known as Mr. Clean."

That was, indeed, to become the favorite tag for EPA's first Administrator. It was not long before the media were portraying William Ruckelshaus as a knight in shining armor charging out to do battle with the wicked polluters of America. By adopting an aggressive stance toward a wide variety of environmental problems, EPA's new Administrator managed to gain headlines for his infant agency almost from the day of its birth.

... Administrator Ruck-elshaus attracted wide media attention when he delivered the keynote address to the second International Clean Air Congress. Ruckelshaus said that he and EPA were starting with "no obligation to promote commerce or agriculture." By promising to enforce "reasonable standards of air quality,"

JoeFox/Alamy

In 1970, "America's leading source of pollution [was] the automobile. The law set statutory deadlines for reducing automobile emission levels: 90 percent reductions in hydrocarbon and carbon monoxide levels by 1975," according to this EPA essay. By the 1990s, SUVs were all the rage in the United States. Should automobile emissions be controlled to reduce air pollution, even if the cost of the automobile is higher than it would be otherwise?

Ruckelshaus positioned himself as the governmental advocate of environmental progress, not merely a mediator between industry and the public. In fact, he seemed to envision for EPA a crucial role in the "development of an environmental ethic" among businessmen and citizens alike.

… the Year of the Environment came to an end on an extremely upbeat note with the signing of a major piece of environmental legislation. The Clean Air Act (CAA) of 1970 was the perfect bookend to balance the National Environmental Policy Act the President had signed with such a flourish on New Year's Day.

The Clean Air Act brought dramatic—and substantive—changes to the federal air quality program. The act required EPA to establish national air quality standards as well as national standards for significant new pollution sources and for all facilities emitting hazardous substances. The CAA took dead aim against America's leading source of pollution: the automobile. The law set statutory deadlines for reducing automobile emission levels: 90 percent reductions in hydrocarbon and carbon monoxide levels by 1975 and a 90 percent reduction in nitrogen oxides by 1976.

… At the outset, President Nixon promised the states a chance to make "a good faith effort" to implement CAA standards, but warned that federal enforcement action against violators would be

> **The Clean Air Act (CAA) of 1970 … took dead aim against America's leading source of pollution: the automobile.**

swift and sure. Alluding to a popular Clint Eastwood picture of the day, the President said that William Ruckelshaus would be "The Enforcer" in cases of air pollution.

215 An early test of EPA's resolve in this matter led to a confrontation with Union Carbide. Under pre-existing air statutes, Union Carbide had been required to submit a timetable for bringing the Marietta, Ohio, plant into compliance with recommended federal standards by the end of 1970.

220 ... William "The Enforcer" Ruckelshaus rejected Union Carbide's schedule for reducing sulfur oxide emissions from its Marietta plant. The company retaliated by threatening to lay off 625 workers. Eventually, EPA was able to forge a compromise that saved the workers' jobs. This was done without jeopardizing the environmental goal of securing from Union Carbide a
225 workable emission reduction plan. The company's Marietta plant brought its sulfur oxide emissions down 70 percent by April 1972.

... Ruckelshaus himself refuses to idealize the early 1970s. In fact, he blames the idealism of the Year of the Environment

230 for many of EPA's subsequent problems: "We thought we had technologies that could control pollutants, keeping them below threshold levels at a reasonable cost, and that the only things missing in the equation were national standards and a strong enforcement effort. All of the nation's early environmental laws
235 reflected these assumptions, and every one of these assumptions is wrong.... The errors in our assumptions were not readily apparent in EPA's early days because the agency was tackling pollution in its most blatant form. The worst problems and the most direct ways to deal with them were apparent to everyone."...

" An early test of EPA's resolve in this matter led to a confrontation with Union Carbide. "

Reading Excerpt 2: Jeremy Bentham, *An Introduction to the Principles of Morals and Legislation* (1781)

INTRODUCTION

Jeremy Bentham was an English philosopher who developed elements of utilitarianism as an ethical theory before John Stuart Mill worked out the theory in more detail. Anticipating the work of Peter Singer almost two centuries later, he uses utilitarianism to argue that we should be concerned that nonhuman animals are sentient beings who can suffer, and thus, that we should take them into account when analyzing the consequences of actions that could affect them.

Jeremy Bentham, c.1829 (oil on canvas), Pickersgill, Henry William (1782–1875)/UCL Art Museum, University College London, UK/The Bridgeman Art Library

Jeremy Bentham, 1748–1832

QUESTIONS FOR REFLECTION

1. Bentham includes "other animals" in his characterization of benevolence and malevolence. How do nonhuman animals experience these activities? Does this set a good foundation for the ethical treatment of nonhuman animals?

2. Bentham thinks that nonhuman animals can experience "happiness," which is part of the utilitarian analysis. What constitutes happiness (and unhappiness) for nonhuman animals?

3. Bentham is troubled that the "sensibilities" of nonhuman animals have been ignored, but he acknowledges differences in the sensibilities of humans and nonhuman animals. What might he mean by those differences? Do these disqualify nonhuman animals from being treated ethically?

4. Why does Bentham seem to think that it is okay to eat animals but not to torment them? Is this consistent with your contemporary reasoning?

5. Bentham uses as an appeal the institution of slavery, which was still prevalent in his day, in urging that our treatment of animals is unethical. Does this suggest that he would agree that discrimination against animals is "speciesism," analogous to "racism"?

6. Appealing to reason and speech in order to distinguish humans from nonhuman animals is inadequate, according to Bentham. Is his comparison with human infants a compelling argument for this claim?

READING

The pleasures of benevolence are the pleasures resulting from the view of any pleasures supposed to be possessed by the beings who may be the objects of benevolence; to wit, the sensitive beings we are acquainted with; under which are commonly
5 included, 1. The Supreme Being. 2. Human beings. 3. Other animals. These may also be called the pleasures of good-will, the pleasures of sympathy, or the pleasures of the benevolent or social affections....

The pleasures of malevolence are the pleasures resulting from
10 the view of any pain supposed to be suffered by the beings who may become the objects of malevolence: to wit, 1. Human beings. 2. Other animals. These may also be styled the pleasures of ill-will, the pleasures of the irascible appetite, the pleasures of antipathy, or the pleasures of the malevolent or dissocial affections....

15 What other agents then are there, which, at the same time that they are under the influence of man's direction, are susceptible of happiness. They are of two sorts: 1. Other human beings who are styled persons. 2. Other animals, which, on account of their interests having been neglected by the insensibility of the
20 ancient jurists, stand degraded into the class of *things*...

Jeremy Bentham, *An Introduction to the Principles of Morals and Legislation,* 1781, excerpts.

> **"** *What other agents … are there, which, at the same time that they are under the influence of man's direction, are susceptible of happiness.* **"**

Under the Gentoo [Hindu] and Mahometan [Muslim] religions, the interests of the rest of the animal creation seem to have met with some attention. Why have they not universally been recognized, with as much as those of human creatures, allowance made for the difference in point of sensibility? Because the laws that are have been the work of mutual fear; a sentiment which the less rational animals have not had the same means as man has of turning to account. Why *ought* they not? No reason can be given.

If the animal eaten were all, there is very good reason why we should be allowed to eat such of them as we like to eat: we are the better for it, and they are never the worse. They have none of those long-protracted anticipations of future misery which we have. The death they suffer in our hands commonly is, and always may be, a speedier, and by that means a less painful one, than that which would await them in the inevitable course of nature. If the animal killed were all, there is very good reason why we should be suffered to kill such as molest us: we should be the worse for their living, and they are never the worse for being dead. But is there any reason why we should be suffered to torment them? Not any that I can see. Are there any why we should *not* be suffered to torment them? Yes, several. . . .

The day has been, I grieve to say in many places it is not yet past, in which the greater part of the species, under the denomination of slaves, have been treated by the law exactly upon the same footing as, in England for example, the inferior races of animals are still. The day *may* come, when the rest of the animal creation may acquire those rights which never could have been withholden from them but by the hand of tyranny. The French have already discovered that the blackness of the skin is no reason why a human being should be abandoned without redress to the caprice of a tormentor. It may come one day to be recognized, that the number of the legs, the villosity [surface traits] of the skin, or the termination of the *os sacrum* [large bone at the base of the spine], are reasons equally insufficient for abandoning a sensitive being to the same fate.

> **"** *The French have already discovered that the blackness of the skin is no reason why a human being should be abandoned without redress to the caprice of a tormentor.* **"**

What else is it that should trace the insuperable line? Is it the faculty of reason, or, perhaps, the faculty of discourse? But a full-grown horse or dog is beyond comparison a more rational, as well as a more conversable animal, than an infant of a day, or a week, or even a month, old. But suppose the case were otherwise, what would it avail? the question is not, Can they *reason?* nor, Can they *talk?* but, Can they *suffer?*

CHAPTER 13

War and the World

> "War is just when it is necessary; arms are permissible when there is no hope except in arms."
>
> —Niccolo Machiavelli

> "In order for a war to be just, ... a just cause is required."
>
> —St. Thomas Aquinas

LEARNING OUTCOMES

After you complete this unit, you should be able to:

13-1 Identify major ethical issues raised by the decision to engage in war and the conduct during a war.

13-2 Explain major philosophical approaches for analyzing the ethics of war, both its initiation and the conduct during war.

13-3 Apply those philosophical approaches to the analysis of the ethics of war.

War seems to be a regular feature of life, despite the advances in contemporary life of diplomacy, communication, and awareness that history provides. The twentieth century opened with "The Great War" (World War I), which was the "war to end all wars," only to lead to World War II. The Korean War, the Vietnam War, and then wars in Iraq and Afghanistan, along with numerous regional conflicts around the planet, make war seem like a never-ending condition for much of the earth population.

Many disciplines study war, including political science, international relations, and history. But philosophers have also taken a special interest in the ethics of warfare and have contributed to the broader cultural dialogue. Ethicists are especially interested in the decision making that leads to war and the conduct during wars.

Overview

In this chapter, we will consider examples of the ethical issues presented by war today. We also will look at several reasoning approaches developed specifically for addressing war, including Just War theory, Realism, and Pacifism. Our case study focuses on an increasingly

What do you think?

War is justified if, and only if, our own country is attacked.

Strongly Disagree						Strongly Agree
1	2	3	4	5	6	7

common element in our discussion of war, namely, terrorism. The readings look at a classic example of Just War theory from St. Thomas Aquinas and a classic example of Realism by Thomas Hobbes.

13-1 MAJOR ETHICAL ISSUES

In previous chapters, issues we discussed raised questions about how persons treat other persons in a variety of settings. They also led us to ask whether our ethical principles for the treatment of persons could be extended to our treatment of nonhuman animals and the entire environment. In this chapter, we want to consider whether principles of ethical treatment of persons might be extended to entire nations in their treatment of each other in times of war. So, we will be extending familiar principles, yet again, to a broader area of consideration.

Under the broad umbrella of the term *war*, we can imagine a huge range of ethical issues that might arise. We will concentrate on a few of the most important issues that have been the subject of extensive discussion by philosophers and other scholars.

Starting in 1991, United Nations inspectors had overseen a program of dismantlement and destruction of any weapons of mass destruction that Iraq might possess. After much wrangling with Iraq over a claimed lack of cooperation, the United States declared that the possible presence of weapons of mass destruction in Iraq was grounds to invade the country. On March 20, 2003, in a preemptive strike, the U.S. military invasion of Iraq began.

Faleh Kheiber/Reuters/Landov

13-1a *Jus ad bellum*

This Latin term is commonly used in international political debates about the justice or right to go to war. It refers to the justifications for entering into a war. It is used in legal, political, and public policy contexts when reasons for declaring war are discussed. For example, the *jus ad bellum*, or justification for going to war, of nation X might be the fact that nation Y invaded a portion of the former. When we focus on jus ad bellum, we are examining what factors justify going to war. For example, if another country physically invades our borders and murders our citizens, are we justified in declaring war? If another country steals our water and food supplies, by rerouting rivers and supply routes, are we justified in declaring war on them to get those supplies back?

What if another country mounts a cyberattack on us, shutting down our computer systems, electrical grids, water purification systems, even though no person from that country physically entered our country; would we be justified in declaring war on that country to get those systems restored? What if we learn of gross human rights violations in another country; are

> When we focus on *jus ad bellum,* we are examining what factors justify going to war.

we justified in declaring war on that country to insist on the restoration of those rights? When we ask these questions, we are discussing jus ad bellum, or the justification for going to war.

13-1b *Jus in bello*

The Latin term *jus in bello* refers to actions that are allowable *within* the context of a war. That is, once we have declared war, what things are we allowed or not allowed to do in conducting that war? When we debate what actions are allowable or justifiable *in* or *during* war, we are debating jus in bello. Can we attack military troops, even though we know there will be "collateral damage" in killing civilians, if there is no other way to achieve our military objectives? Can we use weapons, such as a nuclear bomb, for example, that we know will not only harm civilians now, but also contaminate for future generations the location where they are used? Are we justified in shutting off supply lines to our adversary's troops, knowing that we will also starve innocent civilians in that region? Are we justified in letting an attack on our own troops go forward, if getting them out of harm's way

A U.S. Air Force Predator drone. Air strikes in war are an effective strategy for reaching targets without putting ground troops in harm's way. But, when they result in the killing of innocent civilians, is the so-called war for hearts and minds at risk of getting lost?

Alxpin/istockphoto

would tip off the enemy that we had intercepted their coded messages? Are we justified in using forms of interrogation recognized by the international community as torture, if we think these methods can yield reliable information that would help protect our own people? When we ask these questions, we are debating justice within war, or jus in bello.

In CourseMate, watch a video and take the quiz.

13-2 PHILOSOPHICAL APPROACHES

13-2a Utilitarianism

To work through this range of issues, utilitarianism has obvious uses. Whether we are analyzing a question in jus ad bellum, that is, in the context of the reasons for getting into war in the first place, or jus in bello, that is, regarding conduct within that war, we should always analyze the consequences of all the alternative courses of action. Which will create the greatest happiness for the greatest number of people now and in the future? Or because war involves so much destruction, which alternative will create the least unhappiness for the greatest number of people? As shown in the chapter on animals and the environment, many philosophers will want us to take into account the consequences, not only for people, but

also for nonhuman animals in the environment. When napalm was dropped by the United States on crops in Vietnam during that war, food supplies were destroyed, not only for the Vietnamese people but also for the animals. This destruction also affected plant life in that region. If a terrorist succeeds in exploding a "dirty" bomb in a major U.S. city, horrific consequences will befall not only the human population but also animals and plant life of that region. So the utilitarian would tell us to balance the benefits to the terrorists in promoting their goals, that is gaining world attention to their cause and the resulting positive consequences that would befall people they care about, along with the harm to the people, animals, and the environment caused by that bomb, against the various consequences of not setting off the bomb for all concerned. So our theoretical calculus of happiness and unhappiness will be enormously complex, but it provides us with a framework for thinking through right and wrong action.

13-2b Kantianism

A Kantian approach to human dignity and autonomy is also helpful in analyzing these ethical issues in war. The decision to go to war should be considered in light of the effect it

Napalm is an agent that when mixed with petroleum or a comparable fuel is used in incendiary devices, that is, weapons that produce intensely hot fire when exploded. The fire generates temperatures of 1,500° to 2,200° F (for reference, water boils at 212° F) and causes victims excruciating pain.

Darren Brode/Shutterstock

would have on all people involved, including citizens and residents of the country declaring war, as well as the adversary's population, both when war is declared and while war is being conducted. If another nation physically invades us, they have violated our autonomy and dignity as persons; does that justify our violating theirs in return? Are we sure that all the civilians in that country participated in that decision and deserve being victimized by the conflict? Should we focus our war efforts on the political and military leaders and try to avoid collateral damage to civilians as a way of respecting the autonomy and dignity of these civilians?

> At the heart of the disagreement between just war theorists and realists is whether nations are really like persons ...

war and should therefore conduct wars in whatever way is best for their own nation's survival. Proponents of this view include Niccolo Machiavelli, Thomas Hobbes, and Henry Kissinger.

At the heart of the disagreement between just war theorists and realists is whether nations are really like persons, that is, whether they have ethical rights and obligations. The just war theorists point out that a nation is a collection of persons that have come together to form a government and thus that the government of those persons should be subject to ethical principles, too. The realists agree that individual persons have ethical obligations but reject the notion that a nation, as an entity, is capable of having such obligations.

A different approach is **Pacifism**, which promotes an absolute ban on violence among nations. As alternatives to settling disputes, the absolutist pacifist would urge the use of such techniques as economic sanctions and pressure from the international community. Thus, although both the just war theorist and the realist believe that some wars are justifiable in some circumstances, the pacifist stands in opposition to both of these approaches in believing that wars are never justified.

In CourseMate, apply what you've learned to the real-life scenario in the simulation.

In CourseMate, practice what you learned by taking the chapter quiz.

13-2c Just War Theory, Realism, and Pacifism

In addition to the familiar ethical reasoning frameworks we just explored, we can add some well-developed philosophical theories specifically about war and its conduct. **Just War theory** argues that the conduct of war must be done in accord with the ethical principles we rely on as individuals. This view has been promoted for many centuries. Two of its proponents, St. Thomas Aquinas and Michael Walzer, are discussed later in this chapter. In contrast, **Realism** argues that nations are not subject to ethical rules in

Portrait of Niccolo Machiavelli(1469-1527)Santi di Tito(1536-1603)/Palazzo Vecchio/Palazzo della Signoria)Florence, Italy/The Bridgeman Art Library

An Italian writer and philosopher, Niccolo Machiavelli, 1469–1527, is most known for the suggestion in his infamous book, *The Prince*, that force and violence may be necessary to maintain one's power.

13-3 APPLICATION TO ETHICAL ISSUES

13-3a *Jus ad bellum*

Let us now apply some of these theories to contentious issues about war. Until 2002, U.S. policy was that war should only be entered into in self-defense, that is if the nation was attacked, and military power was important only for self-defense and as a deterrent to others who might be thinking of attacking the country. But in 2002, then-President George W. Bush articulated a new strategy of "preemptive war." He argued that in an age of nuclear weapons, we could no longer wait for an attack to occur because it might be too late for us to respond at all. This, then, was a new approach to jus ad bellum, that is, a new justification for declaring war. George W. Bush is no longer president, but the justifiability of preemptive war in a nuclear age remains a hotly debated topic among the military, government leaders, and the population. How might we think through this issue using our ethical reasoning tools?

Utilitarianism

The utilitarian would ask us to identify the entire range of consequences emanating from this policy. Certainly protecting our own citizens and future generations of citizens from possible nuclear attack is a positive consequence that is important. We also need to consider the consequences for the citizens of the nation that we think might be about to attack us in devastating ways but has not yet done so. Ultimately, we would wish to balance the consequences affecting one's own citizens with those affecting the citizens of a threatening nation. For example, we would ask whether it makes sense, to protect one's citizens from what is expected to be a ground attack that would potentially impose relatively few casualties, to launch a massive bomb campaign that would likely result in a considerable number of fatalities. In other words, we would question whether consideration should be given to proportions and a comparison of likely resulting casualties on both sides. Other consequences include our standing in the world community of nations and the respect we want to command. People might disagree on the extent to which this matters, if at all. But we might consider, for example, whether we will need the help and support of those other nations in pursuing our national goals in this and other military actions. So our standing and trustworthiness would seem to have specific consequences for one's own country in the future. Further, if we take preemptive

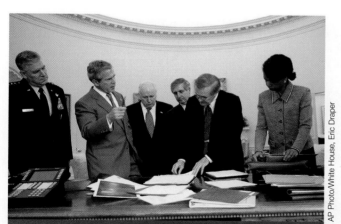

President George W. Bush, with Vice President Dick Cheney and some of his cabinet members. The forty-third president's new preemptive war strategy was a departure from a tradition of self-defense in U.S. policy. How sufficiently sure of an imminent threat ought one be before taking such drastic actions as starting a war?

AP Photo/White House, Eric Draper

action, would we be setting in motion a change in rules for other countries, which might be thinking of adopting this preemptive policy for themselves and use it to justify attacking other nations? This difficult calculus will continue to be debated long into the future. But this framework offers a good idea of the broad range of consequences we need to consider in debating such an issue.

Kantianism

The Kantian would ask us to consider the autonomy and dignity of our own citizens, whom we wish to protect from a possible nuclear attack, for example. But we also need to consider the autonomy and dignity of the persons in the country we are thinking of preemptively attacking. Is this attack, on balance, the best way to address the autonomy and dignity of all those citizens? What of the autonomy and dignity of persons in other countries who might be attacked if more countries adopt this preemptive rationale? Note that the utilitarian is telling us to consider the happiness of all persons as the consequence of most importance. The Kantian is asking us to consider the autonomy and dignity of those persons. Although these two approaches rely on two different ethical frameworks, they might lead to the same conclusions about what to do.

Just War Theory

The just war theorists would ask us whether the threat of attack was sufficiently imminent to support a decision to attack first. They would also want us to make sure as much as possible that the threat was genuine and that we make every effort to gather as much credible and legitimate evidence as possible that the threat was real. They would ask about the intentions of our leaders and whether they were just. They would insist that we have a just cause, the defense of our own nation against actual threats.

Realists

The realists would not worry about the ethics of the choices facing them because they do not believe nations are subject to ethical obligations. But they would worry about the safety and survival of their own nation and the tactics that would best ensure that. Survival would include

KEY TERMS

Just War theory: the political philosophy that ethical standards of just and unjust, right and wrong, should be of central importance in the declaration of war and the conduct of that war

Realism: the political philosophy that ethical standards of just and unjust, right and wrong, are irrelevant in the conduct of war; the only standards that matter are national sovereignty, the nation's self-interest, and whatever it takes to win

Pacifism: the political philosophy that holds that violence is always wrong; in disputes among nations, non-violent actions (such as economic sanctions and international pressure) should be pursued instead

physical survival of their own people in the present, but would also look ahead to the standing of the country in the world community and the possibility of future attacks by others once this rationale were accepted widely.

Pacifism

The pacifist would urge that going to war is not an option, regardless of the evidence we might or might not have for weapons of mass destruction. We should always be able to find an alternative course of action, such as economic sanctions or international pressure. Those measures had been underway when then-President Bush decided to take preemptive action and invade Iraq.

One could consistently urge nonviolent courses of action in a particular situation, such as that facing the United State in 2003 in Iraq, without being an absolutist pacifist in all circumstances. In other words, one could consistently urge nonviolence in that situation but still believe that violence would be justified in a different situation.

Critics of Pacifism argue that by pursuing nonviolence in all situations and stating that as our objective at all times, we might actually encourage other nations to attack us. Because they know we would not respond with violence, they would have no incentive to hold back themselves in using violence. To this argument, the absolutist would respond that few nations, if any, would be in a position to resist for very long the pressure that economic sanctions combined with international condemnation would bring to bear on their people.

Regardless of which theoretical approach is most useful in thinking through these difficult choices, it seems clear that an empirical or factual issue lingers in all of them—with the exception of Pacifism. Just how much evidence do we need that the other country is getting ready to attack with devastating technologies? How solid and reliable should any evidence be? In other words, do we want "the smoking gun to be a mushroom cloud" over one of our cities before we act? If we cannot afford to wait too long, how much evidence do we need to allow us to act before it is too late?

> A subject of much continuing and important debate is the use of torture as an interrogation technique.

13-3b *Jus in bello*

To further apply our theories, let's try a current example of jus in bello, the conduct *within* a war once it is declared. A subject of much continuing and important debate is the use of torture as an interrogation technique. Imagine that we suspect that someone in our custody might know about a ticking time bomb somewhere in our country and we urgently, desperately need to find out where it is so we can intervene before it goes off.

Utilitarianism

The utilitarian would ask us to consider all the consequences that result from our choice to torture or not to torture in this situation. The positive consequence, for a great many people, would consist of the torture yielding the information we seek and allowing us to prevent a catastrophic bomb from hurting our own people. We would balance that against the physical pain and suffering of the person we tortured to get the information, which seems like a clear justification to torture. So our utilitarian calculation from just those factors seems to support the torture. But the utilitarian wants us to look at *all* consequences that result from our choices. What if we are uncertain that a suspected terrorist in our custody has information useful enough to prevent great harm from coming to our citizens and troops? Do

Guantanamo Bay detainees: Are there ethical limits on how we should treat vanquished enemies after winning a war?

Ron Sachs/CNP/Corbis

we engage in the torture of this individual based merely on the possibility that he or she might have such critical information? If we endorse torture, are we exposing our own military personnel to torture when they are captured, and we are left without the ethical grounds for objecting? What are the consequences of our endorsement of torture for our standing in the world community? If our engagement in torture hurts our standing in the world community as a violation of agreements we have made with other members of that community, will there be a ripple effect that ends up hurting us in the long run even more?

Kantianism

The Kantian would find the use of torture a severe violation of the autonomy and dignity of the person we have in captivity. But how about the dignity of our own people, who will not be harmed if we can get that information as a result of torture? A Kantian never says that "the end justifies the means," as a utilitarian would, but we have many persons involved here and need to weigh the human rights violations at stake, including how the respect and dignity of one's own people is affected by the application or the withholding of torture on a suspected terrorist. The Kantian would probably conclude that torture is such an outrageous violation of the suspect's human dignity that we need to find other means to respect our own people.

Just War Theory

The just war theorist would insist that nations follow ethical rules. If we have signed international agreements banning torture, then we should live up to those promises. Keeping commitments is itself an ethical act, along with the decision not to torture. Would the just war theorist tell us that violating one ethical rule is okay if it is outweighed by treating our fellow citizens ethically in protecting their lives? This seems to bring in utilitarianism, which a just war theorist might consistently do. Just war theory says nations must follow ethical rules. Theorists in the just war community seem to agree on some principles, such as proportionality of the action taken within war to the wrong to which it responds. Principles such as the ones included in the Geneva Convention also dictate that the actions within war must themselves not be evil, and torture is identified as an example of an evil that must never be pursued under those principles.

Realists

The realist would say that the nation should do whatever will best promote our survival and the survival of our people. Ethical rules do not apply to nations for the realist and would not apply here. If torture is the best way to get results, then it should be done, the realist would say.

Pacifists

The pacifist would have objected to our being at war in the first place and thus, presumably, would object to the actions within that war as they would involve violence. The pacifists still might find themselves pleading for nonviolence once a country had entered into a war and urge that we extricate ourselves from what they would perceive to be a mistake at all levels.

No matter which reasoning framework we find most satisfactory, we have a crucial need to carefully examine the evidence on which we rely, especially with regard to the nature of whatever threats we consider. How does experience help answer the empirical question of whether torture really gets right answers? Some persons who have endured torture in real life insist that they would say anything at all, true or false, to get the torture to stop; that suggests that torture is not an effective questioning technique, regardless of its ethical nature. But other persons insist they know of examples of persons who were tortured and produced valuable information that their interrogators would not have gotten otherwise. If we further investigate this factual issue, and find better answers about the effectiveness of torture in general, we can then return to our various ethical frameworks for help in refining our conclusions about what to do.

We have looked at two of the most challenging sets of issues in war. There are others and there will surely be more in the future that we cannot today anticipate. But the reasoning tools we work with here should be helpful in addressing evolving issues in this area in the future.

Now that you have studied how various types of reasoning apply to the topics discussed, review Critical Thinking Table 13.1 to follow the process of examining an ethical claim on a related topic.

In CourseMate, listen to the audio summary of the chapter.

EPA/Landov

Khalid Shaikh Mohammed, a member of Osama bin Laden's terrorist organization al-Qaeda, was arrested in 2003. He is alleged to have masterminded the 9/11 attacks in the United States. In 2008, the CIA acknowledged that waterboarding was used on the detainee.

Table 13.1 Critical Thinking Steps and Their Application in an Example: "A Justification for War"

{ "War is justified whenever our country is threatened by people who want to destroy us." }

Critical Thinking Steps	Application
1. Examine and clarify key terms and concepts. 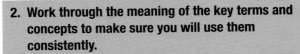 • Look words up in a dictionary as a start if necessary. • Unravel or unpack the complexities and nuances of a central term, such as *justice*, *right*, or *good*.	• What is the meaning of "war"? Do we mean only traditional, physically violent warfare with soldiers and firepower? • What is a "threat"? If someone just says they wish our country were destroyed, is that sufficient? • What counts as "destruction"? Nuclear obliteration? Bombs to destroy buildings and people? Economic collapse? Starvation?
2. Work through the meaning of the key terms and concepts to make sure you will use them consistently. • Consider the ways the term can be used by including it in different sentences and contexts to zero in on the particular meaning you are after. • Ask yourself what words are potential synonyms for the concept. Do those capture everything you want to understand about that term?	• War is used in many senses, both literal and metaphorical. Do we also mean to include newer senses, such as cyberwar or aggressive economic sanctions? Do we mean to include the so-called "war on drugs," the "war on cancer," and the "war on terror," too? • Precisely what threats are sufficient here? What is needed for a more tangible threat to support the response of war? What evidence is needed to count as a credible threat in this context? • Which "people" matter in making these threats? The head of government? Leading political figures? Citizens as polled to gauge popular opinion? What status should these people have to be taken seriously in these threats?
3. Build premises and bring any assumptions to light. • Put together short and clear sentences to build each of your premises. • Think through what you may be taking for granted in your reasoning. What assumptions are you making? • Once you have identified assumptions, articulate them in your premise, so that your audience has the same understanding of a term or a concept as you.	The premises of the argument could be constructed as follows: (i) When our country is threatened by people who want to destroy us, we are justified in taking appropriate action. (ii) War is an appropriate response when our country is threatened by people who want to destroy us. CONCLUSION: War is justified whenever our country is threatened by people who want to destroy us.
4. Test/verify your premises. • Now that you have stated your premises explicitly, do you want to stick with them? • Are you relying on premises drawn from unsubstantiated sources or from questionable authorities?	Both of these premises should be examined: (i) This premise is filled with ambiguous terms: *threatened*, *want*, *destroy*, *justified*, and *appropriate*. Can this premise be justified with the wide range of meaning possible for each of those terms?

Alxpin/istockphoto

Darren Brode/ Shutterstock

Critical Thinking Steps	Application
• Are you consistent in your premises? Or are you appealing to different and inconsistent foundations in your reasoning? • Reformulate your premises if they have proven to be faulty	(ii) Like (i), this premise is filled with vague terms with varying meanings: *war, appropriate, threatened, want, destroy,* and *justify.* Is this premise justifiable for all those broad senses? Another problem with this premise is that it seems to merely be a restatement in a close paraphrase of the original claim we are trying to prove, making this a circular argument; that is, it seems to assume as a premise what we are trying to prove. If you do not accept all of these premises, then you will not accept the conclusion either. But if you do accept all of them, despite the problems identified above, then you would find the conclusion valid and justified.
5. **Confirm that the conclusions you draw are logical. Check for reliance on fallacies and correct any premise that you identify as relying on a fallacy.** 	This argument is especially vulnerable to criticism as the fallacy of equivocation, especially regarding the words *war, destroy,* and *threat*; these terms are used in slightly different ways at different stages of our argument. It also seems to harbor the fallacy of circularity, especially in the second premise: this argument assumes what it is trying to prove.

Michael Walzer

Michael Walzer is one of the most prominent political philosophers in the United States. Sometimes called the "dean" of just war theory, he has published extensively on contemporary development of the theory on the justification of war that traces to Thomas Aquinas and before. Like most just war theorists, Walzer believes that aggression, that is, actual physical attack on human rights, is the only justification for going to war. But much disagreement exists on whether that aggression must first have actually happened or could merely be anticipated. Walzer identifies restrictions on anticipated aggression and does not support unlimited preemptive action against possible aggression. He rejects Pacifism, but insists that ethics must be considered in decisions on declaring and conducting war.

Walzer also has made important contributions on debates around nationality and ethnicity, economic justice, the welfare state, tolerance, and international justice. He has promoted a practical and pluralistic approach to ethics and political and moral life. He rejects what he considers an overly theoretical approach to these issues and grounds his work in the situations of real countries and civilizations. His books include *Just and Unjust Wars: A Moral Argument with Historical Illustrations* (1977), *On Toleration* (1997), and *Arguing About War* (2004).

A Professor Emeritus at the School of Social Science at the Institute for Advanced Study in Princeton, New Jersey, Walzer has received numerous honors for his contributions to intellectual dialogue in political theory.

Michael Walzer (1935–)

CHAPTER 13 Case Study

Racial Profiling in the Age of Terrorism

In the 1990s, profiling by race, especially of African Americans and Latinos, to arrest suspected drug dealers was increasingly recognized as inappropriate. "Driving while black" or "driving while brown" became a familiar cliché to characterize what had been a widespread practice of racial profiling by some law enforcement officers. But just as racial profiling was becoming unacceptable in society at large, the attacks on the World Trade Center on September 11, 2001, rekindled widespread interest in racial profiling. Now, however, profiling also targeted young men who appeared to be of Middle Eastern descent.

On the day of the attacks, Norman Y. Mineta, who was Secretary of Transportation, ordered that there be no racial profiling in the nation's transportation system, including persons who might "appear to be of Arab, Middle Eastern or south Asian descent and/or Muslim." He issued a statement that "In a democracy, there is always a balance between freedom and security. Our transportation systems, reflecting the values of our society, have always operated in an open and accessible manner. And, they will again." Mineta himself, as a child, had been held in the Japanese American internment camps during World War II, along with many others, for no other reason than his ethnic heritage. Though the members of many of those families had been peaceful, law-abiding U.S. citizens for generations, they were relocated to such camps as a result of a kind of profiling, following Japan's attack on Pearl Harbor.

But profiling terrorists and would-be terrorists who seek to wreak havoc on Americans in various ways remains a hot topic. Many insist that airport security should focus their attention on persons who are most likely to be hijackers and terrorists and let people who are obviously "innocent" pass through security without intrusive searches. There is wide disagreement about who really looks innocent. In the past decade, many persons of Anglo descent who were U.S. citizens have been convicted of terrorism. Norway was devastated by the murders of seventy-seven people in July 2011 by a terrorist attack on city buildings and a summer camp.

A Nordic man named Anders Breivik was captured and confessed to the crimes.

Timothy McVeigh was convicted of the bombing of the Murrah Federal Building in Oklahoma City on April 19, 1995, that killed 168 people. Until the 9/11 attacks six years later, this was the worst act of terrorism on U.S. soil in the country's history. McVeigh was executed on June 11, 2001, and his coconspirator, Terry Nichols, was sentenced to 161 consecutive life sentences without the possibility of parole. McVeigh was a native-born U.S. Christian, Caucasian, and an honorably discharged member of the U.S. Army. Nichols was a native-born U.S. Caucasian, who had served briefly in the U.S. Army with McVeigh. Both were members of antigovernment militias.

1. It is true that all nineteen hijackers on 9/11 were men of Middle-Eastern descent who practiced the Muslim religion. If so, does that fact alone support extra scrutiny of persons who match that description at airport security?

2. How would you develop a profile to stop future McVeigh's from committing acts of terror? What information about McVeigh would be most relevant in advance to intercept him?

3. How would you develop a profile that would stop terrorists like Anders Breivik?

4. If you were designing a security system for airports to catch likely hijackers and terrorists, without overly inconveniencing ordinary passengers, what things would you look for and how would you identify the likely terrorists before they could board the plane?

For additional case studies, please see the CourseMate for this text.

Reading Excerpt: St. Thomas Aquinas, *Summa Theologica* (1265–1274)

INTRODUCTION

The writings of Aquinas are studied in previous chapters, and his work remains influential just as well on the question of "just war" as on other topics. His writing follows the same structure here as in the other reading. He states his own position in the middle of this passage, beginning with the words, "I answer that…" followed by his reasoning. He "bookends" his position by first anticipating four objections someone might raise and then finishing by answering those four objections. This is an excellent example of the dialogue of good reasoning. He not only states and defends his own position, but he also anticipates objections and answers them, which makes his position even stronger.

As we saw before, Aquinas always cites biblical passages and the work of previous philosophers. But even without those references, his pure reasoning is worth examining on its own. Here, his three requirements for a just war are well known and defended even today, despite the passage of many centuries.

This 1631 painting by Francisco de Zurbaran shows "The Apotheosis of St. Thomas Aquinas." It depicts the elevation of Thomas Aquinas to a divine status.

QUESTIONS FOR REFLECTION

1. What arguments does Aquinas cite in support of the claim that it is sinful to wage war? How does he respond to those arguments? Do you find his answers persuasive, and why or why not?

2. What are the three things that Aquinas requires himself for a war to be "just"? Are the meanings of all the key words clear and unambiguous? How do we determine the "authority" of a purported "sovereign"? What counts as a "just cause"? What is meant by "rightful intention"? Do these requirements have meaning today in our modern world?

3. Aquinas was writing in a time before the invention of gunpowder or nuclear bombs. Does the existence of these modern warfare weapons alter the necessary tests for a just war, as Aquinas has spelled out? In what ways would you revise his tests for a just war in today's environment?

READING

Article 1. Whether it is always sinful to wage war?
Objection 1. It would seem that it is always sinful to wage war. Because punishment is not inflicted except for sin. Now those who wage war are threatened by Our Lord with punishment…:
5 "All that take the sword shall perish with the sword." Therefore all wars are unlawful.

Objection 2. Further, whatever is contrary to a Divine precept is a sin. But war is contrary to a Divine precept, for it is written …: "But I say to you not to resist evil"; and …: "Not revenging yourselves,
10 my dearly beloved, but give place unto wrath." Therefore war is always sinful.

Objection 3. Further, nothing, except sin, is contrary to an act of virtue. But war is contrary to peace. Therefore war is always a sin.

Objection 4. Further, the exercise of a lawful thing is itself lawful,
15 as is evident in scientific exercises. But warlike exercises which take place in tournaments are forbidden by the Church, since those who are slain in these trials are deprived of ecclesiastical burial. Therefore it seems that war is a sin in itself.

On the contrary, Augustine says in a sermon on the son of the
20 centurion: "If the Christian Religion forbade war altogether, those who sought salutary advice in the Gospel would rather have been counselled to cast aside their arms, and to give up soldiering

St. Thomas Aquinas, *Summa Theologica* (1265–1274).

Augustine of Hippo, 354–430, also known as St. Augustine, held that Christians should be pacifists in their personal lives, but that war may be waged for purposes of restoring or acquiring peace only. These beliefs strongly influenced St. Thomas Aquinas's own views.

Botticelli, Sandro (1444/5-1510)/The Art Gallery Collection/Alamy

altogether. On the contrary, they were told: 'Do violence to no man … and be content with your pay.' If he commanded them to be

25 content with their pay, he did not forbid soldiering."

I answer that, In order for a war to be just, three things are necessary. First, the authority of the sovereign by whose command the war is to be waged. For it is not the business of a private individual to declare war, because he can seek for redress of his rights from

30 the tribunal of his superior. Moreover it is not the business of a private individual to summon together the people, which has to be done in wartime. And as the care of the common weal [general public] is committed to those who are in authority, it is their business to watch over the common weal of the city, kingdom or

35 province subject to them. And just as it is lawful for them to have recourse to the sword in defending that common weal against internal disturbances, when they punish evil-doers, according to the words of the Apostle …: "He beareth not the sword in vain: for he is God's minister, an avenger to execute wrath upon him that

40 doth evil"; so too, it is their business to have recourse to the sword of war in defending the common weal against external enemies.

Hence it is said to those who are in authority …: "Rescue the poor: and deliver the needy out of the hand of the sinner"; and for this reason Augustine says …: "The natural order conducive

45 to peace among mortals demands that the power to declare and counsel war should be in the hands of those who hold the supreme authority."

> " *[I]t is not the business of a private individual to declare war …* "

Secondly, a just cause is required, namely that those who are attacked, should be attacked because they deserve it on account

50 of some fault. Wherefore Augustine says …: "A just war is wont to be described as one that avenges wrongs, when a nation or state has to be punished, for refusing to make amends for the wrongs inflicted by its subjects, or to restore what it has seized unjustly."

Thirdly, it is necessary that the belligerents should have a

55 rightful intention, so that they intend the advancement of good, or the avoidance of evil. Hence Augustine says …: "True religion looks upon as peaceful those wars that are waged not for motives of aggrandizement, or cruelty, but with the object of securing peace, of punishing evil-doers, and of uplifting the good." For it

60 may happen that the war is declared by the legitimate authority, and for a just cause, and yet be rendered unlawful through a wicked intention. Hence Augustine says …: "The passion for inflicting harm, the cruel thirst for vengeance, an unpacific and relentless spirit, the fever of revolt, the lust of power, and such like

65 things, all these are rightly condemned in war."

Reply to Objection 1. As Augustine says …: "To take the sword is to arm oneself in order to take the life of anyone, without the command or permission of superior or lawful authority." On the other hand, to have recourse to the sword (as a private person)

70 by the authority of the sovereign or judge, or (as a public person) through zeal for justice, and by the authority, so to speak, of God, is not to "take the sword," but to use it as commissioned by another, wherefore it does not deserve punishment. And yet even those who make sinful use of the sword are not always slain with

75 the sword, yet they always perish with their own sword, because, unless they repent, they are punished eternally for their sinful use of the sword.

Reply to Objection 2. Such like precepts, as Augustine observes …, should always be borne in readiness of mind, so that we be

80 ready to obey them, and, if necessary, to refrain from resistance or self-defense. Nevertheless it is necessary sometimes for a man to act otherwise for the common good, or for the good of those with whom he is fighting. Hence Augustine says …: "Those

whom we have to punish with a kindly severity, it is necessary to handle in many ways against their will. For when we are stripping a man of the lawlessness of sin, it is good for him to be vanquished, since nothing is more hopeless than the happiness of sinners, whence arises a guilty impunity, and an evil will, like an internal enemy."

Reply to Objection 3. Those who wage war justly aim at peace, and so they are not opposed to peace, except to the evil peace, which Our Lord "came not to send upon earth"....Hence

Augustine says...: "We do not seek peace in order to be at war, but we go to war that we may have peace. Be peaceful, therefore, in warring, so that you may vanquish those whom you war against, and bring them to the prosperity of peace."

Reply to Objection 4. Manly exercises in warlike feats of arms are not all forbidden, but those which are inordinate and perilous, and end in slaying or plundering. On olden times warlike exercises presented no such danger, and hence they were called "exercises of arms" or "bloodless wars," as Jerome states in an epistle.

Reading Excerpt: Thomas Hobbes, *Leviathan* (1651)

INTRODUCTION

The English philosopher Thomas Hobbes is recognized as the first modern political philosopher. His approach to war is referred to as Realism, which rejects the view that war should be conducted according to ethical principles, as just war theorists Aquinas, Walzer, and many others insist should be done. Realists over the centuries have appealed, not to ethical reasoning, but to the practical need for power and security of the state, self-interest of the nation, and whatever it takes to win.

Hobbes's best-known work is the *Leviathan*, which sets out a theory of the state of nature in which we find ourselves until we yield to the authority of a sovereign. The word *leviathan* traces

to a sea monster in biblical writings. For Hobbes, it refers to the body of the state, the structure of society, and the form of government. Among many topics in his book is the necessity of waging war, in the excerpts here, from Chapters 13 and 14.

Thomas Hobbes, 1588–1679

QUESTIONS FOR REFLECTION

1. What factors bring about the condition of war? What are the harmful effects of being in this condition of war? How does a common power over all people change this condition?

2. When people are in a state of war against all other people, why do notions of right and wrong, just and unjust have

no place? What motivates people in this situation? How do notions of justice and injustice arise?

3. Why should all people seek a state of peace? What are the benefits of peace? What alternatives are justifiable if this cannot be achieved?

READING

... in the nature of man, we find three principal causes of quarrel. First, competition; secondly, diffidence; thirdly, glory.

The first makes men invade for gain; the second, for safety; and the third, for reputation. The first use violence, to make themselves masters of other men's persons, wives, children, and cattle; the second, to defend them; the third, for trifles, as a word, a smile, a different opinion, and any other sign of undervalue, either direct in their persons or by reflection in their kindred, their friends, their nation, their profession, or their name.

Hereby it is manifest that during the time men live without a common power to keep them all in awe, they are in that condition which is called war; and such a war as is of every man against every man. For war consists not in battle only, or the act of fighting, but in a tract of time, wherein the will to contend by battle is sufficiently known: and therefore the notion of time is to be considered in the nature of war, as it is in the nature of weather. For as the nature of foul weather lies not in a shower or two of rain, but in an inclination of many days together: so the nature of war consists

Thomas Hobbes, *Leviathan,* 1651, excerpt.

not in actual fighting, but in the known disposition thereto during
20 all the time there is no assurance to the contrary. All other time
is peace.

Whatsoever therefore is consequent to a time of war, where
every man is enemy to every man, the same consequent to the
time wherein men live without other security than what their own
25 strength and their own invention shall furnish them withal. In such
condition there is no place for industry, because the fruit thereof
is uncertain: and consequently no culture of the earth; no navigation, nor use of the commodities that may be imported by sea; no
commodious building; no instruments of moving and removing
30 such things as require much force; no knowledge of the face of
the earth; no account of time; no arts; no letters; no society; and
which is worst of all, continual fear, and danger of violent death;
and the life of man, solitary, poor, nasty, brutish, and short.

Leviathan was published in 1651, right at the end of the English
civil war (1642–1651), a series of conflicts between supporters of
King Charles I and Parliamentarians. The Parliament of England
was a body created by the Crown to help collect taxes. Its power
in practice became its authority to withhold from the king the
financial resources to achieve his political goals. The English Civil
War led to the trial (portrayed here) and execution of King Charles I.

Lebrecht Music and Arts Photo Library/Alamy

It may seem strange to some man that has not well weighed
35 these things that Nature should thus dissociate and render men
apt to invade and destroy one another: and he may therefore, not
trusting to this inference, made from the passions, desire perhaps to
have the same confirmed by experience. Let him therefore consider
with himself: when taking a journey, he arms himself and seeks to
40 go well accompanied; when going to sleep, he locks his doors; when
even in his house he locks his chests; and this when he knows there
be laws and public officers, armed, to revenge all injuries shall be
done him; what opinion he has of his fellow subjects, when he rides
armed; of his fellow citizens, when he locks his doors; and of his
45 children, and servants, when he locks his chests. Does he not there
as much accuse mankind by his actions as I do by my words? But
neither of us accuse man's nature in it. The desires, and other passions of man, are in themselves no sin. No more are the actions that
proceed from those passions till they know a law that forbids them;
50 which till laws be made they cannot know, nor can any law be made
till they have agreed upon the person that shall make it.

It may be thought there was never such a time nor condition
of war as this; and I believe it was never generally so, over all the
world: but there are many places where they live so now. For the
55 savage people in many places of America, except the government
of small families, the concord whereof depends on natural lust,
have no government at all, and live at this day in that brutish manner, as I said before. Howsoever, it may be perceived what manner
of life there would be, where there were no common power to fear,
60 by the manner of life which men that have formerly lived under a
peaceful government use to degenerate into a civil war.

But though there had never been any time wherein particular
men were in a condition of war one against another, yet in all times
kings and persons of sovereign authority, because of their inde-
65 pendency, are in continual jealousies, and in the state and posture
of gladiators, having their weapons pointing, and their eyes fixed
on one another; that is, their forts, garrisons, and guns upon the
frontiers of their kingdoms, and continual spies upon their neighbors, which is a posture of war. But because they uphold thereby
70 the industry of their subjects, there does not follow from it that
misery which accompanies the liberty of particular men.

To this war of every man against every man, this also is
consequent; that nothing can be unjust. The notions of right and
wrong, justice and injustice, have there no place. Where there is no
75 common power, there is no law; where no law, no injustice. Force
and fraud are in war the two cardinal virtues. Justice and injustice

*" Where there is no common
power, there is no law; where
no law, no injustice. "*

are none of the faculties neither of the body nor mind. If they were, they might be in a man that were alone in the world, as well as his senses and passions. They are qualities that relate to men in society, not in solitude. It is consequent also to the same condition that there be no propriety, no dominion, no mine and yours distinct; but only that to be every man's that he can get, and for so long as he can keep it. And thus much for the ill condition which man by mere nature is actually placed in; though with a possibility to come out of it, consisting partly in the passions, partly in his reason.

The passions that incline men to peace are: fear of death; desire of such things as are necessary to commodious living; and a hope by their industry to obtain them. And reason suggests convenient articles of peace upon which men may be drawn to agreement. These articles are they which otherwise are called the laws of nature....

... [B]ecause the condition of man is a condition of war of every one against every one, in which case every one is governed by his own reason, and there is nothing he can make use of that may not be a help unto him in preserving his life against his enemies; it follows that in such a condition every man has a right to everything, even to one another's body. And therefore, as long as this natural right of every man to everything endures, there can be no security to any man, how strong or wise he be, of living out the time which nature ordinarily allows men to live. And consequently it is a precept, or general rule of reason: that every man ought to endeavor peace, as far as he has hope of obtaining it; and when he cannot obtain it, that he may seek and use all helps and advantages of war. The first branch of which rule contains the first and fundamental law of nature, which is: to seek peace and follow it. The second, the sum of the right of nature, which is: by all means we can to defend ourselves.

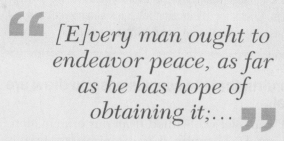

[E]very man ought to endeavor peace, as far as he has hope of obtaining it;...

From this fundamental law of nature, by which men are commanded to endeavor peace, is derived this second law: that a man be willing, when others are so too, as far forth as for peace and defense of himself he shall think it necessary, to lay down this right to all things; and be contented with so much liberty against other men as he would allow other men against himself. For as long as every man holds this right, of doing anything he likes; so long are all men in the condition of war. But if other men will not lay down their right, as well as he, then there is no reason for anyone to divest himself of his: for that were to expose himself to prey, which no man is bound to, rather than to dispose himself to peace. This is that law of the gospel: Whatsoever you require that others should do to you, that do ye to them....

1. Confirm that the conclusions you draw are logical.

In our example, we learned from our examination in **Thinking It Through 5** that one of our premises was flawed. The universal claim in the third premise built in the previous module, **P3: "Any behavior is acceptable in pursuing one's goals as long as one doesn't get caught"** could not be validated or supported and, indeed, clear counterexamples showed it to be false. In turn, that meant that we could not logically reach our conclusion. And finally, that meant that the original statement we were examining could not be supported. We have not proven that it was false, but we have been unable to prove that it is true.

This failure to show that it is true matches with our initial hunch or intuition that the claim could not be supported, even though we sometimes hear statements of this sort from people around us.

Let us imagine, however, that we could have proven the truth of premise **P3.** That would not be the end of our examination. We would still need to check one more thing. We would need to see if our arguments contained any fallacies that would undercut the validity of the desired conclusion.

{ ASK YOURSELF: Do I need to review my premises, their sequencing, and my conclusions once more? }

2. Check for reliance on fallacies and correct any premise that you identify as relying on a fallacy.

Here are some of the most common fallacies we could expect to find in this type of argument:

- **Fallacy of equivocation.** We commit this fallacy when we use the same word with different meanings. We start with one meaning and then shift to another

Because consequences can be particularly dire in certain situations—where human health or even lives are at stake—should one be concerned about strictly applying rigorous and logical reasoning in those situations?

meaning to try to reach our conclusion. Remember how important it was when we began to pay attention to the meaning we were using and focus on precision. We discovered that different meanings could mean different conclusions. For example, when we examined the various senses of the term *acceptable*, we realized that, in the context of our claim, to take this qualifier as meaning *adequate* would not work. In our claim, we observed that there could be no shadings of ethical standards in the case of cheating. Shifting meanings throughout an argument to manipulate the logic and supposedly reach the desired conclusion through this deception yields the fallacy of equivocation.

Let us assume the following: We started our argument with the meaning that cheating is just not working as hard as possible but ended with a conclusion that cheating is plagiarizing a term paper. Then, we would be engaging in the fallacy of equivocation.

- **Begging the question.** When we assume as a starting point precisely what we are trying to prove as a conclusion, we beg the question. Typically, this fallacy is hidden in different language, but when we paraphrase with good synonyms, we realize we are just begging the question.

Let us assume we had argued as follows: "Cheating in college is acceptable because dishonesty is okay, as long as you don't get caught." Our reason (following "because") is a plausible paraphrase or synonym for the conclusion we are seeking to reach. In other words, we have just stipulated and proposed as proof what we are trying to prove.

- **Ad hominem argument.** In this fallacy, one attacks the person rather than the argument.

    Let us assume we had argued as follows: "Cheating in college is okay because my crazy ex-boyfriend says it's not and everything he says is despicable." Here, we are not criticizing the ex-boyfriend's claim (that cheating in college is not okay) but are instead attacking the person who said it.

- **Questionable authority.** This fallacy relies on a suspicious source as proof or evidence of the claim.

    Let us assume we had argued as follows: "Cheating in college is okay because my favorite website says it's okay." Here we are relying on one website that might or might not be the least bit reliable.

- **Hand waving.** This fallacy amounts to being insistent that something is true because everybody knows it is true without any sort of evidence of proof.

    Let us assume we had argued as follows: Cheating in college is okay because that is so obviously true to everybody. Here we are relying, not on argument, but repetitive dogmatic insistence on the claim.

- **Appeal to ignorance.** With this fallacy, we claim that something is true because we have not been able to prove it false, or vice versa.

    Let us recall the following: We noted in the analysis of our sample claim that we could not prove our conclusion to be true based on the premises we were able to formulate. But that does not mean that we have proven that it is false. That would be the fallacy of the appeal to ignorance.

- **Faulty analogy.** This fallacy relies on finding some similarities between two things and jumping to the conclusion that they are similar in other relevant aspects.

    Let us assume we had argued as follows: Hiring a tutor to help me in my classes helps me get good grades and cheating in class helps me get good grades; because hiring a tutor is acceptable, then cheating must be acceptable, too. Here, hiring a tutor and cheating in class do have something in common (help in getting good grades); but that does not mean they are alike in all respects, including acceptability.

{ **ASK YOURSELF:** If I cannot identify a specific fallacy in my argument but sense that there is one, can I correct my argument to avoid using any false premise? }

Conclusion. Once you have gone through every one of these modules's critical thinking steps, you might want to step away from your claim and your analysis for a day or two. Then, return to your work with a fresh perspective and retrace your steps. Keeping a bird's eye view of the process, ask yourself: Is the meaning of ideas or concepts clearer? Do some mechanisms make more sense?

In the end, the critical thinking process endeavors to help you resolve an issue. In other words, it helps you achieve a specific goal. But it also takes you beyond a simple objective, a finite task: it trains you to think more effectively, logically, from a sounder basis. Over time, in continuing to apply this method, as you work through more ethical issues, you will develop more effective reasoning strategies, and widen the foundation of your understanding of today's important ethical problems and the accurate ways to frame them. The quality of your college papers is likely to improve, resulting in better grades, and thus helping you get the job you seek after graduation.

Jeremy Bentham, c.1829 (oil on canvas), Pickersgill, Henry William (1782-1875) / UCL Art Museum, University College London, UK / The Bridgeman Art Library

If we argued that because a car was recalled it meant that the manufacturer of that car could never be trusted, what kind of fallacy would we be committing?

WHY CHOOSE?

Every 4LTR Press solution comes complete with a visually engaging textbook in addition to an interactive eBook. Go to CourseMate for (**ETHICS**) to begin using the eBook. Access at **www.cengagebrain.com**

Complete the Speak Up survey in CourseMate at **www.cengagebrain.com**

f Follow us at **www.facebook.com/4ltrpress**

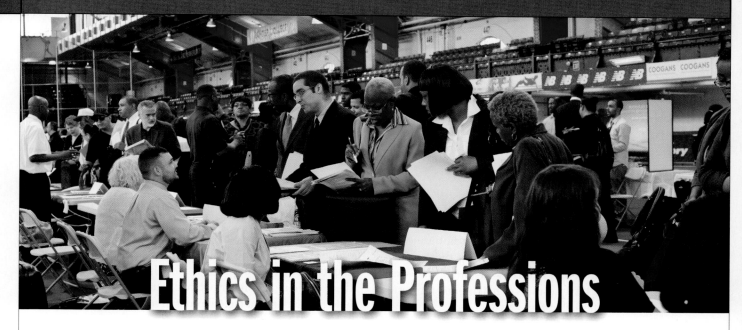

PART III

Ethics in the Professions

This book addresses topics in applied ethics that almost all of you will encounter in your lives at some point, regardless of your profession or geographical location or political orientation. In this final Part, we focus on some questions of special interest for the variety of career paths you might choose.

On average, regardless of the state of the economy, adults change careers three times throughout their working lives—and use many different avenues, such as job fairs, like the one shown in the photo above, to seek a position. The career you are pursuing now might not be the same one you find yourself in when you retire someday. Many of the most promising professions decades in the future are unimaginable now, and some of you might find yourselves shifting gears in your own lives to enter those professions.

Whatever career you hope to pursue now, consider also that you are likely to be a participant in some manner in that activity. You might not be interested in entering a business career yourself, but you will certainly be purchasing goods and services from others in that field. You might not be interested in working in the health care professions, but you will certainly be using the services of their practitioners at various times in your life. You might not be interested in entering the legal profession in some capacity, but the law will affect your life in many ways, regardless of what path you choose— in contracts or real estate or insurance or the many other ways in which the law can impact our lives.

Ethical conduct throughout all aspects of our lives is a goal for everyone. We might disagree on the specific ethical practices we find most justifiable, but awareness of ethics and its pervasiveness in all aspects of our personal and professional lives is essential.

Business Ethics

B1-1 Chapters of Special Interest

In this book, many chapters focus on your relationships with other people, as you will in your career in business, and the principles you develop for handling those relationships will carry through a variety of circumstances. Here are examples of the questions of heightened interest for you in some of these chapters.

B1-1a. *Freedom of Expression* (Chapter 6)

Consider the many ways in which you communicate in your work, from advertising to the general public to one-on-one conversations with employees, coworkers, and clients. Commercial speech is more heavily regulated than the speech in a public or political setting. You will likely be held to standards of factual proof in some settings—that is,

Hemera Technologies

Think of business dealings you have had as a consumer of a service or a product: are there situations where ethical issues came into play that seemed to be "gray areas"? How did such issues compare with others in which ethics were clear cut?

A billboard is one of the many tools used for advertising. Does thinking about the kind of visibility that any content on a billboard gets help you understand the importance of meeting proper standards for commercial communications?

law as well as being unethical. But many more variations of discrimination might be possible, without violating any laws, raising ethical questions instead. For instance, if you refuse to hire persons who are overweight or unemployed for a long time, you might wonder whether you are engaging in unfair and unethical discrimination, or if this is just "good business" that is justified by utilitarianism.

B1-1c. Computer Ethics (Chapter 11)

It is difficult to imagine any business enterprise that does not involve computers in some way and most also rely heavily on the Internet. How do ethical issues arise in your business career where computers and technology are concerned? Do your employees have any right to privacy when they use company computers and Internet connections? What obligation do you have to intervene with online harassment and bullying, whether of employees or clients?

B1-2 Professional Ethics in Business

Almost all professional associations have adopted codes of ethics within that particular domain. These can most easily be located on the websites of those organizations. Here are a few examples with broad interests, but there are many more for specialized work:

- Business: American Chamber of Commerce
- Real Estate: National Association of Realtors
- Insurance: National Association of Professional Insurance Agents
- Marketing: American Marketing Association
- Accounting: American Accounting Association
- Manufacturing: National Association of Manufacturers

Consider these professional ethics codes carefully. Ask yourself whether they cover all the ethical issues of concern to you in your work. Are you clear about what each provision of these codes means? If not, where and how can clarification be obtained? How are these codes enforced? If your work includes a licensing requirement (perhaps in real estate or accounting), could violation of these ethical codes result in loss of your license?

you will need to ensure that data and facts that you provide for business purposes or use to support business claims are accurate and represent truthful information. You will not be allowed to defame your competitors with false and harmful factual claims. But you might also encounter ethical gray areas where you might wonder if resorting to dishonesty regarding your products or services would be beneficial to your profits. For example, you might question whether it would be unethical to sell your product to consumers, if you secretly knew that your newest model will be available in a few months at a much lower price with better quality.

B1-1b. Discrimination (Chapter 8)

Some forms of discrimination in your business life, especially by race, national origin, and gender, will be prohibited by

Health Care Ethics

Many career paths are encompassed in health care, and demand for these services has been growing rapidly with an aging population in much of the world and as a result of developments in medical technology. You might be pursuing a career as a physician, dentist, physician's assistant, pharmacist, nurse, or nurse's aide. You might be looking at health care administration or medical research. Some might be looking at work in developing, marketing, and sales of new medicines and medical technology. The scope of careers in health care is broad indeed.

The type of organization where you work will also vary widely, from hospitals, health maintenance organizations, and medical research corporations, to small businesses, nursing homes, and in-home services for persons who are infirm or elderly. The types of encounters you will have during your career will also vary a great deal: the people, institutions, and organizations you come across will run a large gamut and so will the ethical challenges engendered by the different situations, personalities, and circumstances. New ethical challenges will keep emerging

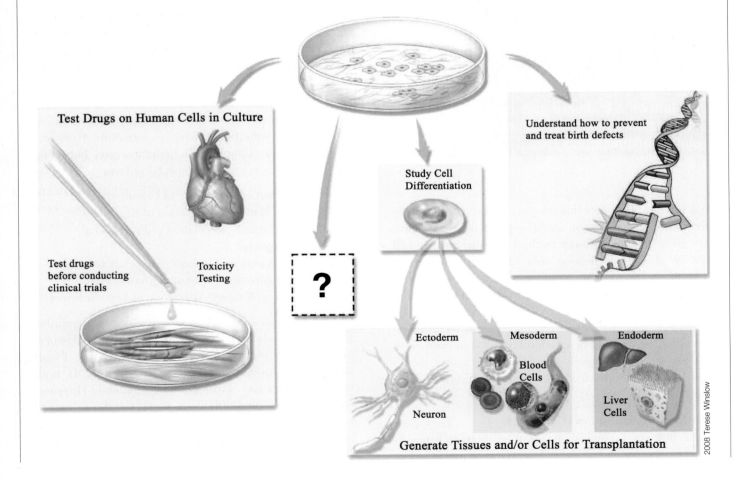

Test Drugs on Human Cells in Culture

Test drugs before conducting clinical trials

Toxicity Testing

?

Study Cell Differentiation

Understand how to prevent and treat birth defects

Ectoderm

Neuron

Mesoderm

Blood Cells

Endoderm

Liver Cells

Generate Tissues and/or Cells for Transplantation

2008 Terese Winslow

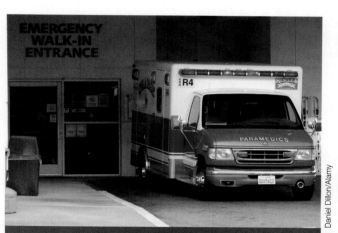

Although some situations will not involve difficult ethical issues, others might. For example, *triage* is meant to ensure that treatment priority is based on the condition of patients. But what if two patients come into the emergency department at the same time and suffering from the same life-threatening injuries: one is a criminal and the other is a minister. Is giving priority to one of them an easy ethical decision?

Daniel Dillon/Alamy

no matter the specific work you do or the setting, as the health care professions and their many components continue to evolve.

B2-1 Chapters of Special Interest

Many chapters focus on your relationships with other people, as you will in your career in health care, and the principles you develop for handling those relationships will carry through a variety of circumstances. Here are examples of the questions of heightened interest for you in some of these chapters.

B2-1a. Human Life: Beginnings and Endings (Chapter 3)

You will likely encounter firsthand the range of the difficult issues we considered, such as abortion, assisted reproduction, euthanasia, and assisted suicide. Although most people will encounter many of these in their personal relationships with family and friends, as a professional

caregiver, in dealing with these life-and-death decisions, you may need to take into consideration standards, regulations, and requirements that private individuals may not have to concern themselves with.

B2-1b. Personal Freedoms (Chapter 5)

Whereas others wrestle with choices on how to behave with regard to so-called "victimless crimes," you are likely to see the results of these choices. Some outcomes you are likely to be called on to tackle might involve emergency department admissions, such as motorcyclists riding without helmets, drivers who operated their vehicles without seatbelts, or drug users who overdosed. You might also handle prostitutes dealing with AIDS or with the aftermath of an assault.

B2-1c. Health Care (Chapter 9)

The general population is concerned about how to obtain health care and whether it is a right or a privilege. In the health care professions, you will be faced with your ethical obligations, if any, to provide health care in certain settings. You might face having to question your rights to economic prosperity in relation to the health care needs of the patient population, regardless of whether they can afford it.

B2-2 Professional Ethics in Health Care

Almost all professional associations have adopted codes of ethics within that particular domain. These can most easily be located on the websites of those organizations. Here are a few examples with broad interests, but there are many more for specialized work:

- American Medical Association
- American Nurses Association
- American Pharmacists Association
- Health Care Administrators Association
- American Academy of Physicians Assistants

Consider these professional ethics codes carefully. Ask yourself whether they cover all the ethical issues of concern to you in your work. Are you clear about what each provision of these codes mean? If not, where and how can clarification be obtained? How are these codes enforced? If your work includes a licensing requirement, as most of these professions require, could violation of these ethical codes result in loss of your license?

Education Ethics

Hill Street Studios/Blend Images/Jupiter Images

Education careers cover a broad range of opportunities. Teachers work at all age levels, from preschool to high school and college, postbaccalaureate specialized graduate training, and classes for adults returning for further education, especially for career changes in a rapidly evolving world. Teachers, teachers' aides, principals, and administrators are common occupations in education. Every conceivable subject matter can be found in different educational settings, from basic skills in language and math to specialized trades and technical skills.

Little one-room schoolhouses have evolved to large bricks-and-mortar buildings and now are expanding to virtual education on the Internet with interactivity unimaginable only a few years ago. Many corporations and government agencies offer in-service education for their employees. You will encounter an enormous variation in issues, but some themes will pervade all of these in the central ethical issues of the education field, especially those involving your relationships with fellow educators, your students, and even the general public, who will reap the results of your work.

B3-1 Chapters of Special Interest

In this book, many chapters focus on your relationships with other people, as you will in your career in education, and the principles you develop for handling those relationships will carry through a variety of circumstances. Here are examples of the questions of heightened interest for you in some of these chapters.

B3-1a. Marriage, the Family, and Sexuality (Chapter 4)

The rights of parents to educate their children as they wish are having a major impact on formal educational settings. Although society at large has obligations to ensure that children all have a basic education to compete in the world, parents face a wide range of options, from homeschooling to private schools and even online high schools.

As an educator, you will have certain obligations to children. In some instances, the rights of these children's parents may also affect your decisions and actions. Parents might have a right to demand that they be informed of certain class topics and activities and require that their child not be exposed to specific subjects and events, involving sex education, for example. They might have the right to demand that their child be transferred to a different classroom or school.

You will be informed of your legal obligations in the setting where you teach, but you will also have ethical obligations. You might, for example, believe that you have an ethical obligation to report apparent issues to your supervisor, even if you are not legally required to do so, such as what might appear to be one of the various forms of child abuse.

What obligations do we have to special needs children? There may be unusual considerations and obligations for those who have the responsibility to educate children who have disabilities.

Spencer Grant/Age Fotostock

B3-1b. Religious Freedom (Chapter 7)

The tension between the right to religious freedom and the prohibition on the establishment of religion by the government of the United States is especially prominent in public educational settings. An educator might face the question of whether the teaching of creationism is an exercise of religious freedom or the imposition of religious doctrine by the government. Educators in public settings also might face demands from students to lead a prayer in class, at a football game, or at a graduation ceremony. All have been the subject of high-profile legal challenges in the recent past and are likely to continue to be in the future. Individual educators sometimes decide that their personal ethical views are so important that they are willing to risk termination or take the lead in spearheading legal fights, but these choices can come at tremendous personal and financial cost.

B3-1c. Discrimination (Chapter 8)
Admissions

Admission to selective schools at any level can be ferociously competitive. How should this scarce resource be awarded fairly? At some schools, including public universities, faculty and administrators are included in setting admissions standards and decision making, putting them into the center of these ongoing debates in the broader society. Should benefits to the greater society be considered in determining who is admitted? Children of wealthy donors might be given an admissions advantage by a private university: is that fair and is fairness a criterion that should even be taken into consideration?

Classrooms

Individuals in the educational sector might be called on to make decisions in their own classrooms as well. Some students might have suffered from racial discrimination and economic hardship when they were younger, which puts them at a disadvantage compared to those who might have had extra advantages with private tutoring and other amenities. In such a case, should the former students be held to the identical testing standards as the latter? Should they be given extra tutoring time at the expense of other students? Does society in general have an obligation to help underprivileged children with extra help, which you as a teacher or administrator might be asked to provide? Is that justified by the greater good to society of the contributions from these future potential business owners or wage earners or as a way to offset previous injustice to those children?

B3-2 Professional Ethics in Education

Almost all professional associations have adopted codes of ethics within that particular domain. These can most easily be located on the websites of those organizations. Here are a few examples with broad interests, but there are many more for specialized work:

- National Education Association
- American Federation of Teachers
- National Science Teachers Association
- National Association of Elementary School Principals
- American Association of School Administrators
- American Association of University Professors

Consider these professional ethics codes carefully. Ask yourself whether they cover all the ethical issues of concern to you in your work. Are you clear about what each provision of these codes means? If not, where and how can clarification be obtained? How are these codes enforced? If your work includes a licensing requirement (especially public school teaching), could violation of these ethical codes result in loss of your license?

Journalism Ethics

Journalism as a profession is changing rapidly as a result of advances in technology. Print newspapers dominated the field for many centuries, but the work of journalists is now found on television, satellite radio, the Internet, streaming video online, and all manner of new electronic media.

You might pursue work as a writer, editor, producer, or technical specialist. The support areas of business, personnel, and finance will be needed in all journalistic organizations. But many of you might be working as entrepreneurs or sole proprietorships posting a blog and hoping to earn revenue from advertising on your site. Yet all these arenas will share rights and obligations to report information to others and to do it fairly and effectively. Your ethical relationships will extend to coworkers, employees, the subjects of your journalism, and the general public who consumes your work.

B4-1 Chapters of Special Interest

Many chapters focus on your relationships with other people, as you will in your career in journalism, and the principles you develop for handling those relationships will carry through a variety of circumstances. Here are examples of the questions of heightened interest for you in some of these chapters.

B4-1a. Freedom of Expression (Chapter 6)

The right of free speech is paramount in journalism, but you will also need to consider its limits.

Although political speech is the most sacrosanct, journalists have no more right to defame people than do ordinary persons. Information obtained in violation of national security laws or that otherwise might put innocent persons at risk must balance the benefits of that information being made public against the possible harm to individual people.

B4-1b. Computer Ethics (Chapter 11)

Computers are ubiquitous in our world today, but their potential for obtaining and spreading information seems especially significant to journalists. Published information can be spread with lightning speed. As a professional in this field, you must consider carefully that if that information is false and harmful to people, retractions and corrections might do little to undo damage.

B4-1c. War and the World (Chapter 13)

War impacts everyone, of course, but journalists have special obligations in this context. They are faced, for

With the "perp walk," American law enforcement often avails itself of the media's appetite for visual "spectacles."

ERICH SCHLEGEL KRT/Newscom

Embedded journalists became a familiar expression in reports on the war following the 2003 invasion of Iraq. The presence of journalists within military units, sanctioned by the U.S. military, was not without controversy. Many questioned whether the arrangement truly permitted journalists to do their job as freely as they might wish and need to.

instance, with weighing how much they should do to ensure that the reasons given for waging war are accurate. Will shirking their obligations result in avoidable deaths among both military and civilians? If journalists learn of secret war plans, are they obligated to tell the public or are they endangering the lives of the military in publishing them?

B4-2 Professional Ethics in Journalism

Almost all professional associations have adopted codes of ethics within that particular domain. These can most easily be located on the websites of those organizations. Here are a few examples with broad interests, but there are many more for specialized work:

• Society of Professional Journalists
• Online News Association
• National Association of Broadcasters
• Online Publishers Association
• National Cable and Telecommunications Association

Consider these professional ethics codes carefully. Ask yourself whether they cover all the ethical issues of concern to you in your work. Are you clear about what each provision of these codes means? If not, where and how can clarification be obtained? How are these codes enforced? If your work includes a licensing requirement (as when licensing is required to obtain a broadcasting permit), could violation of these ethical codes result in loss of your license?

Religious Ethics

Some of you might be pursuing careers related to religion, whether as an ordained minister, priest, rabbi, or the leader in another major religion. Careers might also include positions that support your religion, such as religious educator or administrator at a religious charity. All of the professional areas we are considering have a place for volunteer workers, but perhaps they are more pervasive in religious organizations than elsewhere. Even if you do not receive monetary compensation, you might encounter ethical issues in your relationships with coworkers, clients, members of your group, and the general public.

All major religious groups have their own ethical codes, which are not always consistent with the codes of other religions or general ethical principles in the population as a whole, creating a special set of issues for this career path. Religious freedom is widely protected, under the constitutions of many nations, as well as the United Nations Declaration on Human Rights. So the special challenge is adhering to your own religious ethical code while also respecting the differing codes of others.

embrace it. As a professional in this field, you might be in a position to deal with such an issue. Another ethical quandary you might face could involve needing to follow religious dogma when your personal opinion differs from it. In such a circumstance, you might also need to justify your religion's positions as one of its representatives. For example, you might agree that marriage inequality results in denying some the rights that others enjoy—such as unfettered access to one's hospitalized partner—but must offer those reasons your religion gives for opposing marriage equality.

As a professional in this field, you also might be called on to weigh in on such questions as whether you as your institution's representative believe that the power of government should be used to impose on all citizens the views of particular religions. You might be required to contribute to a debate regarding whether religious marriage, for example, could be distinguished from governmental or civil marriage, as a compromise for marriage equality.

B5-1 Chapters of Special Interest

In this book, many chapters focus on your relationships with other people, as you will in your career in religion, and the principles you develop for handling those relationships will carry through a variety of circumstances. Here are examples of the questions of heightened interest for you in some of these chapters.

B5-1a. Marriage, the Family, and Sexuality (Chapter 4)

An especially contentious issue today is marriage equality, with some religions absolutely forbidding it, whereas others

Bob Daemmrich/Alamy

Like the larger population, prisoners seek spiritual counsel. Prison chaplains play a critical role in helping meet the prison's rehabilitation objectives.

AP Photo/Stephen Morton

We sometimes hear in the news of a religious figure excluded from or reprimanded by his or her church or synagogue because that person publicly spoke out against a religious doctrine. Volunteers also could find their service rejected for publicly criticizing church doctrine. Yet you might seriously consider whether speaking out would likely be vital in helping your institution's religious doctrine evolve in a meaningful way and choose at your own risk to express opinions counter to established church principles.

B5-1b. Religious Freedom (Chapter 7)

This unit looked closely at the tension between religious freedom and the clashes among different religions as well as with secular views. You will likely face resolving how to respect differing religious views concerning ethical conduct while still abiding by your religion's tenets.

If you are an administrator at a hospital of a religion that rejects abortion in all circumstances, even to save the life of the mother, you might be faced with a patient near death in the emergency department and have to decide whether to approve the abortion that would save her life or strictly adhere to the tenets of your religion. Or you might be a volunteer at a religious school and face a difficult choice between reporting an illegal polygamous marriage that has produced some of the children in your

class or just keeping quiet about it. Or an underage child in your class might be in an illegal polygamous marriage and you might wonder whether you should report possible child abuse or respect the religious views of the child's parents.

B5-1c. Capital Punishment (Chapter 10)

Many nations as well as some major religions (such as Roman Catholicism) hold that capital punishment is unethical. In the United States, the death penalty still enjoys widespread support among the general population. One challenge for professionals in religion is whether and, if so, how to shape public opinion. Religious organizations typically have a tax-exempt status that prohibits lobbying the public on political issues. So, if you believe strongly about the death penalty (either in favor or against) based on your religious views, how can you effectively try to change people's views to share yours? Or should you just leave everyone alone to hold their own religious views without trying to change them?

B5-2 Professional Ethics in Religion

Almost all professional associations have adopted codes of ethics within that particular domain. These can most easily be located on the websites of those organizations. Here are a few examples with broad interests, but there are many more for specialized work:

- American Academy of Religion
- National Association of Church Business Administration
- Religious Communication Association
- Religious Conference Management Association
- Associated Church Press
- National Catholic Educational Association

Consider these professional ethics codes carefully. Ask yourself whether they cover all the ethical issues of concern to you in your work. Are you clear about what each provision of these codes mean? If not, where and how can clarification be obtained? How are these codes enforced? If your work includes a licensing requirement, could violation of these ethical codes result in loss of your license? Are these professional codes consistent with the ethical codes of your religion?

Legal Ethics

Practicing lawyers are employed in a wide variety of settings, from law firms and government agencies to public interest organizations and corporations. And the legal profession encompasses many more careers than simply lawyers. Paralegals provide crucial services as assistants in any legal office. Law librarians are important not just in law schools but also in law firms. Most, although not all, judges are licensed attorneys. Many persons with law degrees work in government and corporations, who are not technically "practicing" law, but are using their legal training to function more effectively in those settings. Along with the codes of professional responsibility that apply to licensed attorneys, many of these professional work settings have additional ethical codes that apply to those employees. Ethical questions arise in the myriad of relationships legal employees have with coworkers, supervisors, clients, and the general public.

B6-1 Chapters of Special Interest

Many chapters focus on your relationships with other people, as you will in your career in legal professions, and the principles you develop for handling those relationships will carry through a variety of circumstances. Almost all of the applied ethics questions we have studied also have legal facets, through regulations, laws, constitutions, and enforceable rights and obligations. Here are examples of the questions of heightened interest for you in some of these chapters.

B6-1a. Personal Freedoms (Chapter 5)

With law-related training of some sort, you will be especially aware of activities that are regulated or prohibited by the law, yet that perhaps should be left to personal discretion. Many law enforcement personnel and judges have been speaking out in opposition to strict drug laws, for example, believing that this is a medical problem and should not be a criminal matter. Many also believe in strict gun laws because the easier the availability of firearms to the general public, the more likely firearms will fall into the hands of criminals, which makes their job more difficult and dangerous. In many states, adultery and fornication are still technically crimes, yet they only seem to come before the courts when someone, such as a jilted lover, is seeking revenge.

As a legal professional, you might find yourself having to enforce laws that you personally believe should not exist. One special focus is the issue of whether many admittedly harmful "victimless crimes" are best handled through ethical education and peer pressure or through the strict hand of the government. As a legal professional, you might find yourself in a position where you can speak out about reforms and the ways in which they are handled, whether they concern capital punishment or drug use.

B6-1b. Freedom of Expression (Chapter 6)

Rights guaranteed by law may become more easily enforceable and accepted as a result of the existence of free speech. It is one thing to believe in, for example, marriage equality. But to bring about the change you might wish for in society, you need the freedom of speech to explain why those attitudes should be changed. It is one thing to have the law insist on nondiscrimination in hiring, but the freedom of speech to educate and persuade provides an extra tool that helps educate people on why those nondiscrimination laws matter and should be fol-

REUTERS/Landov

The attorney-client privilege is probably one of the most widely known legal concepts in the United States, the land of "presumed innocent until proven guilty." This guarantee encourages clients to freely disclose information that helps their legal counsel provide informed and effective advice.

made the mistake of hitting "reply all" to an e-mail that we intended to send to only one confidant. In ordinary conversation, this misstep might just cause embarrassment. In a legal setting, it could result in devastating disclosures of confidential information. Ethically, one is also under great pressure to maintain databases with utter accuracy at legal institutions because of the potential harm that would result from a mistake, where, for example, innocent people are arrested because of that error.

B6-2 Professional Ethics in Legal Careers

Almost all professional associations have adopted codes of ethics within that particular domain. These can most easily be located on the websites of those organizations. Here are a few examples with broad interests, but there are many more for specialized work:

lowed as ethical standards, not just legal restrictions. But note that a requirement specific to the legal profession is confidentiality of attorney-client communication, which amounts to a stipulated restriction on free speech for those communications.

B6-1c. Computer Ethics (Chapter 11)

Computers have dramatically altered the legal workplace, as they have so many others. With special obligations of confidentiality, privacy, and timely submission of legal documents, computers and the Internet present both great opportunities as well as added dangers of violations of those special obligations. Most of us have

- American Bar Association
- Association for Legal Career Professionals
- National Association of Legal Assistants
- International Association of Prosecutors
- National Legal Aid and Defender Association
- Federal Court Clerks Association

Consider these professional ethics codes carefully. Ask yourself whether they cover all the ethical issues of concern to you in your work. Are you clear about what each provision of these codes means? If not, where and how can clarification be obtained? How are these codes enforced? If your work includes a licensing requirement, could violation of these ethical codes result in loss of your license?

Criminal Justice Ethics

The criminal justice system employs an enormous range of professionals, with a wide variety of skills. Police officers, at all levels of government, are among the most visible, but they work with prosecutors, public defenders, judges, probation officers, corrections officers, and the many support functions that enable the system to work. Many of these must pass rigorous qualifying exams and adhere to codes of professional ethics for their specialty. Ethical questions arise in the myriad of relationships criminal justice employees have with coworkers, supervisors, clients, and the general public.

B7-1 Chapters of Special Interest

Many chapters focus on your relationships with other people, as you will in your career in criminal justice, and the principles you develop for handling those relationships will carry through a variety of circumstances. Almost all of the applied ethics questions we have studied also have possibilities related to the criminal law, through regulations, laws, constitutions, and enforceable rights and obligations. Here are examples of the questions of heightened interest for you in some of these chapters.

B7-1a. Personal Freedoms (Chapter 5)

With criminal justice training of some sort, you will be especially aware of activities that are regulated or prohibited by the law, yet which perhaps should be left to personal discretion. Many

persons in criminal justice in recent years, for example, have spoken out against what they consider Draconian drug laws, when they believe that drug use should be treated as a medical rather than a criminal matter. One might wonder, then, whether participation in the system shifts one's ethical views on how best to address these issues. You might have different perceptions regarding the legal system's handling of minor infractions than the general population. For example, you might have an opinion regarding the effectiveness and the fairness of "Three-Strikes" laws in effect in certain states. Although most people might think repeat offenders should face the consequences of a stubborn insistence to make the same mistake over and over, you might come to believe that support or assistance to nonviolent offenders would likely

Lisa F. Young/Shutterstock.com

be sufficient to break the cycle of dysfunctional behaviors. The latter strategies would also have the benefit of alleviating overcrowding in the prisons, another issue that has its own ethical dimensions.

B7-1b. Capital Punishment (Chapter 10)

If you work in a country in which capital punishment is enforced, such as the United States, you will experience firsthand the pros and cons of the continuation of this form of punishment for very serious crimes. You will have more awareness perhaps of the brutality of the crimes and also the possibility of wrongful conviction than does the ordinary person. Your familiarity with present conditions

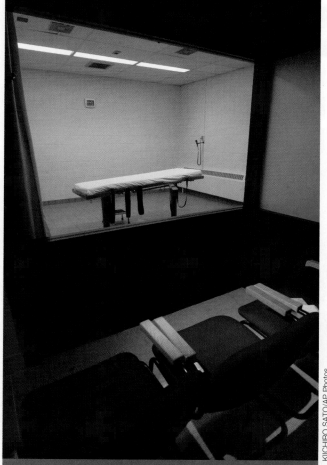

KIICHIRO SATO/AP Photos

An execution witness viewing room. Each state that applies the death penalty has its own selection process to determine who is allowed to witness an execution.

of incarceration might influence your opinion regarding the ethics of the corrections system. Your experience as a witness to an execution also might affect your views on the ethical value of capital punishment. But as a prosecutor, you might also learn hideous details of some crime that would lead you to more strongly support the death penalty.

B7-1c. Computer Ethics (Chapter 11)

Computers have dramatically altered the criminal justice system, as they have so many other workplaces. Simple computer mistakes can result in devastating consequences, such as arresting the wrong person or releasing the wrong person on probation. With special obligations for protection of the public, computers and the internet present both great opportunities as well as added dangers of violations of those special obligations. Mistakenly sending an e-mail to a LISTSERV or to "reply-all" when you intended it to go to just one person could also seriously violate obligations of confidentiality during a criminal proceeding. You will need to make every effort to keep such ethical considerations in mind at all times as you perform your work.

B7-2 Professional Ethics in Criminal Justice

Almost all professional associations have adopted codes of ethics within that particular domain. These can most easily be located on the websites of those organizations. Here are a few examples with broad interests, but there are many more for specialized work:

- Fraternal Order of Police
- American Probation and Parole Association
- American Correctional Association
- American Jail Association
- National Legal Aid and Defender Association
- International Association of Prosecutors

Consider these professional ethics codes carefully. Ask yourself whether they cover all the ethical issues of concern to you in your work. Are you clear about what each provision of these codes means? If not, where and how can clarification be obtained? How are these codes enforced? If your work includes a licensing requirement, could violation of these ethical codes result in loss of your license?

4LTR Press solutions are designed for today's learners through the continuous feedback of students like you. Tell us what you think about (**ETHICS**) and help us improve the learning experience for future students.

YOUR FEEDBACK MATTERS.

Complete the Speak Up survey in CourseMate at **www.cengagebrain.com**

 Follow us at www.facebook.com/4ltrpress

Index

Italicized page numbers indicate materials in features, figures, graphs, or tables.

NOTES

NOTES

NOTES

NOTES

NOTES

NOTES

NOTES

NOTES

NOTES

NOTES

LO 1-1 Explain what philosophy and ethics are, and how ethics fits into philosophical thinking.

NOTEWORTHY TERMS:

NOTE: This list includes Key Terms as well as other important terms found in the chapter

epistemology: theory of knowledge

ethics: the study of human conduct impacting other humans

metaphysics: the study of reality, what exists

value theory: the study of values, such as value in human behavior (ethics) and value in art (aesthetics); sometimes called axiology

REVIEW AND SUMMARIZE:

After reading this section, identify in *complete* sentences:

1. The role of studying "classic texts" in philosophy

2. Current trends in the study of philosophy

3. The most important things taught in philosophy courses

4. Questions of interest in value theory

5. Questions of interest in epistemology

6. Questions of interest in metaphysics

ESSAYS:

1. In a paragraph, summarize the three major areas of philosophy and the central questions of concern to each.

2. In a paragraph, explain why ethics is important in everyday life, using an example as needed.

LO 1-2 State a working definition of what ethics is in everyday life.

REVIEW AND SUMMARIZE:

After reading this section, identify in *complete* sentences:

1. The nature of an ethical choice

2. Choices that seem to impact only our own lives

3. A clash of principles you value

ESSAY:

In a paragraph, explain the kinds of choices which characterize ethics in everyday life.

LO 1-3 Summarize different meanings of what people consider ethics to be.

NOTEWORTHY TERMS:

altruism: the ethical theory that right and wrong action depends on consequences for other persons, but not for oneself

consequentialism: any ethical theory that determines right and wrong action based on consequences (including altruism, egoism, and utilitarianism)

egoism: the ethical theory that right and wrong action depends on consequences for oneself only

moral philosophy: a synonym for *ethics*

utilitarianism: the ethical theory that right and wrong action depends on consequences for everyone, including oneself

REVIEW AND SUMMARIZE:

After reading this section, identify in *complete* sentences:

1. The nature of egoist ethical theories

2. The nature of altruistic ethical theories

3. The nature of utilitarian ethical theories

4. The significance of hidden unethical conduct

ESSAY:

In a paragraph, explain the similarities and differences between the ethical theories of egoism, altruism, and utilitarianism.

LO 1-4 Identify ethical issues that are currently most important to you.

REVIEW AND SUMMARIZE:

After reading this section, identify in *complete* sentences:

1. How ethical issues can vary depending on our age, life situation, and circumstances

2. An ethical issue you are comfortable discussing with classmates

ESSAY:

In one paragraph, discuss how ethical issues vary depending on your age, life situation, and individual circumstances.

LO 1-5 State goals you would like to accomplish this term to develop an understanding of ethics based on personal exploration.

REVIEW AND SUMMARIZE:

After reading this section, identify in *complete* sentences:

1. An urgent ethical challenge in your life that you are comfortable discussing with classmates

2. An ethical issue on which you disagree with friends or family

3. How an ethics course might assist you in your own life, regardless of career goals

ESSAY:

In a paragraph, state the likely benefits of studying ethics.

Chapter Quiz

1. Which of the following is *not* of concern to value theory?
   a. The nature of reality
   b. The study of values in human behavior
   c. The study of values in the realm of art

2. Why do philosophers study "classic texts"?
   a. Because they always have the right answers to important questions.
   b. Because they have proposed ways of analyzing issues that help us develop our own views.
   c. Because they improve reading skills.

3. Increasingly, philosophers have refocused their understanding of philosophy to
   a. put more emphasis on the study of classic texts.
   b. limit analysis of terms to dictionary definitions.
   c. put even more emphasis on good reasoning, regardless of subject matter.

4. What is the *least* important thing taught in a philosophy course?
   a. Factual knowledge about philosophers
   b. Good reasoning
   c. Critical thinking

5. Ethics in everyday life does *not* include which of the following?
   a. Decisions that impact family members
   b. Decisions that impact persons we have never met
   c. Deliberative analysis of classical texts

6. Because we do not have time in daily life to reason through every issue as we might do in class,
   a. we should not bother with ethics at all as it is a waste of time.
   b. we should pursue guiding principles that help us make good decisions on a regular basis.
   c. we should only worry about ethics when it impacts our own personal lives.

7. Most philosophers consider ethics to be synonymous with
   a. moral philosophy.
   b. egoism.
   c. value theory.

8. What does altruism consider relevant to ethical decision making?
   a. Consequences for oneself and only oneself
   b. Consequences for everyone else, but not yourself
   c. Consequences for everyone, including yourself

LO 2-1 Explain how important moral reasoning is and how to apply it.

NOTEWORTHY TERMS:

NOTE: This list includes Key Terms as well as other important terms found in the chapter.

consistency: using terms and principles in precisely the same way

REVIEW AND SUMMARIZE:

After reading this section, identify in *complete* sentences:

1. The best ways to clarify the meaning of key terms

2. The importance of consistency in good reasoning

3. The process of building premises for an argument

4. How to test premises

5. How to avoid fallacies

LO 2-2 Explain the difference between facts and values and why this distinction matters.

NOTEWORTHY TERMS:

facts: descriptions of the way the world is

values: normative statements of the way the world ought to be

REVIEW AND SUMMARIZE:

After reading this section, identify in *complete* sentences:

1. The nature of facts and how they differ from values

2. The meaning of descriptive and normative

3. When factual knowledge matters in ethical reasoning

ESSAY:

In a paragraph, explain the role of facts in ethical reasoning, using examples.

LO 2-3 Assess the use of statistics in ethical reasoning to establish ethical principles.

REVIEW AND SUMMARIZE:

After reading this section, identify in *complete* sentences:

1. The most common mistakes in the use of statistics in ethical reasoning

2. The relevance of shifting public opinion

3. The similarities between legal and ethical reasoning

ESSAY:

In a paragraph discuss the pitfalls of relying on statistics in ethical reasoning.

LO 2-4 State what an informal fallacy is and name several of the most common.

NOTEWORTHY TERMS:

ad hominem **(to the person):** an irrelevant attack on the person making the argument, rather than the argument itself

appeal to ignorance: claiming something is true because we have no evidence that it is false, or vice versa

begging the question: assuming the conclusion that you set out to prove

equivocation: relying implicitly on different meanings of a key term to reach a conclusion

fallacy: an unreliable way of arguing

formal fallacy: invalid logical rule

faulty analogy: misusing reasoning by analogy to exploit irrelevant similarities

hasty generalization: rushing to a general conclusion from a very small or biased sample size

informal fallacy: a wide range of unreliable means of arguing in both everyday discourse and sophisticated argumentation

post hoc, ergo propter hoc **("after this, therefore because of this"):** claiming that one thing caused another because they occurred in sequence of time

red herring: an irrelevant claim introduced to distract focus from the real issue at stake

slippery slope: claiming that some small steps in a certain direction will inevitably lead to other, major consequences

straw man: distorting your opponent's position and then attacking the distortion

REVIEW AND SUMMARIZE:

After reading this section, identify in *complete* sentences:

1. The nature of a fallacy

2. The nature of an informal fallacy

3. Why fallacies matter in good reasoning

ESSAY:

In one paragraph, explain what makes an argument a fallacy, with examples.

LO 2-5 Assess the strengths and weaknesses of ethical relativism as an approach to moral reasoning.

NOTEWORTHY TERMS:

cultural relativism: a factual description of the world, specifically, that different cultures hold different ethical views

ethical relativism: view that there are no universal ethical principles that apply to all people at all times

REVIEW AND SUMMARIZE:

After reading this section, identify in *complete* sentences:

1. The nature of cultural relativism

2. The nature of ethical relativism

3. The relationship between cultural and ethical relativism

4. How to effectively challenge ethical relativism

LO 2-6 State the major principles of Kantianism and of utilitarianism and assess their strengths and weaknesses.

NOTEWORTHY TERMS:

absolutism: any ethical theory that holds that there are universal ethical principles that apply to all people at all times (also sometimes called objectivism)

categorical imperative: a command that applies to all rational beings regardless of their desires

Kantianism: ethical theory developed by Kant focusing on intrinsic value, respect for the dignity of persons, the categorical imperative

as a test of right action, and a rejection of consequentialism to determine right and wrong action

objectivism: any ethical theory that holds that there are universal ethical principles that apply to all people at all times (also sometimes called absolutism)

practical imperative: the statement of the categorical imperative in Kantianism that says all persons should be treated as ends in themselves, never solely as a means to an end

LO 2-7 Identify alternative approaches to ethical reasoning, including Aristotle's virtue ethics, Aquinas's natural law, Locke's social contract, and care ethics.

NOTEWORTHY TERMS:

care ethics: an approach to ethical theory that draws on the rights and obligations of parents to their children and family members

natural law: the view that ethical laws are embedded in nature, as are scientific laws, such as the law of gravity, whether or not we know them or articulate them; ethical principles are not stipulated or created by us, but exist independently of us

social contract: ethical theory that views morality as the product of an agreement among individuals

virtue ethics: ethical theory centering on habits, tendencies, or dispositions that assist us in achieving our goals

LO 2-8 Identify Your Personal Goals.

REVIEW AND SUMMARIZE:

After reading this section, identify in *complete* sentences:

1. Ethical issues that matter most to you personally

2. Goals that will assist you in addressing those ethical issues

LO 3-1 Define the nature of euthanasia, assisted suicide, stem cell research, abortion, and genetic engineering.

NOTEWORTHY TERMS:

NOTE: This list includes Key Terms as well as other important terms found in the chapter.

abortion: human inducement of the termination or expulsion of a fetus before what would have been the natural birth

assisted suicide: suicide committed by a patient with assistance from a physician to obtain the means of death, such as a lethal dose of drugs

euthanasia: termination of a life by another agent, such as death of a terminally ill patient by medical personnel; also refers to termination of nonhuman life

genetic engineering: use of DNA technology to produce desirable changes in organisms

suicide: the intentional termination of a person's life by that person alone

stem cells: unspecialized cells that can be modified into more specific ones, such as nerve skin cells, lung cells, or bone cells; human embryonic stem cells are such unspecialized cells from human embryos that are around a week old and consist of about one hundred cells

REVIEW AND SUMMARIZE:

After reading this section, identify in *complete* sentences:

1. The first step in clear thinking and reasoning

2. The important concepts that make up the definition of abortion

3. The difference between suicide, assisted suicide, and euthanasia

4. The essential material used for genetic engineering and what the goal of genetic engineering is

5. The object of stem cell research and the type of stem cells whose use is controversial

ESSAY:

In a paragraph, explain what the first step in clear thinking and reasoning is and use one of the defined terms as an example to support your explanation.

LO 3-2 Explain the nature of *personhood* and its role in the debates over the ethics of evolving medical technologies.

NOTEWORTHY TERMS:

death: (1) irreversible cessation of circulatory and respiratory functions; (2) irreversible cessation of all functions of the entire brain, including the brain stem

***Homo sapiens*:** the biological category of human beings

person: the comprehensive concept of moral agents with both ethical and legal, as well as biological, dimensions

REVIEW AND SUMMARIZE:

After reading this section, identify in *complete* sentences:

1. The difference between *person* and the biological category of *Homo sapiens*

2. The definition of *death* that recognizes advances in medical technologies

3. The similarities in the famous Quinlan, Cruzan, and Schiavo cases

4. The alternatives for specifying the beginning of "personhood"

ESSAY:

In a paragraph, explain the importance of *personhood* to debates about the morality of abortion, euthanasia, assisted suicide, and stem cell research.

LO 3-3 Use both Kantian and utilitarian reasoning to address these ethical issues.

REVIEW AND SUMMARIZE:

After reading this section, identify in *complete* sentences:

1. Kant's "practical imperative"

2. The ethical issue concerning suicide

3. The principle of utility

4. The utilitarian issue for elderly patients considering assisted suicide or euthanasia

ESSAY:

In one paragraph, summarize how Kantian reasoning can be used with regard to the ethical debate over assisted suicide and euthanasia.

LO 3-4 Explain the relationship of the law to the ethical debates.

NOTEWORTHY TERMS:

penumbra: the shadow created by a source of light; the metaphor used to describe rights not explicitly named in the U.S. Constitution

stare decisis: stay the decision, or let the decision stand

REVIEW AND SUMMARIZE:

After reading this section, identify in *complete* sentences:

1. The "privacy" right claimed in *Roe v. Wade*

2. The "penumbra" of rights in the Constitution

3. The meaning of *stare decisis*

4. The type of reasoning used by the Supreme Court

ESSAY:

In a paragraph, summarize philosophical reasoning methods used by legal courts for these issues.

Chapter Quiz

1. The first step in clear thinking and reasoning is to ensure that
   a. the meaning of key terms is unambiguous.
   b. only the key idea is identified.
   c. "straw men" are injected in the debate.

2. Stem cells
   a. only come from plant life.
   b. are specialized cells that cannot be divided.
   c. are unspecialized cells that can renew themselves through division.

3. What is the relationship between *persons* and *Homo sapiens*?
   a. They are identical.
   b. *Person* includes much more than the biological category of *Homo sapiens*.
   c. *Homo sapiens* is a legal category, whereas *persons* is a biological category.

4. Why does personhood matter in the debate over embryonic stem cell research?
   a. If the fertilized egg is a person, then experimentation is unethical.

   b. If the fertilized egg is a person, experimentation is ethical.
   c. If the fertilized egg is not a person, then experimentation is unethical.

5. Kant's practical imperative says that we should always
   a. treat other persons as a means to an end.
   b. treat other persons as ends in themselves.
   c. treat your enemies as a means to an end.

6. Courts of law often appeal to such philosophical reasoning as
   a. Kantian dignity of persons.
   b. stare decisis.
   c. state constitutions.

7. Assuming there is a privacy or liberty right in the Constitution,
   a. assisted suicide is a guaranteed right.
   b. assisted suicide is not necessarily a guaranteed right.
   c. selling one's bodily organs for profit is a right.

LO 4-1 Identify areas of family life in which our rights to privacy and liberty are central.

NOTEWORTHY TERMS:

NOTE: This list includes important terms found in the chapter.

homosexuality: when a person is sexually attracted to a person of the same sex

in vitro **fertilization:** when an egg is fertilized by a sperm outside the normal biological process

interracial marriage: when two persons of different races marry

privacy: respect for a zone of privacy around the person, whether physical or emotional

REVIEW AND SUMMARIZE:

After reading this section, identify in *complete* sentences:

1. Specific examples of family life in which privacy and liberty are central

2. Types of marriages that are being debated today

3. Controversies concerning children

4. Issues that concern the education of children

ESSAY:

In a paragraph, summarize clearly the areas of family life in which our rights to privacy and liberty are central.

LO 4-2 Demonstrate use of central philosophical reasoning tools to address the rights of privacy and liberty in the context of families (e.g., marriage, children, and education of children).

NOTEWORTHY TERMS:

adoption: when persons who are not the biological parents of an individual legally take responsibility as parents of that individual

homeschooling: when parents elect to educate their children at home instead of sending them to public or private schools

Kantian reasoning: use of Kantian principles such as respect for the autonomy and dignity of persons

surrogate mother: when a woman carries the fertilized egg for another person

utilitarian reasoning: reasoning according to the principle that right action is determined by which action produces the greatest happiness for the greatest number

REVIEW AND SUMMARIZE:

After reading this section, identify in *complete* sentences:

1. The nature of Kantian reasoning

2. The nature of utilitarian reasoning

3. The conclusion in *Loving v. Virginia*

4. A Kantian reason in support of marriage equality

5. A utilitarian objection to surrogate motherhood

6. A utilitarian reason in support of homeschooling

ESSAY:

In a paragraph, explain how a utilitarian would analyze the ethics of homeschooling.

LO 4-3 Explain how ethical reasoning is applied in legal reasoning on these issues.

NOTEWORTHY TERMS:

liberty rights: another term for privacy rights

polygamy: when marriage consists of multiple spouses

same-sex marriage: when two persons of the same sex marry

REVIEW AND SUMMARIZE:

After reading this section, identify in *complete* sentences:

1. A similarity between legal and philosophical reasoning

2. An example of Kantian reasoning in Justice Kennedy's opinion in *Lawrence*

3. The relevance of *Loving* to the issue of marriage equality

4. The use of Kantian reasoning in *Reynolds* prohibiting polygamy

ESSAY:

In a paragraph, discuss the ethics of surrogate motherhood from a utilitarian perspective.

Chapter Quiz

1. Privacy and liberty rights are relevant to which of the following?

    a. Life and death decisions, such as euthanasia

    b. Marriage between persons of different races

    c. Both of the above

2. What is the current status of polygamous marriage worldwide?

    a. No countries recognize polygamous marriage.

    b. All countries recognize polygamous marriage.

    c. Almost fifty countries recognize polygamous marriage.

3. What has been the traditional role of state governments in over-seeing education?

    a. State governments have no role at all.

    b. State governments have the exclusive oversight, with no national role.

    c. State governments have the principal role, with some national participation.

4. What does IVF stand for?

    a. Internal values formulation

    b. In vitro fertilization

    c. International validation formula

5. In *Loving v. Virginia*, the U.S. Supreme Court held that

    a. state laws prohibiting same-sex marriage are a violation of liberty rights under the Constitution.

    b. state laws prohibiting interracial marriage are a violation of liberty rights under the Constitution.

    c. state laws prohibiting interracial marriage are permissible as an exercise of religious freedom by the state governments.

6. Kantian reasoning would identify which reason as an argument against surrogate motherhood?

    a. The surrogacy would result in the most happiness possible for both the surrogate and the childless couple.

    b. The surrogate mother would risk the consequences of her own health because she needed the money for carrying the child.

    c. The baby is being treated like property instead of like a person.

7. In analyzing the ethics of adoption by same-sex couples, which factors are relevant to a utilitarian?

    a. The happiness of the adopted children

    b. The dignity of the adopted children

    c. Whether or not the parents are virtuous

8. In analyzing the ethics of the education of children, which of the following are relevant to a Kantian?

    a. The happiness of the parents in teaching what they believe is important

    b. Bullying from other children in large classrooms

    c. The autonomy and liberty of parents to decide what is best for their children

9. What do philosophical and legal reasoning have in common?

    a. Both sometimes appeal to Kantian and utilitarian reasoning.

    b. Both rely on appeals to authority to prove truthfulness.

    c. Both use *ad hominem* argument extensively and legitimately.

10. In using the decision in *Loving v. Virginia* to support arguments for marriage equality, which reasoning approach is most important?

    a. Deduction

    b. Reasoning by analogy

    c. Ad hominem

11. Which Kantian appeals were used in both the *Lawrence* and *Loving* decisions?

    a. Human liberty and autonomy

    b. Virtuous character

    c. Happiness is pleasure

12. What is the current status of polygamy in the United States?

    a. It is a protected right as an expression of religious freedom.

    b. It is not legal in the United States.

    c. It is legal so long as it is available to both men and women.

13. Which was the first state to legally recognize same-sex marriage?

    a. Massachusetts

    b. Vermont

    c. Iowa

LO 5-1 Identify personal activities that arguably should be free from interference or regulation, whether by the government or community ethical pressure.

NOTEWORTHY TERMS:

NOTE: This list includes Key Terms as well as other important terms found in the chapter.

victimless crime: a wrong that causes harm only to the actor committing the harm

radical libertarian: a person who believes persons should be free to commit harm on themselves

REVIEW AND SUMMARIZE:

After reading this section, identify in *complete* sentences:

1. The central features of a so-called "victimless crime"

2. The main reason why only adults are considered in analyzing victimless crime

3. Several examples of victimless crimes

ESSAYS:

1. In a paragraph, summarize clear examples of victimless crimes, and why they are considered to be victimless.

2. Which of the victimless crimes described in this section of the chapter strikes you, personally, as the most important issue society ought to deal with in the near future? Explain in a paragraph why you believe that is the case.

LO 5-2 Explain major philosophical approaches for analyzing the appropriateness of restrictions on personal freedoms.

NOTEWORTHY TERMS:

harm principle: the philosophical theory that government intervention and restriction of individual liberties is justified only when the action in question would result in harm to another person, and not when the only person harmed is the actor himself or herself

legal moralism: the philosophical theory that government intervention and restriction of individual liberties is justified by the necessity of enforcing society's overall moral codes in the most effective way possible, namely, through the power of government and the criminal justice system

offense principle: the philosophical theory that government intervention and restriction of individual liberties is justified when the action in question causes serious offense to others

paternalism: the philosophical theory that government intervention and restriction of individual liberties is justified when the action in question would harm somebody, whether the actor himself or herself or another person because the role of government is to act as a parent protecting us from ourselves

REVIEW AND SUMMARIZE:

After reading this section, identify in *complete* sentences:

1. Mill's "harm principle" (or "liberty principle")

2. The nature of the harm of concern to Mill

3. The nature of paternalism

4. Why seat belt laws are an example of paternalism

5. The nature of legal moralism

6. How legal moralism would justify outlawing pornography

7. How Kantian dignity can be used to justify some government regulation

ESSAY:

In a couple of paragraphs, explain the nature of the harm principle, paternalism, and legal moralism in your own words. You might highlight their similarities and differences. Also give examples of how each explains an issue today.

LO 5-3 Apply philosophical approaches to important personal freedoms to determine whether they should be permitted.

REVIEW AND SUMMARIZE:

After reading this section, identify in *complete* sentences:

1. How Mill's harm principle would analyze the legalization of prostitution

2. How paternalism would analyze the legalization of prostitution

3. How legal moralism would analyze the legalization of prostitution

ESSAY:

In a paragraph, discuss the ethics of the legalization of marijuana from each of the following viewpoints: the harm principle, paternalism, and legal moralism.

Chapter Quiz

1. What is a "victimless crime"?
   a. An imaginary crime
   b. A misdemeanor
   c. An action in which the only person harmed is the actor

2. Which actors are of principal concern in analyzing victimless crimes?
   a. Consenting adults who can make well-informed decisions
   b. Children without well-developed decision-making capacities
   c. Persons limited in their ability to reason about consequences

3. According to the harm principle, when is government justified in restricting our liberty?
   a. Never
   b. When we act in an immoral way
   c. To prevent harm to others

4. According to the theory of paternalism, when is government justified in restricting our liberty?
   a. When we think bad thoughts
   b. When we engage in behavior that might harm only ourselves
   c. Never

5. According to the theory of legal moralism, when is government justified in restricting our liberty?
   a. When we think bad thoughts
   b. Never
   c. When we act in an immoral way

6. Which theory(ies) could most consistently support making prostitution legal?
   a. Harm principle
   b. Legal moralism
   c. Paternalism

7. What is an example of a victimless crime?
   a. Gambling
   b. Murder
   c. Battery

8. Who is best known for the harm (or liberty) principle?
   a. Kant
   b. Mill
   c. Aquinas

9. What is an example of harm relevant to the harm principle?
   a. Annoyance
   b. Murder
   c. Disgust

10. What is an example of paternalism?
    a. Seat belt regulation
    b. Laws against murder
    c. Laws against burglary

11. Which theory supports making pornography illegal, even for consenting adults in the privacy of their own home?
    a. Harm principle
    b. Paternalism
    c. Legal moralism

12. Which theory is most likely to support the legalization of marijuana?
    a. Harm principle
    b. Paternalism
    c. Legal moralism

LO 6-1 Identify a range of examples of freedom of expression at issue today.

NOTEWORTHY TERMS:

NOTE: This list includes Key Terms as well as other important terms found in the chapter.

expression: understood broadly to include the spoken and written word and symbolic speech, such as artistic expression in paintings, poetry, and the performing arts; synonymous here with *speech*

hate speech: negative speech directed at minority groups, especially concerning race, religion, or sexual orientation

REVIEW AND SUMMARIZE:

After reading this section, identify in *complete* sentences:

1. Examples of "expression"

2. The nature of "hate speech"

3. Examples of current tolerance of censorship

ESSAY:

In a paragraph, summarize the types of expression at issue in the chapter.

LO 6-2 Explain major philosophical approaches for analyzing the right to freedom of expression.

NOTEWORTHY TERMS:

harm principle (or principle of liberty): the principle that government should censor only when the speech at issue would cause real harm

paternalism: the view that government should act as a parent to protect us from ourselves

legal moralism: the view that government should enforce an overall moral code for society

REVIEW AND SUMMARIZE:

After reading this section, identify in *complete* sentences:

1. When the government should censor speech according to the harm principle

2. The claim that pornography should be censored according to the harm principle

3. The use of paternalism in censorship controversies

4. The use of legal moralism in censorship controversies

ESSAY:

In a paragraph, explain how each of the following is relevant in assessing freedom of expression and censorship: the harm principle, paternalism, and legal moralism.

LO 6-3 Apply philosophical approaches to important issues in freedom of expression today.

NOTEWORTHY TERMS:

blasphemy: offensive and disrespectful speech toward religion

shunning: society disapproval and scorn, to censor outside government purview

REVIEW AND SUMMARIZE:

After reading this section, identify in *complete* sentences:

1. How hate speech can be analyzed from a Kantian perspective

2. How to use the harm principle to analyze blasphemous speech about religion

3. How violence in video games can be analyzed according to the harm principle

4. How censorship can be accomplished outside the government purview

ESSAY:

In a paragraph, discuss how hate speech can be analyzed using each of the following: the harm principle, Kantian principles, and shunning.

LO 6-4 Identify possible exceptions to a right of freedom of expression and the justification for making those exceptions.

NOTEWORTHY TERMS:

defamation: words that make false claims of fact that harm the reputation of a person

libel: defamation in the form of written words

sedition: language that advocates the violent overthrow of the government

slander: defamation in the form of spoken words

REVIEW AND SUMMARIZE:

After reading this section, identify in *complete* sentences:

1. Why "causing panic" is an exception to free speech

2. The nature of defamation

3. What must be shown in "incitement to crime"

4. The harm caused by sedition

5. Why Mill thought obscenity should be protected as free speech

ESSAY:

In a paragraph, identify at least two exceptions to free speech and why they are not protected speech.

Chapter Quiz

1. "Expression" here is understood broadly to include
   a. symbolic speech.
   b. the spoken and written word.
   c. all of the above.

2. Pornography should be censored, according to those who believe that it
   a. causes harm in the form of rape.
   b. is offensive, although it causes no harm.
   c. is not protected by the First Amendment.

3. Shunning is
   a. a form of governmental censorship.
   b. a form of censorship limited to the Amish religion.
   c. a form of censorship outside of government purview.

4. The right to freedom of expression
   a. does not exist.
   b. is absolute.
   c. is not absolute.

5. Causing panic
   a. is protected free speech.
   b. is an exception to protected free speech.
   c. never causes real harm.

6. Defamation
   a. is false claims of fact that harm a person's reputation.
   b. is restricted to written harm to a person's reputation.
   c. is protected free speech.

7. Sedition
   a. is protected free speech.
   b. is an exception to protected free speech.
   c. is any language critical of the government.

8. Obscenity
   a. is protected free speech.
   b. is an exception to protected free speech.
   c. is clearly defined in the U.S. Constitution.

LO 7-1 Identify examples of religious freedom at issue today.

NOTEWORTHY TERMS:

NOTE: This list includes important terms found in the chapter.

polygamy: marriage in which one or both partners have multiple spouses

separation of church and state: the doctrine of the First Amendment to the U.S. Constitution that the state may not establish a state religion

REVIEW AND SUMMARIZE:

After reading this section, identify in *complete* sentences:

1. The relationship between religion and morality

2. The difference between the right to hold a belief and the right to act on a belief

3. Thomas Jefferson's view on the relationship of church and state

4. Roger Williams's view on the relationship of church and state

5. Examples of the use of the word *God* in government settings

6. The rights in the First Amendment regarding religion

ESSAY:

In a paragraph, summarize clearly the relationship of church and state in the United States.

LO 7-2 Explain major philosophical approaches for analyzing the right to freedom of religion.

REVIEW AND SUMMARIZE:

After reading this section, identify in *complete* sentences:

1. A positive benefit to freedom of religion

2. The use of the harm principle to analyze the religious practice of polygamy

3. How Kantian reasoning can be used to justify religious freedom

ESSAY:

In a paragraph, explain how a utilitarian would analyze the benefits and harm of religious freedom.

LO 7-3 Apply philosophical approaches to important issues in freedom of religion today.

REVIEW AND SUMMARIZE:

After reading this section, identify in *complete* sentences:

1. The relevant factors for a utilitarian in assessing whether the Islamic community center should be permitted in lower Manhattan

2. The perspective of Kantian reasoning on the proposed center

ESSAY:

In a paragraph, develop a utilitarian analysis of whether the Islamic community center should be permitted close to Ground Zero in New York City.

LO 7-4 Identify possible exceptions to a right of freedom of religion and the justification for making those exceptions.

NOTEWORTHY TERMS:

animal sacrifice: the killing of animals during a religious ceremony, as in the Santería religion

creationism: the belief in the literal creation of the universe in seven days and rejection of evolution to explain the development of the species

REVIEW AND SUMMARIZE:

After reading this section, identify in *complete* sentences:

1. How Mill's harm principle might be used to restrict an exercise of religious freedom

2. Why creationism cannot be taught in taxpayer-supported public schools

3. How utilitarianism can justify requiring photo IDs on all driver's licenses, regardless of the religious views of the applicant

ESSAY:

In a paragraph, explain why the Supreme Court permitted the religious practice of animal sacrifice over the objections of the city of Hialeah, Florida.

Chapter Quiz

1. What is the relationship of religion and morality?

   a. They are always identical for all persons.

   b. They are always separate for all persons.

   c. They are sometimes identical and sometimes separate for different people.

2. What is the source of freedom of religion in most advanced countries?

   a. The Bible

   b. The Koran

   c. The constitution of each country

3. What is the relationship between the right to believe and the right to act on beliefs?

   a. If you have the right to a belief, you always have the right to act on that belief.

   b. If you have the right to a belief, you never have the right to act on that belief.

   c. If you have the right to a belief, you sometimes have the right to act on that belief.

4. The separation of church and state

   a. is guaranteed in the U.S. Constitution.

   b. is rejected in the U.S. Constitution.

   c. is not addressed in the U.S. Constitution.

5. Religious freedom

   a. is absolute.

   b. is nonexistent.

   c. is not absolute.

6. Mill's harm principle would justify restricting some religious freedom

   a. in no circumstances, regardless of the harm caused by that exercise of freedom.

   b. in all circumstances, regardless of the harm caused by that exercise of freedom.

   c. in some circumstances, depending on the harm caused by that exercise of freedom.

7. Paternalism would justify restricting some religious freedom

   a. in no circumstances, regardless of the harm caused by that exercise of freedom.

   b. in all circumstances, regardless of the harm caused by that exercise of freedom.

   c. in some circumstances, depending on the harm caused by that exercise of freedom.

8. Legal moralism would justify restricting some religious freedom

   a. in no circumstances, regardless of the conflict with society's moral code.

   b. in all circumstances, regardless of the conflict with society's moral code.

   c. in some circumstances, depending on the conflict with society's moral code.

9. The Mormon religious practice of polygamy

   a. is protected today as an exercise of religious freedom.

   b. is prohibited as a violation of prevailing community standard.

   c. is prohibited as the establishment of a state religion.

10. The teaching of the religious doctrine of creationism

   a. is permitted outside of public taxpayer-funded schools.

   b. is prohibited in all situations as a violation of the First Amendment.

   c. is permitted only in public taxpayer-funded schools.

11. The requirement for a photo ID on a driver's license

   a. will be waived routinely if it violates the driver's religion.

   b. will not be waived even if it violates the driver's religion.

   c. violates the religious freedom of all drivers.

12. The sacrifice of animals as part of the religious practices of Santería

   a. is unconstitutional in all circumstances.

   b. has been upheld under the Constitution in Hialeah, Florida.

   c. has never been reviewed by the U.S. Supreme Court.

LO 8-1 Specify the nature of discrimination and its various forms.

NOTEWORTHY TERMS:

NOTE: This list includes important terms found in the chapter.

affirmative action: a variety of programs to enhance the hiring of diverse employees and the admission of diverse students to educational institutions

Americans with Disabilities Act: the U.S. law passed in 1990 to prohibit discrimination against individuals with disabilities

unit cohesion: the military term for a unit's ability to work well together

REVIEW AND SUMMARIZE:

After reading this section, identify in *complete* sentences:

1. Relevant characteristics in applications for educational institutions

2. Examples of affirmative action initiatives in education

3. Central requirement of the Americans with Disabilities Act

4. Examples of affirmative action initiatives in employment

5. Examples of discrimination against women in obtaining credit

ESSAY:

In a paragraph, identify and justify appropriate qualifications in applying for admission to educational institutions.

LO 8-2 Explain major philosophical approaches for analyzing the ethical status of the various forms of discrimination.

REVIEW AND SUMMARIZE:

After reading this section, identify in *complete* sentences:

1. How Kantian dignity rejects unfair discrimination

2. How a utilitarian would justify nondiscrimination

ESSAY:

1. In a paragraph, explain how Kantian ethics would analyze discrimination and nondiscrimination.

2. Look for the answer to the following question in a couple of different reference sources and explain it in a sentence or two: What is the difference between *abilities* and *qualifications* as the terms are used in the work world?

LO 8-3 Apply these philosophical approaches to contemporary discrimination issues, including race, gender, and disability.

NOTEWORTHY TERMS:

preferential hiring: a term sometimes used instead of "affirmative action" to address the correction of unfair hiring in the past

REVIEW AND SUMMARIZE:

After reading this section, identify in *complete* sentences:

1. How Kantian principles could reject affirmative action

2. How utilitarian principles could support affirmative action

3. How utilitarian principle could reject affirmative action

4. How the U.S. Supreme Court justified "taking race into account" in *Bakke*

5. The conclusion in *Grutter v. Bollinger*

6. The utilitarian justification for the Americans with Disabilities Act

ESSAY:

In a paragraph, use utilitarian principles to develop arguments both in support of and against affirmative action.

Chapter Quiz

1. The most relevant criterion for admission to college is

    a. wealth of the parents of the applicant.

    b. academic merit of the applicant.

    c. where the parents went to college.

2. The Americans with Disabilities Act of 1990 requires

    a. identical treatment of all students and employees.

    b. nothing because accommodation is strictly voluntary.

    c. reasonable accommodations for persons with disabilities.

3. No women were included in the earliest U.S. space program because

    a. women are too weak to go into space.

    b. only test pilots were considered, and women were barred from being test pilots.

    c. no women applied to be astronauts.

4. When President Harry S. Truman ended racial segregation in the military, critics charged

    a. desegregation would destroy unit cohesion.

    b. nonwhite soldiers were inferior to the white soldiers.

    c. nonwhite soldiers did not want to be desegregated.

5. Affirmative action requires

    a. hiring unqualified persons.

    b. taking positive steps to recruit all qualified people.

    c. nothing because it is strictly voluntary.

6. If a job applicant is rejected solely because she is female, Kant would say:

    a. The rejection violates her human dignity.

    b. The rejection affirms her human dignity.

    c. Nothing.

7. If hiring decisions are made on irrelevant characteristics, a utilitarian would say:

    a. The decisions would result in unhappiness in the workplace and are thus unethical.

    b. The decisions are a violation of human dignity.

    c. The decisions are a violation of virtue ethics.

8. The strongest utilitarian argument in support of affirmative action is

    a. We should respect human dignity and autonomy.

    b. Society as a whole benefits by including previously excluded groups.

    c. Affirmative action demonstrates virtuous character traits.

9. When the U.S. Supreme Court considered utilitarian arguments in *Bakke*, it concluded that

    a. the benefits of affirmative action do not outweigh individual rights.

    b. the benefits of affirmative action outweigh individual rights.

    c. utilitarian arguments are always inappropriate in legal reasoning.

10. In *Grutter v. Bollinger*, the U.S. Supreme Court

    a. overturned *Bakke*.

    b. reaffirmed *Bakke*.

    c. ignored *Bakke*.

11. By enabling the disabled to participate in education and employment, the Americans with Disabilities Act

    a. has backfired and failed to help anyone.

    b. has benefitted both the disabled and society at large.

    c. has violated the autonomy of the disabled.

LO 9-1 Identify examples of current issues in health care.

NOTEWORTHY TERMS:

NOTE: This list includes important terms found in the chapter.

embryonic stem cell research: research conducted on stem cells from fertilized eggs, typically left over from in vitro fertilization

genetic engineering: the manipulation of DNA in humans and plant and animal life

human cloning: the complete duplication of one human being

in vitro fertilization: a procedure in which eggs from a woman's ovary are removed and are fertilized with sperm in a laboratory procedure; successfully fertilized eggs are then returned to the woman's uterus

REVIEW AND SUMMARIZE:

After reading this section, identify in *complete* sentences:

1. The sources of claims that health care is a right

2. The current government policy on embryonic stem cell research

3. The nature of the controversy over embryonic stem cell research

4. The potential benefits of genetic engineering

5. The federal government policy on human cloning

6. The main ethical issues in testing new drugs

7. The possible negative consequences of genetic testing

8. The ban included in the National Organ Transplant Act of 1984

ESSAYS:

1. In a paragraph, identify and discuss the ethical issues surrounding embryonic stem cell research.

2. In a paragraph, discuss some potential dangers associated with genetic engineering.

LO 9-2 Explain major philosophical approaches for analyzing the ethical status of the issues you have identified.

REVIEW AND SUMMARIZE:

After reading this section, identify in *complete* sentences:

1. How Kantian dignity can be used in addressing these issues

2. How utilitarianism can be used in addressing these issues

ESSAY:

In a paragraph, explain how Kantian ethics would analyze the testing of experimental drugs.

LO 9-3 Apply these philosophical approaches to contemporary issues in health care.

REVIEW AND SUMMARIZE:

After reading this section, identify in *complete* sentences:

1. How the test of treating people with respect and dignity addresses the provision of health care

2. The factors relevant to a utilitarian in the provision of health care

3. How the nature of "personhood" affects the debate over embryonic stem cell research

4. How a utilitarian would view the ethics of embryonic stem cell research

5. How Kantian dignity would view genetic engineering, including human cloning

6. How a utilitarian would view genetic engineering, including human cloning

7. The factors relevant to a utilitarian in analyzing the testing of experimental drugs

8. The factors relevant to a Kantian in analyzing genetic testing

9. What factors matter in the ethics of organ donation

ESSAY:

In a paragraph, use utilitarian principles to develop arguments both in support of and against genetic engineering.

Chapter Quiz

1. After World War II, President Harry S. Truman,

   a. succeeded in getting Congress to provide health care to all citizens.

   b. failed in his efforts to get Congress to provide health care to all citizens.

   c. abolished programs providing health care to all citizens.

2. The United Nations' Universal Declaration of Human Rights says that medical care is

   a. a universal human right.

   b. an optional program for government.

   c. a responsibility of each individual alone.

3. Research on embryonic stem cells

   a. is banned by the federal government.

   b. is permitted by the federal government.

   c. has never been addressed by the federal government.

4. Human cloning

   a. is banned by the federal government.

   b. is permitted by the federal government.

   c. has never been addressed by the federal government.

5. Genetic engineering

   a. is the manipulation of DNA in humans only.

   b. is the manipulation of DNA in humans and plant and animal life.

   c. is the manipulation of DNA in plant and animal life only.

6. Genetic testing

   a. can provide information on genetic diseases.

   b. has been banned by the federal government.

   c. has proven completely worthless in identifying genetic diseases.

7. Under the National Organ Transplant Act of 1984

   a. the sale of organs is permitted in the United States.

   b. the sale of organs is banned in the United States.

   c. the donation of organs to anyone other than family members is banned in the United States.

8. In analyzing the ethics of health care issues, Kantians

   a. consider only the consequences of the actions in question.

   b. consider the dignity and autonomy of the persons involved.

   c. reject the relevance of philosophical reasoning.

9. In analyzing the ethics of health care issues, utilitarians

   a. consider only the consequences of the actions in question.

   b. consider the dignity and autonomy of the persons involved.

   c. reject the relevance of philosophical reasoning.

10. Embryonic stem cell research is

   a. strenuously opposed by all abortion opponents, including Nancy Reagan.

   b. supported by some abortion opponents, including Nancy Reagan.

   c. not considered an ethical issue by abortion opponents.

11. The testing of experimental drugs

   a. always violates Kantian dignity of persons.

   b. sometimes respects Kantian dignity of persons.

   c. is irrelevant to Kantians.

12. To treat organ donors with dignity and respect, we must

   a. make sure they are fully informed of the risks.

   b. tell them nothing about the risks so they do not worry.

   c. avoid asking for consent.

LO 10-1 Describe the nature of punishment in general.

REVIEW AND SUMMARIZE:

After reading this section, identify in *complete* sentences:

1. The nature of standards, rules, or laws at issue in punishment

2. The requirement that punishment be inflicted on the wrongdoer

3. The appropriate person(s) to impose punishment

4. The legitimacy of authority needed to inflict punishment

ESSAY:

In a paragraph, identify and discuss the major traits of punishment in general.

LO 10-2 Identify and describe theories of punishment.

NOTEWORTHY TERMS:

NOTE: This list includes Key Terms as well as other important terms found in the chapter.

deterrence: discouraging or preventing an action through threat or example of punishment

prevention: punishing criminals to prevent them from committing similar crimes

prima facie: on the face of it

protection of society: punishing an otherwise innocent but potentially violent person in order to protect everyone else

rehabilitation: education or training to enable someone convicted of a crime of reentering society as a productive member

retribution: punishment a wrongdoer deserves

REVIEW AND SUMMARIZE:

After reading this section, identify in *complete* sentences:

1. Why a theory of punishment is needed

2. The meaning of "eye-for-an-eye"

3. The nature of deterrence to justify punishment

4. Techniques for the prevention of crime

ESSAY:

In a paragraph, explain how the theories of punishment are consistent with utilitarianism.

LO 10-3 Explain how these theories apply to the justification of capital punishment.

REVIEW AND SUMMARIZE:

After reading this section, identify in *complete* sentences:

1. Why critics reject retribution as a justification of capital punishment

2. The difficulty proving that capital punishment is a deterrent to murder

3. Why prevention is effective in addressing crime within prisons

4. The role of rehabilitation in reasoning about capital punishment

ESSAY:

In a paragraph, explain the strongest arguments available for justifying capital punishment, regardless of your personal views on the subject.

LO 10-4 Describe how scientific developments in DNA testing have impacted our thinking about capital punishment

REVIEW AND SUMMARIZE:

After reading this section, identify in *complete* sentences:

1. Why developments in DNA testing have affected current thinking about capital punishment

2. Why capital punishment is unique compared with other punishments

ESSAY:

In a paragraph, explain how recent work on DNA testing and such groups as Project Innocence have contributed to shifting attitudes toward capital punishment.

LO 10-5 Identify situations in which we should make exceptions to capital punishment.

REVIEW AND SUMMARIZE:

After reading this section, identify in *complete* sentences:

1. Why executing the mentally retarded or severely challenged seems unjustified

2. Why executing those who committed murder when they were a juvenile seems unjustified

3. Why executing those who are mentally ill is problematic

LO 10-6 Identify and justify crimes, other than murder, that are subject to capital punishment.

REVIEW AND SUMMARIZE:

After reading this section, identify in *complete* sentences:

1. Crimes other than murder that can be subject to the death penalty

2. The justification for execution after conviction for espionage or treason

3. The concerns over execution for the crime of rape

LO 10-7 Explain how legal reasoning compares with ethical reasoning regarding capital punishment.

REVIEW AND SUMMARIZE:

After reading this section, identify in *complete* sentences:

1. The main difference between legal and philosophical reasoning with regard to capital punishment

2. Examples of similar reasoning in both legal and philosophical contexts with regard to capital punishment

3. The role of precedent or appeals to authority in philosophical reasoning

Chapter Quiz

1. What are examples of the unpleasantness required for punishment?
   a. Incarceration or a monetary fine
   b. A judge authorized to impose punishment
   c. Standards that are violated

2. What is required for violation of established standards, rules, or laws to justify punishment?
   a. They must be passed in a government setting.
   b. They must be understood by potential wrongdoers in that setting.
   c. They must be limited to private rules in a family.

3. What sort of judge is needed to justify punishment?
   a. Someone authorized to determine if rules or laws have been violated
   b. Someone elected in a democratic process
   c. Someone with a strong police force to support the imposition

4. Which theory of punishment can be stated as "eye-for-an-eye"?
   a. Deterrence
   b. Retribution
   c. Protection of society

5. Why is deterrence consistent with utilitarianism?
   a. It is justified by the results of the greatest happiness for the greatest number of people.
   b. It focuses on revenge.
   c. It supports the death penalty.

6. What is controversial about protection of society as a justification for punishment?
   a. Each person should protect himself or herself, rather than depend on the government.
   b. It can justify punishment before a crime has been committed.
   c. It is too expensive.

LO 11-1 Identify major ethical issues presented today by computers and information technology.

NOTEWORTHY TERMS:

NOTE: This list includes important terms found in the chapter.

cyberstalking: stalking, harassing, making death threats on the Internet

intellectual property: creations of the mind, including copyrights, patents, and trademarks

technological divide: the uneven distribution of access to computers and technology, based on economics and geography

REVIEW AND SUMMARIZE:

After reading this section, identify in *complete* sentences:

1. Why privacy issues have escalated with the advent of computers

2. Examples of how cyberstalking occurs

3. What is the nature of the technological divide

4. Examples of intellectual property issues on the Internet

ESSAYS:

1. In a paragraph, identify and explain the ethical issues presented by computers and the Internet.

2. In a paragraph, explain whether Internet providers are ethically obligated to help protect their customers' privacy.

LO 11-2 Explain major philosophical approaches for analyzing the ethical status of the issues you have identified.

REVIEW AND SUMMARIZE:

After reading this section, identify in *complete* sentences:

1. How the Internet affects the use of Kantian reasoning

2. How the Internet affects the use of utilitarian reasoning

3. How the Internet affects the use of virtue ethics analysis

ESSAYS:

1. In a paragraph, explain how the Internet affects our use of ethical reasoning tools.

2. In a paragraph, identify and explain some of the responsibilities individuals have, ethically speaking, when using the Internet, whether for social networking, downloading content, or reading or participating in discussion boards that might constitute cyberstalking, for example.

LO 11-3 Apply those philosophical approaches to contemporary issues of computers and information technology.

REVIEW AND SUMMARIZE:

After reading this section, identify in *complete* sentences:

1. How computers and the Internet alter our ethical analysis of privacy issues

2. How computers and the Internet alter our ethical analysis of cyberstalking

3. Ethical obligations of a speaker exercising rights of free speech

4. Ethical obligations in helping to close the technological divide

5. Ethical obligations in respecting intellectual property on the Internet and with computers

ESSAYS:

1. In a paragraph, provide a Kantian analysis of your rights and obligations in using the Internet.

2. In a paragraph or two, explain why preserving privacy, one's own or someone else's, is important in certain professions.

3. In a paragraph or two, justify the use of anonymous free speech on the Internet, using both Kantian and utilitarian reasoning.

Chapter Quiz

1. Privacy rights violations on the Internet
   a. are unchanged from pre-Internet times.
   b. are much expanded from pre-Internet times.
   c. are not a problem.

2. The technological divide
   a. is a growing problem, based on economics and geography.
   b. is a nonexistent fiction.
   c. is not a problem.

3. Respecting privacy rights of others on the Internet
   a. can be effectively analyzed using Kantian principles.
   b. is a nonissue for the utilitarian.
   c. only matter to a virtuous person if they are caught.

4. If you work at an educational institution
   a. you are subject to privacy restrictions on information about students.
   b. you should feel free to snoop around computer records about students.
   c. federal rules on privacy rights do not apply to you.

5. Cyberstalking
   a. can be great fun and should be pursued without worry.
   b. might be a violation of federal and state laws.
   c. taises no ethical issues.

6. It is a violation of the First Amendment protection of free speech if
   a. a commercial publisher refuses to publish your e-book.
   b. amazon refuses to offer your e-book for sale.
   c. congress passes a law banning publication of your e-book.

7. The technological divide
   a. creates several consequences of great concern to utilitarians.
   b. presents no ethical issues.
   c. is irrelevant to virtuous persons.

8. Stealing someone else's intellectual property on the Internet
   a. violates their autonomy as persons who had a good idea and the potential to benefit.
   b. is permitted without restriction, either ethically or legally.
   c. is much more difficult than it was before the Internet.

9. When you purchase software, you are actually
   a. purchasing the right to make copies to give your friends.
   b. purchasing the right to make copies you sell on E-bay.
   c. purchasing a license to use the software.

10. The privacy of medical records
    a. is not protected in the United States.
    b. is protected both ethically and legally.
    c. raises legal but not ethical issues.

11. The groundwork for the binary language used by computers was developed by
    a. two computer scientists.
    b. two mathematicians.
    c. two philosophers.

12. Harassment can occur
    a. in person.
    b. on the Internet.
    c. both of the above.

13. The Internet was developed
    a. during World War II to decipher Nazi codes.
    b. in the 1960s so the U.S. defense department and universities could communicate without fear of destruction of the physical site.
    c. in the 1980s to facilitate international commerce with the World Wide Web.

LO 12-1 Identify major ethical issues central to animal rights and environmental ethics.

NOTEWORTHY TERMS:

NOTE: This list includes important terms found in the chapter.

higher animals: animals possessing relatively advanced or developed characteristics, such as mammals and other vertebrates

REVIEW AND SUMMARIZE:

After reading this section, identify in *complete* sentences:

1. The issue concerning whether or not animals have rights

2. The issue concerning higher and lower animals

3. Concerns competing with environmental issues today

ESSAYS:

1. In a paragraph, identify and explain one of the ethical issues presented by the environment today.

2. In a paragraph or two, provide an example of the interrelatedness of environmental issues. Specifically, identify an environmental ethical issue that cannot be considered without taking into consideration at least one other ethical environmental issue.

LO 12-2 Explain major philosophical approaches for analyzing the ethical status of the issues you have identified.

NOTEWORTHY TERMS:

anthropocentrism: the view that the interests of human beings always come first over the environment considered as a whole

biocentrism: the view that the health of the overall ecological system should be put ahead of the health and well-being of human beings; also called *holism*

biotic community: a community that includes human beings but puts the interests of humans as just part of that community

holism: the view that the health of the overall ecological system should be put ahead of the health and well-being of human beings; also called *biocentrism*

REVIEW AND SUMMARIZE:

After reading this section, identify in *complete* sentences:

1. Why utilitarian Peter Singer includes nonhuman animals in his ethical analysis

2. The consequences for human beings of different environmental policies

3. How Kantian reasoning is used to argue for animal rights

4. The nature of biocentrism

5. How biocentrism differs from anthropocentrism

ESSAYS:

1. In a paragraph, explain the difference between utilitarian and Kantian reasoning with regard to supporting animal rights.

2. In a paragraph or two, explain how Kantianism can be used to work through ethical issues related to the environment; then explain problems in using Kantianism to address ethical issues related to the environment.

LO 12-3 Apply those philosophical approaches to contemporary issues of animal rights and environmental ethics.

REVIEW AND SUMMARIZE:

After reading this section, identify in *complete* sentences:

1. How a utilitarian would analyze the use of animals in testing new medicine

2. The difficulty attributing identical Kantian dignity to humans and all other animals

3. The challenge using utilitarianism to analyze nuclear power

4. The factors a Kantian would use to analyze nuclear power

ESSAYS:

1. In a paragraph, provide a utilitarian analysis of the ethics of vegetarianism.

2. In a paragraph or two, present the arguments used by supporters of animal testing.

Chapter Quiz

1. The medieval philosopher Augustine argued that animals

    a. may be killed or used for our own purposes because they are irrational.

    b. may not be killed or used for our own purposes because they feel pain.

    c. have all the same rights as persons.

2. The French philosopher Descartes argued that animals

    a. should be treated with dignity because they feel pain.

    b. are incapable of feeling any sensation.

    c. are capable of happiness just like persons.

3. The philosopher Kant argued that animals

    a. are merely a means to help achieve human ends.

    b. should never be treated as a means to human ends.

    c. should be treated with dignity because they are self-conscious.

4. The utilitarian Jeremy Bentham said that animals

    a. do not feel sensation and thus are irrelevant ethically.

    b. do feel sensation and thus must be considered in the utilitarian analysis.

    c. are irrelevant in ethics because they are not able to use language.

5. The utilitarian Peter Singer said that animals

    a. do not feel sensation and thus are irrelevant ethically.

    b. do feel sensation and thus must be considered in the utilitarian analysis.

    c. are irrelevant in ethics because they are not able to use language.

6. Kantian philosopher Tom Regan said that animals

    a. should be accorded the same dignity and respect as humans.

    b. do not deserve the same dignity and respect as humans.

    c. are irrelevant in ethics because they are not able to use language.

7. The biotic community promoted by environmentalist Aldo Leopold

    a. puts the interests of humans ahead of the entire environment.

    b. puts the interests of humans as just part of the entire environment.

    c. concerns only the nonhuman environment.

8. Utilitarians would analyze the use of animals in testing new medicines

    a. by appealing to the autonomy and dignity of those animals.

    b. by appealing to the autonomy and dignity of humans.

    c. by balancing the pleasure and pain of the animals with the humans.

9. One difficulty with the Kantian approach to animal rights is

    a. finding a way to distinguish between humans and non-humans.

    b. measuring pleasure and pain in animals.

    c. measuring pleasure and pain in humans.

10. Biocentrism is

    a. sometimes called holism.

    b. the view that the well-being of humans is more important than that of the environment.

    c. the view that the well-being of humans is equal to that of the environment.

11. Anthropocentrism

    a. rejects the importance of the environment entirely.

    b. rejects the importance of humans in the environment.

    c. says that the interests of humans always outweigh those of the environment.

12. In analyzing the ethics of nuclear power, a utilitarian would take into account

    a. the economic cost of building the plant.

    b. the harm to health of nuclear waste.

    c. both of the above.

LO 13-1 Identify major ethical issues raised by the decision to engage in war and the conduct during a war.

NOTEWORTHY TERMS:

NOTE: This list includes Key Terms as well as other important terms found in the chapter.

jus ad bellum: the justice of war; the justifications or the set of justifications for going to war at all

jus in bello: the justice within war; the justification for acts during the conduct of that war

REVIEW AND SUMMARIZE:

After reading this section, identify in *complete* sentences:

1. An example of an issue concerning jus ad bellum

2. An example of an issue concerning jus in bello

ESSAYS:

1. In a paragraph, identify and explain the difference between jus ad bellum and jus in bello.

2. In a paragraph, provide a couple of real-life examples that illustrate the concept of jus ad bellum.

3. In a paragraph, provide a couple of real-life examples that illustrate the concept of jus in bello.

LO 13-2 Explain major philosophical approaches for analyzing the ethics of war, both its initiation and the conduct during war.

NOTEWORTHY TERMS:

Just War theory: the political philosophy that ethical standards of just and unjust, right and wrong, should be of central importance in the declaration of war and the conduct of that war

Pacifism: the political philosophy that holds that violence is always wrong; in disputes among nations, nonviolent actions (such as economic sanctions and international pressure) should be pursued instead

preemptive war: the theory of war developed by President George W. Bush that a country is justified in going to war if it fears an imminent threat to its existence, even before it is attacked

Realism: the political philosophy that ethical standards of just and unjust, right and wrong, are irrelevant in the conduct of war; the only standards that matter are national sovereignty, the nation's self-interest, and whatever it takes to win

REVIEW AND SUMMARIZE:

After reading this section, identify in *complete* sentences:

1. Factors in war relevant to the utilitarian

2. Factors in war relevant to the Kantian

3. The principal claim of Just War Theory

4. The principal claim of Realism

5. The nature of Pacifism

ESSAYS:

1. In a paragraph, explain the similarities and differences between Just War Theory, Realism, and Pacifism.

2. In a paragraph, explain the nature of Pacifism and how the pacifist recommends a nation respond to threats to its sovereignty.

LO 13-3 Apply those philosophical approaches to the analysis of the ethics of war.

REVIEW AND SUMMARIZE:

After reading this section, identify in *complete* sentences:

1. Whether the doctrine of preemptive war is an example of jus ad bellum and why or why not

2. The factors important to a utilitarian in assessing the doctrine of preemptive war

3. The factors important to a Kantian in assessing the doctrine of preemptive war

4. How a Just War theorist would assess the doctrine of preemptive war

5. How a realist would assess the doctrine of preemptive war

6. How a pacifist would assess the doctrine of preemptive war

7. Why the use of torture is an example of jus in bello

ESSAYS:

1. In a paragraph, use the various theories here to analyze the ethics of the use of torture.

2. In a paragraph, explain what ethical grounds can be invoked to assert that water boarding does not amount to torture and which ones can be invoked to assert that it is.

Chapter Quiz

1. Jus ad bellum refers to
   a. the weapons used in war.
   b. the justification for going to war.
   c. the actions allowable within the context of a war.

2. Jus in bello refers to
   a. the weapons used in war.
   b. the justification for going to war.
   c. the actions allowable within the context of a war.

3. Just War theory refers to the view that
   a. war must be conducted according to the ethical principles of individuals.
   b. nations are not subject to ethical principles.
   c. violence among nations is always wrong.

4. Realism refers to the view that
   a. war must be conducted according to the ethical principles of individuals.
   b. nations are not subject to ethical principles.
   c. violence among nations is always wrong.

5. Pacificism refers to the view that
   a. war must be conducted according to the ethical principles of individuals.
   b. nations are not subject to ethical principles.
   c. violence among nations is always wrong.

6. Analysis of preemptive war theory is an example of
   a. jus ad bellum.
   b. jus ad bello.
   c. Just War theory.

7. In analyzing preemptive war theory, the utilitarian would consider
   a. the entire range of consequences emanating from the policy.
   b. the standing in the world community of the nation using this theory.
   c. both of the above.

8. The preemptive war doctrine was
   a. a continuation of the tradition of war in self-defense.
   b. a departure from the tradition of war in self-defense.
   c. identical to war in self-defense.

9. The use of torture in war can be analyzed
   a. according to Kantian principles.
   b. according to utilitarian principles.
   c. both of the above.

NOTES